D1189559

# THEATRE
## OF
# CRISIS

# THEATRE
OF
# CRISIS

## Drama and Politics in Latin America

DIANA TAYLOR

THE UNIVERSITY PRESS OF KENTUCKY

Copyright © 1991 by The University Press of Kentucky

Scholarly publisher for the Commonwealth,
serving Bellarmine College, Berea College, Centre
College of Kentucky, Eastern Kentucky University,
The Filson Club, Georgetown College, Kentucky
Historical Society, Kentucky State University,
Morehead State University, Murray State University,
Northern Kentucky University, Transylvania University,
University of Kentucky, University of Louisville,
and Western Kentucky University.

*Editorial and Sales Offices:* Lexington, Kentucky 40506-0336

**Library of Congress Cataloging-in-Publication Data**

Taylor, Diana.
  Theatre of crisis : drama and politics in Latin America / Diana
Taylor.
      p.   cm.
  Includes bibliographical references and index.
  ISBN 0-8131-1734-8
  1. Spanish American drama—20th century—History and criticism.
  2. Politics and literature—Latin America.   I. Title.
  PQ7082.D7T36   1990
  862—dc20                                              90-12555

*To*

# ERIC

*and our children*

## ALEXEI and MARINA

# CONTENTS

# PREFACE

Latin American theatre is a relatively unknown field. In order to expand critical awareness of it outside Latin America, I have written this study in English, translating the quotations from the Spanish originals when suitable translations have not been available. Moreover, instead of referring to original editions of texts and plays that may be inaccessible to North American readers, I have chosen to cite easily obtainable editions.

"Every word," according to Merleau-Ponty, "whether we know it or not, is always a word with someone." This book reflects many such words, words with Laurence Davies, Murray Krieger, Beatriz Pastor, Virginia Swain, George Woodyard, and Susanne Zantop, among others. I thank them all.

Nancy Davies, of Dartmouth's Humanities Computing Center, came to my rescue repeatedly. I am grateful for her expertise and good humor. As always, the Baker Library staff, Luis Villar, Patricia Carter, and Marianne Hraibi, have done the possible and impossible to help me. Dartmouth College generously provided a Faculty Fellowship that enabled me to work on the manuscript. And I owe a very special thanks to my family, the Taylors and the Manheimers, for their encouragement and support. Finally, my deepest gratitude to my husband, Eric Manheimer, who makes it all worthwhile.

# INTRODUCTION

THEATRE has played an active role in the continuing colonization of Latin America since the Spaniards used plays to Christianize and colonize the indigenous peoples of the Americas in the sixteenth century. María Sten, in *Vida y muerte del teatro Náhuatl* (14), affirms that "theatre was for the spiritual conquest of Mexico what horses and gunpowder were for the military conquest." [1] For the conquerors and colonizers, theatre was a potent tool in manipulating a population already accustomed to spectacle. Moreover, theatre provided one more stage on which the vanquished were forced to participate in the drama of their own defeat. In 1599, for example, according to José Juan Arrom's theatre history (32), the Jesuits used cadavers of native Americans to portray the dead in their staging of the final judgment.

The end of a colony did not signal the end of colonialism. Latin America remained, economically and culturally, the impoverished and peripheral "other" to the defining European and American "self." Colonialism became internalized, victimizing Latin Americans by means of their own self-hatred. This virulent sense of inferiority has been thematized by major modern plays such as Rodolfo Usigli's *El gesticulador* (1937), Celestino Gorostiza's *El color de nuestra piel* (1952), and Francisco Arriví's *Vejigantes* (1958). In the late 1950s and early 1960s, for reasons proposed throughout this study, several kinds of theatrical activity in Latin America underwent a widespread process of revision, becoming quantitatively different from earlier and generally isolated attempts at forging a constructive native identity. From that time to the present, much Latin American theatre has turned its powers of investigation on itself, both to examine its role in cultural domination and to reshape itself into an instrument of decolonization, a "theatre of the oppressed." [2]

To understand theatre's role in the panoramic drama of oppression, one must analyze the relationship between theatrical performances and the wider uses and abuses of social spectacle. The Conquest did not simply replace the "pagan" productions with indoctrinary Christian plays.

The Conquest toppled various highly ritualized "theatre states," indigenous societies such as the Nahua, the Inca, and the Mayan, in which spectacle provided the vital link between the social and cosmic orders.[3] These societies differed from secular ones in that spectacle for them was not simply *part* of a larger social whole. Rather, these societies considered themselves viable only insofar as their spectacles were capable of harmonizing their material existence with the supernatural powers governing them. Hence spectacle was not a *representation* of power or a *legitimation* of power. Spectacle *was* power. Unlike the society that was to conquer them, these societies did not use spectacle to bolster or justify their violence and warfare but rather the opposite; their war and violence were necessary to fuel their spectacle. They believed that captives were essential for ritual sacrifice; the sacrificial blood fortified the gods and kept them strong, capable of maintaining social stability.

These diverse societies were replaced by a homogenizing system that converted all the indigenous groups, with their many differences, into *one* controllable Other. Colonization entailed the redefinition and renaming of the conquered territory: the "New World," the "Indies," "New Spain." Just as the geographical boundaries were remapped into new political entities, ideology shifted to make way for a new hegemony, drawing new lines of demarcation to separate the "civilized" from the "barbarian," the urban from the rural, the literate from those grounded in orality. (By ideology, I mean simply a given world construct with its prevailing discourse, assumptions, and value systems; by hegemony, I mean the ideology of the dominant group.) The decimated area was inscribed with the new social, political, and religious order, with its own codes and its own spectacular displays of power. Spectacle, though still key, inverted the pre-Columbian pattern. Spectacle was not power, as before; now it supported power. The theatricality, the pomp, and the ceremony of religious and secular celebrations contributed to the legitimation of the new order; they helped recast the indigenous peoples' loss of their world as their gain of Christendom and eternal salvation; they served to maintain order and hierarchies by inspiring terror in the native audience that witnessed public executions, acts of torture, and other spectacles of awesome power. Moreover, by the mid-eighteenth century the monumental theatres themselves bespoke the grandeur of the hegemonic culture. The continuing domination of Latin America is still to a large extent facilitated by the manipulation of spectacle, ranging from political rallies to mass media, Broadway "hits," television, and advertising. As Guy Debord observes in *The Society of the Spectacle* (57), "The society which carries the spectacle does not dominate the underdeveloped regions by its economic hegemony alone. It dominates them *as the society of the spectacle.*" In various ways, then, theatre and the theatricality of social spectacle have historically played, and continue to play, instrumental roles in the cultural colonization of the Americas.

Before analyzing the various interconnections between theatre and theatrical social spectacles, I must clarify three points here: (1) theatre and theatricality are not the same thing; (2) theatre and theatricality are not intrinsically oppressive; (3) they do not invariably work in the same way or support each other.

First, theatre and theatrical social spectacles and ceremonies clearly have much in common: people play roles, set scenarios in motion, wear costumes, construct sets, and so forth. As Jean Duvignaud states in *Sociologie du théâtre* (7), a "tribunal, a jury, the unveiling of a monument, a religious service at a mosque or synagogue, a festival, even a family birthday are all ceremonies at which people play parts according to a scenario which they are in no position to modify because no one can escape the social roles he is obliged to assume." While Duvignaud stresses the dramatic quality of events that individual participants cannot modify or control, in this study I am more interested in the politics of theatricality, the conscious manipulation of social images and situations both by those in power and by those contesting it. Just as theatre controls the audience's perception and directs its attention through the conscious use of movement, timing, light, sound, space, and so on, the theatricality of social events also directs and controls the attention of its population. As in theatre, the political bracketing of events encourages the public to participate in them and accept them unquestioningly. As Elizabeth Burns points out in *Theatricality* (19), "The ad hoc frame (or *epoché*) put around a particular kind of situation and action" allows for the "suspension of belief in the reality of the world and events external to the occasion so framed. For the man within [the frame] . . . the 'natural attitude' is the exclusion of any doubt that the world and its objects might be otherwise than they appear to him." Moreover, the social spectacle, like theatre, not only directs but limits "the spectator's (potentially limitless) responses to it," as Una Chaudhuri proposes in "The Spectator in Drama/Drama in the Spectator" (286). As she and other observers of reader/spectator response point out, specific audience reactions are built into the plays, much as the Aristotelian (cathartic) or the Brechtian (alienation) responses are inscribed within the texts themselves. The same holds true of theatricality: certain displays of power are calculated to evoke foreseeable reactions from the public. The public tortures in seventeenth- and eighteenth-century France (which Michel Foucault, in *Discipline and Punish* calls "the spectacle of the scaffold" [32]), and the state terrorism in Latin America during the 1970s are only two extreme examples of how public displays can atomize or paralyze a population.

The sense in which I use the term "theatricality" differs somewhat from the word "spectacle" as a "specially prepared or arranged display of a more or less public nature"; that which is "seen or capable of being seen" (*OED*). "Theatricality" includes the *mechanics* of spectacle or theatre, the manipulation of images and events behind the scenes which are also capable of *not* being seen. The theatricality of elections, for example, far exceeds the spectacle the candidates make of themselves. Theatricality is not simply what we see but a way of controlling vision, of making the invisible visible, the visible invisible.

While theatricality in general shapes society in that it frames discourses persuasively and evokes the public's emotions and participation, thus forming a collectivity unified by the shared focus, in Latin America the elaborate show of supposedly democratic politics blatantly works to obfuscate the authoritarian reality we are not meant to see. Alain Rouquié, in *The Military and the State in Latin America* (34), notes that the abyss separating political reality from democratic rhetoric characterizes politics throughout modern Latin America—from countries as "developed" as Argentina to those as underdeveloped as Haiti: "Behind the 'public stage' of popular sovereignty there is a 'private stage' based on relations of domination. Every attempt at participation that is not controlled, that is not the result of an agreement by the participants on the 'private stage,' is therefore seen as a threat to the 'pact of domination.' . . . The vertical character of social relations and the almost cosmic distance between institutional ideologies and social conduct produce a political culture of deception. The painted façades of a juridical universalism cover the particularism of personalistic relations and forces. The laws are not only made, as elsewhere, to be broken; they are often adopted, as they say in Brazil, *para inglês ver,* to make the English believe in the perfectly advanced legislation that is never applied."

Second, both theatre and theatricality are socially and politically unstable vehicles for cultural expression, as conducive to supporting the structures and ideologies of power as to challenging or overthrowing them, as capable of aestheticizing and promoting victimization as of demythifying and ending it. In part, this is due to the malleability of texts, performance, and ritual; the fact that both the Nazis and the French resistance groups considered Sophocles' *Antigone* a compelling expression of their fundamentally irreconcilable ideologies is only the most famous example of theatre's political ambiguity. In part, the instability stems from the fact that the public can potentially change its response to a given spectacle; Foucault's analysis of public executions, of "the theatre of hell" (*Discipline,* 46), demonstrates that the participation of the public was both indispensable and ambiguous. Public torture was part of a "policy of terror: to make everyone aware, through the body of the criminal, of the unrestrained presence of the sovereign" (49). Public tortures came to an end in France, however, when the spectacle could no longer be relied on to elicit a foreseeable, politically safe response. In the late eighteenth century, executions increasingly promoted popular disturbances: "It was evident that the great spectacle of punishment ran the risk of being rejected by the very people to whom it was addressed. . . . these disadvantages became a political danger—the people never felt closer to those who paid the penalty than in those rituals intended to show the horror of the crime and the invincibility of power" (63).

Theatre and theatricality have traditionally supported the ideologies of those in power, not because they are inherently conservative but rather because the powerful have generally been able to control most public displays, including theatre. Economic and social factors, indirectly or directly, determine *autho*rity—the production of texts and performances: who has the time and status to write for the public, who publishes or performs the texts, which dramatists are deemed relevant and important, who is canonized as a "master," who attends the performances or reads the texts, and so forth. Clearly, as Edward Said repeatedly stresses in *The World, the Text, and the Critic* (11), "culture is a system of exclusions." However, the instability of the theatrical phenomenon also helps oppositional practitioners in their use of antihegemonic spectacle. In Latin America, theatre can more effectively undermine oppressive forces than can other art forms: theatre is live; live actors affect live audiences in unforeseeable ways; each performance would have to be policed in order to ensure that the actors did not deliver a line or make a gesture that would communicate a politically prohibited message to its audience. So too the oppressed can take up public spectacle to rally support, sympathy, and legitimacy for their position, as attested by the weekly vigils of the Mothers and Grandmothers of the Plaza de Mayo during Argentina's "Dirty War."

Third, marginal groups fight for a theatre that addresses their concerns and interests, that reflects their image and speaks their language as a way of empowering themselves, of fostering solidarity and creating a community. This kind of oppositional theatre, as we shall see, often attacks or subverts the theatricality of social and political rites that legitimate exclusion and mythify oppression. However, marginal groups do not challenge the system only because it excludes them; as Burns (11) suggests: "The theatrical quality of life, taken for granted by nearly everyone, seems to be experienced most concretely by those who feel themselves on the margin of events either because they have adopted the role of spectator or because, though present, they have not been offered a part or have not learnt it sufficiently well to enable them to join the actors." I would agree that those who do not participate in a social system are less likely to see it as "natural" and are therefore more sensitive to its contrived or constructed quality. But the dramatists represented in this study reject the political shams carried out in their countries on the grounds that these are repressive and dishonest (at best) or that, as in the case of Argentina, participation in a criminal system is annihilating. Hence, accepting a role or learning a part is not perceived as a viable option by these groups. Their theatre, then, posits itself as more "real" than the political farces taking place offstage. Through their theatre they alert their audiences to the dangers of political theatricality.

In the following pages I analyze the role and function of oppositional theatre in highly inflammatory sociopolitical contexts, focusing on the work of five playwrights in the five-year period between 1965 and 1970, during which theatrical activity was most heatedly contested in Latin America. This period was one of intense dramatic production: dozens of major playwrights were producing first-rate theatre: university theatres, groups, and workshops sprang up in the twenty-five countries; national and international festivals dedicated specifically to Latin American drama began to take place in these years, temporarily broadening the audiences and building an economic infrastructure that had not previously existed.[4] Significantly, it was also a period of violent political transition and ideological crisis. As artists struggled for self-definition on the one hand, hopes of social, political, and economic self-definition and self-government suffered major setbacks on the other. Dreams of viable Latin American alternatives to authoritarianism faded as the Cuban Revolution became increasingly institutionalized and repressive, as U.S. counterinsurgency undermined Latin American governments and waged undeclared wars against native populations, as new right-wing military dictatorships (beginning in Brazil in 1964) rose up yet again throughout most of the South American continent. These years brought to a head—to a crisis—Latin America's unresolvable tensions and contradictions. "Crisis," as I understand the term, does not signal a specific left-wing or right-wing ideological crisis. Nor can it be pinned down to a specific economic or capitalist crisis commonly explained in terms of market disintegration, inflation, unemployment, Third World debt, and so on.[5] Rather, I refer to crisis in the more general sense of a "turning point" between death and regeneration, taking into account both the *objective* systemic shifts or ruptures (revolution, military takeovers, wars and civil wars) that affect the nature of the society as a whole and the *subjective*, personal experience of disorientation and loss of identity. The classical or general definition of crisis, which I adopt for this study, is James O'Connor's (108): "the turning point of an illness in which it is decided whether or not the organism's self-healing powers are sufficient for recovery." The crisis in Latin America during the late 1960s signaled a growing doubt in the legitimacy of authority and the destruction of one set of values before the new were developed and cemented into a cohesive ideology.

Within Latin America, the widespread manifestations of a theatre of crisis in the 1960s resulted from the rupture precipitated by the rejection of a theatre of oppression which had not yet been replaced by a fully formulated "theatre of the oppressed." The theatre of crisis proposes more questions than answers; it bursts with vitality, with a sense of urgency and aggression that refuses to be sublimated in theatrically "safe" or cathartic ways; it scrutinizes both the violent societies that gave it rise and its own violence, its own role in highly theatricalized societies. The theatre of crisis mirrors the *effects* of sociopolitical crisis—the objective, systemic rifts in combination with the subjective experience of decomposition—without yet evolving *beyond* crisis toward reconstruction.

The inchoate period isolated in this study was both the end of a process and the beginning of several new ones. During this period, dramatists either rejected, dismantled, or transformed traditional theatrical forms and groped for theatrical idioms capable of expressing oppositional world views. At this point, the opposition signaled a rejection of the colonizing, hegemonic world and its supporting aesthetic and valorizing systems. There was a fervent, productive process of theatrical transculturation as dramatists took recognizable "First World" models and changed them into vehicles capable of expressing "Third World" realities.[6]

This theatre tends to be open-ended, episodic, or fragmented, for the dissolution of conventional frames prompts the dramatists to explore alternative modes of bringing previously marginalized realities into focus. They use storytellers, stemming from the oral traditions of the Americas (and not only, as de Toro and other commentators argue, from Brecht's narrators), to make accessible realms of reality that have been pushed aside from the time of the Conquest; they express other ways of knowing and of relating knowledge. Their structural open-endedness resists exclusion and incorporates, rather, the stories and voices of the victims and the downtrodden that have systematically been left out of official and cultural history. The ruptured frames, then, tempt spectators to look beyond their boundaries in order to examine what traditional theatrical genres and well-made plays have kept out, the lacunae, the forgotten areas unmapped, or deterritorialized, by colonization. Consciously anti-Aristotelian, these plays are not depictions of the harmonious universe in which sacrifice is ultimately heroic and inevitable, in which individual death reaffirms the continuation of collective life. On the contrary, the theatre of crisis accentuates the recognition that the contradictions cannot be dismissed, or tied together, by an ending. In the worlds-without-end of oppression and criminal violence explored in this theatre, the many die to secure the stability and harmony of the few. Moreover, the deaths are not portrayed as morally uplifting, aesthetically beautiful, or cosmically inevitable; they could have and should have been avoided. The fragmentation and open-endedness of this theatre, then, serves various functions: it disengages itself from the dependent position of "other" in the hegemonic self/other relationship of cultural colonialism in which the defining group is "self" and the defined is "other;" it attempts to depict worlds, voices, and visions previously marginalized; and it signals its tentative and provisional approach toward the development of "new" or oppositional theatrical theories.

These plays do not work toward a unified vision of Latin American theatre that is as totalizing and rigid in its inclusion as classical theories of "purity" are in their exclusion. The very notion of *a* Latin America, and hence a Latin American theatre or theory, is in itself misleading. It proves more constructive to think of twenty-five different countries—each with its own particular combination of races and populations, languages and dialects, traditions and cultural images—that share a similar history of conquest, colonization, economic and political instability, and continuing sociopolitical and economic dependency. As such, the different Latin American countries are in a similar situation, and thus, to a degree, they resemble each other as well as other colonized countries—*positionally* they are kept on the periphery of a system dominated by a political-economic-cultural *center.* Hence, the cultural manifestations of these marginalized peoples demonstrate similarities—images of political or familial disempowerment and displacement; domination through language and definition; a fragmented and deformed sense of self. So too they develop similar strategies for combatting oppression, subverting cultural hegemony, and struggling for a firm and autonomous sense of self. The similar manifestations of crisis evident in these plays, then, do not result from a shared school or tradition. Rather than squeeze this theatre into the so-called "Western" tradition (the term alone relegates Latin Americans to the nonspace of the non-Western) and continue to analyze it as an offshoot of the theatre of the absurd, or Brechtian epic theatre, or Artaud's theatre of cruelty, it proves more productive to relate this discourse to other minority or marginal discourses inside and outside the West: to black South African theatre, or to black and feminist and Hispanic-American theatre in the United States.

The theatre of crisis is not, however, a cohesive and straightforward theatre of the oppressed as Augusto Boal uses the term. The theatre of crisis is far more complex and contradictory than any purely instrumental theatre. Rather than propose any clear directions or answers, this theatre explores the critical situation with all its ruptures and contradictions, with all its political dangers and ideological blind spots. It differs from other kinds of crisis theatres—the theatre of the absurd or protest theatre—in that it formulates the objective manifestation of crisis as inseparable from the subjective experience of decomposition. As we shall see, the theatre of the absurd reflects a crisis ideology, the personal sensation of decomposition, within a stable, bourgeois context. In protest theatre, the sociopolitical ruptures may be real enough, but the oppositional position is defined and firm. In the theatre of crisis, both the objective context and the subjective consciousness threaten to collapse. The onstage worlds concretize the systemic shifts and ruptures by means of crumbling walls and fragile partitions between inner and outer, walls that neither separate nor protect. The onstage characters, who attempt to situate and define themselves in relation to disintegrating ideological frameworks and faulty social mirrors, appear as monstrous hybrids, as yet devoid of personal identity and incapable of self-government. This inchoate period should not be regarded as a negative state or as an indication that these characters are instrinsically childish or underdeveloped, as their "discoverers," conquerors, and colonizers from the time of Columbus onward have repeatedly argued.[7] Rather, it is a moment of repositioning, of transition between negation and reaffirmation. As Abdul R. JanMohamed and David Lloyd (10) point out, the "minority's attempt to negate the prior hegemonic negation of itself is one of its most fundamental forms of affirmation."

I ground my analysis of a theatre of crisis in major plays written between 1965 and 1970 by five of Latin America's most innovative and influential playwrights: from Cuba, José Triana's *La noche de los asesinos (Night of the Assassins,* 1965); from Argentina, Griselda Gambaro's *Los siameses (Siamese Twins,* 1965) and *El campo (The Camp,* 1967); from Mexico, Emilio Carballido's *El día que se soltaron los leones (The Day They Let the Lions Loose,* 1960) and *Yo también hablo de la rosa (I Too Speak of the Rose,* 1965); from Colombia, Enrique Buenaventura's *Papeles del infierno (Documents from Hell,* 1968); and from Chile, Egon Wolff's *Flores de papel (Paper Flowers,* 1970). These authors use theatre to explore the changing representations of self/otherness in the critical context of shifting sociopolitical and historical power relationships. They approach specific issues that are key to an understanding of Latin America and its cultural images—among them, colonialism, institutionalized violence, revolution, identity and self-definition, and socioeconomic centrality versus marginality—in a variety of strikingly powerful ways.

Buenaventura (born 1925), who writes for a collective and stages his work for Colombia's semiliterate audiences, is commonly referred to as the most "Brechtian" or "popular" of these theatre practitioners (see de Toro and Risk), yet these terms in themselves hardly eludicate his outstanding contributions to theatre. They are misleading: the Brechtian model itself undergoes significant transformation in the hands of Latin American practitioners, and the term "popular" is highly problematic within Latin America. These labels are not, as some radical practitioners maintain, either straightforward, politically "correct," or self-validating. The cycle of plays that constitute Buenaventura's documents from hell scrutinize the role of history as official mythmaking; he produces his own documents to emphasize the stories and perspectives that have been left out of history.

Triana (born 1931), who was exiled to Spain during the last years of Batista's regime, returned to Cuba to participate in the revolutionary society after Castro's triumph in 1959. However, after winning Cuba's prestigious Casa de las Americas award for his *Asesinos*, he was deemed "antirevolutionary" and gradually marginalized from intellectual activity; he again went into exile in 1980. The play introduces the gamut of questions posed about "revolutionary" and "antirevolutionary" theatre argued by people with as diverse backgrounds as Antonin Artaud, Frantz Fanon, and Augusto Boal.

Gambaro (born 1928) has developed a new theatrical language, a poetics of violence, to illuminate and make visible Argentina's politics of violence, which intensified steadily between 1966 and 1982. After receiving multiple death threats, she was forced into exile during the so-called "Dirty War" (1976-82). When she returned to Argentina after three years, the Picadero theatre in Buenos Aires, where her play *Decir sí (Saying Yes)* was staged as part of the Open Theatre cycle of 1981, was burned to the ground. What is particularly interesting about her early plays from a political viewpoint is that they foresee in specific detail the horrors, the abductions, the disappearances that would result from Argentina's continuing fascination with fascism.

Wolff (born 1926) confronts two marginal discourses pertaining to class and gender as the infirm, socioeconomically marginal male of *Paper Flowers*, who refers to himself as a representative of the Chilean underclass, destroys Eva, the prototypical woman, in what he interprets as a politically justifiable attack on the "effeminate" middle class. Wolff won the Casa de las Americas award in 1970.

Carballido (born 1925) draws from Mexico's oral tradition to establish a dialectic with the Brechtian model itself, illustrating that Marxist economic theory and Freudian psychology cannot fully "explain" Mexico's situation, and that its *mestizo* and semiliterate audiences cannot be addressed as if they were 1930s Germans or "children of a scientific age" (Brecht, 183).

The vitality of the drama analyzed in this study stems from the original artistic strategies it devises to survive as an art form that is essential, rather than tangential, to its highly explosive social context. The intense theatrical self-consciousness of this work begs for a new critical consciousness. Theatre not only provides a stage to represent ideological conflict mimetically; it is also a "real" arena in which that conflict is fought out, with real consequences. What does theatrical activity include, what does it exclude in its canon, audience, ideology? Does theatre help audiences deal with their situation, as such practitioners as Brecht and Boal maintain? Or, on the contrary, does it somehow legitimate domination by the repetitive use of images of power? Does theatre allow us an entry into the meaning and significance of violent acts, the theory being (as Elaine Scarry proposes in *The Body in Pain*) that if we could comprehend the reality of suffering, we could and would put an end to it? Does "watching" control violence, as the verbal emphasis on the visual suggests in organizations such as Americas Watch or Klanwatch? Or is watching also its own kind of violence, as attested by voyeurism and the political policing exemplified in the Panopticon?[8] Does theatre make suffering seem trivial and pain entertaining by aestheticizing violence and fueling our desire to see the obscene (literally, the off-scene) or the hidden, that which is normally beyond our vision? Does theatre goad its audiences to greater political involvement, as some governments fear? Or does it incapacitate its audiences by riveting our attention to an image, by involving us emotionally to such a degree that we will accept hierarchies and victimization uncritically? Theatre, after all, "splits" emotions from actions, allowing us as spectators to witness suffering, to participate emotionally yet sit rooted in our seats. Moreover, it permits us to split the real from the unreal in problematic ways. While theatre depends on the spectators' ability to accept dramatic conventions and momentarily believe that the unreal is *real*, the other side of the same phenomenon is equally crucial yet often ignored: theatre simultaneously allows us to erase, block out, and *de*realize the real. This disconnection makes it possible for us to pity the attractive victim and at the same time forget that our money backs the tragedy in the first place. The political implications of theatrical activity that shifts from a theatre of oppression to a theatre of the oppressed are examined throughout this study.

Before addressing these issues in individual chapters, I must note that though questions concerning theatre's role in oppressive societies echo throughout Latin American theatrical activity in general, not all the specific facets and implications of the problem are of equal importance in all countries or to all playwrights. Certain problems—misogyny, racism, and class conflict, for example—are endemic to all the countries, but the urgency of the issues varies according to time and place, even within this five-year period. The problems facing Cuba are vastly different from those threatening Argentina, for example, and even in Cuba the revolution's limitations—signaled out by Triana as early as 1965—became increasingly obvious after 1968 (see chapter 2). If I stress the struggle for culture in chapter 4 and the struggle for history in chapter 5, this should not suggest that the two struggles are not related. Practical limitations preclude the extensive analysis of all the areas of conflict in any one chapter; therefore, I ground the theoretical problems in the contexts in which they figure most prominently. Necessarily, then, certain questions will dominate certain chapters and remain fairly marginal in others.

Some problems facing Latin American theatre are widespread and generalizable, however, and hence best summed up in the introduction. Latin American theatre remains a relatively marginal activity, notwithstanding the dramatic rise in the quantity and quality of the plays produced since the late 1950s. Surprisingly, the aesthetic richness and originality of this theatre have been underestimated by commentators. Though theatre in general receives less critical attention than do the narrative and poetic genres, it remains even more obscure in Latin America than elsewhere. The plays have been underproduced, underpublished, and understudied for several reasons. For one, the dramatic texts were eclipsed by a simultaneous "boom" in the novel. People as a rule read novels, not plays, so the Latin American literature that began to command international attention during this period was the narrative. When people then turned to the theatre, they focused, understandably perhaps, on plays by these already well-known authors. As a consequence, the few plays Latin Americans or Latin Americanists do know have been written by the famous novelists, not by the dramatists. Plays by Mario Vargas Llosa, Antonio Skármeta, Carlos Fuentes, and the like are published and produced both in and out of Latin America without increasing public awareness of Latin American theatre. The focus on the famous novelists only pushes the dramatists into deeper obscurity.

Another obvious reason that this theatre remains unknown is the lack of a constant or ongoing theatrical infrastructure to finance and facilitate the production of these works, both in their home countries and abroad. Thus, people who do not usually read plays do not have access to theatrical productions of these works either. The aforementioned international Latin American festivals, which declined sharply throughout the continent following Allende's overthrow in 1973, were basically the only visible arena for the performance of these works and the establishment of connections and interconnections between different playwrights and groups.

The lack of mutual awareness and understanding between the many Latin American countries, however, reflects not only limited economic means but, perhaps more important, a host of misconceptions, prejudices, and skewed priorities resulting from internalized colonialism. Culturally as well as politically and economically, Latin America has traditionally turned its gaze outward toward Europe and the United States. The manifestations of this attitude are not simply that European and American classics or hits continue to dominate, as they have since the late sixteenth century, the cultural institutions frequented by the ruling class; they are also apparent in the formation and orientation of Latin America's leading dramatists. Gambaro, for example, notes in an interview that she had studied the entire consecrated "universal" (Western) canon before reading one Argentine play (*Teatro*, 10). Triana has cited the importance of Spain's "Generation of '98" and the existentialists and absurdists—notably Sartre, Camus, Ionesco, Beckett, and Genet—on his artistic development (Taylor, *Imagen*, 116). Jorge Díaz notes that the plays he wrote in Chile before leaving permanently for Spain in 1965—perhaps most notably his well-known *El cepillo de dientes (The Toothbrush*, 1962) were Eurocentric, not because he was conscious of his attitude but because Eurocentricism was characteristic of his progressive bourgeois Chilean background.[9]

The dominance of the colonizer's culture has affected the work produced in Latin America in various ways. First of all, foreign models have defined and controlled culture since the Conquest. As the centuries passed, foreign commercial successes (increasingly backed by elaborate marketing mechanisms) continued to displace local theatrical activity, which became a minor or secondary manifestation even in its own context. In addition, theatre produced in Latin America often catered to the consumer market, to the foreign public's demand for exotic otherness, for magic. Sergio Magaña's *Moctezuma II*, an economic success in Mexico for years, staged the grandiose and decorative tragedy of the last emperor to enthusiastic tourist audiences.

No less significant is the fact that Latin American countries are flooded by foreign images transmitted by the mass media, reproduced ad infinitum, and displayed throughout the distant corners of all lands. These movies, television shows, and ads reflect faces, worlds, world views that are alien, if not downright hostile, to native Latin American identities, experience, and aspirations. Roberto Fernández Retamar comments on the irony of colonized populations watching foreign films, such as westerns and Tarzan movies, and clapping at the representation of their own extermination (*Calibán*, 8). Imported cultural representations of otherness often distance, distort, and corrode the image and vision of self, refracted as it is through the powerful foreign optic. Moreover, these widespread images not only alienate Latin Americans within their own countries; they also create and channel desire, thus generating increased demand for more images, which activate more desires. Robert Heilbroner, in "The Triumph of Capitalism" (99), notes that John Maynard Keynes and even Marx himself failed to assess the extent of capitalism's capacity to perpetuate itself in its "never-ending search for overlooked crevices in which capitalism might grow, or for wholly new endeavors it might undertake."[10] And as Guy Debord (28) observes, the society of the spectacle produces isolation: "From the automobile to the television, all the goods selected by the spectacular system are also its weapons for a constant reinforcement of the conditions of isolation of 'lonely crowds.'" The kind of theatrical activity studied here, however, in decoding the oppressive spectacles and challenging the legitimating, reductive, and colonizing role of culture, is generally kept off the main stages. Even on the level of literary production—as manuscripts—the difficulty of getting these plays published and translated impedes their ability to circulate and find an audience.

Another factor contributing to the devalorization of this theatre is the role of dramatic criticism. Latin American drama has generally fallen victim to two conflicting critical perspectives, one that purports to judge the works exclusively as *text,* and one that attempts to judge theatre only as part of a political *process.* Let me begin with a look at the first: American and European commentators of the 1960s and 1970s—and, to a diminishing degree, the 1980s—tended to decontextualize the drama, focusing on universal themes and recognizable theatrical models and traditions. This, after all, is what the academy had trained scholars to do. (The universalizing attitude was so prevalent that the Latin Americans dramatists themselves were not, as I have noted, exempt from it.) When dealing with theatre in the context of colonization and oppression, however, this critical distancing and decontextualizing in itself contributed to continued cultural colonization. While this theatre increasingly tried to free itself and its audience from centuries of domination, its criticism perpetuated a hegemonic, prescriptive role. The critic, perhaps in the name of objectivity, often covered the text with a critical discourse and jargon that further buried the emergent voice.[11] Criticism, as First World scholars have only recently started to point out, can play an important, albeit unacknowledged, political role in marginalizing literary production. As Said (25) notes, "We have reached the stage at which specialization and professionalism, allied with cultural dogma, barely sublimated ethnocentrism and nationalism, as well as a surprisingly insistent quasi-religious quietism, have transported the professional and academic critic of literature—the most focused and intensely trained interpreter of texts produced by the culture—into another world altogether." A certain critical distancing is necessary in balancing ever conflicting versions of realities, but the critics' inability to locate both the text and themselves firmly in the world risks perpetuating the hegemonic versions of reality.

The effect of continued cultural colonization on our understanding of contemporary Latin American theatre cannot be overemphasized. Powerful defining groups outside Latin America constantly reiterate that, judged by their accepted standards of artistic excellence, the theatrical activity of these countries is "underdeveloped." One example suffices, although the tendency is widespread. Erika Munk, editor of the *Drama Review* in 1968, recounting a theatre research trip taken by Richard Schechner and Joanne Pottlitzer to Latin America, summed up in "TDR Comment" what she saw as their experience. For Pottlitzer, said Munk, Latin American theatre was "worth the attention" of our society because, "though it has problems and is a little backward—[it] can be approached and understood in the same ways as United States and European theatre" (33). Not only did such a statement skew Pottlitzer's findings (she explicitly stated that this theatre had to be met on its "own terms"; 35), but Munk did not seem to realize that the very term "backward" subverted her theoretical acceptance of this theatre; as Arif Dirlik notes in "Culturalism as Hegemonic Ideology" (24), the word itself denies "contemporary relevance to the culture of the Other." Richard Schechner, according to Munk (33), left with a different impression: "In the Latin America Richard Schechner visited, there is no theatre. There are some dead shapes moving about on proscenium stages." This commentary, which introduces a special issue on Latin American theatre, demonstrates how hegemony passes as objective criticism, for it depends on our privileging certain models that then become the referents to validate judgments that either legitimate or exclude other cultural manifestations. Only by decontextualizing the plays can Munk allow that they may have meaning in terms of Western background and experience. Only by deterritorializing the works can she justify their existence. Not surprisingly, then, Munk notes the Latin American use of recognizable dramatic forms but concludes that they were "clumsily borrowed" (33) and that the theatre "savors too much of a humble effort to please" (34).

As I argue in this study, however, the plays' multiple uses of recognizable techniques propose visions of reality very different from those advanced by First World authors. With few exceptions, we cannot speak of a Latin American theatre of the absurd, or even a clear-cut Latin American Brechtian epic theatre. Within their specific Latin American contexts, these forms undergo change and become something quite different as they transform the received codes to become intelligible to their own audiences. What the foreign scholars have failed to recognize is that these "borrowings" in fact are part of an ongoing process of transculturation. "Transculturation," denoting the transformation of cultural material as it passes from one society to another, is a term coined by Fernando Ortiz (Cuba) in 1940. Ortiz describes what he sees as a three-part process in the acquisition of foreign cultural material which results in the loss of the autochthonous culture but then yields a new original: "The term *transculturation* better expresses the different phases of the transitive process from one culture to another, because this process does not imply only the acquisition of culture, as connoted by the anglo-american term *acculturation*, but the process also necessarily implies the loss or uprooting of the preceding culture (what one could call a partial disculturation), and, moreover, it implies the resulting creation of new cultural phenomena that one could call *neoculturation*" (qtd. in Rama, *Transculturación*, 32).

Although the foreign critics of the late 1960s did not understand the cultural phenomenon they were witnessing, the concrete ramifications of their deprecating views, expressed through prominent vehicles of cultural authority such as the *Drama Review*, were widespread and hampered reception and research. Who would read past the opening commentary of the Latin American issue? Who would read this backward drama, let alone publish it? Who would produce or direct dead shapes on a proscenium stage? Who would study this area? Who would publish that research? By labeling these works artistically underdeveloped, this kind of criticism added to their marginalization. As Octavio Paz points out ("Invención," 345), the word "underdeveloped" is not a critical term; it is an "excrescence of the idea of economic and social progress" and has no "causal relationship with artistic excellence." Yet we see how this drama was caught in a critical double bind that threatened to erase it: while professing to analyze the texts in isolation and according to universal standards, commentators continued to judge them by norms more in keeping with their socioeconomic context—that is, as underdeveloped. Concurrently, however, the commentators divorced the works from the cultural contexts that gave them rise and evaluated them by universal *Western* standards. Because Munk failed to "see" or recognize the transformation of theatrical forms in divergent cultural contexts—specifically, within the reality of colonization—she concluded that this theatre's "destruction might even be helpful": the dramatists might then "create something real"—yet she immediately tried to dispel the suspicion that the *Drama Review* "was itself exhibiting the putting-down mentality of the colonist" (34).

A secondary manifestation of the same colonializing perspective affects the way Latin American critics view this theatre, the self-deprecating stance that appears to be tied to Latin America's historical process. Theatre produced in the colonial Americas did not reflect its own particular reality. Furthermore, writers born in the Americas during the colonial period, though mostly of European background, were considered inferior and almost entirely excluded from production. When they did write, they were forced to adopt Spanish models (the three-act structure), subject matter (praise of royalty and Christianity), or both. I deal with theatre in the colonial period in chapter 1; it is sufficient here to note that American-born dramatists were forced to adhere to foreign theatrical models. Nor did this domination end with political independence. Theatre that reflected native reality in Latin America—movements such as *costumbrismo* or *indigenismo*, for example—were dismissed by commentators as parochial and folkloric. As Juan Villegas points out in *Ideología y discurso crítico sobre el teatro de España y América Latina* (58), the plurality of Latin America's many realities is typically reduced or rejected in the name of universality. On a subtle level, Latin America's many differences and idiosyncrasies simply failed to interest those who looked for Western equivalents. On a more overt level, however, all theatre was rejected that failed to live up to classical standards. Critics such as the Argentine Alfredo de la Guardia, writing in the 1960s, called for purity in theatre; his theoretic and practical models ranged from Aristotle to T.S. Eliot. Theatre should be sublime, he declared, and consequently is best served by the poetic idiom. If the spectators could not appreciate or understand this art form, then, he quoted Lope de Vega, "people are fools" (Arriví, 64)—even though as early as 1609, Lope (64) had "banished Terence and Plautus from (his) study."[12]

Clearly, then, the criticism that claimed to study these works exclusively as objects of textual analysis—at the expense of their performative contexts, their avowed aims, and their intended audiences—occluded the works' relevance and vitality. However, the opposite position, which posits that this theatre is important only as part of a political process, as a political instrument, a "weapon . . . in the necessary transformations of society" (Boal, *Oppressed*, x), also has reductive results and limits our understanding of the complexity of the theatrical phenomenon. So let us look at this second critical position. Many committed Latin American theatre practitioners, reacting to centuries of colonization, understandably took up theatre as an instrument of liberation. I use Boal's work to exemplify this position, not because he is the most radical of the practitioners (far from it) but because he is the best known and most internationally influential. As Marvin Carlson writes in his *Theories of the Theatre* (475), "no contemporary theorist has explored the political implications of performance-audience relationship in so searching and original a manner as the Latin American director, Augusto Boal." Boal's "theatre of the oppressed" trains the audience to change its role in the oppressed/oppressor relationship. As opposed to an Aristotelian system that divides people into actors and spectators, and further divides the actors into the individuated aristocracy and the anonymous, plebeian chorus, Boal proposes that everyone take a part, everyone become a protagonist in overcoming economic, class, and ideological barriers. He arrives at dramatic strategies to increase active participation on the part of audiences through a series of workshops that devise and rehearse scenarios in which people who are ordinarily passive begin to explore solutions to their problems and learn to act decisively. These presentations are followed (much as in psychodramatic exercises) by group discussion. Because the aim of the workshops is to produce measurable social change rather than plays, the success of this theatre can be evaluated only in terms of its efficacy in achieving specific social goals. If a certain technique or model fails to work, it must be replaced by one that does.[13] The emphasis on theatre-as-process, on context over text, inverts the traditional privileging of literary masterpieces much in the manner of Artaud's impassioned command: "No More Masterpieces" *(Theatre and Its Double)*.

Taken to its extreme, however, though judging theatre's impact on the real rather than the symbolic order (profoundly un-Artaudian) may have positive social effects, it does not always have much to do with *theatre* in the general sense of framed symbolic action. It helps us understand neither scripted theatre nor other kinds of nonscripted theatrical activity. In fact, practitioners in the 1960s who were far more radical than Boal gave up on theatre altogether because it was not reliable or direct enough as an instrument of social change. They often demonstrated hostility toward scripted theatre and contempt for dramatists who were writing texts. In 1968 Pablo Suárez (103) distributed a letter dissociating himself from the prestigious Di Tella Institute in Argentina: "Let those who want to 'get ahead' work in the institute." This position blinds us to the political efficacy of dramatists who do believe in theatre as a vehicle for social change, albeit the slow and difficult-to-measure change of educating an audience. Griselda Gambaro's *Los siameses*, interestingly, opened at the same Di Tella Institute in 1967. Yet even though she is one of the most innovative, experimental, and politically lucid playwrights working today, the radical theatre practitioners could not perceive the value of a play staged in a conventional theatre. The struggles over theatre's function, goals, space, and audience, even within the same context, have contributed significantly to critical misunderstanding.

The radical theatre practitioners were right, however, to despair of theatre's efficacy as an instrument of measurable, foreseeable social change. Theatre is politically too unstable to be an unequivocable, reliable "weapon" in political struggle. Though it can alter the social order through the laborious process of consciousness raising, it is dangerously vulnerable to assimilation by any given social order. Systems and parties appropriate theatre and theatricality (icons, images, plots, rhetoric) to further their own ends, to bolster themselves through images that signal stability and legitimacy. Those in authority not only have the power to silence or censor theatre but can also co-opt its discursive and iconographic techniques to attract spectators, to enthrall audiences, to promote identification and mystification. As the Spaniards found out in the sixteenth century, it is far more effective to preempt images and rhetoric than to attack them. This appropriation can take nonviolent means, as the celebratory nature of much political display attests. However, once the population sees through this level of political mystification and manipulation, those in control often resort to intensifying spectacles of power that atomize and destabilize the population. Dramas of terror and oppression can paralyze the audience by means of real, though highly theatrical, acts of public execution, torture, and terrorism.

This study examines the uses and abuses of theatre and theatricality in relation to the prevalent discourses and ideological tensions of the late 1960s. To analyze the relationship between different examples of the-atrical activity in societies in crisis, however, we must go beyond the two positions posited above: the critical premise that theatre is not or should not be political; and the activist's position that theatre is only a part of the political process. Theatre is always in the world, and always political insofar as it overtly or covertly manifests an ideology. The difference, as George H. Szanto makes clear in *Theater and Propaganda*, lies in the manner in which that ideology makes itself felt by the audience. He distinguishes three kinds of theatre: agitation, integration, and dialectical. Agitation theatre, commonly known as agit-prop, has one specific aim: it "attempts to rouse its audience and society to active ends—patriotism, war, cheering for the home team." Integration theatre, the kind American and Latin American audiences are most familiar with through TV situation comedies, Broadway hits, and the mass media, hides its ideology by depicting what is in fact a social construct as a "universal" or "natural" given. It "attempts to render its audience and society passive; its goal is for its audience to accept unquestioningly and uncomplainingly the social conundrums of the present and not challenge the authority of those who perpetuate the dominant and ongoing social institutions" (Szanto, 9). Integration theatres are often unaware of their ideology, or go to great lengths to attack the concept of ideology altogether. Audiences will often recognize the world-as-construct later, when they see the same images they once deemed *natural* as dated, biased, sexist, racist, or whatever. Other kinds of theatre do not deny or hide their ideology. Contrary to theatre shrouded in magic, or aesthetic mystique, Piscator's "epic" the-atre, Brecht's "dialectic" theatre, Buenaventura's theatre of "deconscie-ntization," and Boal's "theatre of the oppressed" emphasize that theatre is *work:* people produce it; others consume it; it serves specific aims within or against specific institutions. This dialectical theatre "attempts to de-mystify, by depicting separately, interactively, and always clearly, the basic elements which compromise a confused social or historical situation" (Szanto, 75). The plays in this study, with one exception, provide exam-ples of demystifying, though not always dialectical, theatre. They expose the integrating theatricality of their social setting, the political shams and the rhetoric of legitimation that authority figures use to pacify the public and maintain illusions of justice and social well-being.

To keep a firm sense of these works' contextuality, I found it necessary to maintain a tight critical focus on a handful of self-reflective works written within a five-year period. Limiting the time frame to the years between 1965 and 1970 is, in a sense, highly artificial; events never fit into our critical constructs, and one could argue that virtually all Latin Amer-ican periods qualify as times of crisis and violent transition. There were plays written before 1965 and after 1970 that fit into my paradigm of a theatre of crisis. What distinguishes this five-year period from those immediately preceding or following it, however, is the widespread nature of the phenomenon. Although the sociopolitical and economic tensions became even more obvious in Latin America in the 1970s, the years between 1965 and 1970 were the turning point; the hope and exuberance following the Cuban revolution in 1959 coincided and clashed with the grim reality of ever more restrictive totalitarian regimes coming to power after 1964. The inchoate, confusing, contradictory nature of the transition is what I mean by crisis—the turningpoint between life and death, re-generation and repression. The very concept of crisis represents a suspen-sion, a rupture between two states. As new military regimes sprang up, reasserting totalitarian control and fixing rigid boundaries, it became increasingly clear who the "enemy" was. As criminal governments in Argentina, Brazil, Uruguay, Paraguay, Chile, Guatemala, and El Salvador (to name only the most brutal) deliberately used destabilizing tactics to terrorize and atomize their populations, it became evident whose interests the orchestrated crisis of the 1970s was serving. The drama analyzed in this work, then, formulates the prevailing social tensions during a climactic moment, a moment in which old myths and orders fell away but new ideas had not congealed into a seamless, integrative ideology. By situating this period within a larger historical framework, mapping out what came before it and what happened afterward, I attempt to compensate for the limiting temporal frame.

The five-year period examined was also pivotal in the careers of the authors themselves. Their later work indicates important changes in perspective if not always in sociopolitical circumstance; it has taken marked steps beyond crisis toward sharper political and formal definition.

While the specific period under analysis narrows the possible selection of material, I have tried to be as inclusive as possible by studying the works of playwrights from diverse backgrounds, writers who differ both in methodology and, to a degree, intention. In the interest of practicality, I decided to study only one playwright from any one country and only single-author texts (even if they were written for a collective). Regrettably, this meant the exclusion of outstanding collective theatre groups, notably the Teatro de la Candelaria in Colombia and the Rajatabla in Venezuela, as well as major playwrights: Vicente Leñero (Mexico), Virgilio Piñera (Cuba), Luisa Josefina Hernández (Mexico), Elena Garro (Mexico), Eduardo Pavlovsky (Argentina), Osvaldo Dragún (Argentina), Jorge Díaz (Chile), and Sergio Vodánovic (Chile), among others. I also decided against including agitation theatre, or theatre that was univocal and limited to one perspective. The focus of this study, rather, is on the theatre as arena for ideological confrontation and stuggle; hence, the works must necessarily be multivocal and multiperspectival.

While limiting the temporal and material scope of the field on one level, I hope to expand our understanding of a "theatre of crisis" by establishing paradigms of crisis that will elucidate similar manifestions both inside and outside Latin America. Starting from the works' own premises, then, I make connections and signal developments (crisis and beyond . . .) within the Latin American dramatic canon and in theatrical activity elsewhere.

# 1

# THEATRE AND CRISIS: THE MAKING OF LATIN AMERICAN DRAMA

THE STAGE for the theatre of the oppressed was set in the sixteenth century when the Spaniards watched their first indigenous performances. Their response, a mixture of admiration and loathing, affected more than the theatrical activities themselves. Their rejection of the spectacles as godless and "barbaric" justified the destruction of the entire social order that supported and was supported by them. In the confrontation of cultures the Spaniard/spectator won control, cast himself as the defining self empowered to judge and destroy the pagan other. The conquerors imposed their own representation on the natives. They invented and directed the drama that transformed the native into a grotesque other who, in spite of opposition by Bartolomé de Las Casas and others, could be enslaved and worked to death in the name of civilization and Christianity. The rejection of the indigenous, moreover, proved double. On one hand, it was doctrinal—the rejection of an alien belief. On the other, it was instrumental and economic, serving to justify enslavement and forced labor. From that moment onward, the refracted optic as basis for definition and self-definition laid the foundation for future (including current) theatrical discourse.

The similarities between the dramatists presented in this study are more extratextual, contextual, and historical than intratextual. The questions of position (political and cultural centrality versus marginality), definition, and identity, and the concerns with oppression, colonization, self-hatred —in short, many of the issues they articulate—are not simply a product of their own theatrical experimentation; rather, they arise as a consequence of the cultural, economic, and political history of domination. Because Latin American theatre is relatively unknown outside very restricted circles, an introduction to the shifts from a theatre of oppression to a theatre of the oppressed will provide the necessary background material for the ensuing discussion of the theatre of crisis.

The following background, then, is offered by way of introduction to the dramatic revisions in the evolving representations of a Latin American self in the face of a defining and confining otherness. It is not intended as a straightforward historical overview. José Juan Arrom's *Historia del teatro hispanoamericano (Epoca colonial)*, Frank Dauster's *Historia del teatro hispanoamericano*, Agustín del Saz's *Teatro Hispanoamericano*, and single-country histories already provide a historical panorama. Here, I propose to sketch out the changing role of theatre in a context of domination and colonization, the process by which the conquerors imposed a binary frame on the pre-Hispanic world and relegated the vanquished to the position of the barbarous and peripheral other.

## Theatre, Theatricality, and Conquest

Latin American theatre, from its origins to the present, has largely been viewed and defined in terms of otherness. Though scholars such as Riné Leal (*Breve historia*, 9) insist that the conquerers brought *their* theatre but not *the* theatre to the Americas, it is from the perspective of the conquerors and missionaries that scholars today first "see" this indigenous activity. Hernán Cortés, Gonzalo Fernandéz de Oviedo, Bartolomé de Las Casas, Fray Bernardino de Sahagún, Fernández de Alva Ixtlilxóchitl, Fray Diego Durán, Juan de Tovar, José de Acosta, Jerónimo de Mendieta, Fray Diego de Landa, Fray Juan de Torquemada, Fray Toribio de Benavente, and others reported spectacular rituals, festivals, and ceremonies.[1] They involved dance, singing (rather than recitation) of poetry, song, theatrical skits, mime, acrobatics, and magic shows. The performers were trained; they wore costumes, masks, makeup, wigs. Earthen platforms had been erected to enhance visibility. The "sets" were decorated with branches from trees and other natural objects. Some aspects were symbolic: Durán described a little girl "all dressed in blue, which represented the great lake and all the fountains and small rivers."[2]

The vexing issue of definition began when the Spanish conquerors and missionaries tried to find equivalents within their linguistic and experiential frameworks to denote the various kinds of indigenous theatrical activity. These witness-historians are problematic for several reasons. While conceding that numerous aspects of the pre-Hispanic civilizations were marvelous, refined, and entertaining, the Spaniards clearly did not understand or accept the religious system governing those civilizations. In fact, several of them considered the spectacles a form of devil worship.[3] Though the representations to which they alluded played a vital role in the indigenous world, maintaining the social order in harmony with the religious metaphysical order, the witnesses tended to divorce the amusing elements from their socioreligious framework—both because they found them less offensive when viewed separately and because comic routines and role playing corresponded to activities in the Spaniards' own experience of Corpus Christi celebrations and shepherds' plays. It is significant to note that they refer to these activities not as theatre but as "dance" or "sung-dance," "games," "fiestas," and "entremeses." Yet it remains clear throughout their writings that the theatrical skits and representations formed part of a much wider celebration. What they described as a product, a skit, functioned in fact as a process.

What, then, were these activities? The earliest definitions demonstrate that the Spaniards tried to find their own European equivalents for the phenomena. The process of definition always involves equivalents, always uses other words, but the words used to define these activities said more about the Europeans than about the indigenous theatrical process. The conquerors gazed in reluctant admiration at these spectacles and then destroyed them. Aside from the Spaniards' own descriptions, little remains upon which scholars can base alternative interpretations. Few dramatic fragments are extant: the hymn to Tlaloc and the hymn of Netzahualcoyotl, which according to Rodolfo Usigli (23) "were neither hymns nor written by Netzahualcoyotl." The exquisite Mayan piece *Rabinal Achí*, a highly ritualized dramatic dialogue between two warriors, was not published until 1862, by which time it was badly truncated. *El Güegüence* (Nicaragua) and *Ollántay* (Peru), for all their pre-Hispanic elements, are considered colonial rather than precolonial pieces. Recent archaeological research, according to Miguel León-Portilla's outstanding *Pre-Columbian Literatures of Mexico*, has found murals and bas-reliefs of ceremonial processions and rites which may suggest a more apt definition, this time from the point of view of the indigenous people themselves.

Meanwhile, contrary to the widely held view, no evidence supports the hypothesis that these events constituted a theatre, or even predominantly theatrical (rather than, say, ritualistic) performances. All evidence indicates that the festivals, of which theatrical (mimetic) representation was only one component, were extremely complex, highly orchestrated affairs often lasting up to five days. Everyone in the community was involved to some degree in the ceremonies which, grounded in religious imperatives, concerned the well-being of the society as a whole and consequently of everybody in it. Pedro Carrasco, in "La sociedad mexicana antes de la conquista" (235), points to the impossibility of separating out religion from any of the human activities—technological, political, or social—in pre-Columbian societies. Hence, the function of theatricality in these ritualized societies was fundamentally different from what the Spaniards were accustomed to and later imposed on their conquered subjects. Whereas the Spaniards, as we shall see, used the pomp and ceremony associated with theatricality to legitimate and empower their political order, theatricality in Mesoamerica, much as in Bali, served the opposite function: "It was a theatre state," writes Clifford Geertz of nineteenth-century Bali, "in which the kings and princes were the impresarios, the priests the directors, and the peasants the supporting cast, stage crew and audience. The stupendous cremations . . . and blood sacrifices, mobilizing hundreds and even thousands of people and great quantities of wealth, were not means to political ends: they were the ends themselves, they were what the state was for. . . . Power served pomp, not pomp power" (*Negara*, 13).

It is clear, then, that we cannot discuss pre-Columbian theatre as if we were speaking of theatre derived from the Greek classical period. From my point of view, this does not imply a value judgment, although the classical model has historically been used to illustrate the deficiencies of the indigenous. Whatever the similarities—actors, costumes, sets, and so forth—commentators have generally tended to underemphasize the differences. Scholars discussing pre-Hispanic performances point to the existence of actors, for example, but the function of these actors differs profoundly from that of actors in Western theatre. The little girl playing "the great lake" was sacrificed during the performance. So too were the actors embodying divinity. These indigenous performances were primarily presentations to the gods rather than mimetic representations for an audience. Like the Balinese theatre described by Geertz, this was a "metaphysical theatre: theatre designed to express a view of the ultimate nature of reality and, at the same time, to shape the existing conditions of life to be consistent with that reality; that is, theatre to present an ontology and, by presenting it, to make it happen—make it actual" (*Negara*, 104). The way the events functioned reveals a ritual (instrumental) intention. In the minds of the participants the festivals "worked"; they were efficacious; they maintained the cosmic, natural and social rhythms that were, for them, ultimately one and the same. The Nahuas, the Mayas, and the Incas did not allow for a clear-cut separation of the sacred and the secular.

Given the nature of these societies and the role of spectacle within them, it should not surprise us that the indigenous words for these art forms demonstrate that there was no need for the fine-honed aesthetic distinctions and generic hierarchies postulated by Aristotle. *Areítos* (Antilles) derives from *aririn*, meaning "recite, rehearse"; *mitotes* (Nahuatl) derives from *mitotl*, meaning "dance"; *taqui* stems from the Quechua word *taki*, meaning "song"; *batocos* is another word widely used for "song." Just as the words overlap, suggesting a larger activity encompassing many performative elements, so do they represent collective enterprises in which everyone in the society participated to some degree. The powerful priests had as much at stake in the ceremonies as did the lowly; the comic mingled with the sacred. Usigli, in *Mexico in the Theater* (24), quotes an (unidentified) description of this multigeneric performance: "the dance was performed almost always accompanied by singing but the song as well as the movements of those who danced were subject to the rhythm of the instruments. . . . In the spaces between the lines of dancers buffoons usually performed, imitating other peoples in their dress or attempting with disguises of wild beasts or other animals to make people laugh with their antics."

The question of the conquerors' definition continues to pose a problem for twentieth-century commentators, and not only because the chronicles provide the only extant documentation of the actual performances. Were these performances *theatre*? Commentators risk promoting a Eurocentric vision no matter how they respond. Perhaps in retaliation to the conquerors, who considered the performances barbaric, scholars as noteworthy as Angel María Garibay, Arrom, and Sten have implicitly tended to "privilege" them as theatre according to classical Greek models, rather than consider what these works actually represented within their own context. It is as if these commentators do not want to repeat the violence of the conquerors by pointing out the ritual (which for many must still connote "primitive") components of the spectacles. Scholars compete to legitimate the indigenous performances by fitting them into the Western canon. Arrom (21) writes that one "can compare the Inca representations to the ancient Greek tragedies, especially to those of Aeschylus, that are reduced to epic narratives with commentaries by the chorus." Leal (*Breve historia*, 10) calls the *areítos* "representations" but not "*yet* drama" because they lacked conflict (my emphasis). Sten (33) speaks of the theatrical activities as "happenings [*aconteciemientos*] more than representations," yet she affrms that they form a "rudimentary theatre, with all the elements of traditional representations, which, "if it had not been for the Conquest and the following centuries of the Colony . . . might have become spectacles as theatrical as, although very different from, Greek and Christian tragedy." Garibay in *Literatura Náhuatl*, describes songs recited by the chorus, the high priest and the singer as "embryonic" dramatic pieces. Francisco Monterde (xxvi), refers to Pedro Henríquez Ureña's comparison of the *Rabinal Achí* to Greek tragedy: "Not only because it is so similar to Attic tragedy—although this work is not presided over by the Fates—, Pedro Henríquez Ureña, speaking about *Rabinal Achí*, suggests that theatre in Greece, before Aeschylus, could have been like this, with only two actors engaged in dialogue onstage, before the appearance of the third actor, and the *corueta*, a member of the chorus intervened briefly if it was necessary that another character pronounce certain phrases at certain moments of the play, as happens here in a few scenes." "Embryonic," "rudimentary" theatre, defined from the perspective of classical Greek models: the terminology itself betrays these commentators' sense of historical progression as a development from the barbaric to the civilized, from the infantile to the adult. No commentator of these pre-Columbian spectacles has reversed the perspective to propose (as Wole Soyinka does, for example, in "Theatre in African Traditional Culture") that drama is perhaps a *reduction* of the vaster ritual process.[4]

Conversely, theatre commentators run into the same Eurocentrism and limit themselves unnecessarily by considering as "nontheatre" all performative activity that differs in form and source from Greek theatre. By this standard, theatre would exist only in the Western tradition, and everyone else had (or has) something different. This position legitimates the further marginalization of the so-called non-Western. The questions of definition and the seemingly unavoidable Eurocentrism of perspective that complicate discussion of pre-Hispanic performance continue shaping the present discourse. Whether the Mesoamerican activities were "theatre" or "ritual" or something else that we have not been able to define (either because the material has been destroyed or skewed or because we, like the conquerors, lack the epistemic framework to see and understand) seems secondary to the purposes of this particular study. Of primary importance is our recognition of how the colonizing vision has molded perspectives from its first manifestation onward. As with the conquerors, our perspective says more about us than about the performances.

During the colonial period, several major patterns took shape. The Conquest initiated the elaborate play of substitution (one power for another) that continued with the imposition of one structure on another: one culture, religion, language on another; one means of expression (literacy) on another (orality). Just as the conquerors tore down the magnificent *cue* in Tenochtitlán to construct their cathedral with the same materials on the same site, the colonists turned the indigenous theatrical activities (often in the native languages) into instruments of their own power. After the initial displacement, the Colony brought about a double exclusion. On the one hand there was the separation between the colonial cities and economic centers, which, as Jean Franco observes ("Dependency Theory," 68), were controlled by the colonizers through the Inquisition, censorship, and the exclusive use of the printing press. The population living outside these centers was to a degree exempt but also excluded from them. Hence, the indigenous population had no access to the literate culture, and as Franco adds, "the written culture . . . was overwhelmingly associated with domination." On the other hand, the centers of power gradually receded further and further away. Cortés did not simply replace Cuauhtémoc and rule as the new master. He was a representative of another order, the Spanish throne, whose distant nucleus of power decentered the colonies to the political periphery and marginalized the conquered as excentric others.

Not only was the indigenous population dominated by the literate culture through the withholding of literacy, but their own forms of expression were co-opted for the purposes of colonization. For the first fifty years after the Conquest the missionaries used theatre widely to spread the Christian doctrine to a population accustomed to the visual and oral quality of spectacle. Finding it more effective to use the indigenous forms than to put an end to "pagan" practices, the conquerors gutted the content of the spectacles, retained the trappings, and used them to convey their own message. The theatricality of the rituals, which had previously supported the pre-Columbian belief system and sustained a sacred order, now furthered the aims of the Church and administration, undermining the previous system, redefining and redirecting power. The missionaries allowed the theatre to keep some of its pre-Hispanic features; the natives staged biblical stories in their own manner, with their own props and often in their own language. Thus, the indigenous audience became emotionally engaged in an experience that only superficially resembled their own. Motolinía describes how the *auto* of Adam and Eve was "represented by the indigenous population in their own language, so that many of them cried and showed much feeling, especially when Adam was exiled and sent out into the world" (qtd. in Arrom, 28). Adam's loss of paradise in a sense resembles the audience's loss of its world, but the Christian version did not support the reality of the native suffering. On the contrary, Christianity was to a degree the *justification for,* rather than the *reflection of,* the audience's deterritorialization.

While the spectacles were ostensibly promoting a new sacred order, they were in fact primarily serving to support the new secular, political order. Unlike the pre-Hispanic rituals through which the earthly established contact with the divine, theatricality under the colonizers was primarily at the service of the administration. What the Church decreed for the salvation of the indigenous souls and what in fact happened to the colonized were two different things. The purpose of the didactic missionary theatre was to control rather than to educate the natives or assimilate them into Spanish culture. As Kathleen Shelley and Grínor Rojo point out in "El teatro hispanoamericano colonial" (323), the representations taught the indigenous peoples only the minimum required to convert them to Christianity and make them submissive workers: "They were also taught the necessity for obedience, servitude, and respect for legitimate authority (Royalty and the Church), the grave perils of accumulating more goods than were strictly necessary, the small importance of earthly life except in achieving salvation."

Thus, in spite of their indigenous elements, the productions now signaled a vision and a reality that no longer corresponded to the indigenous reality. Their very theatricality, furthermore, facilitated the continuity that to a degree hid the rupture in world vision. The fact that theatricality is in itself potent, even when divorced from its traditional content, explains why it is such an unstable phenomenon and at the same time such a contested and powerful instrument in cementing or undermining social cohesion. The appropriation of spectacle and images to convey a very different world view gradually eroded the beliefs, the memories (conserved through the oral traditions) and the language of the indigenous people and unraveled their world from the inside out.

Toward the end of the sixteenth century, this missionary theatre almost totally disappeared—but by then, so had most of the indigenous population. War, disease, exploitation, "brutality and plain murder for gain, for pleasure, for sport" reduced it by more than 90 percent in the century following the Conquest (Katz, 9).

There was, then, no truly indigenous theatre after the Conquest. There was theatre with indigenous elements and in indigenous languages, as we noted, but its power in maintaining an indigenous consciousness and sense of identity is hard to measure. This is not to suggest that the theatre was totally in the hands of the colonizers, but the texts that remain cannot convey the oral features of the works that must certainly have evoked a sense of collective experience, memory, and history in their audiences. After analyzing the major texts in indigenous languages dating to the mid-eighteenth century—ranging from Alva Ixtlilxóchitl's Náhuatl renditions of Golden Age plays by Lope de Vega and Calderón to the Bible lessons in Quechua by Juan de Espinosa Medrano (1639?-1688) and Gabriel Centeno de Osma (*Yauri Titu Inca* or *El pobre más rico*, 1707)—Shelley and Rojo (344) maintain that the truncated Guatemalan text *Rabinal Achí* (published in 1862) and the Nicaraguan *Güegüence*, published in 1874, while not exactly indigenous theatre, have strong indigenous elements that point the way for future manifestations of popular theatre: "All the other extant works, even when written in indigenous languages and when they contain elements that indubitably belong to that world, form part of a vanquished literature, either entirely or partially alienated from the real circumstances of its (presumed) public." *Güegüence*, they argue, provides the only example of passive resistance to authority, in both theme and style, in the indigenous theatre within this period.

The latter part of the eighteenth century provides an interesting example of theatre playing a somewhat more prominent role in the wider drama of oppression and provoking "real" and devastating political results. In 1780, the Quechua play *Ollántay* (Peru) was first performed for Túpac Amaru II, the leader of the most famous indigenous uprising in the eighteenth century. The point here is not to what degree *Ollántay* is formally an indigenous or, as Arrom (126) argues, a *mestizo* play, "Spanish in terms of structure, versification, the function of some of the characters, certain determined stylistic recourses, but indigenous in all else." More important than the formal elements is the fact that the work is a poignant representation of the marginalization of the noble indigenous warrior Ollántay, who is invaluable in sustaining the king's power but is nonetheless prohibited from marrying the king's daughter.

Though Shelley and Rojo caution that "interpreting the work as a commentary on rebellion is going too far" (350), *Ollántay* was considered a subversive play by colonial authorities, and it precipitated the first case of theatrical banning in Latin America's long history of censorship. Its subversiveness goes beyond its eloquent depiction of the unjustified rejection of Ollántay and the horrific fate of his beloved Estrella. The power of the play, as Arrom realized (126), lies in "the legendary air to the plot, the aching melodiousness of the songs and above all, the climate of rebellion foreshadowing stormy times ahead." The songs and legendary air, more than anything the text handed down to us actually says, perhaps account for the violent reaction it provoked The orality of the work, transmitted through performance, proved threatening to the colonial authorities. As Franco notes in "Dependency Theory and Literary History" (69), the oral tradition, the narrative, songs, poetry, and, I would add, mimetic representation provided the means by which "the Indians were able to maintain a consciousness of their past and build up resentment and subversion over long periods." Moreover, the example of *Ollántay* illustrates that Franco is clearly correct in stating that the "presence of this living history makes the apparent abruptness of Indian rebellions more explicable; the sudden outbreak of armed struggle is in reality the culmination of decades and centuries of latent defiance which oral tradition keeps alive." *Ollántay* precipitated the confrontation between symbolic and political displays of power, the direct confrontation between theatre and an oppressive society with its spectacular power. While the play expressed the wish that Ollántay, the valiant chief of the Andes, "could rule the entire country" (Luzuriaga and Reeve, 171), the Spanish authorities captured the rebellious Túpac Amaru and his family. They were tortured and executed in the public square in Cuzco in a fashion rivaling the 1757 execution of Robert Damiens in France for brutality and theatricality. According to contemporary accounts, Túpac Amaru and his wife, Micaela Bastidas, were first forced to watch his son and uncle have their tongues cut out before they were killed.

Then the Indian woman Micaela was taken up to the scaffold, where, in the sight of her husband, her tongue was cut out and she was garroted, and her sufferings were unspeakable, because as her neck was very slender the screw was not able to strangle her and the executioners had to tie ropes around her neck, and each pulled in a different direction, and with kicks in the stomach and breast they finally killed her. The spectacle ended with the death of [Túpac Amaru]. He was brought into the middle of the square and the executioner cut out his tongue. Then they unshackled his hands and feet and laid him on the ground. They tied four ropes to his hands and feet and fastened the ropes to the girth of four horses, and four mestizos led them in four different directions, a sight this city had never before beheld. Either because the horses were not very strong, or because the Indian was really of iron, they could not possibly tear him apart, even though they tugged at him for a long time so that he was stretched in the air in a way that looked like a spider. . . . A great many people had gathered that day, but nobody uttered a cry or spoke a word. Many observed, and I among them, that in all that assembly there were no Indians to be seen, or at least not in their customary garb; if there were any, they were disguised in capes and ponchos.⁵

The theatrical representations of power offstage clearly overwhelmed the traditionally theatrical ones; nonetheless, the authorities found (and continue to find) theatre subversive and dangerous. They not only executed Túpac Amaru and his family but prohibited *Ollántay* and all theatrical productions in indigenous languages.

Throughout the centuries the inhabitants of the Americas, both the indigenous peoples and the Criollos, witnessed the display of foreign power as passive and silent observers—as audience. The enforced marginalization of the native population is evident in the theatre designed for the Spanish and later Criollo populations, for this was also dominated by church and state. Performances were staged on religious or secular holidays to celebrate the births of princes and the coronation of kings, as well as Corpus Christi (these latter celebrations were recorded as early as 1526, only five years after the conquest of Mexico). These spectacles also served to keep the native-born Americans economically, politically, and culturally other. While Spain remained the center, the metropolis, the peripheral Americas imported rather than produced plays, actors, and producers. American-born authors were almost completely excluded from the production of theatre during the early colonial period. They occasionally wrote for the *corrales públicos* or for specific public occasions when appropriate Spanish texts could not be found, but even these scripts followed Spanish models and reflected foreign rather than local realities. Arrom argues quite rightly that this obligatory adherence to Spanish models restricted the development of a native theatrical idiom. Even major playwrights—and the colonial period produced only two—had to express themselves within the discursive confines imposed by the dominator, as the cases of Ruiz de Alarcón (1580?-1639) and Sor Juana Inés de la Cruz (1648?-1695) illustrate.

Alarcón's theatre, commentators generally acknowledge, rivaled the "masters," Tirso, Lope, and Calderón. However, his success entailed physically and intellectually abandoning his land and identity and moving to Spain. Alarcón's move, combined with the fact that he never wrote about his native Mexico, demonstrates his conscious distancing from his origins in terms of both identity and position. Even so, as Jaime Concha points out in his fine study of Alarcón (361), the playwright was marginalized for being *indiano*, and his plays indirectly bespeak their origins: Alarcón's internalization of the Eurocentric vision of the Americas as a land of monsters, in combination with his own physical deformity (he was undersized and a hunchback), resulted in a dramaturgy that even "within the official orbit of the Church and cathedrals . . . carves out a subterranean world that is a variation and metamorphosis of his monstrous cave. . . . his *cueva indiana.*" The motif of a monstrous native, as we shall see throughout this study, remains constant and disturbing in modern Latin American theatre.

Sor Juana Inés de la Cruz was even further marginalized; she was not only an *indiana* but a woman and also illegitimate. For all her brilliance and beauty, her choices were limited: she could either marry or enter a convent. As a nun, she was able to make a place for herself on the periphery of society and to pursue her scholarly and literary interests, experimenting with a wide variety of literary forms until she was acclaimed as the "phoenix" of the Americas. Yet trying to work within the highly regimented religious system made her triply vulnerable as a writer, for she was not only an *indiana*, like Alarcón, but also suspect for being an intellectual woman, and subject to strict ecclesiastical laws. While she adhered to established models and themes, her own extraordinary voice as a woman and as a scholar, what Octavio Paz (*Sor Juana*, 6) calls her "condemned" voice, drew unfavorable attention to her from others, most important among them Father Antonio Núñez de Miranda, her spiritual director, and Francisco Aguir y Seijas, Archbishop of Mexico. In 1694, under what we assume was considerable pressure, Sor Juana agreed to give up scholarship in a "Profession That, Signed with Her Blood, Sister Juana Inés de la Cruz Made Of Her Faith and Her Love to God, at the Time of Abandoning Humane Studies in Order, Released from That Attachment, to Follow the Road to Perfection." Moreover, she sold her books and her musical and scientific instruments in what Paz concludes was "the gesture of a terrified woman attempting to ward off calamity with the sacrifice of what she most loves" (Paz, *Sor Juana*, 462, 463).[6]

The paradigms established from the time of the Conquest onward signaled exclusion based on conditions of birth, position, class, race, and gender. The exclusion further cemented the binary structure that situated the defining subject as "self" and reduced the other to no more than a malleable object. The indigenous "object" then was deprived not only of the possibility of self-government but also of self-definition and self-expression. The economic and political domination of the native peoples was ultimately inseparable from their cultural subjugation. The voices of the marginalized were channeled through the major instruments of the hegemonic culture, through religious and cultural organs. What we have, then, is a cultural ventriloquism—a native voice that retains some of its distinctiveness behind the religious dogma or conventional three-act forms. This situation did not end with the colonial period and the wars of independence. While some drama slowly began to reflect local realities during the eighteenth and nineteenth centuries, and native-born playwrights gradually became more active in the theatres, waves of European literary currents—the Neoclassicism of the eighteenth-century, the Romanticism of the early nineteenth, and the Realism of the early twentieth—continued to wash over Latin America after independence and long after their popularity had subsided in Europe.

The distinctive Latin American voices become increasingly autonomous from the nineteenth century onward. This cultural distinctiveness was not limited to the widespread *costumbrismo* of the nineteenth-century, which reflected picturesque local customs; it also spawned various "minor" movements. In 1886 in Argentina, for example, the pantomime *Juan Moreira*, which had enthralled a circus audience in 1884, was turned into a play that ushered in a new dramatic genre, the *gauchesco* drama. In 1868 the *teatro bufo* dominated the Cuban stages as "an exclusively national product" that brought together blacks, mulattos, Spaniards, and Chinese in a "cultural melting-pot of marginality that achieves racial integration onstage before it does in real life" (Leal, *Teatro Bufo*, 17). The classical Western influence remained dominant in the twentieth century. It is fascinating, for example, to note the inordinate number of Latin American plays that have reworked classical models: black Medeas, Argentine Antigones, and Cuban Electras are only a few of the Greek protagonists to spring up on Latin American stages. Yet these works, analysis would show, are not imitations of their forerunners but aesthetically new and politically relevant originals.

Commentators have been slow in appreciating the distinctive nature and quality of these minority voices, however, tending to valorize the universal qualities over the decidedly national or local ones. It seems both necessary and timely to invert the perspective and consider this theatre within its own context, from the premises that center it, from the goals it proposes to achieve. This can be done only through an understanding of the realities and effects of colonization. On one level the process involves coming to terms with the distorted image of the colonized—the colonized as monster, "wild man," or grotesque hybrid, cannibal/Caliban.[7] The process also entails the recognition of the counterhegemonic strategies the plays propose in order to disengage themselves from cultural colonization and address their own pressing political reality. In this respect, Latin American theatre has much more in common with other colonized and oppressed theatres than with the dominant European and North American drama.

Even in the move toward self-definition, the use of imposed forms of expression continues marginalizing this theatre. An interesting and important example is that of language. Spanish and Portuguese have been the dominant languages in Latin America for almost five hundred years. Unlike the hundreds of national languages and dialects that actively survive in many African countries, the indigenous languages still spoken in Latin America, such as Quechua and Guarani, are alien to most Latin Americans. African playwrights have an option that Latin Americans no longer have—that of using their native languages in a step toward cultural decolonization. The Kenyan novelist and dramatist Ngugi wa Thiong'o, for example, no longer writes in English but in Gikuyu. This constitutes a significant political rather than symbolic gesture in several respects. He was able to address his native audience first and foremost (although he himself may translate his works into English), and this change of language opened new avenues for literary expression for him: he started by writing drama for the local audience at Limuru rather than novels for foreign readers. The plays he wrote for this audience were his only experiments in dramatic writing. The plays were banned; he was detained without trial and now lives permanently abroad, deprived of his local audience. However, he continues writing nondramatic works in Gikuyu in order to reverse a curious phenomenon also related to colonialism: most scholars consider as "African writers" only those writing in European languages; hence, by continuing to write in English, Ngugi felt that he would eclipse national writers who wrote in their native languages for their local populations. In Latin America, however, most playwrights have no "native" languages to turn to; they would have to learn them, and even then they could address only miniscule populations, such as the Mayan-speaking peoples of the Yucatán or the Andean Quechua speakers. Ngugi's return to a vital autochthonous language like Gikuyu fights against the further marginalization of his fellow African writers, but a similar move on the part of the Latin American dramatists would only further marginalize them. The fact that Latin America was colonized three centuries earlier than Africa explains the differences to a large degree.

A revival of indigenous languages, then, seems problematic and unlikely—yet the dominant language itself continues to function as an instrument of exclusion. This may seem curious, after centuries of use and in the light of the worldwide recognition of Spanish-American literature, especially contemporary narrative. However, as Phyllis Zatlin makes clear, one of the main reasons that Spanish-language theatre from Latin America has rarely been staged in Spain is attributed, ironically, to language: Zatlin (41) cites examples of translations from Latin American Spanish to Castilian! Needless to say, the language issue is the symptom, not the problem. The differences between Latin American and peninsular Spanish, varying according to region, compare roughly with those between British and American English (in which, too, some regional dialects are linguistically more alien than others). But the exclusion of Latin American plays on the basis of language is indicative of a broader cultural hierarchy, more a function of hegemony than of linguistic barriers, as substantiated by the fact that Spanish plays have traditionally found enthusiastic audiences in Latin America.

The language issue has become even more ironic since the 1960s with the rise of Hispanic American theatre in the United States. For writers like the Chicana Gloria Anzaldua, Spanish—as opposed to English—is "the language which reflects us, our culture, our spirit. . . . I feel the rip-off of my native tongue." [8] Spanish, which for Spanish speakers in Latin America is the language of domination, becomes the language of cultural resistance and self-expression for Hispanic Americans in the United States.

The problems posed by the virtual loss of autochthonous languages also hold true in regard to native dramatic traditions. After centuries of colonization, no unadulterated pre-Hispanic dramatic forms remain intact. There is no question, again unlike the case in Africa, of returning to a native drama, even though such notable dramatists as Nobel laureate Miguel Angel Asturias (Guatemala) and Emilio Carballido (Mexico) have experimented with combining indigenous elements—costumes, dance, themes—in modern dramatic form. The use of Western theatrical structures is therefore inevitable, considering that we know so little about pre-Hispanic "theatre." This fact, however, should not lead commentators to conclude that the Western forms are "clumsily borrowed." Cultural systems, as we have noted, undergo processes of transculturation. Marginal societies "are not the passive recipients of ready-made images and consumer goods. Rather, these are complex, sophisticated cultures which filter and mediate first world imports, recreating local meanings, producing hybrid cultural artifacts and subjects."[9] We will see how original these Latin American plays are, exploring radically different issues within the language and theatrical frameworks usually claimed by their colonizers. The works reposition the protagonists in such a way that the marginal and the oppressed dominate center stage in their struggle for cultural and political identity and control.

Colonization not only locks peoples into a binary self/other opposition and distances them as other but also promotes the conflation of all such "others" into a seamless, anonymous group. Even though citizens of the numerous Latin American countries often experience difficulties in relating to or identifying with each other, from the defining perspective outside, Latin Americans are considered the "same." In the time of the Conquest the conquerors erased "difference" between the multiple indigenous groups and reduced them all to other, all "other" being the "same" in subjugation. The defining group actually names that other, as the mid-nineteenth-century French coinage of *Amérique Latine* and the mid-twentieth-century term "Third World" make clear enough. By stereotyping Latin Americans as a single "other" homogeneous group, the dominant increase their power to gloss over complexities and dictate unrealistic policies. The Latin American experience of heterogeneity, on the other hand, with numerous differences not only between the twenty-five countries but between the peoples within them, proves a political liability, as suggested by Simon Bolivar's struggle for a united Latin America. However, while the inter- and intracultural divisions prove the veracity of the "divided we fall" topos, any "united we stand" idea is fraught with antagonism and suspicion. This is because Latin America has historically been united only from afar, by conquerors for whom the conquered were the "same," united in their oppression. Even today, individuals from the numerous Latin American countries feel "Latin American"— rather than, say, Mexican or Peruvian—only when they are far from home, when they view their situation from abroad: Latin American *as opposed to* Anglo-American or European. We might even question whether the term "Latin American theatre" means anything at all. Osvaldo Dragún, one of Argentina's most perceptive playwrights, observes that Latin America has many cultures, many identities, and he doubts that the many parts make up a recognizable cultural whole. A cultural product imported by one Latin American country from another will seem more foreign than a classical import from abroad. Dragún (25) gives a case in point: at the 1983 International Theatre Festival in Caracas, where he was a judge, the German rendition of a Greek trilogy won over a Bolivian play because it was perceived to be culturally closer to the experience of the members of the panel. It seems inevitable, given the oppositional character of most inter-actions between "self" and its many others, that "difference" is seen only in terms of conflict, power, and domination. As the plays themselves suggest, Latin Americans often fail to recognize or respect one another as somehow related. Griselda Gambaro's *Siamese Twins* illustrates that even twins are never similar or "related" enough to avert hatred of the other.

As all the plays in this study show, we cannot entirely separate the colonizing definition of the other from the colonized definition of self as other. The mechanics of exclusion of the colonized other by the colonizer are systematic and straightforward; more disturbing and complex is the secondary manifestation or byproduct of this exclusion, the self-hatred of the colonized. Albert Memmi, in *The Colonizer and the Colonized* (121-22), notes the pernicious outcome when the colonized internalize the defining other: "As soon as the colonized adopts those values, he similarily adopts his own condemnation. In order to free himself, at least so he believes, he agrees to destroy himself." Memmi compares the "Negrophobia in a Negro" to the anti-Semitism in a Jew. Sander L. Gilman's analysis, de-veloped in his work *Jewish Self-Hatred* (2-4), clarifies the phenomenon. He distinguishes between two levels of image projection, which he maintains are universal paradigms "held by any society." On the first level, the outsiders (the socially marginal) accept the insiders or the defining group's view of themselves as other, a view accompanied by stereotyping on the basis of race, gender, class, and so on. The acceptance creates a double fiction shared by outsiders and insiders: first, the myth of communal identity, by necessity a myth since it is based on the acceptance of a stereotypical image; second, the "liberal fantasy that anyone is welcome to share in the power of the reference group *if* he abides by the rules. . . . Become like us" (Gilman's emphasis). By definition, however, the other is "not like us" and therefore cannot share in the power. The other feels that this contradictory signal must emanate from her- or himself, "since that which I wish to become cannot be flawed," and in an attempt to stop being the excluded other, one distances oneself from one's own identity in order to become identical with the defining group. On a second level, the outsiders distance themselves from characteristics they perceive as unac-ceptable to the defining group and project these "defects" as other. They create their own other, an extension of themselves. This distancing, of course, can never be complete, "for even as one distances oneself from this aspect of oneself, there is always the voice of the power group saying, Under the skin you are really like them anyhow. The fragmentation of identity that results is the articulation of self-hatred."

The mechanics of self-hatred are reflected (and sometimes analyzed) in much twentieth-century Latin American theatre. Rodolfo Usigli's *El gesticulador* (1937) takes into consideration the complicitous relationship between the colonizer and the colonized. César Rubio, a dusky, aging, unsuccessful Mexican history professor of questionable integrity, "becomes" the revolutionary hero of the same name during a conversation with a Harvard professor, Oliver Bolton. Bolton, like the agents of power (in Foucaultian terms) before him, "discovers" Rubio. Yet, as Rubio recognizes and tells Bolton, culture is a possession acquired by the powerful: "the codices, the manuscripts, the incunabula, Mexico's archaeological treasures; you'd buy Taxco if you could take it home with you" (749). Bolton's discovery characterizes the unbalanced relationship between oppressor and oppressed. For Bolton the "discoverer," it constitutes a personal victory: that is, recognition and promotion within his academic institution. For the "discovered," however, it alters history; it concerns all of Mexico. In this play, the foreign authority quite literally makes History (with a capital H) happen. The main focus, however, is not on the colonizer but on the colonized, on the complicity of the underdog in his discovery and deformation. Rubio continues his impersonation and speaks of himself in the third person, as other, until he dies a hero's death. Yet, the "real" Rubio, both he and his family agree, is an inadequate, fraudulent nobody. The final image Usigli presents is Rubio's whimpering, betrayed, indignant, but ineffectual son calling for "Truth!" Usigli's final note to the reader, indicative though perhaps unstageable, is that Rubio's shadow will pursue his son forever.

Gradually, however, playwrights propose a more self-conscious context within which to stage and comprehend this drama of oppression. Celestino Gorostiza, in *El color de nuestra piel* (1952), also presents Mexican sexism, racism, and self-hatred. The father, Don Ricardo, himself a Mexican *mestizo*, warns his son to stay away from the filthy "brown" maid, even though "almost all of us Mexican boys were initiated with these lousy Indians" (815). He proposes to send his son to the United States because "three years in the United States makes one see our dark women very differently" (816). Although he is himself dark-skinned, Don Ricardo identifies with the portrait of his white forefather which hangs on the wall. By identifying with the paternal figure of white authority, he can safely distance himself from his fellow Mexicans, stereotyping them as stubborn, stupid, dirty, flea-infested, untrustworthy, indolent, careless, and irresponsible. This play, moreover, points to two kinds of oppression, the deeply ingrained connection between sexism and racism in Mexico best summed up by the term *malinchismo*. If Mexicans are a *mestizo* race produced from Spanish and indigenous stock, Cortés is the male, the white, conquering, powerful father who illicitly couples with Malinche, the Mayan woman who served as his translator (she had learned Spanish from a Spaniard who had been stranded on an earlier exploration to the Yucatán). Insofar as she helped Cortés bring about the downfall of the indigenous worlds, she is considered by modern Mexicans as the dark, treacherous woman. Hence, in the Mexican collective unconscious, to be dark suggests a passive, perverse femininity, and the woman becomes the incarnation of self-hatred, another Eve, another Malinche. Small wonder that cultural philosophers as eminent as Octavio Paz conflate racial injuries with gender violence. In *The Labyrinth of Solitude*, Paz describes the rent in the Mexican identity (Spanish/indigenous; white/dark) in words commonly reserved for the vagina—wound, gash, crack, and so forth.

Unlike Usigli, however, Gorostiza clearly spells out the distortions and violence that stem from self-hatred, at least in terms of race, and points toward a future in which Mexicans will stop thinking of themselves in these annihilating terms. Manuel, whom Don Ricardo suspects is his illegitimate son by an Indian woman, recognizes the mechanism of self-hatred and explains it to Don Ricardo. Even five hundred years after the conquest, Manuel states, "we still don't believe in ourselves. To convince ourselves that we are superior to our countrymen, that we are different from them, each one of us continues allying himself with the foreigner against his own people, that is, against himself. This is no more than collective suicide" (Gorostiza, 830). Again, the final image is violent: the criminal son does indeed commit suicide. But it is not hopeless. There is a faint note of optimism; some of the characters who can recognize what is happening are finally making productive decisions based on the realistic acceptance of themselves and their own needs.[10]

Increasingly, then, Latin American plays focus on an emergent Latin American "self" struggling to free itself from its historically imposed role of grotesque other. One of the problems with the self/other dichotomy is that the terms shift according to who sets up the opposition. Conversely, however, therein lies the possibility of empowerment. The previously marginalized, defined others can fight to gain the power of self-definition by commanding this slippery term, by casting themselves as "self" in their effort to resist continued oppression. While many of the themes remain the same, it is the perspectival revision and widespread search for new strategies for overcoming colonial deformation that lead many commentators to speak of a "new" theatre—not a theatre of the oppressors but a theatre of the oppressed.

## New Theatre

While commentators studying Latin American theatre generally recognize the dramatic transformation that has taken place in the quantity and quality of the plays produced from the 1960s onward, we still do not have a good name to describe the process (or perhaps multiple processes), or a very clear understanding of its (their) complexity or periodization. Various terms have been proposed. Beatriz Risk enumerates them in her work *El nuevo teatro latinoamericano: Una lectura histórica* (19): "theatre of identity, revolutionary theatre, committed theatre, historical theatre, theatre of violence, theatre of social criticism, documentary theatre, avant-garde, popular theatre"; she herself opts for "new theatre." Several studies have traced the history of that term and its practical applications, notably Rosa Eliana Boudet's *Teatro nuevo* and Marina Pianca's *Diógenes*. The term has gradually gained a degree of currency in Latin American studies, although it is doubtful whether everyone using it refers to the same phenomenon. While my use of "theatre of crisis" only partially overlaps with what is generally understood as "new theatre," the latter deserves a brief analysis both because of its widespread use and because it has a certain limited applicability. My comments on the several features characterizing the term will, I hope, clarify my use of it throughout this work and the differences I perceive between new theatre and theatre of crisis.

For Risk and Pianca, new theatre seemingly applies to the entire theatrical movement that developed toward the end of the 1950s (coinciding with the Cuban revolution of 1959), which broke with inherited, especially bourgeois, models and became revolutionary and "dialectical," following Brecht's theatre. The movement spread gradually throughout the Latin American continent and finally reached Hispanic American communities in the United States (Risk, 13). The "new" theatre addresses a "new" proletariat and peasant audience, forming part of a wider socio-economic and political confrontation in which the underclasses struggle for decolonization and for the appropriation of methods of production, including theatrical production. Risk, Pianca, and Boudet all equate new theatre with popular theatre, which does not clarify it significantly because the term "popular theatre" is also open to interpretation.

The definition proposed by Risk, Pianca, and Boudet is, paradoxically, both too general and too specific to prove helpful or meaningful in understanding the profusion of plays produced since the late 1950s and early 1960s. On the one hand, the concept of new theatre signals a widespread commitment to social inquiry and change on the part of the playwrights. In the most global sense, all the serious drama written after the late 1950s which tried to change the situation of the dispossessed is a form of new theatre, characterized by what Leon Lyday and George Woodyard (xiii) describe as "a spirit of revolution, both in terms of aesthetics and often of sociopolitical values." On the other hand, however, the term also refers to a particular methodological approach (a dialectical or

Brechtian model), a clearly defined ideological position (Marxist-Leninist for Boudet), and a specific proletarian audience. So while the dramatists presented in my study unanimously endeavor to demystify sociopolitical obfuscation and alter social attitudes, none of their work—not even that of Enrique Buenaventura, whom Risk uses as her model—falls into the category of new theatre. The use of the term to refer both to a demythifying theatre that profoundly and critically examines society and its own role within it and to a propagandistic theatre that imposes a "correct" political attitude and world view raises a host of contradictions. How can one kind of theatre simultaneously expose and impose an ideology?

The equation of "new theatre" with "popular theatre" further complicates the issue. Questions about what popular theatre is and whose interests it serves are by no means resolved. Discussion about the term's meaning continues in Latin America as well as other parts of the world: for example, in Nigeria and South Africa. Without exhausting all the possible issues the term "popular theatre" raises, two major positions on the subject clarify its use in the context of this study. Many theatre practitioners and scholars accept a "by the people, for the people" definition of popular theatre. Karin Barber's study of the Yoruba traveling companies in Nigeria typifies this stance.[11] Their plays, staged by Yoruba practitioners, reflect the rural audience's values and tastes without attempting to analyze or alter them. From Barber's examples, however, it seems clear that even though these plays are written in Yoruba and performed for audiences unaccustomed to drama, they can in fact reaffirm negative stereotypes and divert the audience's attention from the widespread sociopolitical corruption in Nigeria resulting from the recent flow of *petro-naira* (oil-generated dollars). Though not intentionally "antipopular," such plays can undermine the position of their audience by, for example, idealizing wealth or feminine submission without providing a context for analysis or question. Throughout this study I refer to this "by the people, for the people" theatre as "people's theatre."

The conscious political use and abuse of people's theatre has been noted by such activists as Frantz Fanon and Augusto Boal, who argue that such traditional popular events as carnival and vodun (or voodoo) rites, placed within the framework of colonization, can prove to be antipopular: thus, "the native's relaxation takes precisely the form of a muscular orgy in which the most acute aggressivity and the most impelling violence are canalized, transformed, and conjured away" (Fanon, 57).[12] Those in power not only allow but often promote "native," "folkloric," or "traditional" cultural products and events, thereby controlling, co-opting, and often reifying them. Sometimes the ministries of culture promote this art, claiming to bring it international recognition and thus to secure personal

fame for the artist and good press and tourism for the nation.[13] Sometimes
the promotion of "native" art takes a more sinister turn. South Africa
provides an example of people's culture used against the people: the
Nationalist Party claims that apartheid and "separate development" helps
protect "Bantu" culture.

The other definition of popular theatre, the one I use throughout this
work, takes into account that theatre plays an instrumental part in shaping
ideology, whether it is an agitational, integrative, or demystifying kind of
theatre. Therefore, it defines a theatre as "popular" if it advances and
supports the interests of the oppressed and marginalized groups within a
society. Popular theatre, as Boal and other practitioners recognize, need
not necessarily be written by members of the oppressed classes or even
address a popular audience as long as it furthers the position of the
disadvantaged within the system. Many dramatists want to reach as wide
an audience as possible, hoping to transform the social structure both from
without and from within. Theatre can undermine the assumptions and
expectations of the audience and in this sense, perhaps, can prove most
effective where its efficacy is least anticipated. Popular theatre, then,
refers less to specific spectacles, audiences, and methods of production
than to the *aims* this theatre serves.[14] By means of intense examination and
self-examination, popular theatre attempts to liberate both its audience
and itself from the constraints and blinders imposed (however imperceptibly) by the hegemonic cultural discourse.

Yet like people's theatre, this popular theatre also manifests its own
ideological blind spots, thereby possibly perpetuating oppressive relationships. The black consciousness movement promotes a male ideology
("Black man, you are on your own"), as does its theatre. Male Latin
American political revolutionaries, as Buenaventura points out in *La requisa*, also tend to infantilize or marginalize women. Sometimes, as Wolff's
*Paper Flowers* or Eldridge Cleaver's *Soul on Ice* illustrate, the "revolutionary" discourse can exclude and even actively attack other oppressed
groups—in this case, women. For Cleaver, "rape was an insurrectionary
act" attacking "the white man's law" through his object, woman (26). This
theatre, too, is a product of society and reflects its prejudices. In fact, it is
naive to suppose that "new theatre" can escape the cultural limitations
inherent in any and all art forms.

Again, one cannot overlook the potential political manipulation of
popular theatre. Like people's theatre, it can impose, rather than propose
or expose, a vision. Do the university students and radical intellectuals
have a moral right to instruct the underprivileged on a "better" life? How
does doing so differ from religious proselytizing? Is it merely a coincidence
that a similar conflation of educational and religious zeal occurred after the

Mexican Revolution with the initiation, by José Vasconcelos (Mexico's minister of education) of a program of traveling educators known as "missionaries?" Can the literate, usually from the bourgeois class, even presume to understand or voice the concerns of the illiterate and semiliterate underclass? How does this presumption differ from the official claims that government works in the best interests of the populace? What happens when popular theatre becomes institutionalized? When "popular theatre" groups such as Cuba's Grupo Teatro Escambray and the Conjunto Dramático de Oriente (which Boudet uses as the prototypes for her analysis of new theatre) formally adopt rules that "the actor must possess and practice marxist-leninist principles . . . in a constant and systematic manner" (Boudet, 272), one can again question whose interests are being served.

One of the problems I perceive in the term "new theatre" is the implicit and, in the case of Boudet, Risk, and Pianca, explicit automatic legitimation of theatrical activity perceived as "popular." The terms "new" and "popular," posited in such a way as to reflect and authorize each other, tend to place the subject above discussion and criticism, rather than—as their claims insist—open the field to inquiry. Theatre, precisely because it is process rather than object, always lends itself to multiple uses and abuses, onstage and off. Popular theatre and people's theatre are no exceptions. Without entirely discrediting or discarding the concepts of new and popular theatre, it is important to recognize that they cannot in themselves legitimate or endorse theatrical activity as politically "correct" or socially liberating. Again, as with all theatrical activity, the context defines theatre's ultimate role and character. Popular theatre, then, as I understand and use the term, incessantly questions and rigorously analyzes its own position and ideology.

Another of the major drawbacks in the term "new theatre" is the facile but erroneous assumption made by commentators that if the goals of these plays are similar (social equality, personal and political freedom), their methodology is too. Somehow the diversity and originality with which the plays themselves propose critical revisions of reality has not been duplicated in the criticism. "New theatre" criticism, rather than exploring alternative modes of theatrical discourse, usually legitimates *one,* the Brechtian, claiming that new theatre is epic theatre, collective theatre, and so forth.[15] The repeated critical appeal to specific models or methodologies proves limiting. It fails to account for the multiple anti-Aristotelian, antihierarchical forms that sprang up after the 1960s: *loas* (a form that had almost disappeared after the nineteenth century), farces (by definition an anarchic genre), *el grotesco* (an Argentine genre developed by playwright Armando Discepolo (1887-1971) which advances its own alienation techniques), the *sainete,* short skits or gags dating back to Spain's Golden Age. Conversely, some playwrights (Egon Wolff, for one), take the "well-made play" and demolish it before our eyes. But surely these too are profoundly popular forms and aspirations that continue the earliest attempts made by Latin Americans to express their own local realities in their own voices.

Another disadvantage in the term "new theatre" has to do with periodization: after thirty years, one may justifiably question the validity of the adjective. In a sense, we can say that "new" serves a symbolic rather than practical function. Risk, Boudet and Pianca, as I noted, relate new theatre to the Cuban revolution, and in a sense the word supports the revolutionary aspirations for a new beginning, new dating systems and calendars, new men and women.

Pianca tries to reconcile the symbolic with the practical by dividing the development of new theatre into three consecutive stages: during 1959-68 it developed on a national level; from 1968 to 1974 it became international through Latin American theatre festivals; and from 1974 to the present, it began "under the sign of exile, atomization and repression" but experienced a "restructuring and a new hope."[16] In raising the fundamental issue of periods, Pianca's 1-2-3 approach seems to set up an untenable dichotomy between national and international theatrical development within Latin America. It also introduces a final note of optimism which, given the current reality of sociopolitical acts of repression and continuing genocide carried out in some Latin American countries today (particularly in Central America), seems unsustainable. While she correctly notes that individual theatre groups started working on a national level in universities and cultural centers during the 1960s, the impetus and the energy stemmed from a revolutionary consciousness that was affecting all of Latin America and a large portion of the rest of the world as well. Pianca, like most scholars, recognizes the connection between the emergence of the new theatre and the Cuban revolution in 1959, but she downplays the relationship between the individual national "drama" and what I perceive, in consciously theatrical terms, as Latin America's "major drama of liberation," corresponding to the first stages of the Cuban revolution. The revolution was of course in the most literal sense a national phenomenon— it did not in fact extend beyond the island—but in another sense it was clearly an international phenomenon. As I elaborate in the chapter on José Triana, the revolution proved a suspenseful drama. For Latin Americans who aspired to self-government and self-definition, it was a heroic epic: the oppressed conquered their oppressors; David slew Goliath. For the antirevolutionaries in the United States and elsewhere, the revolution signaled the danger of a "Communist takeover" and led to the disastrous

Bay of Pigs attempt. On the basis of the relationship I see between the new theatre and two stages in the revolutionary impetus of the 1960s (the initial revolution and the subsequent institutionalization or, as some argue, *failure* of the revolution), I would expand Pianca's first stage to the end of the 1960s and divide it into two parallel movements. Even though labeling does tend to be self-legitimating and to promote its own fiction of validity, the need to distinguish between concepts and categories makes it impossible to dispense with the practice altogether. Therefore, I propose the following terms: the theatre of revolution and the theatre of crisis, to signal two general, often overlapping kinds of theatrical activity.

## Theatre of Revolution

As we have noted thus far, most of the serious, noncommercial theatre of the late 1950s and throughout the 1960s was a revolutionary theatre in spirit and form. This is not to suggest that revolution "sparked" this new theatre; several of the plays within the category were actually written before the Cuban revolution. Rather, the conflicts and changing perspectives that led to revolution also shaped this new theatrical perspective. The very constant threat posed by the United States to Latin America throughout this century became increasingly obvious and alarming. I am not referring simply to overt invasions and political meddling—the overthrow of the government of President Jacobo Arbenz Guzmán in Guatemala in 1954, or the thwarted invasion of Cuba in 1963; perhaps of greater long-term consequence was the subsequent CIA counterinsurgency campaign, which initiated the use of terrorist tactics and the now infamous practice of "disappearances" throughout Central and South America. (The term *desaparecido* was used in the Latin American press for the first time in conjunction with U.S. counterinsurgency in Guatemala; see Simon, 23). The increasingly hostile relationship between the United States and Latin America provoked a revision of the colonial self/other tension: the imperialist, now *other,* was to be rejected in favor of the redefined heroic self.

The Latin American revolutionary movement was linked to a larger, polyphonic revolutionary discourse worldwide. According to Fidel Castro and Ché Guevara, political power could be achieved only by means of armed struggle. Régis Debray, the French philosopher and student of Louis Althusser, announced through his *Revolution in the Revolution?* (27) that the 1960s marked the end of an epoch, the "death of a certain ideology" and "the beginning of another, that of total class warfare, excluding compromise solutions and shared power." Previously pacifist approaches such as Martin Luther King's nonviolent civil rights movement became increasingly militant. At this point, there was a romanticization not only of revolution but also of the violence deemed necessary to bring the revolution about. While the escalating confrontations did not meet with the ultimate success that Castro, Ché, or Debray might have desired, in many ways Debray's title itself sums up the proliferating and conflicting left-wing philosophies that sprang up around the world during the 1960s. In the United States, two main lines of revolutionary thinking—best represented iconographically by means of the clenched fist and the peace symbol—typified the discourse. On one hand were the then militant civil rights movement, student rioting on college campuses, the growing feminist movement, and anti-Vietnam protests—only a few examples of political agitation in the United States. On the other was the so-called "sexual" revolution, which many political revolutionaries must have deemed, at best, antirevolutionary and decadent.

Both forms of revolutionary discourse manifested themselves in other countries, sometimes in combination with other kinds of attacks on political and institutional authority. The civil rights movement, influenced by the Cuban revolution, in turn influenced the formation of the black consciousness movement in South Africa in 1968 (Kavanaugh, 158-61). Armed struggle against Portuguese domination during the late 1950s and early 1960s, directly linked Angola's Popular Movement for the Liberation of Angola (MPLA) and Mozambique's Front for the Liberation of Mozambique (Frelimo) to Castro's Marxism, both financially and ideologically. These struggles eventually led to national independence and Marxist governments for those two African countries in the 1970s. The Prague Spring (1968) signaled an internal rupture within Communism itself; it raised hopes of a nonauthoritarian, liberating Communism in eastern Europe, which was then crushed by Soviet Stalinism. The 1968 Cultural Revolution in China also tightened its definition of "revolution" and proposed to "purify" or purge it of stagnating elements. In Paris, during the revolt of May 1968, the student left not only questioned the "the truth of knowledges" and rejected the university (in the words of Althusser) as "the dominant ideological State apparatus in capitalist social formations"; they also contested different varieties of Communism, from Stalinism and Maoism to the cult of anarchism, situationist "created chaos," and Trotskyism (Macdonnell, 14). In Mexico in October 1968 the raised fist emblematized one trend in the revolutionary thinking: left-wing students challenged the Institutionalized Revolutionary Party (PRI), which has dominated Mexico since the 1910-20 revolution. They were massacred in Tlatelolco, a working-class housing compound in the middle of Mexico City, two weeks before the Olympics. Throughout the 1960s, however, the "sex, drugs, and rock-and-roll" trend also affected Mexican youth in what was known as the *onda*, the wave (Monsivaís, 382-94).

The revolutionary movement promised to cast Latin America in a leading role on the world's political and cultural stages. The 1960s provided a new theatrical infrastructure for the marginalized, the oppressed, and the repressed. Radical theatre companies such as Bread and Puppet and the San Franscisco Mime Troupe were on the move; there were national festivals and international festivals. There was renewed hope that Latin America, theatrically as well as politically, would find acceptance not as an inferior other but as a revitalizing, revolutionizing self. Yet, Latin American theatre, with the exception of Triana's *Night of the Assassins* (staged by the Royal Shakespeare Company as *The Criminals* in 1968), was not taken up by the European and U.S. practitioners. And at home, the new feeling of liberation eventually collided with the reality of oppressive power.

The Cuban revolution, aside from providing the hope of viable political alternatives for Latin America, also produced a riveting theatrical image. In other words, though the revolution worked primarily on the real order (a political event, which I leave to political theorists), it had a significant symbolic component. Without reducing the revolution to a spectacle, it is important to notice that its spectacular components served a vital, *real* function. They captured worldwide attention; they rallied followers and admirers by ennobling the revolutionaries while delegitimizing their opposition. The compelling figure of Ché and to a lesser degree the figure of Castro dominated the imagination of a huge portion of the population of Latin America. The revolution generated images of epic proportions, which coincided with Brechtian terminology; Ché's heroic quest embodied the continent's hopes for liberation. The entire sequence was highly spectacular: a new world was being created out of conflict, a new beginning, a new hero or "revolutionary man" (Artiles, 80). The self-representation of the revolution was also powerfully theatrical: the frozen frame of Ché in his beret; the green fatigue uniforms of the *Castristas*; the Brechtian *gestus* as the revolutionary attitude of "men" in action; the episodic plot described by Ché in his diary, his continuing struggle to move the revolution to Bolivia and then to other oppressed regions of Latin America; the enthralled popular audience. Events reactivated the "revolutionary myth" envisioned by José Carlos Mariategui.[17] And just as scholars argue that theatre provides one means of forging a collective identity, the revolution too created a sense of national and international identity mediated through an image. Instead of twenty-five politically marginal, economically and culturally dependent countries, Latin America could envision itself as a united, coherent entity, a producer (rather than importer) of cultural images.

Notwithstanding its epic proportions, the "drama of liberation," even when applied to the revolution, cannot be "read" according to strictly

Brechtian terminology. Although it was a politically liberating event (to a degree), sided with the oppressed against an oppressive and corrupt government, and tried to expose a bourgeois, capitalist, imperialist ideology, it also imposed its own reality. The contradictions underlying many discussions of "new" or "popular" or "revolutionary" Latin American theatre reflect the paradox that lies at the heart of this and perhaps every revolution. If we continue to examine it according to theatrical terminology (discussions of "revolutionary" theatre tend to conflate the two), we detect a significant overlap with Artaud's dramatic theory as expressed in his collection of essays *The Theater and Its Double*. Unlike the Brechtian dialectical theatre, which insists on space for critical distancing—"Spectator and actor ought not to approach one another but to move apart" (Brecht, 26)—the theatricality of the Revolution encouraged an Artaudian identification, even a merging, with those heroic figures "capable of imposing this supreme notion of the theater, men who [would] restore to all of us the natural and magic equivalent of the dogmas in which we no longer believe" (Artaud, *Double*, 32). Artaud's theory calls for collective fusion in the name of metaphysical transcendence; the individual assumes the image and takes on the "exterior attitudes of the desired condition" (*Double*, 80). Likewise, the revolution encouraged subsuming the personal to the collective ideal. The individual surrender to the ideal creates a new real in both theatrical and revolutionary discourse. The actor, committed to the process of creating a new real, "makes a total gift of himself," as Jerzy Grotowski (35) advocated, following Artaud's lead, and "sacrifices the innermost part of himself." But not only in theatre do people give themselves up like Artaud's "victims burnt at the stake, signaling through the flames" (*Double*, 13). The mythification of violence as a source of liberation, whether self-directed or other-directed, in Artaudian theories of a total, essential, and heroic theatre—the "theatre of cruelty"—also forms part of revolutionary thinking, a factor as much in its discourse as in its military strategy. Images of self-sacrifice and surrender characterize works on revolution. Fernando Alegría, in *Literatura y revolución* (11), describes "the bloody operation" of self-examination and recrimination through revolutionary literature, in which authors and their public undergo a painful and glorious striptease: they unmask, "wash, scrub, fumigate themselves, burn their clothing and expose their flesh to merciless scrutiny." Moreover, revolutions themselves are almost synomous with violence; though people do speak of "nonviolent revolutions," the term seems contradictory. Hannah Arendt argues in *On Revolution* (18) that revolutions "are not even conceivable outside the domains of violence." This is a position the Cuban revolutionaries themselves, maintaining that the struggle for political power was inseparable from armed warfare, would have accepted.

This giving oneself up to the revolution, however, is not a Brechtian critical or dialectical position. A sudden linguistic shift occurs at the point where one would follow the Brechtian terminology to its logical conclusion, to critical awareness and emotional distancing. Here, the surrender to the revolution is described in natural rather than theatrical terminology: one *becomes* a revolutionary and creates a new real by giving oneself up to the seemingly irresistible force or process. In this sense, the meaning of "revolution" as the steady motion of heavenly bodies in orbit, which follow laws of physics beyond human control, carries over into the modern usage of the term.[18] For one commentator on Latin American popular theatre, "the new socialist hero" will be neither a pessimist nor a conflicted, tortured individual but "a man caught up in the revolutionary whirl-wind" (Artiles, 80).

Just as the Cuban revolution was theatrical, much of the so-called "revolutionary" theatre of this period incorporated and furthered revolutionary ideology, identity, and images. The theatre of revolution, while functioning primarily on the symbolic order, also aimed at real, political consequences and saw itself as an important instrument in the social struggle. During the 1960s, collective theatres began to reinforce the grassroots movements with their emphasis on leadership, unity, mass mobilization, and combined force. This theatre manifested the widespread preoccupation with war, either reaffirming or decoding military terminology. Augusto Boal, for example, speaks of theatre as a "weapon" in overthrowing systems of oppression and describes theatrical "raids" staged in 1963 during the Cuban crisis: "A group of actors meet on a corner and begin arguing about politics to the point of threatening physical violence; people gather around them and the group suddenly begins an improvised performance that deals with the most urgent political issues. Only midway through the performance does the crowd realize that it is attending a play."[19] In Cuba, theatrical groups such as the Conjunto Dramático de Oriente (started in 1961) and the Grupo Teatro Escambray (1968) gradually moved away from scripted theatre and staged collective acts of group definition and affirmation. Revolutionary theatre is a pragmatic, educational, *useful* theatre, conceived as a practical exercise in learning about the revolutionary process and encouraging "public participation in [revolutionary] solutions. Theatre is an excellent vehicle to detect and combat problems" (Boudet, 12). Theatrical performances also became acts of collective affirmation and group definition.

It is easy to see the considerable overlap and the blurring of boundaries between the theatricality of revolution and the revolutionary theatre. For one thing, both function concurrently on the real and the symbolic level. Both work as double images, W.J.T. Mitchell's "hypericons."[20] They are simultaneously images and generators of images. They provide not only spectacles but scenarios in which one can envision oneself otherwise, take an image and embody it, become it. The theatricality of the roles and parts does not suggest that these are not socially real or efficacious. By assuming the images of power, one can obtain power—therein lies the real power of images: "the robe makes the man" and "a dog's obeyed in office." [21]

The drama of revolution, both onstage and off, orchestrated images to support the revolutionary drive to overthrow both those in power and the ideology associated with that power structure. As the examples noted above suggest, for images to be politically powerful they must be selected carefully; they must signal one unequivocal message. The *theatricality* of revolution, like theatre's *revolutionary* potential, lies in one basic strategy: the elimination (rather than the accumulation) of signs. This theatre, not surprisingly, is often univocal in its attempt to further its ideology. This is its strength as an instrument of change, and its weakness as theatre.

Not all the plays of the 1960s, however, even the socially committed ones, looked to the Revolution for their goals and identity or unquestioningly accepted the revolutionary myth of liberation. Contradictory images, formulated in some of the major plays of 1965–70, reflect the beginning of an ideological crisis. As the revolution within the revolution split factions on the left, the Cuban revolution underwent crisis from within. Opposition also increased from the outside as right-wing governments steadily gained power. The Brazilian military dictatorship of 1964 was the first of a wave of repressive governments that began to take over in Latin America. The triumphalist drama of liberation gave rise to another, far more complex, and problematic depiction of reality. The word "revolution" itself meant no one thing, appropriated as it had been by parties old and new, as varied and unrevolutionary as Mexico's Institutionalized Revolutionary Party, Juan Carlos Onganía's authoritarian Revolución Argentina of 1966, and Guatemala's "third revolutionary party" (1966) headed by Julio César Méndez Montenegro and characterized by death squads. The word "revolution," clearly, had a potent symbolic function that justified its indiscriminate application. As early as 1965 Triana's *Assassins* was already suggesting a disenchantment with revolution in general and with the Cuban revolution in particular, insinuating that "revolution" did not necessarily mean "liberation." The revolutionary process in Cuba was undergoing critical systemic change as it compromised its principles in order to adhere to the Soviet program. Basing its original liberating ideals on José Martí's visions of a revolution grounded in love and self-determination, the Cuban revolution initially considered itself strong enough to tolerate any kinds of ideas. In 1965 with the uneasy reception of Triana's *Assassins* and in 1968 with the famous Padilla affair, [22] it became evident that the *fidelistas*, like Latin American parties before and after them, also felt the need to restrict, censor, and condemn ideas. As Triana's play makes clear, the concepts of revolution and repression, which had in the romanticization of revolution been conceived as antithetical binaries, now seemed indistinguishable. The conflict between the old order and the new had ultimately failed to generate a new language, a new order, new images, new paradigms for historical process.

Dreams of liberation and self-determination gradually gave way to a new authoritarian order, but one which (like the Mexican Revolution) integrated the revolutionary vocabulary and images—new images that also proved re-creations of the old. Ché's heroic though almost predicatable downfall replayed yet again the extinction of a heroic race, another Cuauhtemoc. Like Demetrio, the hero of *Los de abajo*, Mariano Azuela's novel about the Mexican Revolution of 1910-20, Ché and his followers were ambushed in a ravine and fought to the last man. Real events, echoing fiction, acquired a *déjà vu* quality. So too the new image of a Latin American "self" stemming more from a rejection of the other than from any real sense of affinity or identity, proved fictitious and unsustainable. The characters, like the societies they represent, continued to be marginal and economically dependent. One of the hopes for the revolution, as expressed by H.A. Murena in 1960, was that it would "free man from the myths that oppress him," so that he "could become once again his own master." [23] Yet, the revolution seemed to recreate, rather dispel, the old myths.

For many writers who believed that revolution could free the oppressed, the Cuban revolution became another repressive institution. For those who believed that Latin America had reached a new level of democratization and liberty, the 1968 massacre of the students in Tlatelolco proved that neither the powerful elites at home nor the U.S. government supporting them were about to relinquish their grip without open warfare. For those who believed in progress, the new wave of authoritarian governments recalled Bolivar's Sisyphean view of Latin American history, his disillusioned, "I've ploughed the sea." Revolution/repression, self-determination/colonization, progress/repetition, triumph/extinction—the dream of differentiation collapsed into a nightmare of monstrous sameness. The theatre of crisis stems from this collapse.

## Theatre of Crisis

After the brief historical overview of theatre and theatricality as instruments of oppression in Latin America, it may seem arbitrary to designate a body of theatre produced between 1965 and 1970 as a theatre of crisis. And, of course, in a way it is. There have been many periods of crisis, not only in

Latin America but the world over, and hence, one might argue, many theatres of crises. Though in the broadest sense this is true, we can still perceive differences between various manifestations of crisis theatre. What do the theatre of the Holocaust, protest theatre in black townships in South Africa, theatre of the absurd, and commercial "hits" have in common? While we may note that the differences between them are more interesting than the similarities, we cannot overlook that all have been analyzed in terms of crisis, whether political, ideological, or economic. The issues these theatrical activities raise range from ethical ones (Adorno's contention that art after the Holocaust is barbaric) to purely financial ones (how will theatre in Buenos Aires or on Broadway survive as a viable industry if it prices itself out of the consumer market?).

The theatre of crisis that I propose to study builds upon two crisis theories, the social and the scientific. A combined social-scientific theory brings together two determining factors: the *subjective* experience of crisis and personal decomposition with *objective* systemic shifts, ruptures, or delegitimation. In other words, the individual or group's response to crisis is inseparable from the concrete, usually violent or spasmodic, rifts within social systems and institutions. Individuals and groups have boundaries, identities, goals. As Jürgen Habermas points out in *Legitimation Crisis*, the same is true of systems. When those boundaries, identities, and goals are significantly undermined, or when the maintenance of boundaries alters the identity of the system, either ossifying or subverting its structures, we can say that the system is in crisis. However, as Habermas (3) notes, systems can tolerate varying degrees of disturbance without entering into crisis: "Only when members of a society experience structural alterations as critical for continued existence and feel their social identity threatened can we speak of crises. . . . Crisis states assume the form of a disintegration of social institutions."

This objective/subjective definition of crisis excludes from discussion several other kinds of theatre; theatre of protest and theatre of the absurd, for example, express only one of the two facets of crisis, the objective and subjective respectively. Theatre of protest often signals objective systemic strife, as in the case of black theatre in South African townships, yet one of its notable features is its affirmation of personal and group cohesion and identity. The filmed version of Percy Mtwa's play *Bopha!* exemplifies my point. While fighting and explosions turn the streets into a stage for what Wole Soyinka (Foreword, x) calls "the deadly drama enacted daily in the streets and suburbs of South Africa," and while apartheid is recognized as posing a potent and invidious threat to black integrity, the political crisis only accentuates the urgency of reaffirming the blacks' solidarity and sense of identity.

The theatre of the absurd, on the other hand, represents a crisis ideology, the subjective rather than objective experience of crisis. The theatre of the absurd, both as Martin Esslin defines it and as we note in the plays generally associated with it, uproots the disintegrating characters and refuses to recognize the sociohistoric context that gave rise to their rootlessness and existential anguish in the first place. Esslin develops his idea of the theatre of the absurd from Camus's definition of absurdity in *The Myth of Sisyphus*: "In a universe that is suddenly deprived of illusions and of light, man feels a stranger. His is an irremediable exile as much because he is deprived of memories of a lost homeland as because he lacks the hope of a promised land to come. This divorce between man and his life, the actor and his setting, truly constitutes the feeling of Absurdity" (Esslin, 23). This theatre's separation of the subjective and objective factors of crisis, combined with the loss of memory, makes the objective sociopolitical specificity of the catastrophe inaccessible to the characters. Moreover, while the theatre of the absurd reflects the consciousness of a moral and philosophical collapse following World War II, this theatre was produced in a period of social, political, and economic consolidation in Europe and the United States.[24]

The theatre of Holocaust stems from the same sociopolitical crisis that generated the theatre of crisis, World War II, but unlike the theatre of the absurd, it vows never to forget the historic events that gave it rise. In the same "universe" deprived of illusions and light, such writers as Elie Wiesel make a new start: "In the beginning there was the Holocaust, we must therefore start all over again" (qtd. in Langer, 31). The theatre of the Holocaust shares many of the characteristics with the theatre of crisis and, one could argue, is another manifestation of a theatre of crisis as I use the term. Griselda Gambaro's *The Camp* (1967), for example, exposes the concentration camp universe in a way that resembles what Lawrence Langer later called the "literature of atrocity" in his 1975 study, *The Holocaust and the Literary Imagination*.[25] While Langer mainly (though not exclusively) equates the literature of atrocity with the literature of the Holocaust, Gambaro continues the tradition, finding that the *univers concentrationnaire*[26] aptly conveys the horror also of Argentine fascism with its exterminators and death camps (see chapter 3). The main difference between the theatre of crisis and theatre of the Holocaust, then, is that the entire focus of the latter is fixed on one historic event, and it is therefore necessarily more limited in application. Another important difference is that while the theatre of atrocity is a theatre of crisis, the opposite does not hold—the theatre of crisis is not always atrocious. The theatre of crisis invariably deals with violence but with many different kinds of violence, from the subtle, deforming pressures exerted on individuals by oppressive

forces or authority figures (Carballido, Triana), to racial and sexual violence (Buenaventura, Wolff), to the spectacular cruelty of torture and
terrorism (Gambaro, Wolff, Buenaventura). Not all forms of violence
express the hideous, irrational, unmitigated horror that Langer (22) associates with the "aesthetics of atrocity."

Nevertheless, like the theatre of crisis, the theatre of the Holocaust
signals both the objective and subjective reality of crisis. Both (and one
could include most protest theatre as well) emphasize collective suffering,
point to an "official" enemy responsible for the systematic annihilation of
people(s), refer to concrete sociohistoric reality, and combine "historical
fact and imaginative truth" (Langer, 8). Like the theatre of crisis, the
theatre of the Holocaust subverts the lines of demarcation traditionally
used to distance the spectators; on the contrary, it implicates them as
accomplices in the onstage violence. However, one could also argue that
the theatre of the Holocaust takes a step—temporally and ideologically—
*beyond* crisis in that it isolates the problem and assumes a position in the
face of it. And whereas the theatre of the Holocaust fixes its attention on a
historically limited and unique past, and protest theatre generally looks
forward to a happier future, the theatre of crisis is grounded in contradiction; it shapes undifferentiation. We can call it a theatre of crisis precisely
because the historic point of reference, like all else, blurs into decomposition.

The theatre of crisis by definition, then, involves objective systemic
change: that is, the dissolution or the transformed identity of social
institutions and structures attempting to cope with or stave off systemic
rupture or collapse. Crisis is not linked to the collapse of any specific
political ideology, however, of either the left or the right. It can, for
example, result from other, nonpolitical factors. Sophocles' *Oedipus Rex*
(430 B.C.), perhaps the prototypical model of the theatre of crisis, a play *of*
and *about* crisis, was written during an outbreak of the plague and against
the background of the Peleponnesian wars (431 B.C.). It manifests the
characteristics associated with crisis thus far—the loss of identity and the
collapse of boundaries leading to "contagious" crimes such as parricide and
incest.[27] The subjective and objective factors of crisis are inseparable and
mutually fueling. Oedipus's crimes ostensibly "cause" or provoke the
Theban crisis, and his own crisis (his own awareness of his unhappy
situation) directly stems from his attempts to resolve the social catastrophe. Not only is the play overtly violent—Oedipus stabs out his eyes, and
Jocasta hangs herself—but Thebes as a city is drowning in a sea of violence
and disease. Or, crisis can result from the fracture between competing,
irreconcilable ideologies or "isms." The abyss into which the *indiano* Don
Alvaro hurls himself, in Duque de Rivas's *Don Alvaro o la fuerza del sino*

(Spain, 1835), represents the no-man's-land, the ruptured ideological, political and cultural frames of the early nineteenth century.[28] Chekov's plays also belong, in a general sense, to a theatre of crisis. They focus on the moment of transition between two economic and cultural systems, a moment that provokes feelings of decomposition and despair in those caught in the middle of the social transformation. However, the violence in Chekov's plays, the murders and suicides, can hardly be called atrocious; nor does the chopping down of the cherry trees, though violent within the context of the play and world-shaking in its sociopolitical implications, constitute what we normally think of as a hideous act of violence. Chekov's disintegrating characters and waning worlds quietly fade away.

During the period under examination in Latin America, the *causes* of system transformations and disintegrations vary from country to country— from the crisis within the revolution on the left to the rise of quasi-fascist totalitarianism on the right. In Cuba the entire social apparatus taken over from Batista was dismantled and restructured to serve the sociopolitical and economic ends of the new revolutionary government. Early in its history, however, the Cuban revolution underwent major internal, structural changes as it increasingly compromised its original agenda and became incorporated into Soviet Communism. In Argentina, Onganía's government (which came to power with the repressive *coup d'état* of 1966) called itself "the Argentine revolution" and intended not only to eliminate and reconstruct existing institutions but to override constitutional limits and remain in power indefinitely. Colombia, in the 1960s, saw the end of a decade of widespread civil strife known simply as *La Violencia*, which had left 300,000 people dead. It also experienced the intensification of other kinds of violence associated with the growing drug trade, which escalated to such a degree that at present murder is the leading cause of death in males between the ages of eighteen and forty (Lernoux, 512). Mexico, by comparison, seemed relatively stable, yet the PRI government (an undemocratic oligarchy) came under extreme fire during the late 1960s. Civil confrontation became critical in 1968: government tanks patrolled Mexico City's main streets; hundreds (some estimates say thousands) of students were massacred in Tlatelolco, and their bodies were burned or dumped into the ocean. The crisis in Chile did not occur until slightly later, but ideological confrontations had gradually intensified through the late 1960s. The heated competition between the PDC (the Christian Democratic Party, heavily backed by the U.S. CIA) and the FRAP (the anticapitalist, antiimperialist socialist-communist alliance) led to the victory of the PDC in the 1965 elections and then, because of increased dissatisfaction among major elements of the population, to the election of the FRAP and Salvador Allende in 1970. Before Allende's presidency could be ratified by the Chilean Congress, however, the Chilean military with United States backing initiated the series of assaults that led to Allende's death in 1973 and the imposition of Augusto Pinochet's military regime. For all their differences, then, many Latin American countries in the 1960s underwent profound crisis; their societies were either threatened with civil war or became embroiled in revolution culminating in military dictatorships.[29] What we are dealing with here is full-fledged sociopolitical and economic crisis, rather than a subjective crisis of consciousness or ideology.

Notwithstanding the different *causes* of crisis in these various contexts, the *effects*, as manifested through the theatre of crisis, remain surprisingly constant in both content and representation. The similarities, quite obviously, were not intended. Nor do they reflect a school of thought, a dramatic tradition, or even a coherent, shared ideology—except perhaps the shared rejection of Western hegemony evident in these Latin American plays—but rather a crumbling set of beliefs and structures: myths of democracy and personal freedom, progress and utopia, Marxism, liberal humanism, and revolution. The inability to subscribe to them as possible solutions leaves a void, attesting to the difficulty of finding another sustaining ideology. The concept of liberal nationalism failed early in the century, creating its own disillusionment. Democratic socialism had no roots in Latin America. Therefore intellectuals found themselves floundering, seeking a nonmythifying ideological basis in which to ground beliefs. The common denominator of these plays, then, is not intertextual but extratextual.

Still, common denominators do exist, and the analysis of the similarities in conjunction with the differences allows us to map out the parameters of a Latin American theatre of crisis between 1965 and 1970. Produced in the moment of suspension provoked by a systemic schism, this theatre shows society balanced between destruction and renovation, subject to change and open to question. The moment of crisis is one of rupture, of critical irresolution, the "in between" of life and death, order and chaos. And because these plays combine feelings of decomposition with the threat of imminent extinction, they often reflect the moment of annihilation and/or terror. The characters, locked in a dreadful present, perceive time as a contradiction. The historical moment is lived as ahistorical. As Anthony Kubiak (82) notes, the "moment of terror, like the instant of pain, is a moment of zero time and infinite duration. Although terror can only exist in history, it is felt as naked singularity, existing outside all possible representation." The temporal displacement implicit in crisis is accompanied by spatial dislocation as well; the characters in the plays presented in this study have no safe home of their own—they live in houses either owned or taken over by someone else. Nor do the houses shelter or protect; often they are prisons, with barred windows and locked doors. Sometimes, the house itself becomes a weapon, an instrument of oppression or torture. Often, too, the structures collapse: walls fall in or break down, either crushing the inhabitants or exposing them to the violence from outside. The inner spaces merge with the outer; the sociopolitical conflicts are fought out on city streets, in homes, on human bodies. Crisis, as rupture, suspends boundaries, denying the characters the possibility of temporal and spatial shelter; there is no place to hide, no future to look forward to. "To think disaster," as Maurice Blanchot observes in *The Writing of Disaster* (1), "is to have no longer any future in which to think it." The theatre of crisis is fragmented, inconclusive. It offers no resolution, no restorative harmony, no cathartic relief.

René Girard, in *The Scapegoat*, notes the uniformity in various and culturally divergent depictions of crisis, suggesting that the similarities in the social and personal experience of crisis lead to similarities in its representation. What, then, are the effects of crisis? What happens to individuals in a society whose boundaries, goals, and identity are being attacked? Societies that are not in crisis respect authority and maintain hierarchies, resort to a judicial system in times of conflict, tolerate diversity, "name" and differentiate between members; societies confronting crisis initially—for that second of suspension—do none of the above. When systems are attacked, the effectiveness and legitimacy of authority become suspect and, as frequently happens in Latin America, vulnerable to violent contention. The notion of legitimate government, of due process and judicial integrity, of moral and ethical safeguards all interconnect to such a degree that the challenges posed to one threaten the others.

When all basis for positive (noncrisis) differentiation has been undermined, these societies respond in two sequential ways. First, they experience the "monotonous and monstrous" sameness of crisis (Girard, *Scapegoat*, 13) that negates difference; they fail to name, differentiate, valorize, or make distinctions. Michel Foucault's description of the plague in seventeenth-century France reveals all the stereotypes of crisis: the "suspended laws, lifted prohibitions, the frenzy of passing time, bodies mingled together without respect, individuals unmasked, abandoning their statutory identity" (*Discipline*, 197). Artaud also describes the plague as a crisis in which "social forms disintegrate. Order collapses"; crisis is accompanied by "every infringement of morality, every psychological disaster" (*Double*, 15).

Second, because this sameness is threatening and intolerable, those who exert some power combat disorder with a vigilant, oppressive order. This is the deadly "society shrouded in an order so orderly that its chaos was far more intense than anything that had preceded it" described by

Michael Taussig in his *Shamanism, Colonialism, and the Wild Man* (4). If crisis provokes disorder, then, the "solution" to crisis would seemingly entail the imposition of strictest order, states of emergency, law, and penalties, and the application of what Foucault calls the "disciplinary mechanism" that monitors individuals precisely by naming them, locating and compartmentalizing them, and controlling their movements by means of either visual surveillance (the Panopticon) or computers (the threat to black liberation posed by computers in South Africa). People are compartmentalized, subjugated: "All events are recorded . . . [the] uninterrupted work of writing links the centre and the periphery . . . power is exercised without division, according to a continuous hierarchical figure" (Foucault, *Discipline*, 197). Crisis, experienced as a profound disorder that threatens power, hierarchy, social systems, and individual identity, sets in motion an "ordering" mechanism of surveillance, of social and individual control.

Aside from the imposition of centralized, vigilant order, which epitomizes crisis governments from South Africa's Afrikaner Nationalist party to Pinochet's military regime, societies in crisis also set in motion a mechanism of exclusion; they invent false differences and convert members of society into grotesque and apparently threatening others. Initially, this attack on the other also passes as a solution to crisis—if crisis is equated with undifferentiation, surely the politics of differentiation provides the way out of crisis. Systemic crisis often results in persecution and scapegoatism because selective violence, as Girard argues in *Violence and the Sacred*, is conceived as channeling the community's aggression. Instead of destroying each other, members of the community agree to focus their aggression on a "safe," expendable victim. Moreover, as these plays demonstrate, violence is perceived as a *defense* against crisis, rather than as an *effect* of it. By participating in the creation of difference and in the politics of segregation and exclusion, people can comfort themselves that they are doing something to solve the problem; they not only differentiate but rigorously maintain boundaries. Yet because the "difference" is generally a false one, a created one, the hatred, exclusion, and persecution of the other often masks a deeper hatred and self-hatred. The violence associated with sociopolitical crisis, then, is self-perpetuating, coming back to destroy the individuals who initiated the violence as a form of self-defense.

The similar depictions or descriptions of crisis evident in this theatre reflect the uniformity of the experience of social, systemic crisis. In the theatre of crisis analyzed in this study, the sets concretely depict the struggle for spatial control in the face of structural collapse. When walls cave in, crumble, or disappear, inner is inseparable from outer and private from public. The blurred and obliterated boundaries reveal worlds in ruin, both onstage and off. The physical destruction reflects disintegrating judicial, moral, and physical frameworks, distinctions that will not hold, partitions that fail to separate or protect.

The same annihilating undifferentiation is evident in the depiction of the characters. The overwhelming majority of characters in these works have no distinguishable identity; few even have names. They are socially marginal, physically infirm, or malformed to the point of monstrosity. Waves of violence wash over previous distinctions and hierarchies: children kill their parents; the police violate the innocent; personal violence and state violence mingle and feed on each other.

One of the significant features of crisis, as attested both by this theatre and by theorists as divergent as Girard and Habermas, is that it incapacitates the subject to deal effectively with the situation. The theatre of crisis abounds in examples of passive characters unable to react constructively to the situation at hand. The characters' ineffectuality may stem, in part, from powerlessness. Habermas, who introduces the concept of crisis in medical terms, compares the subject of crisis to a patient in critical condition: "Crisis cannot be separated from the viewpoint of the one who is undergoing it—the patient experiences his powerlessness *vis-à-vis* the objectivity of the illness only because he is a subject condemned to passivity and temporarily deprived of the possibility of being a subject in full possession of his powers" (1). It is only later, when the characters are in a sense beyond crisis, that they can gain the lucidity to assess what occurred. However, we should resist interpreting this powerlessness and passivity as either historically or biologically determined. It is not a personality defect on the part of the victims, as critics of the indigenous victims of the Conquest or of the Jews in the concentration camps (to signal out only two groups), seem to suggest.[30] Rather, it is situational, positional; the victims are caught in a deadly and complex web of circumstances and cannot effectively judge, from their position *within* it, how to best extricate themselves. Usually, they need outside help from those who are not themselves trapped in the critical situation.

The characters' sense of being trapped, of being unable to deal with crisis, results in the creation of both victims and victimizers. Several of the most vicious characters in these plays see themselves as victims of crisis and claim to be coping with their predicament when they attack others who, they feel, are responsible for provoking it. As Girard (14) notes, "Rather than blame themselves, people inevitably blame either society as a whole, which costs them nothing, or other people who seem harmful for easily identifiable reasons." Hitler, in *Mein Kampf* (229, 232-33), exemplifies perhaps the most extreme position of crisis culminating in mass victimization, blaming what he saw as the humiliation of the German nation after World War I not on military defeat (the "outward symptom of decay") but on "toxins," "harmful poisons," and an "alien virus" undermining the national "body." Only the extermination of the Jews, according to his thinking, could restore "health." Unable to identify the true causes of crisis, the "victims" can become the victimizers, willing to kill for a "cure." Within the context of the plays, the protagonists who experience crisis—Lalo, the Torturer, the Hake, Lorenzo, and even SS Officer Franco—consider themselves its victims. In order to "defend" themselves, they rationalize exterminating others on the grounds that they are "Communist" (Buenaventura and Gambaro), or "bourgeois" (Wolff), or hurtful and harmful in some way (Carballido and Triana). Therefore, it is deemed necessary to marginalize the "dangerous" individuals or kill them. While the individuals thus singled out as victims may in fact be guilty of some crime, it is not the catastrophic, earthshaking crime for which they are being persecuted and punished. The victims of the kind of violence associated with persecution, as opposed to judicial law, are usually members of marginalized social groups: poor, black, female, and so on.

It is interesting to note throughout these plays that the objects of attack in times of crisis are precisely the boundaries—physical, moral, legal, or discursive—that previously maintained social hierarchies, family and personal integrity, law and order. All the crimes associated with crisis, such as parricide, infanticide, and incest, "seem to be fundamental," Girard notes. "They attack the very foundation of the cultural order, the family and the hierarchical differences without which there would be no social order" (*Violence*, 15). Buenaventura's cycle of plays depicts violence as both the result of the imposition of social and class boundaries and an attack on those hierarchies regarded by the outcasts as exclusionary and oppressive. In *The Menu*, the boundaries are literally painted on the stage in the shape of various colored circles; the Beggars are fumigated before they are permitted to cross from one ring to another to pick up the leftovers that the charitable ladies graciously throw their way. Notwithstanding the insistence on maintaining difference, however, the enforced distinctions only underline the fact that all these characters are very much the same. While the poor are unwashed, infirm, greedy, deformed by poverty and degradation, the wealthy ladies themselves are freaks and hybrids: the Wo/Man, the Fatso, the Dwarf. The colonized, having internalized the colonizer, incarnate contradiction; they are simultaneously victim and victimizer, the embodiment of the two-in-one, grotesque self/other. The monstrosity and violence in the privileged circle is no different from the monstrosity and violence of the beggars. The painted lines maintain power rather than difference—or, more precisely, they maintain power by insisting on false difference. In Triana's *Assassins*, Lalo's "crime" reeks of incest; he pretends to penetrate his parents with his knife and roll in their blood. His world becomes a nightmare of undifferentiation in which life is indistinguishable from death and refuse. The bedroom, as site of reproduction and incorporation, "becomes" the bathroom, the site of excretion and expulsion. In Gambaro's *Siamese Twins*, Lorenzo's personal need to annihilate his twin is physically carried out by the police who, though theoretically upholders of law and justice, torture and kill Ignacio and dump his body in an unmarked grave. The play opens up spiraling worlds of violence in which the violence *inside* the home and the individual and the violence of the systems and structures *outside* augment each other. Ultimately, the violence ends in a whirlwind of terrorism, which, by invading the streets, homes, and private lives of individuals, "gets us where we live" and deterritorializes us. In Wolff's *Paper Flowers*, the Hake's destruction of Eva attacks both class and gender, for he substitutes the real, tangible woman's body for an incorporeal, "effeminate," middle-class body politic. Wolff has so effectively—that is, so *invisibly*—transposed one site of aggression (the middle class) onto another (the woman) that almost without exception commentators read the The Hake's violence as a political act, the more-or-less justifiable attack by a social underdog on an exclusive system of power. The fact that it is also a misogynist act (in which a physically powerful man destroys a powerless woman), and an example of scapegoating, has passed without comment.

The plays examined in this study, while not all violent, are about violence, a term that is hard to define in the best of times and almost impossible to pin down in a discussion of oppression and crisis.[31] I discuss the various kinds in individual chapters and in the concluding remarks, but it is worth noting here that the plays as a whole emphasize two major, interrelated spheres of violence: crisis and oppression. The paradigm of crisis, as I have noted, includes the initial subjective-objective collapse that provokes disorder and undifferentiation, followed by the implementation of the strictest order, the differentiation and exclusion of a group into a grotesque other, and the persecution and scapegoating of the marginalized group or individual. The paradigm of oppression includes the deforming, though often less overt, violence that casts the victim as grotesque other in the repressive self/other binary—the distanced, underdeveloped, childlike, ignorant, inferior, helpless, passive, feminized, persecuted other whose "permanent dream," according to Frantz Fanon (53), is to become the self, the defining power, "the persecutor."[32] In connection with these two major paradigms, we see numerous secondary manifestations: revolutionary violence (response to oppression), institutionalized or professionalized violence (criminal governments, torture and terrorism associated with both oppression and crisis), behavioral disorders and seemingly gratuitous acts of cruelty (again, related to both crisis and oppression).[33]

While there is significant overlapping between the two paradigms of violence, crisis and oppression, they are not inherently connected. Crisis, as I noted, can stem from factors such as plague or war that are not directly or even indirectly related to oppression. Moreover, even when crisis derives from clear sociopolitical clashes resulting from oppression, crisis threatens the legitimacy of the ruling power (insofar as it threatens all objective and subjective frameworks), while oppression need not. This is not to say that oppressive societies are morally or ethically "legitimate" but merely that their existence is not questioned or contested in any manner that will seriously jeopardize their continuity. Oppressive systems are usually so consolidated, so deeply cemented in institutions, laws, and ideology, that their legitimacy is taken for granted not only by the oppressors but often by the oppressed themselves. These systems can last decades without experiencing or provoking crisis, in part because their violence has been rendered natural, almost invisible. It was long considered "natural" for women to serve men, for blacks to serve whites, and so forth. Studies in law, history, human nature, and biology among others—by means of which "man" came to represent "mankind," proved how natural a state it was. Some scholars go so far as to deny that we can use the word "violence" to describe institutionalized oppression. Even Hannah Arendt (*Violence*, 42) states that a "legally unrestricted majority rule, that is, a democracy without a constitution, can be very formidable in the suppression of the rights of minorities and very effective in the suffocation of dissent without any use of violence." Here I disagree with Arendt; rather than thinking in terms of violence and nonviolence (power) in regard to oppression, we might more accurately think in terms of explicit and implicit violence. Explicit, or overtly physical, violence is easy enough to recognize. No less real, though perhaps just as damaging in the long run, is the implicit violence of naming and directing the other, of *naturalizing* distinctions based on gender, race, and class, of limiting the others' options and casting them in symbolic if not literal servitude. My broader definition of violence includes the violence Emmanuel Levinas refers to in *Totality and Infinity* (21): "Violence does not consist so much in injuring and annihilating persons as in interrupting their continuity, making them play roles in which they no longer recognize themselves, making them betray not only commitments but their own substance, making them carry out actions that will destroy every possibility for action." While I oppose Levinas's downplaying of explicit violence, I believe that no one has better delineated the corrosive effects of what I call implicit violence.

Even though oppression and crisis are not necessarily related, this study illustrates the process by which implicit violence becomes explicit, by which the age-old violence associated with oppression bursts into the reactive violence of the oppressed. The process of decolonization is violent and perhaps, as Fanon (35) suggests, *"always* violent" (my emphasis). What interests me here, however, is that the violence of decolonization precipitates crisis. Fanon describes the objective systemic shifts and the subjective transformations I have associated with crisis as inherent in decolonization: "A whole social structure [is] being changed from the bottom up," and "there is a total, complete, and absolute substitution" by means of which "a certain 'species' of men" is replaced by another. That crisis, then, marks both the culmination of distress and the uncertainty for the future—the question of "whether or not the organism's self-healing powers are sufficient for recovery." Recovery here should not signal a return to an earlier noncrisis state in what would constitute the politically conservative or reactionary move toward reestablishing the status quo. Rather, "recovery" and "self-healing" suggest that the state and individual strive for self-definition, autonomy, nonviolence. The problem, of course, is that the process threatens to be circular and self-perpetuating. If decolonization precipitates crisis, and if crisis (as the paradigm indicates) throws systems and individuals into abeyance and undermines structures of definition (which is not necessarily bad, as Fanon points out, but always critical), resulting in a situation that then triggers strict repressive measures, where will it end? That is what these plays ask us to consider.

# 2

# THEATRE AND REVOLUTION: JOSÉ TRIANA

THROUGHOUT HIS CAREER as a dramatist, from the 1950s to the present, José Triana (born 1932 in Cuba) has examined the relationship between theatre and revolution.[1] What is the nature and function of theatre in periods of revolution? What do we mean by "revolutionary" theatre? How is revolution, specifically the Cuban revolution, *theatrical*? Triana's plays pose these questions, those written both at the peak of his influence within Castro's revolutionary party (*Night of the Assassins*, 1965) and later, when he was deemed an antirevolutionary and completely marginalized from the revolutionary movement (*War Ceremonial*, 1968-1973, and *Worlds Apart*, 1979-80).

The examination of these questions is fundamental to our understanding of Triana's work, illuminating its aesthetic originality and political importance, as well as the marked decline in his theatrical production after 1965. A failure to comprehend Triana's theatre in the context of the Cuban revolution has led to critical misunderstanding; Cuban commentators rejected his work on the grounds that it was antirevolutionary and had nothing significant to say about revolution; foreign commentators, however impressed by his plays, examined them in isolation from their politically loaded context. The misinterpretation of Triana's position vis-à-vis the revolution led to his political and intellectual ostracism and his exile which, by denying him his native audience, further affected his subsequent theatrical production. This chapter argues that Triana's theatre is politically and aesthetically revolutionary, although not in the sense that his critics recognized or were prepared to accept.

Commentators' views of Triana's position vis-à-vis the Cuban revolution have shaped his critical reception. Within Cuba, his work was rejected on the grounds that he was antirevolutionary and hence had nothing of interest to contribute to the new society. Ché Guevara, without mentioning Triana specifically, stated in "El hombre y el socialismo en Cuba" that "the fault of many of our intellectuals and artists lies in their original sin: they are not authentically revolutionary. We can inject maples so that they give pears, but at the same time, we have to plant pear trees. The new generations will be free of this original sin" (qtd. in de Campa, 14). Putting this general condemnation into critical language, some commentators spoke of Triana's inability to develop aesthetic resources capable of representing the revolutionary reality. While they admired his dramatic techniques in the prerevolutionary plays such as *The Major General Will Speak of Theogony* (1957) and *Medea in the Mirror* (1960), noting that "he maintained a critical attitude toward the national past," they lamented that "the critical vision of the prerevolutionary past maintained by Triana was static; it did not permit him to evolve; hence it was impossible for him to reflect the new social reality transformed by the new system" (de Campa, 14). Other critics tried to reconcile their support for the revolution with their recognition of Triana's work by claiming, as Hernán Vidal (12) does, that *Night of the Assassins* was in fact a reflection on the degradation of Cuba's *pre*revolutionary period. Set in the 1950s, during Batista's regime, the play "is a concrete judgment against Cuba's prerevolutionary society and history." Triana himself actively promoted this view, repeatedly stressing that he began writing *Assassins* as early as 1957-58.[2]

Román V. de la Campa (14) observes that the issue of Triana's revolutionary position led to a critical bifurcation: though *Night of the Assassins* received the widest international reception and reached the largest audience of any Latin American play between 1965 and 1970, was put on in Stratford-on-Avon by the Royal Shakespeare Company in 1967 (as *The Criminals*), and published in the *Drama Review* in 1970, it was ignored in Cuba—in spite of the fact that an international jury awarded it Cuba's prestigious Casa de las Americas prize in 1966: "From that moment onward, instead of bringing him fame, as had happened in the United States, and situating him in the vanguard of Cuban dramatists, his works stopped being produced in Cuba and became only a remnant of a period that had been overcome." Foreign critics by and large received *Assassins* enthusiastically as a "universal" play, as an example of Artaudian theatre of cruelty, as theatre of the absurd, as Genetian ritual, and as *danse macabre.*[3] In short, they tended to ignore the loaded political context and debate and placed the work instead in the European dramatic tradition or, more universal still, in "a planet-wide culture, whose common denominator, in the western world, seems to be the individual's show of alienation" (Murch, 369). And even when a foreign scholar as eminent as Richard Schechner did mention *Assassins* in the same breath with the revolution, he failed to see the connection: Stating that he was not impressed with Triana's plays, he adds, "What I am impressed about in Cuba is the fact of the revolution, and I think the children are marvellous. . . . If there is to be a Cuban theatre it will come in the next ten years or fifteen years—there is none now. . . . [Theatre] must develop its own forms, and the people we met were wandering in the wilderness because they were attached to bourgeois forms, and, therefore, they are irrelevant" (Interview, 39).[4]

I disagree with commentators who place Triana outside or *against* the revolutionary discourse, as well as those who study his work in isolation from it. Triana had, and continues to have, something important to say about the Cuban revolution, about " revolutionary theatre," and about theatre in periods of revolution. Moreover, he says what he has to say in a theatrical language that only superficially echoes the existentialists (Sartre specifically), the absurdists, or Genet and only playfully makes use of bourgeois forms. Rather, he converts First World artistic products into vehicles for the expression of his own specific cultural and historical concerns.

Triana's *Assassins* is particularly interesting in that it is one of the first works to raise the most urgent questions about the nature and meaning of revolution from within the very frame of the revolutionary movement. It is important to stress that Triana's work was not politically reactionary or antirevolutionary, as its critics at the time suggested. He was not "outside," removed from, or against the movement. On the contrary, when he describes that period, he always speaks of himself as *in* the revolution (*dentro de la revolución*),[5] an idiomatic construction echoing Castro's famous axiom: "Inside the Revolution, everything. Outside the Revolution, nothing." Triana participated actively in restructuring Cuba after the revolution as a founding member of the Union de Escritores y Artistas de Cuba (UNEAC). His critical inquiry into the nature of revolutionary roles and discourse does not indicate that he was experiencing personal disillusionment or crisis. Rather, the Cuban revolution and the very concept of revolution were undergoing crisis from within, a result of the gradual institutionalization of the revolutionary process. Triana initially believed that the Cuban revolution, as Castro had claimed, was following the doctrine of José Martí calling for political, economic, and cultural independence and an ethos of love and creativity. Like Yevgeny Zamyatin, who in the 1920s was considered "a Soviet heretic," Triana felt that the revolution had not gone far enough and thus it had betrayed Martí's vision of Cuban self-determination by conforming to Soviet communism. Zamyatin comes closest, to my mind, in describing the obsessive "heretical" drive for a permanent revolution that characterizes both him and Triana (perhaps a romantic recycling of a concept of *révolution en permanence* that had been popular in the nineteenth-century): "Revolution is everywhere, in every-thing. It is infinite. There is no final revolution. . . . The flame will cool tomorrow, or the day after tomorrow. But someone must see this already today, and speak heretically today about tomorrow. Heretics are the only (bitter) remedy against the entropy of human thought. When the flaming, seething sphere cools, the fiery magma becomes coated with dogma—a rigid, ossified, motionless crust" (108).

*Assassins* is a play about revolution written at the height of Triana's influence in the *fidelista* party, yet the ambiguity of his formulation of "revolution" precipitated an estrangement from that movement which culminated in the playwright's exile to France in 1980. UNEAC consid-ered ambiguity itself antirevolutionary, arguing that "the problems of our times are not abstract; they have names and are concretely localizable. We must define that against which we fight as well as the name in which we fight."[6] However, the systemic shifts within the revolutionary movement during the mid-1960s made it difficult for those involved to declare in whose name they fought (Martí, Castro, Ché, Marx, Lenin, Kruschev?) and to demarcate the revolution's boundaries (national or international revolution?). *Assassins*, in its very ambiguity, emphasizes the ambiguity of this particular phase of the Cuban revolutionary movement as well as the ambiguity of the term "revolution" itself.

## Crisis, Revolution, and *Night of the Assassins*

The "problems of our times" as represented by Triana's *Assassins*, includ-ing the nature and character of revolution, are anything but namable and localizable. We, as audience, look on while three adult children (Lalo, Cuca, Beba) lock themselves in a filthy basement or attic and reenact or rehearse Lalo's murder of their parents. Judging by the nonchalant attitude of the sisters, and by their words, Lalo's "representation" takes place time and time again. Cuca and Beba assume supporting roles in Lalo's drama, alternately playing along with and antagonizing him. Although everything takes place in a closed space, and no one ever passes through the door that connects this peripheral room to the house proper, the three characters take turns playing out several of the key figures in their lives: parents and neighbors. The end of Act 1 coincides with the end of the siblings' representation, the climactic moment when Lalo goes to murder his mother and father. In Act 2, Cuca and Beba, as policemen, supposedly find the butchered bodies and arrest Lalo. As prosecutors, they keep after him to confess his crimes. His confession again calls for role playing: the siblings "become" the parents and represent scenes of familial anger and unhappiness leading to the crime. Lalo's participation in the conflict ends with a whimper of defeat and despair: "If only love were enough, for after all, I love them" (201).[7] Beba now resumes the onslaught: "We must tear this house down!" (200). Lalo precipitates the first act (the murder); Cuca takes control of the second act (the trial). Lalo, Beba, and Cuca act out a crime-and-punishment cycle in which they take turns purging their environment alternately by means of anarchy and order. Lalo, in Act 1, attacks the foundation of the social structure. By "killing" his parents he avenges the sacrifice of the individual in a dehumanized family setting. In Act 2, Cuca reinforces the social edifice with concepts of institutionalized justice and collective well-being. When Beba at the end of the play announces, "Now it's my turn" (201), we, as audience, can only speculate what direction the action will take.

The play gives us nothing to hold on to. We never know where, when, or what—if anything—actually *happens*. Have they killed their parents? Are they acting? Playing? We lack either the perspective (like Triana's foreign commentators) or the critical distance (like his Cuban colleagues) to discern what is taking place. Audience and characters are trapped in a totalizing, closed world that refuses to let us see beyond the limiting discursive and perceptual frames. Like the six blind "men of Industan" who theorize about the nature of an elephant after touching parts of it, we are hard put to decide whether what we have before us is spear, wall, tree, snake, fan, or rope: "And so these men of missing sight / Each argued loud and long. / Though each of them was partly right, / They all were in the wrong" (John Godfrey Saxe). We can speculate, but we cannot know.

By situating us in the middle of a closed world and depriving us of all knowable links to the outside, *Assassins* calls attention to the unlocalizable nature of this space, to the simultaneous and paradoxical centrality and marginality of the onstage world. All markers orienting us have disappeared. Like Lalo, we cannot find our bearings in this womblike world: "We float, with our feet in the air and our heads downward" (140). Like the fetus in the uterus, these characters are central to the larger body, *within* yet not *in* the world. Is this an island (Cuba) paradoxically in the middle of nowhere? The disorienting inclusion works also as a form of exclusion— banishment, exile, exclusion with all its political, existential, archetypal, psychological, sexual overtones. The characters try to orient themselves in a space that is not their own, like Oedipus, Lucifer, Sartre's Garcin, Triana himself. Like Plato's cave, this womb-attic-basement-theatre is both a metaphor and a generator of images; it is a double image, a hypericon. The presence of a door only heightens the in-between feeling of the space. As in Plato's image of the cave, we can never know the truth inside this room without crossing the threshold to the light outside. Yet in *Assassins*, as in Luce Irigaray's interpretation of Plato's cave (*Speculum*, 247), that passage outward is the forgotten passage, the "forgotten vagina . . . between the outside and the inside, between the plus and the minus," between this devastating, annihilating uterus and the outside world. Is this dark space the matrix from which the child starts off, or the one to which the incestuous matricide (Lalo, Oedipus) returns? The end of the journey or the beginning? Are fantasies born in or projected onto this dark theatre?

The play displaces us in time as well as space. While focusing on one event, the murder, it resists our temptation to place the action either "before" or "after" it. Again, this ambiguity fractures all readings. Is the action preparatory, a rehearsal for murder? Is it expiatory, a cathartic release, an atonement for the crime? Is it compensatory, a substitute for murder? The before/after question obfuscates political interpretations. We have noted in Ché's statement how very important the concept of *beginnings* is for revolutionary thought, the urgency of symbolically separating present from past by starting a new calendar or celebrating the birth of a new hero or being. Any faults, any ideological shortcomings, can be placed outside the revolutionary frame, *before* the revolution. *Assassins*, set in the 1950s, but written in the 1960s, blurs the slash in the Batista/Castro opposition central to all histories and interpretations of Cuba. If the action takes place before the murder, Triana's play could be seen as a representation of the children's suffocation, thus justifying their need to overthrow the deadly social structure: "We must tear this house down." (This view, as I mentioned, redeems Triana's work for those who, like Hernán Vidal, argue that *Assassins* depicts a prerevolutionary Cuba that desperately needed radical change.) If the action takes place after the murder, Castro's revolutionaries could be seen as the assassins, having brutally usurped power from Batista. Worse still, this reading implies that the children, having won their own territory, free from parental (governmental) oppression, are incapable of creating a better world; rather, they replicate the violence and pettiness they had wanted to leave behind. (This reading was most common among Triana's Cuban colleagues.) The self-referential onstage world floats in this double dislocation, turning our markers upside down and undermining all grounds for interpretation.

*Assassins* offers a biological, cyclical model of human history. The three children, confined in their dark room, repeat the prototypical act of parricide that dates back to the three Cyclopes. The biological pattern—parents give birth and identity to children who will rebel against the father in their struggle to acquire a separate identity—itself gives birth to a political model dating back to antiquity. As Aristotle notes, "The patriarchal family supplies the primal model for political government"; Having overthrown the father, the children band together in criminal conspiracy, and the new society they form, according to Freud, is "based on complicity in the common crime" (qtd. in Brown, 16). In Triana's play, the crime gives the children their identity; they are "assassins," partners in crimes, embarked on the mythic task of creating the new out of the ashes of the old, order out of chaos.

In this play-within-a-play, the characters repeatedly act out a series of roles that undermine rather than establish identity and context. As in all theatre, we try to make sense of the relationship between the characters and of the roles they play, but in *Assassins* the action falls in the undifferentiated gap between murder-as-event and murder-as-metaphor. The dividing line between the frames of this metaplay proves more tenuous than Julio Ortega proposes in his essay on the play: "Reality, that is the normal or believable level, lies in the ruptures between role-playing" (263). Cuca-as-policeman discovers the murdered bodies and tells policeman Beba to take a look. Beba reacts as we expect but not in the role we expect: "Beba (*Entering. No longer acting as the other policeman*): It's horrifying" (178). The metatheatrical levels, like interfacing mirrors, refract infinitely. Lalo, confessing his crime, recounts how the idea of murdering his parents originally occurred to him: "One day, as I was playing with my sisters, I suddenly discovered . . ." (189). Weaving between different levels of action, trying on roles that seem too big for them, speaking in voices other than (and silencing) their own, the characters forget their lines and wander between text and context, between fictions and what they tantalizingly propose as facts.

The ambiguity erases generic distinctions. Different commentators, basing their arguments on different assumptions as to what takes place, call the action a ritual, a rehearsal, a game, a black mass. Are the children reenacting and purging themselves of a murder they have already committed—a mimetic representation? Are they preparing to murder their parents—a rehearsal? Can we, like Kirsten Nigro ("La noche," 46), classify the work as "a preparatory rite, doomed to be repeated again and again, until the children can finally consummate their criminal act"? We would have to assume, like Frank Dauster ("Game," 180) that the "bloody dress rehearsal" will culminate in performance, in the original meaning of the word *parfournir,* "to carry out," *llegar hasta el final* (169). Triana situates his work in the ground common to games, ritual, and drama. These activities involve framing, the demarcation of space free from the exigencies of ordinary life; they unfold in "pure" time, the contradictory no time or antitime, the intersection of time and the timeless. All involve repetition, impose rules, and alternately dismantle and reconstruct order. And although participants know that these activities are not "real" and have no direct or measurable repercussions on the existing social order, they can be important and fulfill serious personal and social functions. Triana deliberately returns to the inchoate phase of these activities in which games, ritual, and drama were most alike—so much so, in fact, that what Roger Callois writes about games could pass as Aristotle's defense of drama in the *Poetics* or the *Politics* and René Girard's observations on the beneficial nature of ritual in *Violence and the Sacred*: "Games discipline instincts and institutionalize them. For the time that they afford formal and limited satisfaction, they educate, enrich, and immunize the mind against their virulence. At the same time, they are made fit to contribute usefully to the enrichment and the establishment of various patterns of culture" (Callois, 55). Games, like ritual, like drama, are safe and constructive; they neutralize rivalry, hostility, fears, and violence by displacing them, by containing them in a separate, signifiable space outside the mundane bounds of the community. They allow the terrible to occur through an elaborate process of substitution whereby actors "die," goats replace humans on the sacrificial altars, and tokens go to jail without passing "Go." (Even when humans were sacrificed, ritual still represented an act of substitution: the individual took the place of an entire community that felt threatened by catastrophe.) With its ritualistic, playful, and theatrical overtones, *Assassins* resists any but the most general, antigeneric descriptions. The play too works through displacement, through an elaborate process of substitution, metaphorically, *as if,* negating the illusion even as it creates it.

As if aspiring to Aristotelian grandeur, Lalo stresses the tragic and terrifying dimension of "a spectacle worthy of being seen. It makes my hair stand on end" (142). He is simultaneously the spectator relishing the horror, the director controlling it, and the actor living it. With all the care of a director he dominates space, closing the door, framing the playing area, setting the stage, accentuating boundaries of separation. He dominates time, structuring events in dramatic beats that deliberately highlight their theatricality: "End of part one!" (168). Like Oedipus and Hamlet, he plays both executioner and victim in his attempt to reorganize a world in crisis. He is the actor who plays all the parts (mother, father, assassin, fetus, victim) in a drama that is only partially his own. He is a double, triple, quadruple figure, split to the nth degree, simultaneously innocent and guilty, terrifying and pathetic, in control and helpless, violent and defeated. As in Genet's *Maids* (which Triana had seen in Cuba in 1950), the action weaves between a desire to steep oneself in violence and the desire to liberate oneself from oppression. As in Genet's *Balcony,* the characters search for identity and power through the absolute identification with an image. As in Sartre's *No Exit,* the infernal, repetitious action goes on obsessively behind closed doors. As in ritual drama and the theatre of cruelty, Lalo experiences cathartic relief after the murder: "Now I feel calm. I would like to sleep, sleep, sleep forever" (167).

As in a game, the players take their turns. The alternation undercuts the linearity or circularity of action we associate with theatre; the play "ends" with Beba's words: "Now it's my turn" (201). The characters, through their different voices, refer to the action as "a monstrous game" (186). The stakes are high; the repercussions range from the subjunctive mode of possibility, "as if your soul were at stake" (170), to the indicative mode of fact: "Life or death. You can't escape" (173). Furthermore, the work explicitly stresses the ambiguous ludic/theatrical nature of "play": "We were playing . . . that is, we were acting" (189).

As in a ritual, Lalo invokes the gods and accentuates the ceremonial nature of the action and the objects, lending the work a sacred quality. Yet even on this level the play is split. Is it a sacred, religious, or transcendental ritual, or a secular ritual or ceremony unfolding within a personal and social context? [8] The representation seems designed instrumentally, designed as a means of provoking "something," making "something" happen. With all the pomp of a high priest, Lalo presides over the sacrifice, controlling those around him: "Lalo (*Holding the knife in his hands*): Silence. (*The two sisters begin to murmer softly*)" (167). The play focuses on separation and liminality, two of the three stages Van Gennep discerns in ritual. The children close the door that supposedly links them to the parental home and establish an alternate world, another "area of ambiguity" between forces of structure and antistructure. [9] Cuca puts things in place, advocates respect and order; Lalo rearranges everything and threatens to disrupt the family structure. The physical separation in *Assassins* exactly echoes the "opening of doors . . . the literal crossing of a threshold" (Turner, 24-25) associated with liminality. The action unfolds in sight of and in relationship to the door, which dominates the play both visually and thematically. Not only is it the one fixed object in sight (the only unblurred boundary of separation between inner and outer); it objectifies the very concept of liminality. We can define the characters as "borderline" or "liminal" because of their position vis-à-vis the door. Will they cross its threshold into the larger world and be reincorporated into their society, thereby completing the ritual process? Or will they remain in limbo, undefined, undifferentiated? By shutting the door, the characters try to gain control of themselves, of their space, and thereby rebel against their lack of definition, their personal indeterminacy. The third phase of incorporation, representing "the return of the subjects to their new, relatively stable, well-defined position in the total society" (Turner, 24), is conspicuously missing, aborting the ritual process.

For all its ritualistic overtones, the endless structuring and restructuring in the play works less as a transformation from one state to another (associated with ritual) than as a response to crisis, a struggle for definition and meaning, "a declaration against indeterminacy" (Turner, 83). In the face of crumbling social and personal frameworks, Lalo tries to create an alternative spatial and temporal frame from which to stage an act (however dangerous) of personal affirmation. He rejects the ambivalence that, according to him, plagues Cuca: "You want and you don't want. You are and you aren't. Do you think that being like that is enough? You have to take risks. Win or lose, it doesn't matter" (148). Perhaps herein lies the power of theatre during periods of crisis. In the face of rupture and decomposition, theatrical representation lends form, structure, organization, hierarchies, plots, inversions, roles, lines, attitudes, symbols. Yet in spite of Lalo's attempts to combat crisis by imposing form, the representations melt into each other; the boundaries blur between inner and outer, between action and reaction. The stage directions and dialogue accentuate the ambiguity of space, leaving us wondering where Lalo goes, for example, when "he hurries off toward the back," or where he comes from when the directions tell us "Enter Lalo" after stressing that no one passes through the door. The walls fade into the dark corners, illuminated only in spots by the flashlights Cuca and Beba, as policemen, use in their investigation. The borderline protagonists fight to define themselves in a crumbling world of partitions that do not separate, distinctions that do not hold, levels of action and intentionality that melt into each other.

By using the forms of games, drama, and ritual as though they were interchangeable, Triana does far more than complicate our reading of the text. By blurring generic distinctions and forcing us to question the terms themselves, the formal antistructure of the work brilliantly echoes the play's thematic concern with boundaries of demarcation. The play's focus on liminality (thematically and formally, as related to ritual) ties into its physical concern with blurred spatial limits, pointing back to the etymological kinship between *limes* (boundary) and *limen* (threshold). This serves as yet another example of the play's thrust back to embryonic, undifferentiated form. Its unfinished quality tempts us to label the nature of the action and then demonstrates the impossibility of doing so. In order to interpret this play we must go beyond the ambiguous frame or, rather, the *frame of ambiguity* and insert our own "facts." We can call it a game only if we maintain that the children do not murder their parents; a preparatory rite only if they do; a rehearsal only if the culminating act is theatrical rather than criminal, and so on. The juxtaposition of the inner and outer levels in the metatheatrical frame blurs all frameworks, undermines all readings. The play, unfolding in the common ground of game, drama, and ritual, refuses to develop into differentiated form. By dislocating our frame of reference, Triana's particular theatrical inquiry highlights our inability to locate, to define, for the "secret" or "answer" seems to lie just behind the door, just beyond our view, launching "desire beyond what it permits us to see" (Barthes, 59). As a meditation on the political exigencies of naming and locating within the revolutionary discourse, Triana's *Assassins* calls attention to the contradiction of the undertaking. On one hand, the ambiguity within the frame cannot be clarified unless we see beyond the frame, for we cannot judge what it includes until we understand what it excludes; we cannot interpret what goes on onstage until we know what lies beyond the door. Yet the revolutionary discourse demands unequivocal definition and localization: is one *in* the revolution or *outside* it? *For* the revolution or *against* it? A revolutionary or an antirevolutionary? The impossibility of critical distancing within the confines of the revolutionary frame creates the very area of ambiguity that the revolution attempts to combat through nonambiguity: that is, through naming and locating.

The blurring of boundaries and the collapse of the frameworks that would allow for differentiation, associated with the objective systemic rifts in crisis, are accompanied by the subjective, personal experience of crisis in *Assassins*. Lalo, Cuca, and Beba try to define themselves in the absence of a concrete, objective *other,* either individual (parents) or social. While closing the door on otherness at first seems to facilitate the liberation of self and self-determination, the exclusion or disappearance of the real, objective other signals the crisis or death of self. As the protomyths of Oedipus and Lucifer indicate, the revolt against the father denotes the striving for alterity, every human being's need to be other than an extension or sign of parental desire. It also involves substitution of role and/or place. Oedipus *becomes* king; Lucifer falls from heaven to become lord over hell. The substitution involves an element of transgression, of violation, in both spatial and ethical terms. Representations of parricide traditionally tie images of territorial conflict and exclusion to physical and spiritual putrefaction and abjection. Lalo, like Hamlet, feels embodied in a solid/ sullied body that he fears (rather than wishes) will melt. Like Oedipus, Lalo finds himself trapped in a world in ruins. The disintegration of his world, plagued by mice and cockroaches, is due (again as with Oedipus and Hamlet) to his relationship to his parents: "This house is my world. And this house is getting old; it's dirty and it smells bad. It's Mother and Father's fault" (150). The transgression reflects the blurring of boundaries in the parent/child relationship, for it simultaneously involves the excessive proximity of incest and the radical separation of murder. The crime suspends all bounds and undermines all borders. The contamination (associated with both incest and murder) from the outer world invades the inner; the inner overflows into the world outside.

Lalo tries to define himself in terms of his territory, distancing himself, circumscribing and controlling the space around him, creating a personal frame of reference. "Put the ashtray in its place!" he demands. "In this house the ashtray goes on the chair, the flower vase belongs on the floor" (140). Lalo, like the "deject" whom Julia Kristeva describes in *Powers of Horror* (8), questions his identity in terms of *where* rather than *who* he is: "I didn't know where I was, nor what all those things were," he says. (191). As "a deviser of territories, languages, works, the *deject* never stops demarcating his universe whose liquid confines . . . constantly question his solidity and impel him to start afresh. A tireless builder, the *deject* is in short a stray. He is on a journey, during the night, the end of which keeps receding" (Kristeva's emphasis). Lalo's journey through the interminable "night" is a search for meaning through control of form, a construction of an identity ("assassins") inextricably linked to the existence/disappearance of the other, the victim.

The relationship between *where* and *who* is reciprocal. The play's set description underlines the reciprocity: "They are figures in a museum in ruins" (138). *Where* shapes whoever inhabits it; the characters are reified into figurines. *Who*, in turn, shapes the environment; the museum pieces precede the structure housing them. In *Assassins*, it proves impossible to separate subjective from objective, personal crisis from social decomposition. Lalo's opening command, "Close that door," signals the paradoxical position of both the characters and the room; they are separate yet belonging; excluded yet entrapped. By closing the door, Lalo attempts to regulate the manner in which outside meets inside and self faces other. The offstage cast of characters—the parents, the police, Margarita and Pantaleón—"enter" the set only through representation, enacted by the onstage characters. Moreover, the door signals the fragility, the penetrability, of the border between inner and outer. In their attempt to keep domains apart, the characters actually bring together the horrors they can neither forget nor assimilate. What has been left out of the frame— parents, neighbors, police—comes in to plague them. Stocked with rejects and harboring rats, cockroaches, spiders, and termites, the room stands as a concrete reminder of the centrality and the predominance of things (metaphorical and physical) they cannot get rid of, cannot deal with, and consequently attempt to push out of sight.

The uncontrollable merging of the inner and outer world, explored spatially through the hazy lines of demarcation and structurally by means of overlapping levels, suggests both objective social crisis and personal decomposition. The disintegration around Lalo underlines his own lack of solidity. His sense of self is so tenuous that he fades into the other: "I stood in front of the mirror and saw my mother dead at the bottom of a coffin" (190). He is "going down, down, down" (149), back into his mother. The mirror, surface of reflection, reveals the depth of the despair. Paralyzed in and by crisis, Lalo cannot separate from his parents; he cannot simply walk away from the house. Rather, be becomes caught in the circular process of internalization and expulsion. He internalizes his parents by means of role playing and expels them, makes them separate. Through murder he transforms them into things—corpses, rejects. His psychodramatic attempts to shake himself free of his parents by means of internalization and expulsion function as a grotesque inversion of gestation—incorporation and expulsion by the parental body. For Lalo, giving birth becomes confused with defecation, a substitution expressed in spatial terms when the bedroom "turns into" the lavatory. The onstage world resembles a decaying body whose borders, the "bladders" and "sphincters," no longer separate—hence the pollution of both outer and inner, life merging with death: "I don't know why I didn't drown you at birth" (193).

Lalo feels simultaneously trapped in and excluded from the maternal body. He experiences the collapse of a world without boundaries to such a degree that even the human body, the only remaining boundary, has been taken over and threatened with disintegration. His role as his pregnant mother on her wedding day shows him in and central to her body. He "plays" her carrying him. He is simultaneously a part of her and himself, a state of utter undifferentiation and dependency foreshadowing his present condition. The maternal body gives him being, but his being in turn (his imperceptible presence as fetus) sets everything else in motion: his parents' wedding, their subsequent misery. Though the maternal womb gives him birth, Lalo experiences bond as bondage, as a devastating uterine labyrinth engulfing and destroying him. So too he feels that his very existence repulses his mother, who revolts against him and rejects him as if he were the Minotaur, the product of a monstrous coupling: "Nine months of dizziness, vomiting. . . . I don't know how I stood you that long in my belly" (192-93). He is the monster abhorred by his parents, a reject in a room of rejects. Though expelled from the parental body, he in no way feels autonomous or capable of living in the world. He is embryonic (floating head downward), unfinished (a thirty-year-old child), a distorted image in a faulty family mirror. His ambivalent feelings reflect both his extreme dependency (for as is the case with a fetus or infant, the parents' death would mean his own death) and his equally urgent need to separate from them in order to live. He acutely needs to be other than the sign of parental desire: "I wanted . . . life . . . I wanted, needed, longed desperately to do things for myself" (187). But he can only define himself in response to their existence—their son, their murderer. Like Michelangelo's slaves, struggling to pull free from the marble engulfing them, Lalo tries to throw off the dead weight of his parents: "I suffered every morning when I awakened: it was as if I arose from death weighed down by the two corpses that followed me in dreams" (190). In a kaleidoscopic world, people and objects, inner and outer conflate: "The chair wasn't the chair, but my Father's corpse. If I held a glass of water, I felt as though my hands were gripping my dead Mother's clammy throat" (191). The disintegration around him threatens his own solidity: "It's as if I were vanishing" (153). Having no firm sense of identity, Lalo reverts to the familiar role of "object" and casts himself as the knife, a sacred object "saturated with being" (Eliade, *Eternal Return*, 4), an instrument of separation.

Lalo's inclusion/exclusion in relation to the parental body functions as the model for the larger power network alluded to in the play. Locked in the onstage world, the characters constantly hint at other worlds beyond the door. The parental world, as depicted by the children, manifests all forms of deceit, ranging from polite hypocrisy to gross betrayal. Manipulative/manipulated, infuriating/furious, violent/self-sacrificing parents scrimp and scrounge to make ends meet. Their world, in turn, opens up to a larger world of tortuous city streets, humiliating jobs, degrading extramarital relationships. The complex social network appears both hostile and unknowable to the protagonists, principally Lalo, who states, "I don't know how to walk through the streets; I'm confused, I lose my way" (153). These different worlds are presented spatially (womb, room, house, city) as concentric spheres of authority, closed structures different in degree but not in kind. In each, everyone vies for control, suspects and dislikes everyone else, maintains conflicting views on what the world should be and what should go on in it. Together, they do not represent a pluralistic vision of existence, divergent modes of being and diverse values, but a monistic, totalizing system in which each component threatens to absorb and nullify the others. The passing from one circle to another is depicted as a violent invasion. Just as Lalo grew inside his mother's womb against her wishes, imaginary characters invade Lalo's inner space much against his will and authority. So too the parental world cannot protect itself from the censuring gaze of the outside world, even though the parents hide behind hypocritical roles and impose them on others. Outsiders seem ever ready to penetrate, to "stick their noses" (153) into other people's business. Yet while the social structures cannot defend against malicious social intrusion, the dirty windows and the grimy walls keep out the sunlight.

Authority within these concentric worlds seems basically intrusive, patriarchal, and hierarchical. It invades the space of the other and takes over, marginalizing and oppressing the disempowered. The need to maintain power breeds violence, from the overt physical violence inherent in defending the system to the insidious violence of fostering crippling dependency in its members, denying them the possibility of meaningful action and uncompromised discourse. In *Assassins* the father (as represented by the children) speaks in the yours-is-not-to-reason-why tone of authority figures everywhere: "Lalo, you will do the washing and the ironing. . . . Then you'll clean the toilets. You'll eat in a corner in the kitchen. You'll learn. I swear to God you'll learn! Do you hear me?" (152). Yet the father is no freer, no more individualized or autonomous than the children. He, too, is an object, a reject. Cuca, playing the role of the mother, defines their father as "a piece of trash. He's useless. He's always been a Mister Nobody" (195). Triana's use of names indicates the "progression" from the childish diminutives (Lalo, Beba, Cuca) to the ridiculous, anonymous Mister Nobody. The father is merely a larger version of Lalo, described in words echoing those Lalo uses to describe himself. And so, we assume, the circle widens across the society to include larger and larger versions of the same pathetic beings, and it spirals temporally as generational, biological self-perpetuation.

In this insistence on circularity, *Assassins* simultaneously reflects and challenges the biological model of historical process. Lalo is both a product of past events and, at the same time, the being who perpetuates the past into the future. As with Oedipus, the biological fact of his existence generates history and sets in motion a series of foreseeable events, the petty domestic miseries decreed before he was born. Although Lalo kills his parents—symbolically if not literally—the killing itself is not the main problem. (The entire issue of the killing seems more practical than ethical; it is not so much a question of whether they should or should not as of whether they can or cannot.) The problem is that he and his sisters cannot find new ways of acting in order to devise new strategies for reorganizing their territory once they have conquered it. Should they tear down the house—revolution? Should they improve on what they already have—internal reorganization? Should they leave the house forever—exile? But the endless abreactions seem to preclude the possibility of action altogether. One of the most striking features about this play is the limitation of choice and absence of viable alternatives. The characters repeatedly act out a series of roles that undermine rather than establish identity and context. Lalo, playing father at the end of the play, replaces his father in true Oedipal fashion, substituting one power figure for another. But is this revolution? Lalo fights with his sisters, hits them, orders them around, steals the show, and thus reproduces the male-dominated, violent world he had tried to leave behind. So while he may be capable of violence and murder, he is incapable of radical change. Here, I feel, Triana expresses his views on the recently triumphant revolution. The violent usurpation of political power did not guarantee social renovation. The challenge of the revolution was to create a new system of power that would not reproduce the oppression and dependency of the ones before. But Lalo reiterates the words spoken by his father before him: "We should have cleaned the house. . . . We should have replaced the furniture" (199). The father, incapable of directing his own life, crumbles under the challenge. So does Lalo. Like father, like son. "If love were enough . . ." (201), says Lalo at the end of the play. But love has failed. So has the struggle for personal autonomy and self-determination. The utopia envisioned by José Martí has failed. Lalo remains trapped in a parental body that rejects him, locked in an annihilating family structure that deforms him: biology as history and history as biological process. Here, then, we have repetition not only as circularity and substitution but also as degeneration. Each new revolution bespeaks new failures, deeper depths of despair.

Triana offsets the circular, downwardly spiraling motion of a degrading biological process by juxtaposing another model of repetition and recreation: theatrical rehearsal. Repetition signals more than a simple replay. The theory behind theatrical repetition—the French *répétition*—is originality and pefectibility, but this linear, progressive improvement is possible only within the framework of a repetitive structure. Practice makes perfect; rehearsal culminates in performance. "One day," the children keep reassuring themselves, "we'll go through with it." The hope is that instead of being dwarfed by inherited biological and theatrical roles—father, mother, Pantaleón, the maids, Garcin—the children may try on and eventually assume roles that allow them to break out of the circular patterns, that through theatrical repetition they may be able to generate a new Ideal, out of which will grow a new Real. This is revolution's utopian project. In this sense, revolutionaries are absolutists and romantics. This is also theatre's utopian project as described by Artaud's "life renewed by theatre, a sense of life in which man fearlessly makes himself master of what does not yet exist, and brings it into being" (*Double*, 13).

However, *Assassins* illustrates that there are at least two major problems in the theatrical model of progress and re-creation. The first (though from the perspective of *Assassins* not the most important) is that the theatrical model of self-engendering, of conceiving oneself otherwise and merging with a theatrical image, necessarily encourages a degree of mythification. Triana is aware of both the positive and the negative implications of creating and assuming new roles. On the positive side, research by psychologists (notably J.L. Moreno, who in the 1920s developed the psychodramatic technique for altering human behavior) and theatre therapists (for example, John Bergman of Geese Theatre, who works with criminals in penitentiaries) indicates that individuals can increase their options for functioning in the world by assuming new roles. But whereas these examples presuppose that the individual is the deviant who must adapt to social reality, not all those who use theatre techniques to change the role of the individual in social systems share that assumption. Boal's "theatre of the oppressed" bases itself on the opposite premise, that many individuals are excluded from sociopolitical circles that should rightfully be open to them. Taking on new roles, according to Boal, is not an adaptive but a revolutionary technique to help individuals change the system. On the positive side, Triana, like Boal, shows the world improving as a consequence of the children's ability to find more independent and better-directed ways of acting. The negative aspect of taking on theatrical roles is that though only new roles will allow the children to change their sociopolitical situation, the characters' uncritical identification with heroic images threatens to trap them in a totalitarian fantasy. Thus, as heroic citizens, these "new men" feel not only entitled, but morally obliged to exclude those who fail to live up to the fantasy. As Cuca asks the imaginary jury: "Can we allow such a person [as Lalo] to share our hopes and ideals at a time when humanity, that is to say our society, should be marching toward a shining future, toward a golden dawn?"[10] The danger is that the thrust for liberation hides a far deeper need for submission, that the vision of collective harmony merely disguises and legitimates the mechanisms for excluding others, and that what promises to be revolutionary activity proves only an adaptive measure.

Ultimately more self-defeating, from the context of *Assassins*, is that the paradigm of theatrical self-engendering only revamps an old, basically misogynist model of historical process. Like the Hegelian and Marxist theories of human perfectibility through conflict, work, and thought, the theatrical model also maintains that humans (specifically males) can eschew biology and bring themselves into being. Lalo (the mover and doer in the play) believes he can overcome biological determinism through theatrical representation by casting himself in desired roles varying from high priest to assassin. Artaud, too, fantasizes about recreating himself and pronounces the rejection of his mother and his biological birth in terms similar to those expressed by Lalo: "This is no way to be born, to be copulated and masturbated for nine months by the membrane which toothlessly devours . . . I know that I was born otherwise, born of my own works and not of a mother. . . . I was born only in my own labor pangs" (*Anthology*, 83). Moreover, Artaud's search through theatre for a way of recreating himself, extreme as it is, strangely echoes Hegelian and Marxist political thought. Hegel states that man "comes to light" only in his fight to the death against the other.[11] Sartre, in his introduction to *The Wretched of the Earth* (14), praises Frantz Fanon for being "the first since Engels to bring the processes of history into the clear light of day." Sartre's Hegelian view of historical process shows the revolutionary as the "man recreating himself" through his own "labor," through work and conflict.

Rather than signaling a new self-conception, however, these repeated images of self-engendering obfuscate what is basically the male appropriation of the process of gestation and birthing, revealing perhaps not so much a new historical paradigm as a profound fear and hatred of women. In other words, the image of the man giving birth to himself does not alter the biological model so much as simply eliminate woman from the process. The model not only excludes women; it is a negative inversion of the biological process of gestation itself. Instead of giving birth and life, a *man* can only "come to light" through a fight to the death. By defeating the Master, the Slave "himself creates himself" (Sartre, Introduction, 21). Lalo too acquires his identity (assassin) by killing his "masters." Like Hegel's "Slave," he imagines he can bring himself into being only through his own actions, through his willingness to risk his life rather than accept servitude. As he tells Cuca, "You have to take risks. Win or lose, it doesn't matter" (148). The first problem with the self-engendering myth, which according to Hannah Arendt "is the very basis of leftist humanism," is that it is patently wrong. As Arendt points out, "nothing is more obvious than that man, whether as a member of the species or as an individual, does *not* owe his existence to himself" (*Violence*, 12-13; Arendt's emphasis).

The skewed version of historical process in *Assassins* is consistent with the world view in the play as a whole; the children's failure to create new roles is linked to their inability to go beyond old paradigms of history; their definition of self (whether individually or historically) still depends on the elimination of the (m)other. The revolutionary act becomes conflated with the misogynist act. In order to "become" a man, the hero must abandon woman: Lalo's father should have walked out of his home and abandoned his wife. For Lalo, autonomy comes only through the radical separation from parental bonds, exemplified in maternal engulfment (pregnancy); as in Plato's simile of the cave, enlightenment comes only upon leaving the uterine dwelling; in historical paradigms, revolutionary man becomes self-engendering through his own labor. As Lalo's predicament indicates, it proves impossible to envision new roles without also devising new constructs that allow new ways of thinking about such concepts as origin, progress, revolution, and history.

How, then, can the children create new roles that will permit freedom of action and self-definition without reproducing the violence and limitations of the old? How can they devise a different way of thinking about individual and historical process that does not lead back to the old dead ends? How can revolution create a new society without recreating the problems of the previous one? The roles, images, and ideas produced and reproduced in *Assassins* illustrate that without a conceptual breakthrough, progress is illusory. The illusion of progress is maintained through a process of repetitive substitution rather than by linear development. The creation of a fictitious, theatrical self is only a re-creation that hinges on the elimination of the real other, which is then replaced by a false other and a false self. Instead of the past, the home, the parents, we have the present, the room, the children—who then generate their version of history. Yet the past melts into and is indistinguishable from the present. The room beyond the door, the parents, the past—in short, everything we can suppose to represent the real other in *Assassins*—proves only a refraction of self: *that* room is probably no different from *this* room, so the problem is not only *there* but *here*; the parents are probably no different from the children; the present represents the past. The doubling is theatrical both in the sense that it mimetically represents and, at the same time, historically actualizes the past. The past does not simply "appear on stage wearing the mask of the preceding scene." This replay is not only an optical distortion, as Régis Debray argues in *Revolution in the Revolution?* (19), produced by "our vision, encumbered with memory and images learned in the past. We see the past superimposed on the present, even when the present is a revolution." The point of Triana's play is that the present *re*produces the past, in the sense of reactivation rather than mimesis. The problems have not been solved. The questions have not been answered. (Twenty years later, in *Worlds Apart* [14], Triana continues to emphasize this point: "War? Again? And what did the last two solve? Just more blood, more deaths!") Unless something radically alters the situation, the past is repeatedly actualized as present and as future, generation after generation. But what is that something? Revolution? Is revolution the awaited radical upheaval or yet another repetitive cycle, one more substitution?

*Assassins* incessantly brings us back where we began. The play not only thematizes parricide as a form of ultimate self-annihilation; it works as theatrical and historical parricide/suicide. What we see in *Assassins* is an elaborate play of substitution. To begin with, the play kills off (literally shuts the door on) the real other. In the absence of the real other, the play presents a false other (Lalo *as* father, Cuca *as* mother, children *as* self-engendering). The substitution operates through metaphor, in itself the vehicle for substitution. The other is recreated through role playing, which substitutes for the absent real other. This fictitious, theatrical invention becomes the mirror through which the characters try to define self. Having eliminated the real other, Lalo can only hope to see (though he *fails* to see) himself in this imagined other: looking in the mirror, he sees his dead mother. Hence, unlike the mirror stage that Lacan considers vital to ego formation, this mirror deforms the ego by reflecting self as absent, completely out of the frame. Only a false or nonself can evolve through identification with the false other—and that false self cancels the real through theatrical substitution. Who are these children? How old are they? What do they think about themselves, each other, the world they live in? The process we see in *Assassins* is one of double elimination, double substitution in that the banished real *other* also makes impossible the existence of a real *self.* The children, too, are absent, rendered invisible through role playing. All we see are the roles, and the roles are too big for them. We hear different statements through disembodied voices that cancel themselves even as they speak. The theatrical recreation of other destroys the self. The roles the children reenact challenge us to pose theatre's own self-annihilating question: if these people could stop acting, could they start living?

*Assassins* problematizes the revolution's failure to create new roles, new constructs, a new real; however, it also problematizes the role of theatre in the revolutionary process. The juxtaposed circular and linear models not only illustrate conflicting ways of thinking about history—the biological-ahistorical and the linear-triumphalist respectively—but also signal the two major assessments of theatre's political effectiveness, which were then and to a degree still are being debated by theatre practitioners in Latin America and elsewhere. The aim of the representations, the characters tell us repeatedly, is to "carry through" with their act, to kill their parents—which, within the context of the play, seems equivalent to the prototypical, revolutionary act. The action, then, claims to concentrate tension, rather than diffuse or release it, in order to bring about specific social change. This linearity seems to support the revolutionary view of theatre as an instrument in social struggle as expressed by people such as Augusto Boal, T. Philemon Wakashe (South Africa), and Ngugi wa Thiong'o (Kenya).[12] But the play professes two antithetical goals. The second undercuts the first; the action seems cathartic and circular, designed to release tension through repeated abreaction. Lalo expends his energy on obsessive representations that incapacitate him, one might conclude, for real action. On this level, *Assassins* insinuates its concern that theatre serves to exhaust and pacify the suffering of the oppressed without improving their situation. As Fanon says of dance and possession, "The native relaxation takes precisely the form of a muscular orgy in which the most acute aggressivity and the most impelling violence are canalized, transformed, and conjured away" (57). Boal issues a similar warning about carnival ("Teatro popular," 32). *Assassins* manifests both the linear progression associated with revolutionary theatre and the circular, exhaustive aspects of cathartic theatre. Is this a preparatory (revolutionary) theatre, or a substitute for real action (antirevolutionary)? The ambiguous relationship between theatrical representation and real action in the play raises questions about the possibility of action (as opposed to reaction) in a closed political system. By participating in the enactment of the murder, what do the children accomplish? If the "play" is a rehearsal, can we believe these aging adolescents capable of ever changing their environment? In other words, is there anything to suggest that theatre prepares an audience for political action and precipitates radical social change? If the play provides cathartic release, the anarchistic onslaught serves only—ironically—to strengthen the hated social structure. By exhausting their hostility in a "safe" (theatrical) setting, the children manage to live in a world they perceive as unlivable. In short, we could argue that instead of affecting the system as they suppose, their obsessive representation allows them to adapt to it. *Assassins* asks us to consider whether, for these children, theatrical re-creation is not the ultimate form of violence, nullifying the possibility of real action, "making them play roles in which they no longer recognize themselves . . . making them carry out actions that will destroy every possibility for action" (Levinas, 21). Is drama (*dran* = to do, to act) their *un*doing?

*Assassins*, however, is not a play that denounces theatre. It offsets its concerns about the futility (and perniciousness) of dramatic action precisely by posing them through theatre. In spite of the seeming impossibility of maintaining an *other* in a totalizing world, the work's unfinished and ambiguous nature in fact points to an *other* way of being. Because it undermines frameworks that allow us to formulate meaning in any clear, unequivocal way, the play resists assimilation. The play is untotalizable and, as such, external to the totalizing world it portrays. The play speaks, yet its disembodied voice cannot be pinned to any one speaker; it responds, yet no one is responsible. The only way to be *other,* the play suggests (in spite of the many overt attacks against indeterminacy), is through ambiguity. Ambiguity, by nature untotalizable, threatens the very notion of totality. When revolution offers no possibility of critical distancing, when there is "nothing" outside the revolution, when all discourse is subsumed by the revolutionary frame, then the only *other* space is the area of ambiguity within the confines of the revolutionary frame itself.

*Assassins*, then, creates its own space and a language of ambiguity that cannot be absorbed by the larger political or theoretical structure or terminology. It sidesteps the political demand that art name and locate. But why the importance of creating an *other?* Is ambiguity meaningful only as a strategy for disrupting political complacency, in the sense Barbara Johnson refers to in *A World of Difference* (30-31): "Nothing could be more comforting to the established order than the requirement that everything be assigned to a clear meaning or stand. It is precisely because the established order leaves no room for unneutralized (i.e., unestheticized) ambiguity that it seems urgent to meet decisiveness with decisiveness.

But for that same reason it also seems urgent not to." Could it also be that by remaining *other,* the play can be not *anti-* but in a sense *independent of* the revolution, posing a dialectical tension with the stasis of revolution. This dialectical otherness may seem unreasonable, even heretical, for as Herbert Marcuse (vii) notes, revolutionary discourse "seems promising and productive enough to repel or absorb all alternatives. Thus acceptance—and even affirmation—of this reality seems the only reasonable methodological principle. Moreover, it precludes neither criticism nor change; on the contrary, insistence on the dynamic character of the status quo, on its constant 'revolutions,' is one of the strongest props for this attitude. Yet this dynamic process seems to operate endlessly within the same framework." Hence, by remaining outside the revolution, the play threatens not the revolution but the stasis of revolution, the totalizing tendency of revolution, and provokes rather an ongoing dialectical process—a permanent revolution. For that reason, Zamyatin ruefully observed, heretics are "exterminated by fire, by axes, by words" (108).

If the play maintains a position other than that assigned to it by revolution, does that make it antirevolutionary? Initially, the *fidelistas* advocated complete intellectual freedom, declaring that the revolution could tolerate all manner of divergency. But by 1965, the "seething sphere" of revolution had cooled to dogma, Zamyatin's "entropy." The tensions between what the Cuban revolution could and could not accept focused on Triana. He was simultaneously accepted and rejected; he received the coveted Casa de las Americas prize and yet was gradually ostracized from intellectual life. His play not only depicted the difficulty of being other in a totalizing system that insists on defining and situating everything; it also activated the problem. The play simultaneously *presented* the problem of alterity in a totalizing structure and *represented* it. In the 1960s it was generally accepted by Latin American intellectuals that politically and socially committed artists should support the Cuban revolution. Fernando Alegría, for example, while noting that literature is revolutionary in various ways, states that "an author who lives in the revolution cannot, if he is sincere, help but ask himself how his work functions within the new social organization and what is expected of him within the revolutionary dynamics" (10). *Assassins* is a revolutionary work of art, but not in the sense that its commentators expected or were prepared to accept. The play speaks to the ongoing dialogue about dramatic and social action, but not in a voice we would recognize or from a position we can localize. The play's definable or localizable generic and political "character"—its inquiry into the nature and efficacy of the Cuban revolution, its political urgency and romantic intensity—disappear (like the play's characters themselves) behind its formal ventriloquism. It is not, like the revolutionary theatre discussed previously, immediately *useful* as a work of art; on the contrary, the revolutionaries found it harmful and disturbing. It proves disturbing, however, precisely in its revolutionary questioning of the revolutionary process itself. As Zamyatin (109) concludes, "Harmful literature is more useful than useful literature." And because *Assassins* problematizes the boundaries of the system's discursive and perceptual frames, it is also a destructive play. But then dialectical thought, as Marcuse (xii) states, is "necessarily destructive . . . it reveals modes and contents of thought which transcend the codified pattern of use and validation." Yet out of the destructive comes the potential for a renewed union of theory and practice, thought and action. What has to change in order for Castro's Cuba to avoid repeating the corrupt and totalizing systems it replaced? How can we learn to think and to be otherwise so that we do not replay the past? This is the truly revolutionary question, and insofar as the Cuban revolution failed to answer it, it was also the pro-foundly heretical one.

In the same vein, *Assassins* is also an aesthetically original piece of theatre. It presents itself as an avant-garde play in the tradition of the French existentialists, of the absurdists, of Jean Genet, whose work Tri-ana encountered first in Cuba and later in Spain ("Entrevista," 116). Yet though it shares many similarities with their works, here too Triana carries out a complicated play of substitution. *Assassins* "looks" like other plays, but the resemblance is only a political necessity, a means to challenge the complacency of the revolution without obviously transgressing the limits of the revolutionary discourse. But the politically grounded nature of Triana's preoccupations point away from, rather than toward, the issues that concern Sartre, Ionesco, and Genet. Sartre's *No Exit* is also a cruel striptease, a play of endless self-examination and self-recrimination. The three characters "peer" into themselves, "into the secret places of [their] heart[s]"; they reveal what they see, and it makes them "faint with horror" (43). Like Lalo, Cuca, and Beba, they use their knowledge as a weapon and take turns ganging up on each other. They vie for control and dream of liberty under the shadow of the door, which leads, as in *Assassins*, to a labyrinthian passage and from there to "more rooms, more passages, and stairs" (6). In Sartre's play, the characters' eternal acting-out also under-mines the possibility of real action. Like *Assassins*, *No Exit* blurs distinc-tions between inner and outer: the characters can look back on earth from their position in hell, and hell is a direct consequence of their acts on earth. Hence, as in Triana's work, the past is actualized in the present; only *now* do the characters realize the full extent of the horror of what they com-mitted in life. And all the while the door between the two worlds remains firmly shut. However, even though Sartre pins down certain historical details—Garcin, interestingly, is a Brazilian journalist shot to death by the military for fleeing the country during a period of political crisis—the thrust of the play is not so much about humans trying to create better roles and better worlds as a depiction of constant, ubiquitous human suffering. The theme is universal, existential: people make themselves suffer; they create their own hells, here and always. The characters are dead; they are beyond the possibility of action, beyond change. Nothing could be further from Triana's utopian project. For him, theatre is not a representation of an infernal condition but a site for generating new, real, redemptive images.

Triana's concept of theatre as a site for generating images is what brings him close to Genet, the playwright with whom he is most often compared. Genet too is acutely aware of the political importance of spectacle in society: power is maintained through the manipulation of images—Queen, Bishop, Judge, General, Chief-of-Police. Political conflict, Genet perceived perhaps better than anyone, is a battle of images. The revolutionaries in *The Balcony* convert Chantal into the image of revolution, another "Liberty Guiding the People" à la Delacroix. The images engage in the battle for control of the symbolic order; the image of the Queen, proving most powerful, appropriates the revolutionary image and uses it toward its own ends. Ultimately, Genet proposes a vision of power that Triana consciously struggles against and denounces. For Triana, the simulation, the incessant and ambiguous playing, is that "which conceals the truth," the specific, historically grounded failings of the Cuban revolution. It is that which enables him to speak "the truth" without coming straight out and saying it. Yet truth is real. For Genet, the simulacrum is the "truth which conceals that there is none. The simulacrum is true" (qtd. in Baudrillard, 1). For Genet, the battle of images does not create a utopian real, but a postmodern "hyperreal." Baudrillard (2-4) defines the hyperreal as "the generation by models of a real without origin or reality. . . . It is no longer a question of imitation, nor of reduplication, nor even of parody. It is rather a question of substituting signs of the real for the real itself." The *image* of the Queen plays as important and politically real a function as the Queen herself—or more, in fact, insofar as real queens can die and images can be produced (through theatre, photography, and so on) and technologically reproduced and projected infinitely. Genet was fascinated with the political use of these images, particularly in fascist and totalitarian states. In *The Balcony*, those who control the fantasies, the little theatres in which the images are generated and lived out, control the population. Irma, like the watch guard in the panoptic prison, controls the "visitors" by keeping them in separate studios, each one equipped with a viewfinder. Irma's centralized scrutinizing machinery, in turn, is at the service of the state. She is power's whore, literally the Chief-of-Police's whore; to him she passes all the valuable information, and he protects her "house of Illusions," which continues producing the images people live by.

Genet's model, even though based on the technological production and reproduction of images, applies primarily (though not exclusively) to the advanced "societies of the spectacle" described by Baudrillard's predecessor, Guy Debord (6): "The spectacle, grasped in its entirety, is both the result and the project of the existing mode of production. It is not a supplement to the real world, an additional decoration. It is the heart of unrealism of the real society." Genet's model also holds an important political lesson for developing countries. In South Africa, for example, computers are currently used as instruments of social control much in the manner of Irma's viewfinders. Genet's image of the studios, which Irma tirelessly endeavors to keep separate, represents the compartmentalization and constant surveillance that writers such as Fanon (38) associate with colonialism: "The colonial world is a world cut in two. The dividing line, the frontiers, are shown by barracks and police stations." Yet though it applies to developing countries, this particular model does not apply specifically to the problems Triana associates with Cuba, either in the early 1960s or today. Cuba was trying to get beyond the internal divisions, the conflict and oppression that characterize both the South African and the colonial model. Triana was interested in theatre not as a coercive totalitarian tool (or a model for one) but as an arena for generating real sociopolitical change. As I have insisted previously, Triana believed in the revolutionary project. Ideologically, he was much closer to his colleagues at UNEAC than to Genet or Sartre; he believed in the real as well as in the reality and necessity of radical social upheaval. For Triana, the battle was one not of fabricated, artificial images but of new political roles, visions, and options. Like one member of the Grupo Escambray, Triana too probably would have scoffed at the irony of someone rehearsing an Ionesco piece while engaged in revolution.[13] What could be more foreign to Triana, who was producing a play in the context of the revolution for an audience that had committed itself to a radical social overhaul, than Ionesco's notion of "objective reality, outside time, eternal" and his concept of art as "an autonomous creation, an independent universe with its own life and its own laws"?[14] What Triana criticizes is the limiting, controlling aspect of discursive and perceptual frames, the enforced naming and localizing. In this sense, Triana's position is "absurdist" only in that it dialectically opposed the "reasonable" path of the *Castristas*. Hence it was irrational, politically *absurd*, "to speak a language which is not the language of those who establish, enforce and benefit from the facts. As the power of the given facts tends to become totalitarian, to absorb all opposition, and to define the entire universe, the effort to speak the language of contradiction appears increasingly irrational, obscure, artificial" (Marcuse, x).

In short, the fundamental difference between Triana and the avant-garde playwrights with whom he is compared is his fervent belief in the importance and possibility of sociopolitical regeneration. The repetition of the piece expresses a disillusionment, but also a hope. As Debray (23) points out, failure is not the end of the revolution; "For a revolutionary, failure is a springboard. As a source of theory it is richer than victory: it accumulates experience and knowledge." For Triana as for Zamyatin, literature should be harmful, the more destructive and dangerous the better. Literature should stay not within the revolution but outside it, keeping it going, keeping it honest, leading it onward toward the creation of new images and constructs that it helps bring into being. For Zamyatin in 1923 as for Triana in the 1960s, what was needed was a literature capable of exploring "vast philosophic horizons . . . we need the most ultimate, the most fearsome, the most fearless 'Why?' and 'What next?'" (Zamyatin, 109-10).

During a decade (the 1960s to the 1970s) in which Latin American artists and intellectuals believed in the Cuban revolution with almost religious zeal, Triana problematizes the increasingly dogmatic nature of that revolution as well as the static/dynamic tension inherent in all revolutions. Does revolution refer to a radical political upheaval, fought in the name of liberation and social justice, which culminates in the creation of a new state? Can the new state, on settling down to follow its new agenda, ever avoid what some thinkers consider the unavoidable ossification that accompanies the "laborious, slow, useful, most useful" evolutionary process? After all, is not the concept of a *permanent* revolution a contradictory one? Revolutions and revolutionaries, as Mexico's "institutionalized revolution" demonstrates, are often trapped and die in the systems of power they fought so hard to win. Revolutions seem heroic and laudable when they remain outside the system, struggling to get in, fighting to introduce such concepts as liberation, freedom, and equality. Upon winning power, however, they too must cement their policies through the laborious restructuring process that is grounded in the real. To varying degrees they renounce their ideals for a pragmatic, workable program. This is the reasonable, practical, necessary course; no party could remain in power without taking it. Rather than face the contradictions posed by reality, the "reasonable," "useful," productive course is to eliminate the subversive, destructive dialectical questioning—what Marcuse calls "the power of negative thinking" as "the driving power of dialectical thought" (viii). And so, back to entropy. Can revolution ever break out of the repetitive cycle?

Rather than profound social upheaval, does revolution signal circular repetition, as in the revolutions of the earth around the sun? Or does it denote substitution, the process by means of which one power figure merely replaces another? Is revolution inevitably the "spectacle that has fallen under the sign of Saturn: 'The revolution devouring its own children'"? (Arendt, *Revolution*, 49).

The existence of *Assassins* as a self-reflective piece of theatre that keeps asking "Why?" and "What next?" (rather than anything it actually *says*) makes it a highly political work that carves out for itself a separate place. *Assassins* is an *historia* (in both senses, history and story) *of* and *about* exile. Written both before and after Triana's exile (before Castro and again after Castro), it dislocates us, erasing the slash in before/after. *Assassins* is revolutionary, a play *of* and *about* revolution. It is profoundly revolutionary in the sense that it is "harmful," "heretical," and utopian; thus, it eludes being trapped in the revolutionary frame. *Assassins* is metatheatrical, a work *of* and *about* theatre. It warns of the dangers of playacting but does so in the only role open to it, through play. The play, like the characters, simultaneously "is" and "isn't" (148). The play gives us the slip. Through its metaphoric substitution, *Assassins* as game, as ritual, as rehearsal, is a play that absents itself even as it speaks. And yet, it speaks.

Triana's *Night of the Assassins* is theatre of crisis. Suspended between life and death, locked in an area of ambiguity, it presents a world turned upside down and inside out. The dark, closed chamber in which the children obsessively act out their drama is a camera obscura, the dark space in which images are simultaneously generated (from the inside out) and projected (from the outside in), a cave. The room is both a political metaphor for claustrophobic, totalitarian space *and* the scene or site of image-production, the matrix/womb, the revolution, the theatre in which matricidal figures and histories originate and die.

## Mapping the Revolution: Crisis and Beyond

If *Assassins* is a "harmful" and heretical play set in the moment of crisis, in the rupture between thought and action, theory and practice, *War Ceremonial* (1968-73) goes somewhat beyond the ambiguity of crisis to map out and "prepare the ground for their possible reunion" in which it is possible for "thought to develop a logic and a language of contradiction" (Marcuse, xii). While reexamining the connections between theatre and revolution already explored to a degree in *Assassins*, the plays *War Ceremonial* and *Worlds Apart* indicate the changes in Triana's position in Cuba during the three years after he won the Casa de las Americas award. Triana no longer feels trapped within the theatre but rather feels left outside it. *Ceremonial*, by representing a wounded revolutionary whose fellow revolutionaries have left him behind to die, offers a very personal, albeit fictionalized, description of Triana's situation after the reception of *Assassins*, his gradual marginalization from all intellectual activity as he was forced to do manual labor in a factory, and his going into exile in 1980. The obsessive, confessional tone of the play is nightmarish (Triana describes *Ceremonial* as a recurring nightmare of betrayal and paralysis ["Entrevista," 122]), its introspective quality accentuated perhaps by the fact that Triana had no hopes of staging any more plays in Cuba and had no audience in mind while writing it.

Autobiographical elements notwithstanding, it is clear that the basic conflicts and paradigms we find in *Ceremonial* were already present in *Assassins*, although superficially, *Ceremonial* looks like an entirely different play. Aracelio, a revolutionary soldier, a *mambí*, has been wounded in the leg during Cuba's war of independence. His companions abandon him until they realize that Aracelio has the map indicating the way to the fort, the Candelaria. Not only are the enemy's military supplies and food kept there, but the fort also represents a microcosm of Cuba, "the image of our island" (6). Whoever has the map, they say, controls the country's future. Aracelio has been entrusted to direct a heroic mission, "the Revolution's greatest epic," to take the fort and, hence, the country: "It would be as if you had taken possession of Cuba" (34). Just as it proves impossible for him to undertake the task single-handedly, especially with his injury, it also proves impossible for his fellow revolutionaries to take the fort without the map. Throughout the two-act play, Aracelio's companions use fiction, role playing, and theatrical ceremony to try to win over the map, and Aracelio.

*Ceremonial*, however, is less ambiguous than *Assassins*. In *Assassins* the political meditations on revolution hide behind the dominant Oedipal motif; in *Ceremonial* the biological is almost totally transposed to the political body. The word "revolution," never once mentioned in the earlier play, is repeated some fifty times in this text. Aracelio depends on the political body (revolution) for his existence and identity. The revolution becomes the "mother" that gives birth to the new being, only later to reject her offspring: Saturn devouring his children. Aracelio is defined by his revolt; he is a "revolutionary" much as Lalo is an "assassin." He incorporates himself totally into the larger political body and claims to surrender his individuality; he recognizes that he "belongs" to the revolution (90) and commits himself "unconditionally" (82) to it. Yet he feels betrayed and rejected, having been abandoned to die of his wound, another Oedipus. He passionately longs to merge with the revolutionary ideals and heroic images, yet he despises the body that expelled him. Like

Lalo, both incorporated by the mother and loathed by her, Aracelio experiences annihilation as both inclusion and exclusion: he is a revolutionary trapped in a rotting body; he has been left behind by the revolution to die alone.

Like *Assassins*, *Ceremonial* is also about revolution. While the former focuses on the limiting nature of the revolutionary frame which makes it difficult to see beyond it or to think critically about it, the latter analyzes revolution-as-spectacle, revolution-as-icon. The ceremonious, repetitive, almost ritualistic quality of the revolutionary war is already suggested in the title: *War Ceremonial*. Its perfectible, utopian nature (as rehearsal) is made explicit in the epigraph to the play, taken from the Spanish Civil War poet Miguel Hernández: "If revolution is the stuff of theatre, let us make sure that our theatre, and hence our revolution, is exemplary—then maybe, maybe, our world will be too" (1). As in *Assassins*, Triana uses a double time frame to temporally dislocate his discourse. Though the action takes place during Cuba's war of independence (in fact, two wars: the "Ten Years War," 1868-78, and the successful rebellion of 1895-98), everything the play says about that struggle applies at least as much to the revolution of 1959. In *Ceremonial*, however, the displacement is not primarily a means of avoiding criticism and censorship (we recall that he had no hopes of publishing or producing this work); rather, Triana sees the struggle itself as repetitive insofar as it seems irresolvable. The period of bitter struggle in the late nineteenth century (inspired by the ideals of Martí) ended in the questionable "independence" that freed Cuba from Spain, only to make it a protectorate of the United States; the revolution of 1959 moved it from the American to the Soviet orbit. The use of the same technique, temporal displacement, now takes on a different function.

Perhaps the most significant step beyond the ambiguity of *Assassins* is the acceptance in this later play of that old Marxist concept, contradiction. While the characters of the early piece despair at their lack of determinacy, in *Ceremonial* Aracelio finally acknowledges that revolution is unthinkable without the acceptance of contradiction. Although revolution's power to attract attention and draw followers to its ranks lies in its theatrical framing, in the careful selection of roles and the simplification of images signaling one unequivocal "revolutionary" message, these images are necessarily ambiguous; they must unite disparate collectivities under one banner, and they can do so only if they are equivocal enough to mean different things to different people. Aracelio, who at the beginning of the play clung to his notions of "revolution" and "truth" (as if they were identical) like the revolutionary absolutist and romantic he is, now realizes that truth is relative and revolutions are not absolute. "Truth" is self-legitimating, and the potent symbolic function of the word "revolution" lends itself to indiscriminate application, but neither means any *one* thing. "Revolution" is simultaneously a "holy word" (79) that motivates people to higher actions and sacrifices *and* a word to camouflage the basest self-interest, treason, and lies. Instead of a monolithic notion of a truth, perhaps it makes more sense to speak, as Aracelio finally does, of a personalized "*my* truth" (93), or of the changing truths described by Zamyatin (110): "All truths are erroneous. This is the very essence of the dialetical process: today's truths become errors tomorrow; there is no final number." If we can accept this contradiction, it may be possible to recognize that the problem in using these words lies perhaps less in their fluidity than in their fixity. Truth and revolution, while apparently antithetical to dogma and institutionalization, nonetheless become dogmatic and institutionalized when they are fixed, made permanent, as in *the* truth and *the* revolution.

Other contradictions must be faced as well. How can a dynamic process of revolution be contained in a static image? How can revolution, theoretically a collective process, subsume the many to the one—one image, one slogan, one leader? How can an agenda based on higher social truth, freedom, and justice be based on fiction—the fabrication of images? Is unity always and necessarily the most important political posture, or does a movement have to allow for pluralism? Is revolutionary ideology what holds groups together, or is it rather idolatry, the worship of the image, the icon, the golden calf? The way the characters fling the word "revolution" around makes it resemble a banner whose appearance commands reverence and obedience. Aracelio wavers between betraying the revolution by withholding the map and betraying himself by cooperation with the revolutionaries who betrayed him. Unlike Lalo, however, he is not hopelessly paralyzed by contradiction. By handing over the map, he tries to go beyond the gap between theory and practice, thought and action. The map then provides not only a guide to the territory, indicating pitfalls, but also symbolizes a generative, almost utopian projection toward the future, a new Cuba. It is a blueprint for the future which is only partially based on the past.[16]

The most fundamental problem in *Ceremonial*, and in the very concept of revolution, is manifested in the tension between the fluidity of the process and the rigidity of the program, between the idea of a guide and the concreteness of a map, between truth as goal and truth as dogma. Maps fix boundaries; their purpose is to divide, to delineate, to set down. While the world's surface, political boundaries, and human concepts change, maps remain fixed. They do not change; they are replaced. Maps are ideological insofar as they depict dominant perspective (powerful countries are represented as unduly large and on top, though there is no scientific basis for having the north "on top" of the south/north axis). When maps fail to correspond to contemporary reality, they are superseded by ones that do. In short, there are no flexible maps; they are rigid (the concrete equivalent of Zamayatin's entropy); they distort (they represent the world as static when it is in constant movement). Yet we need maps. We cannot get around, or overcome, contradiction. Rather we need the "language" and "logic" of contradiction that allows us to accept the need for maps and truths in spite of their limitations and because of their limitations. Faced with countless possible routes, we need direction, the limitation of choices. We also need truths—collective, distorting, and limiting though they may be. The individual *my* truth does not motivate armies until it becomes *the* truth, a generally accepted collective truth; but collectives do not run revolutions, as Castro's revolution makes clear. However, as Triana protests in *Ceremonial*, the personal must be added to the collective, and the collective must respect the personal. The revolution cannot move until the revolutionaries stop to reintegrate the man they left behind.

If crisis is the moment of suspension between death and regeneration, *War Ceremonial*, like *Assassins*, remains in abeyance. It is not until Triana writes *Worlds Apart* (1979-86) that he moves beyond crisis, that he acquires the critical distance and declares his separate peace by deciding to go into exile, to live "worlds apart." Or, to use the original title in Spanish, *Palabras comunes* (*Common Words*), Triana had accepted by 1979 that the heretic, the man excluded from the revolution, could not lead the revolution with his Zamyatinesque prophecies. He did not have *palabras divinas* to say to his fellow Cubans but only *palabras comunes* for a foreign audience: *Worlds Apart* was staged by the Royal Shakespeare Company at Stratford-upon-Avon in 1986. The play is a kind of leave-taking, a panoramic view back over Cuba's history between its war of independence and World War I. In this work he ties his country's past into his own past; historical allusions blend with allusions to his personal situation and his own earlier works. We hear echoes of the three children in *Assassins* except now, in *Worlds*, it's Beba's turn: Victoria looks back on her life while her two siblings, Alicia and Gaston, play supporting roles. Unlike Lalo, however, Gaston finally has the autonomy to open the door and walk away. The links between personal and national history have no projection toward the future. Leaving Cuba, Triana realizes that he has ceased to exist in and for Cuba: "I've left no footprints in the sand." Here too, however, I see Triana's leave-taking less as an antirevolutionary rejection than as a profoundly revolutionary aspiration, the kind described by Zamyatin (112): Most people "lack the strength to wound themselves, to cease loving what they once loved, to leave their old, familiar apartments . . . and walk away into the open field to start anew" (112). Lucid? Yes. Romantic? Undoubt-edly. But *antirevolutionary?*

Rather than antirevolutionary, I would argue that *Assassins, Ceremonial,* and (though to a far lesser degree) *Worlds Apart* are revolutionary texts, dramatic processes that attempt to envision a better real. Like the map, like the cavelike room, this theatre is both an image of the world and a generator of new images. As Fredric Jameson (81) observes, "We will have to begin to think of the Real, not as something outside the work, of which the latter stands as an image or a representation, but as something born in and vehiculated by the text itself." The repetition in these plays is not merely the incessant representation of what already exists but a striving for creation and regeneration. And for Triana's characters, the challenge, like the performance itself, has always just begun.

# 3

# THEATRE AND TERROR:
# GRISELDA GAMBARO

GRISELDA GAMBARO (born 1928 in Argentina), scrutinizes the role of theatre and theatricality in Argentina's criminalized society of the 1960s and 1970s.[1] Throughout more than twenty-five plays produced between 1963 and 1986, she examines the way in which the representation of violence in theatre limits and controls an audience's responses. Moreover, her plays specifically call attention to the backdrop of real political violence taking place offstage, also designed theatrically to elicit specific public reaction. As early as 1963, Gambaro's plays were depicting the abductions and concentration camps, the victims and victimizers, the escalation of political violence that became the grim reality of Argentina's "Dirty War" in the 1970s.

Argentina itself has increasingly become an arena of confrontation. Since 1963, it has had thirteen heads of state, each promising (though failing) to take charge of the critical situation.[2] While all these governments have needed the pomp and ceremony associated with theatre to legitimate their regimes, Juan Perón "raised" politics to an art form. During his terms in office (1946-55, 1973-74) he relied heavily on theatricality as a means of building public cohesion, of creating a popular audience, of forging a national sense of identity and destiny. Starting with his dramatic rise to power, celebrated in the demonstration of *17 de octubre*, he staged massive rallies in the Plaza de Mayo; he directed the public's attention through slogans, posters, and propaganda of national unity under *El Líder* (*The Leader*); he cast his wife, Evita, in the redemptive role of a "Madonna," a "Lady of Hope," a "Standard-Bearer of the Poor" (Rock, 307). His monumental staging of national mourning and solidarity at her death was a stage production in its own right. Unlike conventional dramatic activity, however, this fervent theatricalization sought pragmatic rather than aesthetic ends; it served to cover Argentina's growing economic and political crisis.[3]

Competing displays of power became increasingly evident after Juan

Carlos Onganía's particularly repressive coup in 1966 and his "ostentatious parade" of power (Rock, 347). Riots and strikes staged by students and workers broke out in Córdoba in 1969 and turned the city into "a theatre for pitched battles between rioters and police" (Rock, 349). The rampant political violence of the 1960s developed into orchestrated terrorism in the 1970s. (See Rock, 353-57, for a description of the rival factions.) From 1976 to 1983, when the military dictatorship waged its Dirty War against the civilian population, the theatricality of terrorism endowed the national frame with a strange spectacularity. A tragic aura enveloped the country; the tension mounted; the population—riveted to the terrible image of the men in the raincoats and the Ford Falcons—was paralyzed by terror and suspense. The Mothers of the Plaza de Mayo, like the Greek chorus, were a physical reminder of the people, the facts, the values that violence threatened to erase from history.

Gambaro's work has captured the *constants* associated with so- ciopolitical and personal collapse, as well as the changes in perspective that lead to an understanding of what crisis means and whose interests it serves. The perspective from which her characters view their predicament de- velops from a passive acceptance of catastrophe in the 1960s to the acute awareness in the 1980s that their passivity had disempowered them, that they had contributed to their own annihilation. This awareness permits the characters to oppose those in power and fight back. Although the evolution in her dramaturgy occurs gradually, and many of the themes, constructions, and technical devices remain recognizable throughout, it is nonetheless possible and helpful to divide her work into three stages.

The plays of the 1960s are theatre of crisis. They depict the combina- tion of objective, systemic rifts and the subjective experience of personal dissolution that I associate with crisis. The characters know that their world is chaotic, menacing, incomprehensible, yet they cannot make out the causes of the crisis. They try to make themselves unobtrusive and, as a result, end up participating as victims in the drama of their own demise. It is important to note that the irrational and unknowable nature of these works does not link them (as commentators have suggested) to the theatre of the absurd. In *The Walls*, the bedroom becomes the site for torture and extermination. In *The Blunder,* the round metal trap engulfing Alfonso's foot is not an "absurdist" image but the sign of a new womb/weapon that gives birth to a new life/death. Gambaro's early work signals the beginning of a national death-oriented trajectory in which all relationships of produc- tion and reproduction realign toward death. Rather than place her early dramatic production at the end of a literary tradition, the theatre of the absurd, we must recognize that it is embryonic; it develops into a new discourse on fascism and atrocity.

By the 1970s, Gambaro had begun to separate the objective and

subjective components of crisis. As the violence associated with sociopolitical, systemic disintegration became even more intrusive and appalling as people were snatched from their houses and terrorism was
carried out in homes and city streets, Gambaro's theatre no longer focused
primarily on the experience of the victim. Rather, it became the drama of
disappearance, obsessed with the "missing": the missing people, the
absent values, the nonexistent judicial and moral frameworks, the un-
fathomable reasoning, the grotesque national and international indifference toward the situation.

The plays of the 1980s have greater insight into the mechanics of
objective and systemic crisis. They examine causes and effects, the political advantages of permanent crisis to a warrior caste, the military. Crisis is
not necessarily something that "just happens"; it can be a national drama,
conceived and set in motion by those in power. What Martin Anderson
calls the "dirty secrets of the 'dirty war'" became public: the leftist guerilla
opposition, while real in itself, had been largely manipulated by the
government in order to justify the outright elimination of all suspected
"subversives"; Mario Firmenich, leader of the Montoneros, the largest
antigovernment group, was in fact a government agent working for the
military (Anderson, 340). As Suki states in Gambaro's 1984 play, *From the
Rising Sun*, the military "told us that not *that* many people had died. They
told us it was necessary. Those things happen in war. People . . . die. They
. . . want us to keep quiet" (144). Now, the public understands its role in
the atrocity; it has gone along with the drama as *audience*, respectfully
suspending its disbelief.

In focusing on the period between 1965 and 1970, I deal here primarily
with Gambaro's two major plays of that period, *Los siameses* (*The Siamese
Twins*, 1965) and *El Campo* (*The Camp*, 1967). *Los siameses* offers a fine
example of Gambaro's theatrical formulation of crisis, the self/other rivalry
and hatred that exist not only between race, class, or gender *others*, but
between *same*, between Siamese twins. *El campo* shows Argentina's growing fascination with fascism and the appearance of Nazi-like concentration
camps; moreover, because it consciously echoes the theatre of the Holocaust, it provides an excellent basis for exploring the differences I perceive
between the theatre of crisis and the theatre of the Holocaust. (The shift in
Gambaro's dramaturgy from crisis to atrocity and disappearance is exemplified here by her 1972 play, *Information for Foreigners*).

Gambaro's early plays—*Las paredes* (*The Walls*, 1963), *El desatino* (*The
Blunder*, 1965), *Los siameses* (1965), *El campo* (1967)—reflect the inchoate,
monstrous undifferentiated quality associated with the theatre of crisis as I
defined it. The onstage worlds, inverted and nightmarish, depict the
erasure of life-promoting norms and values. Children kill their parents;

parents annihilate their children. The police participate in private conflicts and are incapable of distinguishing guilt from innocence. Social
safeguards and systems erected to protect individuals and institutions
against violence fail. Homes become indistinguishable from concentration
camps; the production of death eclipses the production of life. Society
undergoes a normative transformation as the abnormal becomes the norm
and the unnatural replaces the natural. As all basis for differentiation
vanishes, it becomes increasingly difficult to distinguish inner from outer,
private from public, self from other. The world melts into a terrifying void
whose parameters recede and contract. The seemingly private room in *The
Walls* becomes a prison cell in which the walls physically move in and crush
the inmate; the Siamese twins' room gives way to a detention camp; the
violence practiced in the inner spheres, as in the family setting of *The
Blunder,* proves as devastating and systematic as that carried out in the
concentration camps.

The objective manifestation of societal and systemic shifts proves
inseparable from the subjective experience of crisis. The spatial undifferentiation stands in a real, rather than a metaphoric, relationship to
the psychological disintegration of the characters. Alfonso, in *The Blunder,*
regresses to infantilism; his foot, inexplicably caught and rotting in a metal
trap, makes it impossible for him to move or tend to himself. Like the room
in *The Walls*, Alfonso's world becomes smaller and smaller. The individual
desire for autonomy and self-definition crumbles, as in *The Siamese Twins*,
into a self/other undifferentiation that destroys both. Throughout these
plays, contradictions and confusion multiply. The known universe becomes unknowable, populated by monsters as freakish as Siamese twins,
as familiar as husband and wife, mother and son.

Gambaro's protagonists are a deformed cast of characters; they are
generally anonymous, adolescent, passive, and grotesque. They respond
to crisis in two distinguishable ways. The victims, incapacitated by crisis,
cannot orient themselves. The Joven in *The Walls*, Alfonso in *The Blunder,*
Ignacio in *Siamese*, and Martin in *The Camp* have no idea what is happening
to them. Like patients suffering from a critical disease, they endure the
catastrophe passively. But the crisis also creates victimizers who, perceiving themselves as victims (Lorenzo in *Siamese*, the SS officer Franco in *The
Camp*), adapt to crisis by deflecting the violence toward others. As Gambaro makes emphatically clear, victimizers and torturers are made, not
born. She does not portray them as psychopaths; we cannot comfort
ourselves by distancing victimizers as monstrous others. As a survivor of
Auschwitz said of his tormentors, "It is *demonic* that they were *not* demonic" (Lifton, 6). The hybrid, grotesque characters we see onstage are
the products of adaptation to a disintegrating system.

Crisis sets in motion a "pathetic drama"[4] of extermination. The theatrical terminology describing the operation is not accidental. From her first play onward, Gambaro points to the fact that victimizers and victims are strangely theatrical, both accepting their parts in this *pas de deux*, though in significantly different ways. The victimizers, referred to in the stage directions of several of her early plays as "theatrical" (one is even called a "director"), are inherently theatrical insofar as they adapt to their roles by a splitting and doubling mechanism that allows one part of the personality to take over the atrocious role without destroying the whole person. *Splitting* breaks off a part of the personality, allowing for what Robert Jay Lifton, in *Nazi Doctors* (420) calls "psychic numbing". The deadened part of the personality atrophies, while the dominant looms larger. The reduction of a complex personality into one stock trait is a phenomenon traditionally associated with theatre, where we have no trouble recognizing, or accepting, that someone is "all bad." *Doubling* works in a similar manner, though it maintains two, almost separate "wholes." In Brecht's *Good Woman of Setzuan*, the "good" Shen Te can remain "the angel of the slums" only because the "bad" Shui Ta does the dirty work. The grotesque reality onstage, then, is a product of this appalling adaptation to crisis. The theatrical aura of the victimizers should not suggest that they are fantastic, "absurd," or symbolic of "the irremediable nature of the human condition."[5] These plays warn us that on the contrary the theatricality of the victimizers is *real*; victimization could not continue without it. Victimizers, however theatrical, do not represent something else, such as the "human condition"; they are not make-believe "bad guys" that delight audiences. They kill people. But it is precisely our inability to credit the reality behind their theatricality that allows extermination to continue.

The theatricality of the victimizers sets the drama in motion. The script is straightforward. The victimizers see themselves as victims defending themselves from annihilation: that is, from dangerous *others*. The splitting and doubling mechanisms, evident in the victimizers' psychic functioning, pertain to the entire process of victimization. The split or double part of the personality that participates in the violence is bolstered by language that justifies the proceedings as something else—a "job," or an act of national defense. The linguistic ruptures or splits divorce the signifier from the signified and bury reality beneath innocuous words. By fictionalizing the lethal process of extermination, the victimizer manipulates the victims into starring in dramas that they fail to recognize as the tragedy of their own persecution and annihilation. The glaring theatricality of the sets—a cell disguised as a luxurious room in *The Walls*, or the concentration camp that passes for an office in *The Camp*—actually lulls the protagonist into passive acceptance. Even the antagonist's hideous costumes, the Functionary's outlandish Master of Ceremonies outfit in the former play and Franco's Gestapo uniform in the latter, fail to alert the protagonists to the gravity of the situation. On the contrary, the theatricality *itself* makes the entire scenario possible by signaling to the victims that the visible threat is not "real."

The criminals control the action, forcing the victims, like actors, to take their parts in the "dramatic knot" (*Las paredes*, 17).[6] In *The Camp*, Franco stages a concert in which the emaciated, flea-infested Emma gives a piano recital for a "select" audience of fascist tormentors and fellow prisoners. The piano does not work; the flowers he gives her are artificial; but the victimizer, "for all the world like a theater director" (72), demands that the victims play along.[7] And they do. Fastening a train to her prison uniform and covering her shaved head with a ridiculous wig, Emma attempts to mask the painful reality with the desired image. She mimics the nonexistent music with her frail voice. Anyone comparing Gambaro to the absurdists would stumble against the historical and contemporary sociopolitical reality of this image, against the reality of human degradation and pain in this horrifying rendition of a bald soprano. What becomes clear through the double frame of concentration camp–concert hall is not the absurdity of the singer or of art in general, or even the meaninglessness of life, but the embodied, physical, and sociopolitical reality of victimization.

The theatrical postures that the victimizers force upon their victims serve a vital function in continuing victimization. By making them assume roles in the process, the victimizer converts the victims into accomplices in their own annihilation. The farce, of course, tries to turn the victimizer-victim relationship into a sadomasochist one, suggesting thus that the victim craves, even needs, to be hurt. This radically alters the nature of the relationship; it introduces the fiction of *consent* and necessarily changes the audiences' response to it. Who is going to interfere with two consenting adults? Like children stumbling upon the primal scene, we blush and look away from this sexual terra incognita. But the truth of the matter is that there is no such consent; we are witnessing annihilation, not titillation. The fact that the distinction is subtle and easily lost in the theatricality of violent acts explains why there is a tendency to eroticize victimization, why critics speak of atrocity as "tacitly pornographic" (Sontag, *Saturn*, 139) and why most depictions of victimization (such as Liliana Cavani's film *The Night Porter*) lead us further away from, rather than closer to, understanding and combatting victimization.

The process of victimization unfolds concurrently on the theatrical and real planes. While the violence is real and life-threatening (that is, not a "performance art"[8] or mere spectacle), the victims are asked to deny the reality they see with their own eyes and believe in happily-ever after. Hence, the victims are both actors in this lethal sham and spectators of it, either refusing to see the horror that awaits them or suspending their disbelief if they do. In *The Walls*, the fiction handed to the Young Man by his abductors is that he is temporarily a guest in the Functionary's luxurious home;[9] he will be free to leave as soon as the Functionary satisfies himself that the Young Man is not Ruperto de Hentzau o Hantcau, a villain in a novel (18). The Young Man, knowing for a fact that fiction is not life and that he does not belong to the universe of *The Prisoner of Zenda*, finds comfort in the hope that he will be released as soon as the Functionary recognizes the truth. The myth here, of course, is that the victim recognizes the truth while the victimizer does not. The Young Man clings to traditional wisdom and values: fiction is distinguishable from truth, and innocence "normally" guarantees freedom. The room (cell, set, torture chamber), however, functions as a transformer of norms—nothing comes out "normal." The very concept of normal dies in that room. The play maps the "unmaking of the world" described by Elaine Scarry in *The Body in Pain*, the backward thrust from civilization to disorder and chaos. The set is gradually stripped of its reassuring trappings, the curtains and furnishings disappear from view, the walls contract as the room itself becomes an instrument of torture and demolition on a par with Poe's in "The Pit and the Pendulum."

What we are witnessing, of course, is a case of abduction, a crime that became increasingly common in Argentina during the two decades following the play's appearance in 1963. Those involved in the unmaking, however, attempt to convince those undergoing the experience that everything is, in fact, "normal" and that this is not "a country of madmen" (58). Like the spectator at the theatre, the Young Man can no longer believe his eyes or ears. The lights go on and off, establishing an independent, unnatural order. The Usher convinces him that he cannot interpret what he hears; that the screams filtering in from outside, against all logical evidence, have nothing to do with violence. Similarly, the Young Man's words fall on deaf ears, for he cannot make himself understood by those who have no interest in understanding him.

The chilling dissonance of victims like Emma and the Young Man is that they cling to scripts which, on another level, they know are "untrue" and, for all their fictitiousness, will inevitably culminate in their deaths. The language and actions of the victims, borrowed from happier scripts, clash with the devastating reality we see onstage. We see two frames; the "normal" and logical (fictitious) arguments advanced to explain the situation prove pathetic in the face of the terrifying reality. As the Young Man waits, the scene acquires the static quality of a tableau. He resembles the "languid young man looking out of the window" (9) in the painting that hangs in his room. Even as the frame closes in on its subject, as the room gets smaller and the painting, curtains, and props disappear, the Young Man refuses to abandon his fictions and recognize his impending extermination. After agreeing to go along with the drama thus far, the Young Man cannot at this point respond to truth even when he hears it from his tormentors. Even after the Usher informs him that the walls will cave in on him and crush him to death at midnight, he still waits patiently for his release.

Doubling and splitting are instrumental in victimization; they are also potent instruments in seeing through and ending the drama of victimization. Gambaro's juxtaposition of two frames in this first play marks the beginning of an inquiry into the nature of theatrical representation and perception (with all its metapolitical implications) which characterizes her work as a whole. Her framing of the two images of young men in *The Walls*—one theatrical, one painted—illustrates her technique. The apparent tranquillity of the young man in the lovely painting with the heavy ornate frame functions as a background for the young man in the luxurious room framed by the heavy curtains. Placing the two images together demonstrates how theatre, by shaping perception, can either obfuscate or clarify a dangerous situation. Combining the two images—the victim set against the backdrop of the painting—blinds us to the lethal situation. It seduces the spectators, as it does the victim himself, into accepting what is in fact a horrifying situation. It soothes the spectator: surely there is no danger here, it all looks so normal.

This superimposition of the banal and the dangerous, as recent studies demonstrate, forms the basis of fascist iconography. Alice Yaeger Kaplan's *Reproductions of Banality* and Saul Friedländer's *Reflections of Nazism* show how the juxtaposition or "binding" of the innocuous and the dangerous, disarms us.[10] The double image gives a mixed message, hiding what is threatening behind what is harmless. A similar example of "binding" operates in the play's final image. The Young Man dies, obediently holding his landlady's porcelain figurine in his arms. The figurine, a perfect example of kitsch, is, as Friedländer (25) notes, "a faithful expression of a common sensibility, of harmony dear to petit bourgeois, who see in it a respect for beauty and for the order of things—for the established order and things as they are." So while the image signals a reaffirmation of the normal, it obscures the fact that the values and systems associated with the normal fail to govern the situation. While the victims can only delude themselves by upholding "things as they are," the tormentors have the power to unmake the world, to make concrete objects disappear, to derealize them.

Just as juxtaposing images can blind us to the lethal, separating or decoding them can alert us to danger. Gambaro reproduces and dismantles the treacherous icon. By placing the painting and man side by side, by having each of the three characters refer to the painting, and by making the painting vanish, Gambaro encourages the spectator to look back and forth between the two images. As in the children's game "What's wrong with this picture?" we check for similarities and discrepancies. What differences do we perceive between the two images? Within the universe of the play, one is art, the other is "real." From the point of view of the spectator, both painting and theatrical scene are artistic representations, while we, the spectators, are "real." As spectators, what difference do we see between the two forms of representation? None—unless we understand the context. On one level, both images represent rather shallow young men gazing out toward false freedom. But the juxtaposition does not serve to support the apparent conclusion of contextualization, that art is "permanent" while the young man in the room faces death. Though the painting's frame emphasizes its aesthetic autonomy, separating it as a world or work unto itself with its own laws and unity, à la Ionesco, the painting too will come and go at the will of the Functionary. It vanishes as the room moves in on its inmate; it reappears to lull the next victim into complacency. Art can be manipulated, and it plays a role in ongoing power struggles whether the artist intended it or not. Art is neither immune nor separate. And while art "is an icon of our control of the flux of reality," as Sander Gilman notes in *Disease and Representation* (2), in this context it occludes the public lack of control. It is precisely because the seemingly autonomous frames between the aesthetic and political are intricately connected that theatres in Argentina are bombed and theatre practitioners attacked or silenced.

Yet the frame draws our attention away from this vital connection; it dissociates us, splits us from everything surrounding it. The separation proves not only untenable but dangerous. By concealing the connections, the frame creates a perceptual blind spot that makes the spectator incapable of dealing with the larger picture. Framing does not protect the victims from harm; it does not keep violence out. By calling attention to the artificial confines of the frame, Gambaro urges us to go beyond it, to examine not only what the "sumptuous sculpted frame" (9) and the curtained room *keep in* but also what they *keep out:* the facts of abduction and torture, the screams from the neighboring rooms, the violent deaths— in short, everything that we cannot see but that we know exists. Those realities are out there, and as Gambaro's work evolves, she warns us more and more directly that we ignore them at our peril.

By placing the two images side by side and insisting that they have to be understood both separately and in conjunction, Gambaro enables us to apply to the larger sociopolitical arena what we have learned from the examination of them in theatre. Social spaces, like the onstage room, are also made and unmade before our eyes. As cultural materialists remind us, there is nothing permanent or immutable about the social constructs we see before us. Just as the self-contained painting literally disappears from the scene, so does the Young Man and so, over the next two decades, did 30,000 Argentines. We spectators, seemingly protected by the proscenium arch, are neither separate nor safe. The fact that the victims are themselves spectators watching the unthinkable happen as well as actors experiencing it should lead us to suspect that the audience too plays a greater role than it suspects in the process of erasure. *The Walls* illustrates that the things that disappear from consciousness (the painting, the shrinking social space, logic, coherent language) must be understood in relation to the disappearance of humans, of consciousness, from the world.

By calling attention to the steady disappearance of things from the room, Gambaro also draws out attention to the mechanics of disappearance, which we take for granted in theatre. Theatre, like magic, fascinates us with its visible and invisible acts. By exclusively privileging the lighted areas, by carefully directing our attention, theatre and magic permit us to think of nonvisible spaces as nonspaces. What happens to the characters who walk offstage? What do magicians do with all those bunnies? The offstage screams, however, caution us against accepting the theatrical illusion of nonspace. Actors go backstage to dressing rooms, bunnies go back to their cages, and abduction victims end up in torture chambers and unmarked graves. By pointing out the theatrical illusion involved in making people "disappear," Gambaro illuminates the very real presence of deathly spaces beyond the confines of the lighted stage into which people and art itself vanish. Theatre and political theatricality, both of which determine and control what we see and what we cannot see, can effectively mask disappearance. But theatre can also do the opposite: it can convince us of the existence and, often, perniciousness of the hidden.

The relationship between the terrifying onstage and the terrifying (and real) offstage spaces in Gambaro's work signals her departure from other kinds of theatre that also call attention to offstage violence. Unlike the violence taking place offstage in classical and neoclassical theatre, which is described in detail onstage in deference to convention and decorum (the elaborate accounts of Hippolytus's destruction in Euripides or Racine, for example), the violence intruding on Gambaro's stage represents the systematic politics of violence plaguing Argentina. The aesthetic off-scene of Aristotelian drama has become the politically criminal or obscene. The factual reality of the sociopolitical background differentiates Gambaro's work also from, for example, Jean Genet's. *The Balcony* also represents a large house with individual rooms, each dedicated to private acts of violence and transgression, but Genet eroticizes violence in both his dramatic and his autobiographical writings. His "house of illusions" generates the offstage screams and revolutions associated with the *hyper-real*,[11] the frenzied, postmodernist battle of images associated with European and American politics, rather than the more overtly violent Latin American *real*. The revolution going on outside the brothel seems controlled from Irma's little theatre and is no more "real" than the simulated acts inside the studios. Again, this image says more about the "silent," theoretically "apolitical" American population for whom reality, mediated through television images, becomes "unreal," even as its tax money goes to control revolutions. The clips of the Vietnam War shown on television demonstrate how "real" death and "real" war can become as vacuous as the ads framing them. Herein lies the truly obfuscating potential of theatricality: the media undermine the message; the spectators, seeing the "real" in this format, are blind to its significance. Gambaro's work, on the contrary, developing within the very arena of confrontation, refuses to perpetuate insubstantiality. Rather, her insistence on the danger offstage underlines the historical veracity of unseen crimes and the political urgency of combatting the dangers she alludes to.

Gambaro's plays of the 1960s call attention to the created blind spots and the ruptures between frames that obscure the causes of social crisis. Crisis and conflict, as we have noted, are generated offstage, in the "invisible" spaces that neither theatre nor social inquiry can easily illuminate. Characteristically, societies undergoing crisis concentrate on the effects, the manifestations of social disease. Even before Onganía's military coup in 1966 unleashed political violence, clandestine acts of abduction and torture had already disrupted the population of Argentina. Gambaro's plays themselves serve as evidence of the individual experience of threat and impending doom. Crisis, however, throws us into temporal abeyance; the doom, or the disaster, as Maurice Blanchot would say, had in a sense already happened. "The infiniteness of the threat has in some way broken every limit," he writes in *The Writing of Disaster* (1). "We are on the edge of disaster without being able to situate it in the future: it is rather always already past." Although the worst was yet to come, criminal politics had already become an accepted part of political struggle and had already corroded the moral and judicial frameworks erected to contain violence. Unable to isolate the true causes of the problem, society inverts cause and effect and, as Girard observes, blames the victim for causing or provoking crisis: "The persecutors always convince themselves that a small number of people, or even a single individual, despite his relative weakness, is extremely harmful to the whole of society" (*Scapegoat*, 14-15). By blaming the Peronists or the Communists or the proliferating right-wing and left-wing "subversive" groups and finally indiscriminately turning on the general population, the military government after 1976 carried out an undeclared, basically one-sided "war" against its own people.[12] Yet while the population experiences the effects of crisis, the understanding of its causes comes only later. Gambaro's plays of the 1960s examine the phenomena associated with crisis, the isolation of victimizable individuals and groups, the process of stereotyping, persecution, and scapegoating. Unlike her plays of the 1980s, her earlier work does not propose that social crisis serves a very real political function: that is, diverting social attention from concrete, irresolvable political contradictions. The paradigms of persecution used by Gambaro are not overtly political contradictions. The paradigms of persecution used by Gambaro are not overtly political at this stage. Rather, they lean toward mythical and psychological armatures within which to place Argentina's ongoing practice of political repression and extermination.

## *The Siamese Twins:* The Drama of Victimization

*Los siameses* (*The Siamese Twins*, 1965) depicts Argentina's escalating fratricidal violence through the love-hate relationship between two brothers, apparently born Siamese twins though now *physically* separate. The play can almost be read as a continuation of Triana's *Night of the Assassins*; having killed the parents, the children turn on each other. Lorenzo, like Triana's Lalo, claims he has committed parricide, suggesting thus that all succession involves criminal violence and that murder is a rite of passage—a compelling theory, given the realities of Argentina's radical political transitions. "After the killing of the father," Freud writes, "a time followed when the brothers quarrelled among themselves for the succession" (qtd. in Brown, 17). As in Triana's *Assassins*, the new criminal onstage society is grounded in violence and violation.

Ostensibly, the bone of contention between the brothers in *Siamese Twins* is the parental home, a small room with two cots and a few other sticks of furniture. Again, as in *Assassins*, neither of the adult children seems capable of leaving home behind. Ignacio explicitly expresses his desire to be autonomous, to lead his own life, marry, and bring his wife to live in "my house. My parents' house" (125). Yet he feels morally and financially responsible for Lorenzo, who appears to be the more helpless of the two. Lorenzo, of course, claims that the home belongs to him, and he alternates between the need to separate from and cling to his brother. When the play begins, the room is empty. The twins, we soon learn, have been out in the street, and Lorenzo has just thrown a stone at a child. The child's father runs after him, but Lorenzo succeeds in getting back to the room before his brother, and locks the door behind him. As Ignacio beats on the door and begs Lorenzo to open it, Lorenzo dawdles and asks him questions as to the whereabouts of his opponent, until the father finally catches up with Ignacio and beats him senseless. Thus begins the drama of victimization whereby Lorenzo establishes himself as master of the territory, the defining self, and casts Ignacio in the role of the dangerous other, to be eliminated at all costs. In the effort to free himself permanently from Ignacio, Lorenzo conceives and directs the drama that Ignacio dies by: he engineers events so that Ignacio will be rejected by his girlfriend, arrested by the police, and killed while in custody.

*Siamese* is a representation of victimization stripped down to the core. There is no race, gender, or class dimension to complicate the process. Although, unlike that of most Latin American countries, Argentina's population consists predominantly of white European immigrants (the indigenous population was almost completely exterminated by the mid-nineteenth century), Gambaro is not suggesting that there is no significant racist, misogynist, or class-related violence in Argentina. Her later work makes it clear that there is a very special hatred of women, Jews, and people of color and, hence, a special kind of violence reserved for them. However, in this play she stresses that *perceivable difference* (race, gender, class) is not necessary for victimization to occur. Even societies that are basically homogeneous are vulnerable to violence. Victimization, this play shows, *invents* difference and fabricates an enemy other even when that other is identical, or even inseparable, from the self.

Lorenzo's ambivalence toward Ignacio illustrates the problematic symbiosis between self and other which, the play proposes, lies at the root of victimization. The two young men portrayed separately in *The Walls*, one in the picture and the other in the room, now both live in the same frame, turning the abstract doubling and identification into open rivalry and aggression. The self/other relationship perhaps inevitably leads to one of victimizer/victim, given the social context in which power equals domination. However, the victimizer/victim relationship still involves identification and doubling, even beyond the obvious doubling in the image of Siamese twins. The victimizer (Lorenzo) needs the victim in order to establish his own identity as the active, powerful, defining self. Lorenzo, cowardly and impotent, can feel masterful only by annihilating his brother, whom he acknowledges as more worldly and successful. The process involves identification (Lorenzo wants to be successful like Ignacio) and distancing (he can be successful only by demolishing Ignacio; only thus can Lorenzo be more powerful than Ignacio).[13]

The tension between the simultaneous desire to fuse (to be like Ignacio) and to separate (to kill Ignacio) is concretely reflected theatrically in the opening scene. The slash in the self/other and victimizer/victim opposition, like the door that Lorenzo locks and barricades with his body, concurrently binds and splits the two entities. Lorenzo keeps Ignacio out, but at the same time he mirrors Ignacio's movements down to the last detail. Lorenzo imitates Ignacio's prostrate position, his thrashings, his groans. This mirroring suggests a profound identity between the two men, a deeper identification than simple mimicry, since Lorenzo's vision of Ignacio is limited to peering at him through the keyhole. Although he leaves his battered brother outside all night, when he finally lets him in the next day, Lorenzo fantasizes that they are one being. He now wants to incorporate his twin. He lies next to Ignacio on the cot; he insists on their walking together around the room leg to leg, as if they were joined at the hip. Lorenzo also claims that they are "one" in the eyes of the world, maintaining that outsiders cannot tell them apart: "But who is capable of distinguishing between us? I can't. We're the same. That's our tragedy. We're so similar that our actions become confused" (100). He carries this line of reasoning to the extreme of almost convincing himself that it was Ignacio, rather than himself, who threw the stone.

The play's title image not only reflects the violent and grotesque unity of two men joined into one; it also reflects the opposite, the "one" entity violently struggling to become two autonomous beings. Whether we accept Lorenzo's version that they are Siamese twins surgically separated at birth or Ignacio's perception of them as still joined in his repeated longings to "cut the cord," the unity, presented as an ironic ideal in Lorenzo's fantasy, is concurrently perceived by both brothers as a life-threatening liability. Ignacio wants to separate and make his own life, but his inability to do so costs him his life. Conversely, Lorenzo privately insists on their inseparability but publically denies the tie and provokes the incidents that lead to Ignacio's arrest, torture, and death, thereby promoting a radical separation.

Siamese twins constitute an especially apt parallel with Argentine victimization by combining the violent symbiosis of self/other with the myth of unity (oneness) and the fictions of shared origins, history, and destiny characteristic of fascist discourse (fascism, etymologically, means "uniting"). Lorenzo, in the manner of fascist leaders, belabors the story of their shared birth, past, and future—particularly in times of trouble, when Ignacio gets angry with him and threatens to separate. The image of the Siamese twins, moreover, captures the *doubling* (the two-in-one) and the *splitting* (the one-into-two) that I have associated with fascist iconography and discourse. Like the theatrical victimizers in Gambaro's earliest work, Lorenzo inverts the script, calls himself the victim, and actually dresses up as various victims: Lorenzo as Jew, as blind man, as prisoner from the concentration camp. These representations are openly theatrical; the audience is expected to see through them and establish, in turn, a double distancing from the play. The play (any play) necessarily imposes the primary distancing inherent in the acknowledgment "We know this is a play, but we'll momentarily accept it as real." The double distancing distinguishes between the play (as real) and the theatrical (false even within this context of "play"). This is a basic operation, an automatic response on the part of theatregoers accustomed to theatrical conventions.

The innocuous theatrical convention easily becomes a potent tool in obfuscating violence, however, whether or not costumes are involved. Lorenzo's childlike and "brotherly" weakness in insisting that Ignacio walk around the room leg-to-leg with him disarms both Ignacio and the spectator: surely the request is infantile—but *dangerous?* The earlier, very real aggression that Lorenzo demonstrated toward Ignacio begins to fade. We look on Lorenzo as a spoiled child—naughty, perhaps, but not criminal. Ignacio, misreading the situation, confesses that he wants to separate, to "cut the cord," as if Lorenzo could respect his right to autonomy, as if Lorenzo were not his mortal enemy. Ignacio's disclosure only accelerates his annihilation. Doubling makes the deadly seem nonthreatening. The reality of the tormentor "disappears" behind the images of the tormented, childish Lorenzo; the deadly rival slides invisibly behind the image of the childlike brother.

The doubling and splitting in language hides the fatal reality in a similar manner. In the opening scene, one of the most excruciating in the play, Lorenzo calmly writes a note to his brother, who is being beaten behind the door. The image of Lorenzo quietly going about his business and calmly writing a note somewhat pacifies the spectators, negating to some degree the reality of the horror beyond the door. Theatre usually asks us to believe what we see even when we know it is not "true"; here, on the contrary, we must reverse our theatrical perception and accept what we know to be true even though it is not what we see. Lorenzo's letter writing does not (as we believe) relieve the agony; it accentuates it. Not that Lorenzo says anything openly hostile or inflammatory. On the contrary, he congratulates himself that the note is well thought out, an epitome of good taste and manners: "Dear Ignacio: I'm asking you if he [the opponent] is close by. . . . *(He lifts his head and ponders, while he rubs his chin thoughtfully. Suddenly, the sounds of Ignacio's screams can be heard, accompanied by the poundings of a body violently banged and beaten against the door. Lorenzo, self-absorbed)* Should I mention the thing about fear or not? No, he'll get offended. I must be thoughtful! *(He raises his head and listens. Calmly regretful)* They're going to break the door. *(He rises and pushes the note beneath the door.)* Wait, I'll pass you the pencil. *(He pushes the pencil beneath the door.)*

Answer in writing!" (117). The juxtaposition of the two levels of functioning, the innocent and the malevolent, is more than an example of the traditional theatrical irony, where the audience is privy to information denied the characters. Here, the innocent image tries to negate the existing malevolence. As opposed to irony, which enhances the audience's capability of deciphering the situation, doubling makes reality more resistant to decoding.

Behind the banality of the letter writing hides an act of torture. We do not immediately recognize it as a prototypical act of torture: the victimizer and the victim are not in the same room; the victimizer holds a conventional pen rather than an instrument of torture; Lorenzo acts like a thick-headed clod rather than a cruel, imposing executioner. The fact that the violence does not look like violence in general or torture specifically, however, speaks to its efficacy. But even though the success of torture depends on its ability to hide violence behind the language of bureaucracy and social necessity, we can get to the truth of the situation by inverting the theatrical perspective and refusing to suspend disbelief. Lorenzo's incessant "questioning" in this scene, as in acts of torture, attempts to cover the cruelty and render it either "necessary" or somehow justifiable. "Are you alone? Are you listening to me? Are you alone?" (96), Lorenzo asks his terrified brother time and time again. Studies of torture show that victimizers undertake and continue artocious acts while pretending that they must extract information from the victim. Clearly, the questioning is only one more instrument of cruelty, a means of prolonging and intensifying physical pain. The fact has been well documented that actual acts of torture rarely have anything to do with obtaining information.[14] Lorenzo's questions, not to mention the note he pushes under the door ("answer in writing!"), illustrate the gratuitous and torturous nature of the interrogation. The banality of his questions serves to invert the vicious process. Theoretically, the victim, not the victimizer, is now in control of the situation; as soon as he decides to speak, the pain will end. Hence, the questioning appears to grant an option which, of course, the victim does not have. It shifts the moral weight and responsibility from the victimizer to the victim. "Why didn't you open the door?" asks the battered Ignacio. "Why didn't I open the door?" echoes Lorenzo. "I explained it to you in writing. You didn't even answer. *(Goes to the door, opens it, looks for something on the floor and comes back with a wrinkled piece of paper.)* You got water on it. I can't read a word. Why do I bother?" (103). Along with the (false) element of choice enter notions of responsibility: if the victim *chooses* to suffer rather than answer or "confess," we (as spectators) are relieved of the moral responsibility of interfering with that choice. Good audiences stay in their seats and let the actors fight it out.

The drama of torture, then, inverts the "interpretation" and "critical reception" of the atrocious procedure: the victim, not the victimizer, is in control of the situation; the victim, not the public, is responsible for ending it. Torture, as Ignacio's feigned concern for the well-being of his brother illustrates, relies on role playing to turn the act of cruelty into something else, something the torturer and the public can accept. For Lorenzo, the questioning passes as an act of self-defense: "What if I open the door and he pounces on me?" (97). Whether the act of torture is staged in its own set, with its painful props and paraphernalia, or in a room with a few sticks of furniture, the script neutralizes the image. The language of torture belies the spectacle of suffering, turns it into something else that protects the victimizer and the spectator by misrepresenting the reality of the victim's extermination. To hear Gambaro's tormentors talk, they are actually doing the victim a favor, trying to help him or her resolve a nasty situation. The ungrateful victim, they argue, refuses help, will not cooperate, and in fact both deserves and provokes the violence.

At this point in her dramaturgy, Gamabro focuses on the two obvious participants in torture, the victimizer and the victim. Her portrayal of the twins indicates that the differences in their response to crisis distinguishes the victimizer from the victim. While both brothers are at first potential victims of the barbarous police, Lorenzo survives because he is able to comprehend the policemen's incomprehensible speech and can then join in their conversation. He can adapt; he can "speak their language." Ignacio dies because he cannot understand what is happening; he cannot believe what he knows to be true (that Lorenzo is setting him up); and he refuses to believe that the police will not see through Lorenzo's sham (129-37). Even after Ignacio shows the police how Lorenzo set the stage to deceive them and manufactured the evidence against him, they suspend their disbelief and give themselves up to the drama. Lorenzo's props and script transform Ignacio into a terrible criminal while hiding the very real violence that Lorenzo is practicing on his twin. The point that Gambaro makes here is important (although she does not elaborate on it until her next play, *The Camp*): the bureaucratic, legalistic, moralistic, entertaining sham surrounding torture does not have to be convincing—everyone knows what is going on—but must simply offer the opportunity for torturers and participants (here, the police) to justify their action and carry on with the show.

The doubling in the image of Siamese twins, then, far exceeds considerations of plot and specific biological-biographical issues as to whether the men are twins or brothers or simply fellow human beings. The stage directions make clear that the battered Ignacio who enters the room looks nothing like Lorenzo. Questions as to whether the physical differences date back to birth or result from the disfiguring attack on Ignacio's face and body, or whether the struggle for the house is literal or figurative, fail to recognize the image as a metaphor for undifferentiation (implicit in the image of identical or Siamese twins) and its relationship to personal and social crisis.[15] The image of the "unnatural" twins illustrates the monstrous undifferentiation, the suspension of "difference," the inability to differentiate or separate that is associated with crisis.[16] These men, according to their own perception of the situation, are concurrently *separate* and *inseparable*; they are *two* individuals and yet indistinguishably *one* and the same.

This personal experience of crisis, moreover, is inextricable from the widening spheres of social violence. Lorenzo, for example, feels that the violence from the "outside" (sociopolitical sphere) will attack him; it will annul all boundaries and intrude into his house, penetrating into his own skin. He interprets the assassination of John F. Kennedy as the signal that social safeguards fail to function: "If they can do that to Kennedy, what'll they do to us? He had body guards. I don't have anything! I don't have anything! This is getting out of hand, and look at me, alone and helpless. Look at my skin, Ignacio. It's nothing. You scratch me and I bleed" (106). One of the responses to crisis, particularly of the victimizer, that we have noted throughout is to deflect the violence to another—a scapegoat. Ignacio does not realize that he in fact fulfills this function for Lorenzo. When he tells Lorenzo: "Don't worry. . . . I'm . . . I'm here" (106), he fails to recognize the irony of the remark. He is indeed Lorenzo's safeguard against crisis, not as bodyguard but as expendable victim. By sacrificing Ignacio, Lorenzo can channel the violence away from himself and toward his brother.

The violence associated with sociopolitical crisis, then, attacks outer and inner; it suspends boundaries, annuls ties; it simultaneously destroys the body, the house, and the society. The doubling, moreover, calls attention to the fact that the spheres of violence are inseparable. Whether we see the conflict between the two men as an intrapsychic conflict between parts of one whole, or as an interpsychic confrontation between two men who are somehow joined or related, or as a symbol of fratricidal violence through which the powerful self persecutes and kills its (br)others, the violence associated with crisis must be understood to operate concomitantly in the social and personal spheres. Although we can approach this violence from diverse analytical perspectives—the psychological, the cultural anthropological, the psychohistorical, the historical—we keep coming back to the fact that violence nullifies boundaries and overflows the barriers that have been erected by individuals and society to protect them from its virulence.

On a psychological level, for example, the tension that exists in doubling suggests that people do not even need "real" others to generate animosity; the mere *consciousness* of otherness suffices to cause misery and death. Whether it is Narcissus looking at his image (as beautiful, elusive other) in the water, or the perception (real or imagined) of one's own inadequacies in the Lacanian mirror, the consciousness rather than the material existence of otherness creates the problem. Although both paradigms of destruction are grounded in the field of vision, they differ in an interesting way: Narcissus loves the reflected other and dies in his attempt to join it—an example of misery and death but not of violence. For Lacan, however, violence too stems from visual perception: the initial love and idealization of the reflected image gives way to a sense of inadequacy and rage in the viewer. In his essay "The Mirror Stage," Lacan posits that the child's first visual experience of self as "whole" in the mirror jars with the physical experience of self as fragmented, in that the child looking at itself without a mirror can see only disconnected limbs, toes, and fingers. The whole self in the mirror is initially (like Narcissus) seen as an ideal other. As Lorenzo spies on Ignacio's lovemaking, he too identifies with this ideal, virile other and wants to be "one" with him, or "be" him. But the whole, ideal other is also a rival that only accentuates the child's feeling of lack and nonwholeness. So too Lorenzo, spying on Ignacio, is increasingly aware of his impotence and lack. The other may be imaginary—either a reflection in the mirror or the product of a brother's idealization—but the rage, frustration, and alienation which, according to this theory, originate in the field of vision are real enough.

A Lacanian reading of *Siamese* then, could on one level seem a consistent one. The two men may be seen as two parts of one whole, much as the image of Siamese twins suggests. Lorenzo tries to manipulate Ignacio as he would the reflection in the mirror, imagining Ignacio a "whole" and social "I," out there, autonomous, in the mirror, as opposed to the "specular I," the I-Eye that sees, the Lorenzo who lives from and through Ignacio. The specularity promotes mimetic rivalry with oneself (the self in the mirror) *and* others, producing aggressivity and feelings of lack. Lorenzo feels lacking and inadequate compared to Ignacio and wants to "be" Ignacio. Failing this ultimate identification or oneness, Lorenzo wants to destroy a quality associated with Ignacio's way of being which he covets yet cannot emulate. Lorenzo senses that his lack is somehow a consequence of Ignacio's wholeness. This imbalance, of course, is characteristic of twins in general, in that one is usually larger and stronger than the other, and of Siamese twins in particular, especially when they cannot be separated without killing the one lacking a vital organ. Here, the imbalance is metaphoric rather than biological. Ignacio's laughter, Lorenzo confesses, somehow impoverishes him: "I like . . . how you laugh. . . . Everytime you laugh, you take something away from me, something that's not mine . . . I want your way of laughing" (142). Violence, then, results from the initial identification with the other, followed by rivalry and rage. Though one may want to separate from or kill the other, the two are never entirely separate; the death of one leads to the death of the other. At the end of the play, Lorenzo lies huddled over Ignacio's grave, a mirror image of his dead brother lying in the ground. The text, then, provides an exemplary model for a Lacanian analysis of the origins of violence.

However, it is important to remember that the hostility affects more than a symbiotic self/other; the character does not simply fall into the pool and drown. Given the sociopolitical context, we must be wary of derealizing or fictionalizing the world of outsiders, both the individuals and the institutions that carry out the annihilation. Violence may originate in the scopic field, but it plays itself out in the social field and involves a number of other people, from the man who first beats Ignacio to the police who kill him. Ultimately, the psychological and sociopolitical spheres of violence prove inseparable. (Perhaps more interesting than a Lacanian "psychological" reading of *Siameses* would be a Lacanian "theatrical" one—a reading that considers what, according to Lacan's theory, seems an inevitable violence linked with the scopic drive. As Gambaro becomes increasingly concerned with the spectators in her later works, I discuss below this aspect of the theatregoers' necessary *scopophilia*—(necessary, or they would not go to the theatre, a place *to see*.)

The personal realm of violence remains inextricably linked to the social if we maintain, with René Girard, that violence originates in mimetic desire, desire for what the other desires. What could be more personal, we might argue, than desire? But desire, according to this theory, is not necessarily personal; it is mimetic, an imitation of someone else's desire. Lorenzo wants what Ignacio wants; they compete for the same goals, vie for the family home and women. It does not matter that Lorenzo does not actually want what Ignacio desires; the fact that Ignacio desires it is enough. After eliminating Ignacio, Lorenzo does not return to the house he fought so hard to win, and as his attempts to prove his sexual prowess illustrate, he feels nothing but contempt and repulsion for women. As Paul Dumouchel (12) explains Girard's theory, violence stems from wanting what the other wants, and creates "doubles" of the antagonists: violence is mimetic both in *origin* ("two greedy hands mimetically attracted to the same object") and in *operation*: "one blocks, the other hits, and vice versa, as one hits the other blocks. A violent exchange is always a dumb repetition of the same gestures. . . . In the end, violence reduces both enemies to mirror images of each other."[17] Inside the door, Lorenzo mirrors his beaten brother, who lies outside. On the grave, Lorenzo mirrors his dead brother, who lies in it.

Violence does not limit itself to the mimetic dyad, however. Progressively, as *Siamese* illustrates, more and more people are drawn into it, resulting in constantly escalating violence. Violence can end if social institutions and laws are capable of containing it, but in times of crisis, when institutions fail, no one can put an end to the violence. Everyone is drawn into the fray—the father, the police. Violence becomes "contagious": "Only violence can put an end to violence, and that is why violence is self-propagating. Everyone wants to strike the last blow" (Girard, *Violence*, 26). As *Siameses* makes clear, in the universe of the play the judicial system is already indistinguishable from personal violence. For Girard, then, violence originates in the intrapersonal sphere and brings into existence the social institutions needed to curb it.

On a more specific social level, Lorenzo's cruelty bespeaks the dangerous politics of Argentina's civil conflict. Lorenzo describes the "operation" of differentiation whereby the twins are separated: "What happens, in operations like these, is that they can't save them both. One of them is ruined. In order to leave one of them in perfect condition, they have to ruin the other. They have to" (107). Ignacio becomes transformed into an enemy other by means of the operation of differentiation, the creation of "difference." This is the negative side of what is normally the positive process of individuation, the process whereby individuals in a society are differentiated from each other. The positive, identity-giving process of individuation includes the formation of the ego and the adaptation to exterior reality as well as the knowledge and self-knowledge derived from inner reality.[18] This positive individuation is radically theatened in times of crisis, when both outer and inner "reality" change drastically. In the face of nonindividuation (the monstrous undifferentiation of Siamese twins), crisis triggers a secondary, apparently defensive response—enforced difference. This reverses the process of individuation. Instead of naming, we have *labeling*; instead of respect for autonomy, we have *stereotyping*; instead of ego formation, we have ego deformation, the destruction of all frameworks that allow for positive identification, decision-making, and action. Instead of developing speech to formulate thought and communicate with others, the victim is either deprived of speech or forced to mumble answers to a question.[19] Instead of being permitted to adapt to exterior reality, the individual finds the outside a bizarre, unnatural, and terrifying place; those who adapt do so only by splitting, doubling, becoming as grotesque as their surroundings. The policeman at the end of *Siamese* orders Lorenzo to hurry up digging the hole for Ignacio's corpse: "I like to see my kids before they go to bed" (141).

In this operation, one of the two is saved, as persecutor or victimizer. One of the two is "ruined," persecuted, labeled as enemy, and destroyed. In crisis situations, persecution substitutes for individuation. Enemies are singled out, marginalized, stereotyped into others. Such exclusion keeps "them" out and allows the defining group to forge an identity—or an anti-identity, a negative "not-them," rather than the positive identity resulting from ego formation. Lorenzo locks his brother out so that he will be beaten, literally defaced, reduced to a nonrecognizable other: "His face has changed. They won't mistake us any more" (101).

What makes the operation of cruelty particularly interesting in this play is that Gambaro's image of the Siamese twins points to both the personal and the sociopolitical realms of violence; it refers both to the crisis (undifferentiation) and to the response (the engineered "difference," the separation of the twins that leaves one dead). The biological nature of the image calls attention to the danger of applying biological terminology to the sociopolitical "body." While the separation of twins resulting in the death of one of them may be a necessary evil in preventing the death of both, the same "operation" is a euphemism for extermination along the lines of Hitler's medical solutions. The image also depicts the simultaneous though conflicting pulls—fusion and separation—that theorists such as Klaus Theweleit associate specifically with *fascist* murder. The victimizer, according to Theweleit (1:204), "finds himself in a state of dissolution . . . both the killer and his victim *lose their boundaries* and enter into union" (Theweleit's emphasis). It is this fear of dissolution, "the fear of the 'floods' and the 'lava'" inundating boundaries (1:256), that leads to the need to murder (to differentiate, to separate radically) in the first place. The image of Siamese twins also conveys the fact that Argentina's population is basically homogeneous (what could be more identical than Siamese twins?) and that homogeneity is no defense against the violence of persecution and scapegoating associated with crisis. We generally think of persecution as directed toward others on the basis of race, gender, or class; perceived "difference" usually "explains" violent attacks. In *The Camp*, the fascist Franco asks his victim, Martin: "Jew? or Communist?" However, as the indiscriminate violence of Argentina's undeclared civil war demonstrated, even such age-old rationalizations as "difference" are essentially meaningless. Martin answers: "Tell me, does it matter?" (52). People are not necessarily persecuted because they are different; it is simply safer to persecute members of minority or socially marginal groups than to attack members of the dominant group. No matter how much the "same" people are, *Siamese* illustrates the certainty that some will always find a reason to annihilate others.

Undifferentiation leads to violence within the broader political context as well. It not only undermines the identity of the insiders, the twins trapped in the dyad; it accounts for the violence that befalls that dyad from the outside. Lorenzo explains that his brother's assailant could not distinguish between them and therefore struck the wrong twin. The inability to differentiate has repeatedly been used to justify unwarranted displays of cruelty. Franco, in *The Camp*, makes the political repercussions of this more explicit: "Now you take the Vietnamese and North Vietnamese. It's all one to me. Who knows them? Who's read anything they've written? What language do they talk? The whole thing's a mess!" (54). He therefore has no objections to the violence annihilating them. The lack of positive differentiation (North Vietnamese and South Vietnamese are indistinguishable) combined with created difference (they are both *other*) converts them into expendable victims. Such designations expose victims to persecution and annihilation on both personal and international levels. The image of the Siamese twins, then, refers not only to the rivalry between two brothers; it refers to the entire process of victimization, from the individual to the political, from Lorenzo and Ignacio to the marginalization of Latin America. Forcefully and "unnaturally" binding the two in the one, subsuming many countries with their numerous differences under a fiction of *a* Latin American identity, culminates in violence, not unity. The inability of an outsider to differentiate between the parts (be it the father in *Siamese,* Franco in *The Camp,* or the foreign observer of Latin America) exposes the parts to indiscriminate policies and violence.

It proves impossible to separate the psychological and sociopolitical manifestations of violence, regardless of how we explain the connection. We can view the social as a product of or a response to the individual's inclination toward violence, as in Girard's theory. Like Klaus Theweleit, we can argue that in the fascist imagination the body is both product and producer of the social. The "new" fascist man is a robot, a machine "whose interior has lost its meaning" (2:162). Furthermore, the inner has been projected or externalized onto the social, the "fear of the inner body with its inchoate 'mass' of viscera and entrails, its 'soft' genitalia, its 'lower half,' is translated into the threat of the 'masses' in the social sense of classes or— especially in those chaotically mixed groups with women and children in the forefront—mass demonstration" (1:xix). Like Gilles Deleuze and Félix Guattari in *Anti-Oedipus* (30), we could posit that the individual is a product of the social, that the "desiring-production is one and the same thing as social production. . . . Thus fantasy is never individual; it is group fantasy." Robert Lifton also sees the personal as a product of the social. He describes the doubling and splitting of individual personalities in critical situations not so much as "character disorder" but as a disorder which is "more focused and temporary and occurs as part of a larger institutional structure which encourages or even demands it" (*Nazi Doctors*, 423). No matter how we formulate the connection between the personal and the social, *Siamese* indicates that the interconnected spheres of violence fuel and maintain each other.

It is important for our purposes here to recognize that Lorenzo not only fantasizes on a personal level about exterminating his brother; the fascistic military did come to power in Argentina and did engage in the widespread extermination of its people. Moreover, the fascistic fantasies of mythical origins, unity, destiny, and history are compelling on both a personal and a national level, and it is lethal to underestimate their potency. Lorenzo's myths successfully manipulate Ignacio, who succumbs to them against his own judgment. They cost him his life. And since the 1930s, Argentines have found it hard to resist the fascistic fictions belabored by their leaders.[20] Again, many people have died because of them. Violence in the name of love within the family functions like violence in the name of national security in the political arena.[21] The biological metaphor of monstrous unity underlines the sociopolitical dangers of creating both fictitious unities and fictitious differences. Each contributes to the destruction of the other.

Even when the relationship between the personal and the social is not clear-cut, we must resist separating the levels and opting for one interpretation as opposed to another. Gambaro herself has illustrated the folly and shortsightedness of seeing frames separately rather than together. Moreover, the efficacy of fascist discourse depends on our seeing one facet of the image to the exclusion of the other. In a study of theatre of crisis, perhaps the conflation of personal and sociopolitical "bodies" itself bespeaks the complexity and pervasiveness of a violence as archetypal and universal as Cain's killing of Abel, as politically urgent and specific as an understanding of Argentina's outbursts of fascism.

For all its universality, the image of the twins reflects the "real" disappearance of the other, the criminal commonplace of Argentina in the 1970s. Myths of fraternal bonds proved fictitious. Outside forces were summoned to cut the cord, projecting violence into the public sphere. The drama went beyond familial violence and became one of torture and official terror. The death of Ignacio signals both an end and a new beginning, but not in the positive religious, mythical, or even revolutionary sense associated with rebirth and regeneration. Rather, it marks "the final closing of one historical cycle and the beginning of another,"[22] the escalation of violence culminating in the Dirty War. Instead of being given a proper burial, Ignacio's body is dumped in an unmarked pit, foreshadowing the real events that followed: people were thrown from airplanes to their deaths; bodies were burnt or disposed of in communal graves. As in

*Siamese,* the home gave way to the graveyard. Lorenzo's remarks to his brother in the opening scene—"we respect what we kill . . . you're not dead yet; if you were, you'd be safer" (99)—is echoed in General Lanusse's famous statement: "If this continues, we'll have peace, even if it's the peace of cemeteries."23

## *The Camp:* Crisis and Holocaust

By the time *The Camp* appeared in 1967, following the especially repressive military coup of 1966, the "deadly toxin" had corroded the "Argentine body politic" (Skidmore and Smith, 103). "Contagious" violence further undermined distinctions between social, family, and personal space; each became one more arena to conquer, to invade, to terrorize. Gambaro's plays of this period reflect the intensification of annihilating violence as boundaries totally disappeared between private and public. In *Siamese,* the home that the men originally fought over is abandoned as the final scene gives way to the makeshift burying ground. In *The Camp,* the process takes the opposite direction. The action begins in the concentration camp, and the "released" prisoners fantasize that they still have a home to return to. In fact, however, the home Emma and Martin run to at the end of the play is as unfamiliar, and as lethal, as the concentration camp they thought they had left behind. The very idea of release seems hopelessly nostalgic in a world in which the home, traditionally the space reserved for individual shelter and reproduction has become indistinguishable from torture chambers and death camps. The home in the final scene foreshadows Gambaro's use of a house as a theatre space in *Information for Foreigners* (1972). In *The Camp,* thugs from the concentration camp enter Martin's desecrated home and brand a number on him. The personal, familial, and social spaces are turned inside out and upside down. As terrorist attacks, abductions, and violations decimate families, the home itself becomes the site of official terror. Human bodies are literally inscribed with political insignia. The spectators enter the *univers concentrationnaire* (Rousset) associated with the Holocaust and the literature of atrocity.

The similarities between Gambaro's work and European depictions of fascism and Nazism are not accidental. The ties between Argentine and European fascism are old and strong. As early as 1930, General José F. Uriburu modeled his semifascist state on the doctrines spreading through Germany, Italy, Spain, and France. And, as *The Camp* illustrates, even after fascism subsided in Europe, fascism, "Franco," and the concentration camps lived on in Argentina, where fascist war criminals and their ideologies found a receptive home.24

Gambaro's inquiry into the nature of fascism and the conscious modeling of her play on Nazi practices in part account for the many similarities between *The Camp* and theatre of the Holocaust. Robert Skloot titles his anthology of plays *The Theatre of the Holocaust,* using the term to designate plays of "diverse styles and artistic strategies" that thematize the Holocaust (4). Elinor Fuchs also notes the "surprisingly varied theatrical approaches" (xi) in the introduction to her anthology *Plays of the Holocaust.* A specific historical reference point determines this theatre. For those writing these plays after the end of the war, the year 1945 marks the historic, if not the personal, end of suffering. The survivors, looking back, have a temporal and spatial separation from the terrifying events which the theatre of crisis lacks. They have a defined moral commitment to speak out, never to forget. They have achieved a clarity of vision and a direction absent in those playwrights who write within the disorienting moment of crisis. Basically, then, a sense of distance (critical or historical, not emotional) separates the two theatres, for most of the canon now referred to as "theatre of the Holocaust" was written either after the end of the war or, like Nelly Sachs's *Eli,* from the physical distance of exile. History, held in suspension during the erasure of European Jewry and the assault on everything that attested to its culture, traditions, and history, seemed tentatively to begin again after the war. Elie Wiesel's words "In the beginning was the Holocaust . . . we must invent reason, we must create beauty out of nothingness" (qtd. in Langer, 31) indicate a new age coming *out* of crisis, *out* of chaos, an age determined to remember its dismembered past.

Notwithstanding the historical specificity limiting the thematic scope of the theatre of the Holocaust to the 1930s and 1940s, it has much in common with the theatre of crisis. Both set the imaginary stage world against a background of concrete sociopolitical crisis. The individual experience of decomposition is inseparable from that of widespread social crisis. There is also an important awareness of collective as well as individual suffering in these plays. The playwrights depict the victims as representative of a larger historical confrontation. Both the theatre of the Holocaust and the theatre of crisis struggle intently to develop aesthetic forms that will render artistically intelligible what the artists, and the victims they speak for, experience as unintelligible: the gratuitous extermination and/or oppression of a people.

Here, there is a slight though significant divergence between the two kinds of theatre. The playwrights of the Holocaust face the moral dilemma of whether they should be writing at all, whether the experience of the Holocaust can ever be appropriately expressed or any writing do justice to the victims. Theodor Adorno (159) provocatively proposes that art after the Holocaust is barbaric in that it denigrates suffering and victimization:

"The aesthetic principle of stylization, and even the solemn prayer of the chorus, makes an unthinkable fate appear to have some meaning; it is transfigured, something of its horror removed. This alone does an injustice to the victims." The very act of representing atrocity aesthetically, through theatre, poses the ethical problem that the formal appeal may contradict or undermine the moral condemnation of atrocity. As Susan Sontag notes, simulating atrocity risks "making the audience passive, reinforcing witless stereotypes, confirming distance and creating frustration." Moreover, she adds, "the display of atrocity in the form of photographic evidence risks being tacitly pornographic." (*Saturn,* 139).

These reservations, while applicable to all forms of artistic stylization, are especially appropriate in regard to theatre. The theatrical event operates, at least on some level, on the buying and selling of pleasure. Furthermore, theatre in itself tends to establish the (false) complicity between the victimizer and the victim that I noted earlier. The actor, playing victim, is actually onstage by choice; the real victim is not. The fact that audiences and critics find the representation of violence "tacitly pornographic" comes partly from this insidious, albeit unintentioned, shifting of consent.

How, then, can a dramatist represent a terrifying reality in a way that permits the audience to comprehend its significance without allowing for the *pleasure* that theorists from Aristotle to Brecht argue is theatre's only "passport?"[25] And granting that the dramatist can achieve this, who is going to want to attend the performance or read the script? If theatre's "passport" into our world is "fun" (as Brecht states), how can we possibly be expected to "like" these plays? The fact that the theatre of the Holocaust, like many of the Latin American plays examined here, are about violence—that is, they are not "likable," and unlikable theatre for all practical purposes becomes equated with "bad" theatre[26]—keeps them out of production. The problem of reception, then, complicates what already seems an impossible mission.

The notion of further desecrating the victims haunts playwrights of the Holocaust precisely because the event is in the past. The political emergency staged in Gambaro's theatre, however, precludes the option of remaining silent. For all the difficulties involved, playwrights caught in the middle of an annihilating situation simply feel they have no *choice* but to write about violence. While Gambaro's plays explicitly call attention to the potentially perverse or voyeuristic scopophilia of the spectators, she nonetheless insists that the audience must *see* the criminal violence of its moment and, more important, *recognize* it for what it is. The audience must not be allowed to transform, or assist in the transformation of, the deadly into a spectacle that diverts public attention. For those who commit themselves to responding, through the theatre of crisis, the theatre of the Holocaust, or protest theatre, the problem lies in *how* to allow outsiders an insight into the insane reality of victimization and genocide without trivializing, distorting, mythifying, or sexualizing the brutality—all without losing the audience. The challenge for these dramatists, then, lies in representing, without reproducing or adding to, the fascist's "fascinating" discourse.[27]

Setting the play against the historical fact of disintegrating moral, judicial, and personal frameworks poses other aesthetic problems for both the theatre of the Holocaust and the theatre of crisis. Aesthetic frameworks collapse along with all others. Traditional dramatic forms, with their own historical contexts and ideological assumptions, no longer serve to depict the horrifying new reality. In an age that fails to valorize life, the concept of tragedy and the idea of heroism are romantic if not meaningless.[28] The systematic production of mass death invalidates aesthetic valorization. Dramatists experiment relentlessly, not for any art-for-art's-sake devotion to form but to find a new theatrical idiom that can express what has hitherto been deemed unspeakable. It is not surprising, then, to find diverse treatments of extermination and oppression illustrated by both these theatres. There can be no one form, for the ungraspable, irrational nature of the reality evades ready formulation. The violence at work in genocide and other kinds of victimization is difficult if not impossible to represent; it works on the real rather than the symbolic order. It does not *mean* or *signify* anything else, and we have seen already how dangerous it is to "interpret" or "see" violence as a metaphor, as a "solution" to something else. Moreover, even forms that find a way to enter into the significance of violence soon become inadequate. Once the audience anticipates the violence or recognizes the artistic techniques, the revelation once again disappears into the ordinary, the expected. The repeated depiction of violence, even the "real" violence of newscasts or the televized Vietnam War, encourage "psychic numbing" and allow spectators, like victimizers, to split off from its significance.

Notwithstanding the diverse aesthetic resources, however, both the theatre of the Holocaust and the theatre of crisis tend to depict nightmarish onstage worlds. "Grotesque, ridiculous, crazy, mad" (Langer, 36) are adjectives that apply to both. All moorings have been lost, all boundaries violated. The nightmare quality of these works not only stems from the insane violence and the disappearance of moral and judicial frameworks capable of sustaining difference but makes itself felt through monstrous images and double sets. The combination office and gas chamber in Peter Barnes's *Auschwitz* (1978), for example, works in much the same way as doubling does in *The Camp*. It is characterized by aural and visual disorientation: the screams, the disintegrating walls, the nonrealistic staging techniques required to represent this grotesque reality.

Even beyond these features shared by the theatre of the Holocaust and the theatre of crisis, *The Camp* accentuates the links between the two by setting the action in a modern Argentine neo-Nazi concentration camp. The noise of machine guns, the smell of burning flesh, the allusions to the showers, the reference to the school-children "being led to a . . ." (57) leave no doubt that this camp is modeled after its German original. However, it is fundamental to recognize that *The Camp* is not about the Holocaust. Although it deals with the historical fact of Argentine fascism and criminal politics, it has no historical documentary intent. Unlike the theatre of the Holocaust, it is not a testimonial; it need not face the challenge of depicting "a sense of what it must have been like in the ghettos and the camps" (Friedländer, 99). Rather, it looks ahead to where the escalating violence will lead Argentina. The play's depiction of a death camp in fact precedes the appearance of actual concentration camps in Argentina by a decade. As in her earlier plays, Gambaro juxtaposes two frames—Nazi Germany and Argentina—so that we can read them in conjunction, so that we can discern the similarities and the differences and so understand the nature of fascism in Argentina today.

Set against the background of fascism generally and the Nazi variation specifically, *The Camp*, then, is not a play from or even about the Holocaust. From the very beginning, Gambaro historicizes the event. World War II has come and gone; the Vietnam War is in full swing. It becomes increasingly clear to Martin that the "office" in which he has just been hired as an accountant is in fact a concentration camp, in spite of the strange theatricality and insularity of the room. Everything that he hears or sees seems regulated by the intercom device situated on Franco's desk. Martin hears peasants singing in the field, but when he looks out the window, he sees "nothing" (55). The window, as in theatrical sets, only suggests the existence of an external, visible reality. When Martin pushes the button on the intercom, the singing stops. The sounds of children screaming, of people running in the halls, of ferocious dogs "barking and growling. . . as though they were attacking someone" suddenly break in through the white noise, the "soporific, well-scrubbed music"—yet in relation to the clean and orderly setting the groans, harsh reprimands, and screams "almost seem an illusion" (51).

The carefully staged effect of the scene goes beyond the technologically controlled surroundings. The characters that Martin encounters in the camp, specifically Franco and Emma, are also consciously theatrical, modeling themselves on recognizable roles. When Franco appears, he is wearing a shiny Gestapo uniform, complete with boots and whip. Yet he smiles benignly at his new employee, and "there seems to be nothing threatening about his demeanor . . . his face is almost kind" (51). Martin is thrown into a state of confusion; he cannot interpret what he sees with his own eyes, hears with his own ears. As in Gambaro's earlier pieces, the victim has stumbled onto the wrong stage.

Again, the theatricality of the scene lulls the victim into believing that the deadly situation is not "real" and hides no actual danger. In *The Camp*, Gambaro focuses particularly on the sexualization or eroticization of brutality as a means of disarming the victims and spectators. The first three scenes illustrate concretely how an act of torture can be transformed to look like an erotic fantasy.

In the first scene, Franco tries to convince his victim that, in spite of his Nazi uniform, he is in fact quite harmless; he refers to his uniform almost as if it were a costume, as if it signaled merely a personal fantasy, "a harmless little quirk" (58). "Why didn't you choose another one?" Martin asks. "Another one?" asks Franco. "Why? They're all alike. The only difference is that this one has a history." Franco implies that he is drawn less to the uniform's history than to the pleasure it gives him: he dresses up, he confesses, because "I like it. And you damn well better indulge your taste while you're alive!" (52). The uniform, Gambaro recognizes, simultaneously signals two messages. One is the horrifying history of Nazism. The other is a fetish, a "harmless" though decidedly odd element associated with sexual "taste," commonly in conjunction with sadomasochistic sexual practices. In "Fascinating Fascism," Susan Sontag notes that while "there is a general fantasy about uniforms" which suggest order, community, and identity as well as the "legitimate exercise of violence," there is a special fascination with the well-cut, "stylish" SS uniform. However, she continues, there is an even greater fascination with *photographs* (and, I would add, *representations*) of uniforms, especially SS uniforms; they "are units of particularly powerful and widespread sexual fantasy. Why the SS? Because the SS was the ideal incarnation of fascism's overt assertion of the righteousness of violence, the right to have total power over others and to treat them as absolutely inferior. . . . The SS was designed as an elite military community that would be not only supremely violent but also supremely beautiful" (*Saturn*, 99). Dressing up in Nazi uniform, then, becomes a means of self-representation for Franco that concurrently allows for the image of violent domination and sexual prowess. The fact that he continually refers to his costume, plays with it, exhibits himself by undoing the buttons and taking off the jacket, the boots, the socks, emphasizes the sexual nature of the fantasies associated with it. The scene becomes grossly exhibitionistic, a grotesque striptease.

But why? If Gambaro's challenge is to depict the atrocity of Argentina's growing fascism without reproducing the fascination with violence and power it tends to provoke, why deliberately sexualize it? In scene 1, Franco's eccentric behavior might pass for a bizarre, sadomasochistic fantasy, complete with whips and leather, in which violence arouses sexual titillation. He "likes" it. It turns sexual violence into what Sontag also calls a "taste . . . a self-conscious form of theater which is what sadomasochism is about . . . a master scenario available to everyone" (*Saturn*, 105). But though Franco is undoubtedly eccentric, Martin, like the audience, is disarmed when the officer attributes his "quirk" to pleasurable rather than annihilating activities. Who can argue with sexual preference? The point, of course, is that the play is neither about sex nor about specifically sexual violence.

It becomes evident in scene 2 that the sexualized fantasy is only a strategy for disguising acts of torture and fascistic violence. Franco informs Martin that he has invited a woman ("Venus, a frivolous element") to spend the evening with them—"I invited her just for you. . . . Be nice to her. I'll be dressed in a minute" (61)—and then he leaves to change back into his Nazi outfit. What has been set up supposedly as a sexual encounter, whether a blind date or act of prostitution, is actually something quite different. Emma is shoved into the room. She is shaved, emaciated; she wears a prisoner's smock; her right palm is marked by "a livid wound"; her "face bears the ravages of long suffering. She is barefoot." Her body itches and she scratches herself until she bleeds. Her body, in fact, has been converted into a surface of living pain which the text equates with the concentration camp itself: "It's not lice," she explains to Martin. "Oh, no, that's not it at all. They've been exterminated from the whole area" (62). The linguistic ambiguity annuls the distinction between body and camp. What area is she referring to? However, this woman, whose body itself has become a source of torment, is obviously expected to seduce Martin exactly as if she were a movie actress: "She makes a terrible effort, as though she were about to act a role"; "All the while she continues smiling and talking with artificial and mannered high spirits"; she "walks in the manner of a movie star" and touches her shaved head as though she were arranging a full head of hair"; she speaks of her admirers, her secretary, her impossible social schedule (62, 64, 65). The scenario is a cruel parody of the sex symbol who must please her fans; without her admirers she is nothing. It also painfully reflects the gender-specific condition of woman as desired object, all "lack" to be filled by the male. If Martin does not "like" her or find her attractive, she is nothing.[29] Her body has been transformed into the source of her pain; her femininity is split (image/ degradation) in a grotesque reflection of the splitting associated with adaptation to an annihilating situation.

Emma's self-conscious though apparently chosen or accepted role as society lady and gifted pianist situates her almost alongside Franco within what appears to be a perverse fantasy.[30] She is trying to seduce Martin in what seems an effort to please Franco; she pulls up her skirts; she strokes Martin. She attributes her intolerable itching to her excitement: "But just now the itching is driving me crazy. It must be because I'm excited, and the blood flows more rapidly. I do so want to please you" (66). The violence and perversity of the scene seem on the level with the "erotic daydream" described by the psychiatrist Robert J. Stoller in his study *Sexual Excitement* (xi): Belle's daydream was that she "was being raped by a horse while a group of silent men watched, the performance controlled by a sadistic Director."

Franco enters the room and indeed takes on the role of the sadistic director:

Emma     *(Martin sits down. Emma moves behind the chair. She hesitates in the choice of hands and then, with her good hand, begins to caress Martin's face and hair, all the while scratching herself with her other hand):* Darling, you're a dream!

Franco   *(interrupting her, for all the world like a theater director):* Not like that. That's too crude.

Emma     *(meekly):* I'll improve. *(She starts once more.)* When the music starts . . .

Franco   I vomit! . . .

Emma     *(in anguish, to Martin):* Please don't push me away. No matter how much you want to, please don't push me away.

Franco   Stop begging! The most desirable woman in the world! Why do you resort to methods like that?

Emma     *(straightens up with great effort, raises her head, and again addresses Martin, with the falseness of a movie star):* Kiss me!

Franco   *(softly):* Disgusting. *(Then, changing his manner altogether)* Your nerves are frayed, my dear. [72]

It is clear, however, that this is not just another sexual fantasy of humiliation and violation á la Stoller's Belle. First of all, this is not Emma's fantasy but Franco's. She did not choose her role; she does not find sexual pleasure in seducing a man in front of a sadistic spectator. She is a victim of Franco's fantasy; he conceives and directs the action, and as Theweliet's *Male Fantasies* makes clear, fascist violence involves a strong dose of misogyny and perversity. Second, in spite of the perversity of the scene, it is not principally about sexual violence. This scenario, unlike true erotic fantasies and daydreams, is not a means of sexually arousing the dreamer— Franco. The purpose of this playacting, rather, is to ensure that Martin will not leave the camp, as he has already threatened to do. Emma is the lure.[31] She is not an accomplice in perversity but herself a victim of torture; her body itches because her tormentors have applied an irritant. However, this scene is not set up by Franco primarily to hurt and humiliate her further. She is bait, live bait. Martin, not Emma, is the intended victim of this scene. Franco strikes at Martin (the innocent bystander, the spectator) through her. Martin is horrified by her: "It hurts just to look at you. You remind me of . . ." (66). He cannot speak the unspeakable; he too resists thinking and speaking about violence. The live bait "catches" him, but not through the grotesque sexuality. "Martin *(pulling her skirt down):* What are you doing? Now stop it! Here you are showing me your legs and you look like someone who's escaped from a . . . *(He halts, surprised, as though he had not realized until that moment that she appears to be an inmate of a concentration camp)*" (65). He feels compassion for her. Not once in the course of the play does Gambaro eroticize or romanticize their relationship. Martin sides with Emma as a fellow human being, and he feels rage at her tormentors. He has seen and understood the nature of her suffering. He is engaged, no longer free to leave.

This scene of torture grimly dressed up as a sexual fantasy inverts the relationship between excitement and violence in sexual perversion. Excitement, in erotic scenarios, derives from the anticipation of pleasure; the fantasies involve an element of risk and danger. As Stoller (*Excitement*, 19) indicates, the trick to erotic daydreaming lies in maintaining "the delicious shudder—while at the same time minimizing true risk. So one writes in *safety factors* that reduce danger to the *illusion* of danger (Stoller's emphasis). Torture, this scene illustrates, does the opposite. The excitement in this case anticipates real danger. Moreover, the point of staging this sexual fantasy is not to introduce danger as a "delicious" illusion but to disarm Martin, to prevent his recognizing the very concrete threat facing him and Emma. If we, as audience, dismiss the encounter as a frustrated attempt at seduction, then we can ignore the torture by arguing questions of choice, taste, perversity, and responsibility. Why, we could ask, does Martin—or even Emma for that matter—simply play along? Why is he, or she, incapable of leaving?

Gambaro's method of depicting this torture scene is a variation on a well-known form of torture used in Latin America, one that destroys the victim and the spectators at the same time. "Family torture" consists of raping, brutalizing, and killing the woman in her own home in front of her children and husband. While this practice dehumanizes and kills the woman, and attacks all concepts of family and home for present and even future generations, the tormentors' aim is ostensibly to extract information from the male. For the explicitly *macho* and misogynist military men, women are only objects, the "body" part of the body/brain, female/male dyad. It proves more effective to torture the female body in front of family members than to torture the man himself. The female body is seen as providing entry into the male psyche. This is not to imply that women are destroyed only insofar as they are perceived as extensions of the persecuted man. Women are also tortured if they are politically aware or active (and thus, in the military government's equation, subversive). As Ximena Bunster-Burotto documents in "Surviving beyond Fear," women in the countries of the Southern Cone (Argentina, Chile, Uruguay, Paraguay, Bolivia) during the 1970s were not simply exposed to the "daily terror" of "generalized violence" ("massacres, attacks on churches during mass, and the burning of villages"), as they were in Central America; they were especially singled out as enemies of the state: "Women are systematically identified—with names, address and family composition—as 'enemies' of the government. They are methodically tracked down and incarcerated. There are institutions within the military government dedicated specifically and exclusively to this task" (297-98). Thus, women are doubly victimized—victimized (like men) for what or whom they theoretically know; victimized (unlike men) as a means of torturing the men who look on.

The implications of the fact that "watching" can be turned into a form of torture are far-reaching. The only way that Martin could conceivably extricate himself from the situation would be by not caring. He could ignore Emma's plea ("No matter how much you want to, please don't push me away"); he could reject her, leaving her to her fate. Now turning one's back on the victim is hardly a viable solution to victimization (and *The Camp* does not really offer Martin the possibility of walking away), but the widespread belief that it is a solution shapes the public's response to torture. Most people feel that it is dangerous to sympathize or side with the victim, dangerous to really see what is happening, dangerous seeing. It is safer to disengage, to turn one's back on the problem. But what actually happens to the public involved, directly or indirectly, in situations of torture?

Gambaro explores the broader political implications of public lack of interest in acts of torture, perceived as a means of self-protection in terrorized countries (*The Camp*) and as a means of protecting one's peace of mind in nonterrorized countries (*Information for Foreigners*). In scene 3 of *The Camp*, she introduces a wider audience to the spectacle of torture. Emma must give a concert for her fascist "admirers" and fellow prisoners. Franco, as always, directs the show; Martin, once more, is forced to witness. Franco choreographs the scene in a way that transforms victimization into a bizarre parody of entertainment. The torture involves the actual infliction of real pain: Franco "treats" Emma's open wound in front of the audience, pouring liquid onto her raw palm. It also involves the destruc-

tion of Emma's sense of self through the violence and humiliation directed
at her as a woman. Again, she must act the part of a sex symbol or "star."
She must dress up: that is, pin a filthy rag on her prisoner's outfit by way of
a train, cover her shaved head with a wig. The piano does not work, so she
must "pretend" by creating the music with her thin voice. As before, the
grotesque manipulation of a gendered role (the sex symbol) forces her to
live up to the cultural stereotype of attractive femininity ("Venus") that
only accentuates her "disgusting" and inadequate condition. The torment
involves splitting Emma in two, rupturing her sexual identity: the ideal
woman is gracious, talented, frivolous, and beautiful; the real Emma is a
failed woman, clumsy, ugly, and painful to watch. Moreover, Franco calls
attention to the discrepancy between Emma and her role model: he steps
on her train so that it detaches from her smock; he pats her head to dislodge
her wig, which he then holds in the air. He "looks at it, amused, and
deposits it on the piano" (82). He makes certain that the piano does not
work. The ridiculous image of Emma shifts the responsibility in the scene:
instead of blaming the torturers for destroying Emma, the audience feels
justified in jeering as she makes a pathetic spectacle of herself. The
performance is aimed specifically at undermining her as a woman, and it is
as a woman that the audience of prisoners attacks her: "Let her play with
her ass! Let her play with my . . ." (80).

The show involves three sets of spectators (although the play as a
whole points to five): Martin, the other prisoners, and the fascist officers.
Martin, who cares for Emma as a human being, is forced to sit through her
torment. When he protests, the fascist officers pin him down and scratch
his face until it bleeds.[32] The spectacle, for him, is a form of torture.

Emma's fellow prisoners, eager to avoid an unpleasant fate, obediently
participate in the production. The violence they witness paralyzes them
by means of mimetic identification—this could be happening to them—
so they disengage from the reality of Emma's suffering, even contribute to
it on demand. They become impatient when Franco suggests they do so;
they quiet down at his instruction; they applaud on cue. They drown
Emma's voice with their jeers and insults. After Franco warns Emma that
the spectators "bought their tickets . . . you must please your public" (82),
they begin to demand their money back. Studies of victimization point out
that the reaction of indifference and even hostility on the part of fellow
victims is an adaptive measure resulting, perhaps not surprisingly, from the
fact that they "were driven to choose survival at the expense of their
humanity" (Langer, 6). Fellow victims, then, sometimes adapt to the
situation by participating in the torture.

The third set of spectators consists of those who in fact run the show,
the fascist victimizers. For them, on the one hand, the show is a display of

power. They can make Martin, Emma, and the other prisoners behave as they want. This is not a negligible attraction, for we see from Franco's first encounter with Martin that he is a man who needs to dominate and control. He is also exhibitionistic, always present, visible, audible during the recital. The entire spectacle focuses not so much on the degradation of Emma as on Franco degrading Emma—pulling off the wig, stepping on her train, "treating" her hand, talking incessantly to the audience, and so on. Just as he claims center stage in the cruel proceeding, he controls his audience by imposing theatrical convention and decorum on a situation that is not a traditionally theatrical one. He insists that the audience behave in a manner in keeping with the loftiness of the cultural event: "You must have more respect. Martin, do you wish to hear the young lady?" (81). An officer warns Martin: "We'll have to eject you from the theater. You should know how to behave . . . at a concert" (82; suspension marks do not indicate an omission from the text). On the other hand, the show is a strategy to keep public attention off the sociopolitical reality of overt violence and extermination. The infliction of physical pain on Emma, for example, is administered as something other than physical violence; it passes for medical treatment, a means of "helping" the victim. As Franco approaches the stage with his bottle of "medicine," he hisses at Martin: "I don't take care of her, huh? You say I don't take care of her? You bastard" (79). Furthermore, the fascist officers take advantage of the spectacle onstage to attack Martin and scratch his face.

The most glaring example of the executioners' manipulation of performance arts as a diversionary tactic is only passingly referred to in the play. I set it aside in a paragraph of its own not only because it is the most important but also to avoid the danger of rendering it invisible in my own text: the entire performance occurs just as bodies are being burned in the crematorium (84).

*The Camp*, then, suggests that theatre taking place in a criminal context can contribute, willingly or not, to covering up violence. Theatre, as an institutional bright space, the "flower" of our civilization, obscures its opposite, the institutional attempt to sweep brutalized bodies into a historical, visual, and even physical nonspace. The staging of atrocious acts also succeeds in drawing attention away from the real power or authority behind the show. In spite of the fact that the tormentors may derive personal and perverse pleasure from the domination and victimization of others, they are not in fact solely, or even principally, responsible for the proceedings. They run the show, but they are not the ones who orignally devise policies or ultimately benefit from them. It is indicative that the actual "producer" of this atrocious show, the fourth audience, is nowhere near the concert and is mentioned only indirectly. Martin at the beginning of the play asks Franco: "Is this establishment yours? Or are there other owners?" (57). Franco's response (in the English translation) that a "corporation" owns the camp captures one essential component of the setup: it is tied into financial interests. He admits to Martin: "We were making money. What did we care about keeping records?" (60). The financial gains to be had through controlling and if need be annihilating uncooperative sectors of the population—factory workers and union leaders labeled "subversive"—inexorably linked violence and financial "stability" in Argentina during the 1970s. As David Rock (369) observes: "The Army's war on subversion and Martínez de Hoz's [economic] program elicited opposite responses from outside observers, who detested the extreme brutality of the former but generally praised the latter. In many respects, however, the two policies were complementary and inseparable." The English word "corporation," however, leaves out one vital factor connoted by the Spanish original: *"sociedad anónima"* does denote "corporation," but its literal meaning is "anonymous society"—which introduces an entire new group of spectators into the equation, the fifth audience.

The "anonymous society" refers to the "silent majority," both inside and outside Argentina, that is only indirectly involved in the horror. Inside Argentina, as we shall see, torture effectively silences an entire population that visualizes *itself* in George Orwell's Room 101—the worst place in the world. Outside Argentina, the majority sit quietly (clipping coupons or not) while their fellow human beings are exterminated. Society at large is involved in these terrifying tactics—as "outside observers," as financial investors, as innocent bystanders, as readers of newspapers. The mixed public reaction to foreign divestment of capital from South Africa is only the most obvious example of people's hesitation to give up financial gains, even when they know that their benefits cost an entire people its freedom. Our situation as spectators (outside the context, looking on) in this atrocious drama is only fleetingly referred to by Emma's image of the fireflies with the "little light on their bodies." The image speaks not only of a world without hope but of the spectators' response or, more accurately, *lack* of response to that hopelessness: "The little light goes on and off, as though they were calling for help. What help? No one knows. The night goes on, dark and silent, and we look on" (63).

Elaine Scarry's fine study *The Body in Pain* repeatedly refers to torture in the language of theatre. She writes of torture as the "mime of uncreating" (20), as an "acting out" (27), as an "obscene and pathetic drama" (56); "the torturer dramatizes the disintegration of the world" (38). Scarry also notes characteristics of torture that I would call theatrical: for example, an obsessive display of instruments to instill terror in the watching victim.

She writes about torture as "many endlessly multiplied acts of display" and notes that torturers speak of the "production room," the "cinema room," and "the blue lit stage" (28). And though she proposes that torture assists in "the conversion of absolute pain into the fiction of absolute power" (27), Scarry focuses on the victimizer/victim relationship to the extent that she understates two vital aspects of torture, both having to do with the spectator. Who is this grotesque and obscene drama for? And how does the public assist in the conversion of pain to power?

Torture cannot be explained in terms of only two participants, victimizer and victim. Torturers are not self-employed; they work for a state. Torturers may be sexually perverted, although usually they are not. They may believe they are fighting a dirty but necessary war against enemies of the state; they may go to torture school (Peters, 179-84). The point is that torture, as an instrument of the state, is tied into power structures far exceeding the most bizarre fantasy. Ridding society of "dangerous elements" (read, *human beings*) seems to be a top political priority for one of every three governments in power today. Governments using torture claim to be ensuring the safety of their population and, in Argentina and South Africa, the safety of foreign investment. We cannot understand torture unless we place it within its larger socioeconomic and political context.

From this play onward, Gambaro points to at least five participants involved in torture, all five caught up, in different ways, in its theatricality: the "producer," the victimizer, the victim, the victimized public, and the general public. Perhaps it would not be out of place, after so many allusions to the theatricality of torture, to state the obvious. Torture is not theatre; it is torture. It would not help our understanding of the phenomenon to reduce it to a "performance art." Torture is real; it destroys and kills *real* people. Nor would we withstand Gambaro's plays if they were themselves torture. However, I do not believe we can understand either the plays or the continuing practice of torture without understanding what Gambaro perceives as the theatrical elements of torture and the torturous potential of theatre.

While the theatricality of the torture act is key in creating and maintaining the victimizer/victim relationship, as Gambaro illustrates in her earliest plays, the roles of the producer and the audience are also theatrical, also vital for the continuing horror show. For the producers, torture offers an effective way of controlling a population while they themselves almost remain invisible. When we think of torture, we think of sinister figures wearing dark hoods, not of businessmen working for United Fruit or IT&T. Theatre, we must remember, can make the invisible visible only by making the visible invisible. As in most shows, the producers keep far from the production itself. The role of the audience (national and international) in acts of torture and terrorism is a more complex and challenging one and, as such, the subject of Gambaro's most complex and challenging play.

### *Information for Foreigners:* Dangerous Seeing

Gambaro's first play, *The Walls,* began an inquiry into the nature and dangers of perception, the "what we see" and "how we see it" in both theatre and society (Quigley, 53). That play situates two frames side by side—the young man in the painting and the Young Man in the room—but the visual framing leads us beyond the artificial boundaries of the frame itself toward the dangerous, invisible spaces into which people disappear. *The Camp* again presents two frames, the Argentine death camp against the backdrop of Auschwitz. As before, the juxtaposition does not suggest that we stop our inquiry there but rather demands that we make the connections with the broader picture. Anyone staging the play today in the United States (or France, England, Germany or any other country loath to acknowledge its fascist subgroups and elements) could suggest analogous frames. How can this play be interpreted in the light of the neo-Nazi groups parading in middle America? Skinheads? David Duke's election to the Louisiana state legislature? The Nazi sympathizers in the current Republican administration? Or William F. Buckley's call for AIDS patients to be tattooed?[33]

Gambaro's *Información para extranjeros* (*Information for Foreigners,* 1972) pushes her inquiry into the politics of perception even further. Instead of presenting two images set side by side onstage, safely separated from the space of the audience offstage, this "chronicle in 20 scenes" dealing with torture and terrorist acts pulls the audience itself on stage. The audience becomes the main protagonist, *not* the audience made up of torturers, torture victims, or producers of the deadly productions we saw before but the audience of innocent bystanders, compassionate onlookers, invisible members of the *sociedad anónima* or silent majority—that is, *us.* Gambaro explicitly reminds us that we do not have to live in a criminal society in order to be a part of it. The "foreigners" of the title emphasizes that we, as readers, also make up the silent, invisible, anonymous audience.

*Information* is staged not in a conventional theatre but in a house, and the action takes place in the various rooms and corridors. The spectators are warned before they enter that what they are about to see is unsuitable for any audience: "The show is restricted, prohibited to those under thirty-five and those over thirty-six. . . . Everyone else can come in without difficulties. No obscenities or strong language. The piece responds to our way of life: Argentine, Western, Christian. We're in 1971. I ask you not to separate, and to remain silent" (*Information*, 70).[34] Instead of the dislocating vacuum associated with crisis earlier, Gambaro now ties her play to the specific sociopolitical crisis that gave it rise. The crisis, then, has not changed; if anything, the escalating violence is only growing worse. However, the protagonist's attitude toward the crisis changes as it becomes clearer who is destabilizing society and whose interests such orchestrated violence serves.

The spectators are divided into groups upon arrival, each group differentiated by a number or a color, each led through the house by a Guide introducing the different scenes with short excerpts about abductions and murders taken from actual contemporary newspapers—"information" for foreigners.[35] The information the Guide reads out is verifiable, accessible both to the audience in the house and to the reading public inside and outside Argentina. The question is, how can people deny the reality they know to be true, whether or not they see it with their own eyes?

The audience follows the Guide down long, dark passageways cluttered with corpses and prisoners, up and down steep staircases, in and out of small rooms in which isolated acts of torture or theatrical rehearsals are forever being played out. In one room a group is rehearsing the final moments of *Othello*; in another, a mother sings a lullaby from Federico García Lorca's *Blood Wedding* to her child. Elsewhere a young woman is being subjected to the *submarino*, a form of torture in which the victim's head is submerged in a tub of water usually mixed with urine, blood, and vomit. A mother and father are forcefully taken from their home along with their young children. A member of the group (actually an actor posing as an audience member) is attacked and abducted by unidentified men.

The Guide, however, encourages his charges to overlook the violent intrusions. He dispels the incessant, unexpected outbursts of violence as marginal or accidental in relation to the audience's right to entertainment. As the spectators turn their heads to see what is happening, the Guide breaks in: "You must be saying . . . 'We should have stayed home. This is dangerous.' I'll bet that's what you're thinking, 'Television is safer,' eh? But no, gentlemen. All is not lost" (90). He draws their attention to the safe or undisturbing features of the house and then leads them to the catacombs in the basement, the tombs of martyred Christians. This site of historic interest is the highlight of the tour. Still, screams and shouts echo through the halls, and as the lights go on and off throughout the house, the Guide objects. He clamors for amusement and "a little gaiety, dammit!" He grumbles about the bad scripts and the unsavory subject matter. Complaining that "modern theatre is like that! No respect" (107), he nonetheless points out to the spectators that now that they have paid for their tickets, they may as well enjoy the show.

*Information* goes further than Gambaro's previous plays in depicting the erasure of boundaries between private and public, between theatre and society. Society as a whole, Gambaro stresses, has been transformed into a terrifying theatrical set, giving new meaning to the term "environmental theatre," so popular in the late 1960s and early 1970s. Unlike "the term used by Richard Schechner and others to refer to a branch of the New Theater movement," connoting "the elimination of the distinction between audience space and acting space, a more flexible approach to the interaction between performers and audience and a substitution of a multiple focus for the traditional single focus" (Wilson, 378), *Information* signals not only a new kind of theatre but a new kind of world being created before our eyes. Not only is theatre an arena for intense political confrontation, as attested by the policing of theatres, censorship of scripts, and harassment of writers and practitioners, but political violence is itself played out theatrically, on the public streets, in private houses, on human bodies. If the acts of terrorism Gambaro depicts are flagrantly theatrical, like the abduction of the family in scene 9, it is not simply that she is experimenting with a new kind of theatre, rather, she is depicting a new kind of violence, a terrorism that is itself highly theatrical.

In terrorism, as Gambaro demonstrates in *Information*, spectacular acts of cruelty take place offstage, not on. Antagonists appear on the scene as if by magic; victims disppear into thin air only to surface dramatically, like the corpse of the tortured girl, at the appropriate moment. The terrorists, like Gambaro's police in the raincoats, burst onto the scene and set the drama in motion. The victims, like Gambaro's actors, stand in (albeit unwillingly) for something or someone else—hostages, bait, pawns. Terrorism atomizes the audience. It precludes the possibility of solidarity and mobilization. Everyone is vulnerable; the unexpected attack could come from anywhere, anytime. In this house, where the Guide warns his group to "watch your step and your pocketbooks," anyone could be a thief, an assailant, an informer. As a man is chased through the enormous house, his screams echo down long corridors: "Oh my God, why did I run, why did I run?" (87). The theatricality of terrorism, like theatre, however, allows the authorities as well as the audience to deny the reality of what we see with our own eyes. When the stage characters in scene 12 report that they have witnessed an abduction, the official sends them away: "I'm not interested in what you saw. If there's been harm done, I'll deal with it" (99). State authorities assure shattered populations that everything is under control. The witnesses, like obedient spectators in the theatre, are encouraged to "suspend their disbelief."

Gambaro again, though now much more directly, calls attention to the way that the public's perception is directed and controlled by those in power. The Guide, for example, physically ushers his group from room to room; he tells them where and when to look; he censors what they can see: "Not the ladies, please. Sorry, but ladies can't see this. The men can, if they like" (89). Much of this "guidance" may seem inoffensive, perhaps even necessary. The Guide, after all, does this for a living; we have never been in the house before and we do not know our way around. Who can we trust? However, while this may be Hell, this Guide is no Virgil. When he steers his group away from an atrocity, it is only to protect the perpetrators. He himself participates in the violence, pushing the corpses out of sight with his foot as he flashes "a wide, fake smile" at his group (88). He constantly reveals his hatred of women; he omits (the literal translation is "eats" ("me como las señoras") the "ladies" of "ladies and gentlemen," claiming that it takes too long to say the whole phrase (90); he thrusts his hand under the tortured girl's skirt; he complains about the "ungrateful" girl, muttering, "Who understands women? Difficult gender" (89). However, as women are raped, tortured, and killed throughout the house, we realize that these seemingly trifling "personal" remarks and gestures in fact tie into a rampant national misogyny. Like Lorenzo's fantasy of eliminating his brother, the Guide's allusion to "eating" and thus omitting the "ladies" is profoundly indicative of a group fantasy for the dehumanization and elimination of "subversive" women, the "enemies" of the state. When he grabs under the girl's skirt, he in fact signals that women's sexual organs are the target of most attacks on women. Theweleit's *Male Fantasies* (1:191) articulates and theorizes a fact substantiated by most Latin American reports on violence against women, that violence is usually directed at women's genitals, buttocks, and breasts: that is, specifically at their femininity.[36] However, *Information* also demonstrates that the distinction between "good women" and "bad women," at least tentatively upheld by the protofascists in *Male Fantasies* (1:183), has been subverted in Argentina. The scene in which the mother is abducted in front of her children dispels all myths about differentiation between "subversive" and "motherly" women, a distinction that has been particularly rigid in Latin America.[37] The mother in *Information* may remind her abductors that "no one would harm a mother!" (92); the police may cling to the fiction that no one is punished unjustly, "an eye for an eye" (94); but the mother is stripped and raped just the same.

Respect for the authority of those in power, Gambaro illustrates, can be dangerous indeed. It can lead innocent bystanders to become indirect and even direct participants in torture. The Milgram experiment is underway in one of the rooms, a restaging of an actual experiment carried out by Stanley Milgram at Yale, Princeton, and Munich in the 1960s.[38] The pseudoscientific trappings of the process veil the fact that it actually tests an individual's capacity for inflicting pain and even death on a stranger at the command of an "expert." The young man playing "pupil" is strapped to a chair and given electric shocks by the man playing "teacher." Though the pupil is known to suffer from a bad heart, the experimenter urges the teacher to increase the voltage, on the traditional grounds that obedience to authority supersedes personal responsibility: the experiment is necessary; it's for the greater social good (defined as *knowledge* in scientific experiments and *social stability* in torture); the man dialing up the lethal voltage is not responsible for the victim's death. How can a person deny a reality he or she knows to be true? By listening to an expert asserting that it is really something else, by participating in a drama that inverts roles and changes names to create the illusion of innocence. The theatricality of the proceedings, on a practical level, admirably fulfills its real function. It makes people participate in an act they would otherwise find repellent. While most people probably disagree with the Massuist position that "torture is not merely permissible but morally mandatory,"[39] the experiment suggests that a majority of the population can potentially be deformed into torturers: 65 percent of Milgram's American participants and 85 percent of the German were "fully obedient" (Milgram, 609). So torture and torturers are not quite the monstrous others we like to imagine. And the audience obediently moves from room to room.

One might ask if Gambaro's depictions of torture and terrorism in these and other plays are not themselves a variation of a form of torture called "showing the instruments." Does Gambaro want to terrorize further an already terrorized audience? Are we now victims who have stumbled into the wrong play? Or does she suggest that we are complicitous in the atrocity? By stripping the spectators of their invisibility and placing them in the (Lacanian) lethal field of Other, or as (Sartrean) objects of another's gaze in a situation where danger and death are everywhere, is she not victimizing them? On the contrary, Gambaro's depictions of atrocity are not life-threatening but potentially life-saving. The subject matter is unpleasant, and we, like the Guide, can complain about the unsavory scripts. Her intrusions into traditional realms of pleasure are as unwelcome as the mandatory review of emergency procedures on our pleasure flight. The Guide, in fact, jokes about this: "Come in," he says to to group, "watch your step. All that's missing is a 'fasten your seat belts and refrain from smoking'" (95). However, given the waves of indiscriminate violence washing over Argentina, and other parts of the world, Gambaro warns that we must learn to see violence in its many guises; we must recognize our role and the role of people "just like us" in maintaining it. She is not demanding "information" from us but offering it: "information for foreigners." As R.I. Moore points out in his preface to Edward Peters's *Torture* (vii), "Ignorance has many forms, and all of them are dangerous." No-where is this admonition more appropriate than in regard to torture.

The emphasis in *Information* is not on the violent acts themselves but on the audience's role as spectators watching the violence, on the act of watching. There are many ways of watching, some empowering, some disempowering, some associated with wisdom (clairvoyance), some with perversity and criminality (voyeurism). A widespread theory is that watch-ing is empowering: that is the theory behind panopticism, in which surveillance functions "ceaselessly" and "the gaze is alert everywhere" (Foucault, *Discipline*, 195). Watching is a powerful tool of totalitarian states: Big Brother is watching. Gambaro, however, challenges the dangerous fiction that watching in itself can somehow empower the spectator or control violence. In scene 3, a guard asks the tortured girl, "Why so sad? Nothing is going to happen to you. Look at all these people. They're watching us" (72). The word "watch" in the names of groups dedicated to ending political and racial violence (Americas Watch, Klanwatch) indicate the quasi-magical power we attribute to watching. The play shows, how-ever, that *watching*, in and by itself, never saved anyone. Americas Watch, Klanwatch, Amnesty International, and similar organizations do not sim-ply watch. The girl's corpse turns up before the end of the play. In another scene, a young woman reminiscent of Ophelia sings sweetly: "My death will be as simple as if I had never lived" (105). A man from the audience walks up and suffocates her in front of everyone, then calmly turns and walks out of the room. Four hospital attendents zip her body into a plastic shroud and cart her away. So much for Ophelia. No scenes at her grave, just disappearance, "a cup of *café con leche* that nobody will drink, absence" (106). Did the audience's presence save her? No. But the danger is that the audience may feel that by watching it is at least doing something about the violence. Watching, potentially empowering when it forms part of a broader network, can be extremely disempowering when reduced to the spectator's passive "just watching."

Conversely, can watching itself be a form of violence? Is this the "unauthorized" or even criminal scopophilia of voyeurism? (Metz, 63). The Guide's flashlight accidentally falls on a prisoner, cowering in a corner, "who raises his head, surprised and terrified. He covers his sex with his hands" (71). The spectators, paying customers, are suddenly cast in the role of peeping Toms. Worse still, having paid for tickets to a restricted play, we may have anticipated nudity and violence, indisputably the two major selling points of commercial theatre. John Berger states it simply in *Ways of Seeing* (58): "We want to *see* the other naked" (Berger's emphasis). Here, however, we catch a glimpse of things we do not want to see: a body under a tarp, a naked man gagged and stuffed in a cage, a murder. Faced with this twisted version of what we were paying for, we are shocked into considering, perhaps for the first time, what our expectations were and what we thought we were buying. What are we doing in the theatre? After paying for our tickets, do we merely feel an obligation to get our money's worth? Are we perverted? We are on dangerous ground.

Nowhere more than in theatre (or cinema) is the desire to *see* so prominent. We go to the theatre to see, to hear. Christian Metz writes in his study of cinema, *The Imaginary Signifier* (58-59) that cinema (the same holds for theatre) "is only possible through the perceptual passions"; seeing and hearing are sexual drives, powerful but sublimatable, different from other sexual drives in that they function through distance and absence. Metz notes the importance of *lack*, of *absence*, in fueling this erotic desire: perceptual drives "always remain more or less unsatisfied . . . the lack is what it wishes to fill, and at the same time what it is always careful to leave gaping, in order to survive as desire." Roland Barthes, in *Camera Lucida* (59), also links desire to absence and distance in describing an erotic photograph: "The erotic [unlike the pornographic] photograph does not make the sexual organs into a central object; it may very well not show them at all; it takes the spectator outside the frame, and it is there that I animate this picture and that it animates me—as if the image launched desire beyond what it permits us to see."

Gambaro does not allow for the distancing of scopic pleasure, or the more vital distancing of voyeuristic pleasure. If, as Metz (following Freud) argues, "voyeurism, like sadism in this respect, always keeps apart the *object* (here the object looked at) from the *source* of the drive (the eye)" (59), Gambaro abolishes that distance by having us stumble on what we do not want to see. We are in the same room. The cinema and photography both, to paraphrase Metz (61), bolt desire to lack in that the object looked at is not physically present. But this naked body does not, as in cinema, exist in the realm of the imaginary, pure celluloid; it is materially present. And unlike the spectators in traditional theatre, which still maintains distance even as the actors and audience coexist within the same four walls, members of this audience actually knock into or stumble against a naked body. Unlike theatre that eroticizes or aesthetizes nudity and violence by "covering" as much as it reveals, Gambaro's theatre simultaneously exposes and draws us in. The audience sees the utterly raw nakedness of another human being without the erotic distance, the accompanying sympathy, love, or desire that renders the sight tolerable or titillating. There is nothing safe, erotic, innocent, or gratifying about this vision that inverts the traditional theatrical perception, producing pain and perhaps even shame, but precluding pleasure. It is intolerable sight, sight that traps both seen and see-er, that captures both the revolting sight and the viewer's revulsion, all in the same frame.

Moreover, Gambaro calls attention to the fact that those perceptual desires or "passions" have already been socialized and politicized in ways we do not realize. Metz's "perceiving drive," which "concretely represents the absence of its object" (59), and Barthes's "blind field" of the erotic (57), desire launched beyond what one is permitted to see, fail to account for what we feel standing in front of the half-open doors of torture chambers. Is the "beyond" here a visual lure? Is our reluctance to "look" a reluctance to satisfy our desire, to see lest we satiate (terminate) desire itself? Is it not, rather, the horror of witnessing real *absence,* a case of political absenting— that is, disappearance? If we actually saw it, we might have to do some- thing about it. The lack, then, is of a fundamentally different nature when we move to the physical and political arena of abductions and atrocity, precluding the voyeuristic pleasure in this (not in all) theatre.

The same holds for the audience's feelings of trangression. Creeping through the halls, peeping into dark rooms, the spectators feel like intru- sive children stumbling on the primal scene. Originally, however, trans- gression, much in the manner of taboos and other prohibitions, was conceived by populations as protecting humanity. Theatrical representa- tions and rituals originally mediated between the human and the divine, shielding humans from the awe-full (the holy). Examples as culturally diverse as Euripides' *Bacchae* and the pre-Columbian rituals stress the danger of transgression, of *seeing* that which exceeds human comprehen- sion. The power of the superhuman, like Zeus in all his splendor, threat- ens to blind and destroy the human.

Now, on the contrary, Gambaro demystifies the notion of transgression and challenges its politics: what is behind those doors, and why do we not have legitimate access to it? Transgression shields the mechanics of power rather than the sensibilities of humanity. Whether the sanctum sanctorum is the pre-Hispanic *cue,* the parental bedroom, the masking societies of West Africa, the Pentagon, or Oz, the public is excluded from the produc- tion and reproduction of power—hence the masks, the hideous sculp- tures, the admonitions. The politics of the awe-full have given way to the politics of the awful; political secrecy replaces taboo; the off-scene has become the obscene; terrorism, like ancient gargoyles, compels us and repels us with its horror.

Much as in the "seduction" scene in *The Camp,* Gambaro illustrates that torture, abductions, and other scenes of atrocity frighten us away from seeing and recognizing them by appealing to ways of seeing that we, consciously or unconsciously, associate with *bad* seeing, perversion, voy- eurism, and transgression. We are socialized to avert our eyes from sexually charged sights. Binding the sexually charged image with annihilating violence tempts us to look away. We do not want to feel like peeping children at keyholes, like voyeurs, like perverts. We do not want to feel complicitous. Yet the identification with peeping children and perverts is a misleading one; though spectators have no place in the bedroom, the same does not hold for the political arena. There, the public gives up its place and its right to participation at its peril. Thus torturers get away with murder.

The incapacitated spectator plays a major role in what Scarry (27) calls "the conversion of absolute pain into the fiction of absolute power." The spectator, whom she does not mention, is the only one capable of assisting in the conversion of pain to power. Torture is not designed to prove to the *victims* that the regime has the power to exterminate them; that proof is manifested in the act of torture itself. The aim of torture is to prove to the population at large that the regime has the power to control it absolutely. As in *The Camp*, no one can escape the long arm of the victimizer. The terrorist attacks we associate with Middle Eastern violence clearly illustrate that no one is safe from terrorism. As in *The Camp*, scenes of torture and terrorism use the victims as bait, as hostages to incapacitate the wider audience. The public is the intended spectator of this "pathetic drama." And just as torture destroys the victim, it destroys the spectator who has not learned how to react.

Torture works on several levels simultaneously. It annihilates the victim; it destroys the victim's family, sometimes into the next generations; it undermines the immediate community, which, however threatened, is unable to put an end to torture; it affects the larger international community, which, even when not immediately threatened, still feels powerless to put an end to it.

The amplification of torture, by means of which twenty victims can paralyze an entire community or country, functions by means of its theatricality. Confronted with the reality of torture, our tendency as audience, as in traditional theatre, is to identify with the protagonist, the victim. The identification with the victim, however, is both misleading and disempowering. Scarry (29) mentions that torture collapses the world of the victim, as *The Walls* literally depicts. But torture also threatens to reduce the world of the public. People do not like to talk or think about violence; hence, there is less and less that people *can* think about, watch, read, say. As the tour through the house illustrates, there is less and less safe ground. Those in charge of imparting information (like the guard), can squeeze us into ever tighter corners and make us hold our tongues. The equation established by Scarry is that "the prisoner's steadily shrinking ground . . . wins for the torturer his swelling sense of territory" (36); innocent bystanders too make it possible for torture to continue by giving up ground, by not daring to venture into that realm of knowledge. The aim of torture is, according to Peters, to reduce the victim to "powerlessness" (164) and "to transform forced cooperation and broken-willed assent to the principles of the party" (162); this holds true for the *spectator* as well. Torture and terrorism, as those who orchestrated Argentina's Dirty War knew, destabilize the population and make it easier for the government to maintain power by creating "a climate of fear in which subversion would be impossible" (*Nunca Más*, xvii). Moreover, foreign audiences, having turned away from the atrocity, are no longer in any position to understand or combat it. As in the case of the Young Man in *The Walls*, it becomes increasingly difficult to object or react to what one has systematically failed to credit as real, as menacing. The audience sitting in distant lands may not fear the violent intrusion of victimizers into their homes, but they do fear giving up their peace of mind. If they understood that the practice of torture is tied to financial interest, that torturers are not monsters but people who are trained to do what they do, and that the lack of public interest makes atrocious policies possible, the public might have to do something about it or consider itself complicitous. The very existence of torture, whether one openly confronts the practice and its implications or denies them, threatens to undermine one's sense of well-being, one's comfortable moral and ethical principles, one's easy assumptions about human nature and the civilization we live in.

Terrorism deconstructs reality, inverts it, transforms it into a grotesque fiction. Accounts of terrorism show that victimized populations write their own dramas: these "disappeared" people must have moved; they must be someplace—anyplace except in that no-place in which they are being brutalized and assassinated. Torture and terrorism create their own looking-glass world—a real world, even if it does not appear on city maps. Old maps no longer correspond to or guide us through this world. The theatricality of torture and terrorism tempts us to rethink our world, to somehow accept or make room for these performative acts within our canon of the admissible, thus producing normative changes. Torture and terrorism exploit age-old fears with a theatrical flair. Their efficacy depends largely on triggering and manipulating the population's unexamined fears, the racism and sexism, the fear of the dark and dangerous other. In the *Blood Wedding* fragment of *Information*, the traditional theatrical plot flows imperceptibly into terrorism, a "modern" drama. The father tells his child a story, but the narration completely revises the events we see before us. Two men are attacked and abducted. But that's all right, the father explains; they were bad guys, dark, Bolivian, had lots of children; they deserved to be punished by the good guys. The unacceptable (the abduction) becomes not only acceptable but necessary. So too, as another scene shows, a tranquil image can be turned into a terrorist act by reporters. Terrorism, then, is not simply a political perversion. It serves also as a discursive site for terminating discussion and exterminating others: labeling others "terrorists" allows them to be erased without a trace.

The theatricality of terrorism exceeds the practicality of staging atrocious acts. Terrorism functions like a social transformer. It manipulates social fears and inverts cultural symbols. For torture victims, Room 101, Orwell's torture chamber in *1984*, is the worst room in the world: there each victim encounters what he or she fears most profoundly. Torture and terrorism also represent the worst fears of the general public. As the tour through this house illustrates, terrorism plays with potent images of the unknown, the pit, darkness. It capitalizes on infantile fantasies, and the torturers exploit fears of destruction, dismemberment, and suffocation. It works through amplification: twenty victims can hold an entire society hostage. Phantoms loom over a cowering population. The hideous intrusion of children's songs and games in Gambaro's *Information* illustrates how terrorism pushes the population to regress to those early areas of experience that prove most overwhelming and hardest to decode. One approaches as an adult and turns away as a frightened child incapable of action. Cultural concepts and norms enter and come out skewed. The innocent are called enemies. And as I have noted, the transformation is real, not illusory. It actually changes society. The general public does in fact become complicitous and guilty, denying the gruesome reality it knows to be true. The public begins to accuse the victims of disturbing the peace, of fabricating accounts.[40]

Two examples must suffice here. Amnesty International was not allowed to convene at UNESCO's facilities in Paris because its 1973 report on torture reflected unfavorably on some sixty countries then using torture. Rather than blame the perpetrators in an effort to end torture, UNESCO further silenced the victims with its rule that "an outside conference at UNESCO" should not "use material unfavorable to any member state" (Peters, 160). Another case in point concerns Jacobo Timerman, a journalist who was abducted, imprisoned, and tortured by Argentina's military government in 1977, accused both of being subversive (as editor of the newspaper *La Opinión*) and of being a Jew (another example of the strong anti-Semitism in Argentina). While many of the torturers and criminals involved in the Dirty War were never punished, Timerman was severely criticized by reviewers for his book *Prisoner without a Name, Cell without a Number.* "Many reviewers," writes Peters (160-61), "condemned Timerman's treatment outright and unqualifiedly. Others, however, both wrote milder criticism of the regime that tortured Timerman and focused their concern upon Timerman himself, suggesting that he may somehow have invited and perhaps even deserved what in any case was necessary, exceptional and uncharacteristic treatment—in effect, that

Timerman had brought his own troubles, including his own torture, upon himself." The innocent are found guilty; the torturers are acquitted. Light becomes dark, the visible becomes invisible. And we participate in the violence if we fail to see through the manipulations and inversions; if we believe the assertions that everything is under control, that violence is erotic, that the victims actually bring on their victimization, that Latin Americans are violent "by nature," that the torturers are "unnatural" monsters, that crimes just happen as if by magic.

So the theatricality of torture and terrorism, capable of inverting and fictionalizing the world, lies not necessarily in its visibility, but rather in its potential to transform, to recreate, to make the visible invisible, the real unreal. I disagree with Anthony Kubiak's assertion (84) that while anti-state terrorism has performative qualities, "state terrorism (by far the more virulent of the two forms of terrorism) typically relies on the non-theatrical in-visible techniques of torture, clandestine operations, disppearances, and night-time bombing runs." Aside from the fact that night bombings are highly visible, dealing in disappearance and in making the visible invisible is also profoundly theatrical. Only in theatre can the audience believe that those who walk offstage have vanished into limbo. Perhaps the fact that we know what is going on and yet cannot see it makes the entire process more frightening, riveting, and resistant to eradication. As with erotic art, the power lies not in the visible but in the innuendos that exceed vision, that accentuate what we cannot see.

How can an audience avoid participating in violence? As Gambaro's work has shown, there are no easy choices. We can do something about victimization: we can be involved directly (as torturers) or indirectly (as participants) *at the risk of our humanity;* we can pretend it is not happening (like the Young Man in *The Walls*)—or we can reclaim the territory won by victimizers. This involves recuperating everything that criminal societies have taken from us, especially a sense of community and solidarity. In order to *see dangerously,* to look back at the gargoyles without turning into lifeless stones, Gambaro insists that we must see beyond the theatrical frames and decode the fictions about violence, about torturers, about ourselves as audience, about the role of theatre in this "pathetic drama." She develops a dangerous theatre, one that provokes audiences to resent and reject theatrical manipulation, one that shocks and disrupts, that breaks the frames of theatrical traditions in order to make the invisible visible once again. In order to do this, Gambaro draws elements from recognizable traditions. As in Aristotelian drama, the spectators participate vicariously in terrifying deeds. As in Artaud's theatre of cruelty, however, they are not immune to the contagion; the formal and spatial boundaries separating the audience from the action have dissolved. As in Brechtian theatre, the narrative discourse coexists with the dramatic; the Guide functions almost as a narrator, and the episodic plot negates a finished version of the conflict. Like Brecht, Gambaro cautions that mimetic identification with dramatic characters can be disempowering to the audience. But unlike Brecht's work, this play does not submit any coherent, rational political agenda. We walk through a house of ghosts, of the dead and the dying, old forms, old plays, vanished worlds. However, forms do not entirely disappear because they collapse. The memory of these forms, and the world views supporting them, linger in the air like the lost voices. We can remember, if only through art, that other worlds existed.

Gambaro's theatre then, is a theatre of disruption and fragmentation. She pushes theatre to the limits of representation and, some might argue, beyond. Almost like the guerrilla theatre so popular in Latin America during the early 1970s, *Information* "raids" theatrical traditions. Spectators never witness a complete scene; events fail to link up in any coherent or causal way. By interweaving fragments of theatrical scenes with acts of criminal violence, Gambaro indicates the degree to which theatre in Latin America is an arena of intense and dangerous ideological conflict. As Desdemona lies dead, the police burst onstage to arrest Othello. This incident signals more than the failure to accept theatrical convention, more than an ironic reminder that only in drama do the police protect the victims. The policing of theatre, the censorship of scripts, and the harassment of theatre practitioners illustrate that authorities regard theatre as subversive. Radical practitioners, on the other hand, see theatre as one more stage for continuing oppression and cultural colonialism. Desdemona will continue to die on Latin American stages, and Emilia will continue to defend the noble man's right to murder his wife. For others, theatre is (or should be) merely entertainment.

From the understated juxtaposition of two frames in *The Walls* to the bombardment of disrupting and disturbing scenes in *Information*, Gambaro's work develops from a theatre of crisis to a theatre *about* crisis and orchestrated destabilization. As her work progresses, and as the sociopolitical situation in Argentina becomes more clearly defined, the plays that at first depicted irrational decomposition and death give way to those pointing toward the source of the violence and demanding an end to the atrocity. Her work as a whole provides a guide to victimization, from the dramatically "inevitable" annihilation of the Young Man in *The Walls* to the institutionalization of mass murder in *The Camp*; the persecuted Christians whose heroic martyrdom is attested by the catacombs are now the persecutors, the Argentine military that in the name of Christianity precipitates the degrading murders in *Information*. These deaths are no longer aesthetically (or politically) necessary or inevitable; they could have and should have been avoided. And even though the aesthetic rendition of

Desdemona's demise and the tour of the catacombs provide a historic reference to a past in which death was perceived as meaningful, in another sense the observation of that past is ahistorical, a red herring. It diverts our attention from the atrocious present in which teeth are simply recuperable objects and bodies pose the nasty problem of disposal.

As the spectators of *Information* move physically from one room to another, one frame to another, Gambaro leads us from Aristotelian theories of pleasurable and uplifting depictions of terror to the atrocity of the Holocaust and beyond. Robert Skloot in *The Theatre of the Holocaust* (10), asks: "How could these horrifying events occur in one of the most civilized and advanced nations of the world? Why did most of the free world remain aloof to the plight of the Jews and other persecuted minorities. . . . Had we been involved in the events of this time, how would we have behaved?" The point, Gambaro makes clear, is that these questions are not hypothetical. This in no way suggests that the terrorism holding Argentina hostage in the 1970s compared to or was "like" the Holocaust, although John Simpson and Jana Bennett (9) maintain that "what happened in Argentina in the years that followed 1976 was probably closer to what happened in Germany after 1933 than anything else in the Western world during the past four decades." The Holocaust was a unique historical event. It ended, but atrocity and fascism live on; the tactics of terror and the bureaucratic and systematic extermination of countless victims continue today in camps and torture chambers in various Latin American countries. Did any informed person either in Argentina or the United States and other Western countries (the implied "foreigners" of Gambaro's title) *not* know that the Argentine military government terrorized its population from the mid-1970s to the early 1980s? Did any one *not* know that the American government supported the military with economic aid and training? [41] By juxtaposing the catacombs with traditionally theatrical scenes, with torture, with terrorist attacks, Gambaro forces us to relinquish our comforting assumptions about violence, our claims to deniability, innocence, and quietism, and urges us instead try to understand what prompts it and how we participate, either as voyeurs, as investors, as uninterested bystanders, or as victims. In a way, Gambaro's play submits the audience to its own Milgram experiment. Will we continue to follow the Guide and passively participate in the situation? Will we ask for our money back or walk out of the show? As the spectators move from room to room, or turn the pages of the newspaper for "information," the question is being answered. The response is not hypothetical; the play will not allow us to split off. We are involved; as the phrase "information for foreigners" makes clear, *we* are the spectators. Whether we peep through those half-closed doors or glean our information from the newspapers, this is our show. Can we put an end to it? If not, as the Guide says, we might as well enjoy it; we're paying for it.

# 4

# THEATRE AND TRANSCULTURATION: EMILIO CARBALLIDO

READERS of Latin American theatre may be surprised to find a chapter on Emilio Carballido (born 1925 in Mexico) in a study of theatre of crisis.[1] Carballido's plays, especially the two emphasized here—*El día que se soltaron los leones* (*The Day They Let the Lions Loose*, 1957), and *Yo también hablo de la rosa* (*I Too Speak of the Rose*, 1965)—are playful and expansive, calling for elaborate and complicated sets, large casts, bright colors, and music. These plays do not seem to belong to a violent, grotesque world of oppression and crisis. No one overtly torments or tortures anyone else; death comes only to those who deserve it. Compared with much Latin American drama in general and with all the other plays included here in particular, Carballido's theatre seems joyful, almost optimistic. This is no "poor" theatre; there is no call to action associated with "revolutionary" theatre. Nor are Carballido's plays "committed," "popular," or didactic in any straightforward sense. But commentators will be deceived by Carballido's playfulness if they do not recognize that these plays speak to revolution; they are profoundly "popular" as I defined the term in chapter 1; they offer a liberating vision of Mexican culture which evades the tugs of the West and yet resists the temptation to fall back onto some native traditionalism.

Carballido's theatre is deceptively frivolous; it deceives both in style and in subject matter. In part, this is because Carballido openly questions the *efficacy* of didatic theatre. Although he calls *Lions* "a didactic farce . . . with a strong social commitment, a reflection on the 'Third World,'" he asks whether univocal, agitational theatre does more than simply convert the converted (Velez, "Entrevista"). The political impact of his work, he would argue, lies in the breadth of the audience receptive to his work, rather than in the directness of the message itself. In his theatrical production of more than one hundred plays since 1946 he has addressed a wide variety of audiences. He is Mexico's best known and most influential playwright, head of the theatre department at the National University of Veracruz and founder and editor of Mexico's largest theatre journal, *Tramoya*. He has a broad student and intellectual following; he holds regular workshops in playwriting throughout the country; he has the works of young playwrights published and produced yearly in conjunction with the publishing house Editores Mexicanos Unidos. He also has a wide middle-class appeal; he has written theatre for children; and in 1984 he compiled a volume of theatre for workers.

Perhaps a more important reason that commentators have been deceived by Carballido's theatre, however, is that his focus—culture—has been underestimated by Third World theorists and practitioners concerned primarily with Mexico's pressing economic and political problems. Though culture is generally considered important in the context of revolutionary change (as attested by the very concept of "cultural revolution"), people usually think of it as something that happens after the revolution. Carballido, however, recognizes the importance of counterhegemonic cultural activity as *fundamental* to a people's struggle for liberation.[2] He not only examines the role of theatre in a Third World country such as Mexico in which individuals feel oppressed and marginal, obliterated by foreign rulers, policies, ideologies, and art forms; he also points to a way of coming out of the crisis that involves recasting the indigenous self as *central* to Mexico's quest for identity, self-representation, history, and knowledge.

The strategies that Carballido proposes to liberate Mexico from its position as dependent and peripheral vis-à-vis First World powers are not military; they call for neither war nor revolution. Rather, he emphasizes that in spite of its long history of colonization, Mexican culture (and the same holds true for other Latin American cultures) is neither moribund nor a poor imitation of a foreign original. It is an energetic, vital, ongoing activity: the absorption and selection of foreign ideas and influences received through the centuries; the merging of the received cultural material with ideas and world views deriving from its autochthonous traditions; the transformation of this material into an original, creative, culturally specific product. In other words, Carballido goes beyond the binary self/other frame imposed on economically underdeveloped countries by colonization to explore the independent development of a cultural heritage that is tied into but not subservient or inferior to the global cultural development. Using foreign material, he argues, need not be merely derivative borrowing on the part of economically underdeveloped countries but ongoing, intercultural reciprocity. What would Western theatre be without Aristotelian tragedy, Stanislavski's method acting, or the transcultural raids of Artaud and Brecht? By rethinking culture, Mexicans and Latin Americans can rethink their relationship with the dominant powers, for culture "is not a thing . . . but a relationship."[3] Hence, rather than continue to internalize the colonizer and accept the external view of themselves as *inferior others* (let alone the other terms of self-hatred used, as we have seen, by Mexican playwrights such as Usigli and Gorostiza), Mexicans can see their world from their own perspective; they can stop seeing themselves as excentric to their own history, their present, their future.

Carballido's concentration on culture as an arena for ideological debate does not imply that he ignores the very real political and economic problems facing Mexico and Mexicans either in the 1960s or today. Anyone carefully analyzing his work would realize that the social, political, and philosophical questions posed by his plays are as critical and as urgent as those in more apparently serious Latin American drama. The confrontation between individuals and society, for all Carballido's humor, proves as life-threatening in *Lions* or *Rose* as in Triana's *Night of the Assassins* and Wolff's *Paper Flowers*. But by focusing on culture "not only as a way of seeing the world, but also as a way of making and changing it" (Dirlik, 14), Carballido offers other than military solutions in the perennial struggle for liberation. Culture, he proposes, not only participates in systems of domination but can also provide a way out of them. In *The Day They Let the Lions Loose*, Carballido lays bare the network of power structures, institutions, and traditions that oppress individual existence and suppress identity in Mexico. In *I Too Speak of the Rose*, he indicates how rethinking culture and repositioning the indigenous self as central in it can provide strategies to liberate the dominated from the restrictive hegemonic/counterhegemonic binary.

## Cages, Big and Small: *The Day They Let the Lions Loose*

The farcical nature of *Lions* is immediately apparent in Carballido's stage design calling for "painted trees" and lions "played by two actors per lion."[4] The play opens with a dialogue between the Aunt and the Neighbor. The invalid Aunt suffers from "a most unusual pain" that has plagued her since puberty: "It runs up my back, then it grabs me around the shoulders, after that it digs into my joints, and when it goes away for a bit it comes back around my heart!" (7). The Neighbor has left her child tied up, attacked by rats and screaming for liberation, in order to tend to the ailing woman. The Aunt constantly shouts for her sixty-seven-year-old niece Ana, whose position in the household resembles that of a maid rather than a relative. Ana prepares tea, talking to and caressing the cat she keeps without the Aunt's knowledge or consent. The Aunt, fed up with waiting for her tea, enters the kitchen, finds Ana with the cat, and throws the cat out of the house. Ana, after a second's hesitation, leaves the house to look for the cat. Her search takes her to the lake in Chapultepec Park, where she meets the Man, a hungry, outcast poet. Together they capture a swan from the lake and roast it over a fire for breakfast. In another part of Chapultepec Park, the Teacher leads his military cadets through the zoo. While the instructor pauses briefly to chat with his fiancée, the Young Girl, the students throw stones at the animals and engage them in a rock fight. One mischievous student, López Vélez, hits the Young Girl; then, afraid of the Teacher's punishment, he opens the lions' cage and runs away. The lions escape to where Ana and the Man are preparing their meal and frighten them into taking refuge in the trees. The Woman, a widowed housewife who inadvertently stumbles upon the scene, faints when she sees the lions. Ana comes out of hiding and chides the lions for threatening to devour first the roasted swan and then the Woman. The first act ends as Ana, the Man, and the Woman share a meal in the company of the peaceful lions.

In the second act the police and the Teacher begin their pursuit of the lions and, by extension, of Ana, the Man, and the Woman as accomplices, but the fugitives escape to the island in the middle of the lake. In the confusion the Teacher is wounded by police bullets—intended for the lions—and dies.

In the third act, Carballido juxtaposes the confusion of the police activity (sirens, megaphones, searchlights) with the intimate conversations of Ana, the Man, and the Woman, in which they question the pressures, fears, and attitudes that have skewed their lives. The Woman realizes that she has "belonged" to someone all her life—first her parents, then her husband—and that she has never done anything for or by herself. Still, she cannot live without her role as housewife, even when there are no children or husband to take care of, so she decides to go back to her house and the only role she knows. Setting off in a rowboat, she tips into the water and is rescued by the child López Vélez, whose bravery is rewarded with a medal. The police begin their attack on the island. In order to escape, Ana and the Man ride the lions back to the mainland. Hemmed in by police, they run toward the lions' cage. Ana and the lions enter the cage, but the police catch the Man at the door. When he claims to have captured the lions and returned them to their cage, he is rewarded with a job as zoo keeper. Ana opts to live in the cage with the lions, even though she learns from the Neighbor that her Aunt has died and bequeathed her the house. As the play closes, Ana knits a sweater for a baby bear and converses with the Man, who now wears a uniform. She warns him to beware of institutionalization. She screams insults at the military cadets as their new teacher leads them through the zoo.

*Lions* juxtaposes two worlds which, though apparently contradictory and mutually exclusive, are very much the same. The first world is the Aunt's house, a constricted, restrictive domestic prison. Like Triana's characters, Ana is a grownup child, a sixty-seven-year-old woman who has been infantilized and controlled all her life. The oppression she experiences at the hands of her Aunt is not overtly violent, but as Carballido signals throughout, there are different kinds of violence. Some kinds do not look like violence, and some people might argue that they are not. Of the two paradigms of violence I set forth in chapter 1—crisis and oppression—Carballido focuses particularly on the latter, which is at times less easy to identify than the former. The use of language is an example: the Aunt calls Ana "Anita," the diminutive, which in Mexico is usually an affectionate way of addressing a loved one but in this case forms part of the Aunt's exploitation of her niece; it is somewhat akin to calling adult black men "Boy." The power exercised on the body is another. Ana's body is literally shrouded in custom; she has dressed in black mourning since she can remember: "If it isn't one relative, it's another. I wore mourning for six years for my parents; for my sister, three. Aunts, uncles, nephews, and nieces, two years each. Six months for first cousins; and for close friends of the family, three months. I've gotten used to black" (24). She has never understood her body or her sexuality. Like a prepubescent child, she ponders the mysteries of life: "I don't believe people really do all those things." [5] She danced once when she was young and pretty, and even then her Aunt pinched her, hissing that she would get back at her (25). The play also depicts the power and violence associated with censorship, surveillance, and control. Ana has never been allowed to read things of her own choosing, to go where she wanted to, to eat the things she liked; she has never had friends or, until now, a pet. She has suffered violence in the name of love. As the Aunt tells her, "You always kill the thing you love" (31). This, then, is the kind of violence described by Emmanuel Levinas (21): "Violence does not consist so much in injuring and annihilating persons as in interrupting their continuity, making them play roles in which they no longer recognize themselves, making them betray not only commitments but their own substance, making them carry out actions that will destroy every possibility for action." Carballido compares the Aunt's controlling "love" for Ana with the violence of forcing people to accept lifestyles incompatible with their own needs and nature. "Imagine," says the Man to Ana, "giving a farm to a tribe of gypsies, or what's worse, forcing those gypsies to *work* that farm" (30). What could be crueler than pressuring gypsies into settling down to till the soil?

Carballido does not mythify the stifling oppression of Ana's existence by suggesting that freedom and hope reside elsewhere. On the contrary, the second world, the park that Ana flees to, is as repressive as the situation she has tried to leave behind. The park *seems* freer; the trees, the lake, the "early morning light," the mist, the swan going by, "exaggeratedly delicate and poetic—reminiscent of Pavlova and Tchaikovsky" (5). But Carballido warns rather than seduces us through these images. This is no magic realism; the oppression and violence are real enough. Instead of the house, we have Chapultepec Park with its famous gates; instead of the Aunt's *tinaco* or water tank, the artificial cement-lined Chapultepec lake; instead of cats, lions living in a cage.[6] Instead of a censoring Aunt, there is the Teacher telling the youngsters what they can know; instead of Ana's black dress there are the military uniforms of the children. The Neighbor's child is tied up; the schoolchildren are threatened with court martial. So even though the Aunt's home seems more repressive than the magical outdoors, the opposition between oppression and liberty is more complex than a straightforward inside/outside dichotomy. Ultimately, there is little difference between inside and outside, since the characters cannot escape from the social constraints that hamper or work against their needs and their nature. The idea of choice collapses if both options are identical; the possibility of differentiation or individuation is belied by the fact that only a few characters—those who defy the totalizing system—have proper names.

Carballido's depiction of power and oppression indicate that they are not localizable in any one spot, institution, or person. The Aunt, Neighbor, Teacher, police are not individually responsible for the oppression; they *all* are, in conjunction. The power associated with the inside—domesticity, family, home, education, religion, and custom—reinforces and is in turn reinforced by the power of the outside with its educational, scientific, religious, military, and governmental institutions. In this play, Carballido is suggesting something very similar to Foucault's statement: "Power must be analyzed as something which circulates, or rather as something which only functions in the form of a chain. It is never localized here or there, never in anyone's hands. . . . Power is employed and exercised through a net-like organization" (*Power/Knowledge*, 98). But Carballido is not referring to abstract power; he is decoding the particular configuration of forces at work in Mexico.

Set in modern Mexico City, *Lions* evokes centuries of destructive displays of power. The area of Chapultepec, where most of the action takes place, has historically been the scene of brutal confrontation; it indicates not only the sacrifice of the individual in modern Mexico but sacrifice as a persistent theme in Mexican history. Ana and the Man realize that the ground they sit on is "slightly rotten." [7] The ground, the leaves, the air, the water retain the memory of violent, unnatural deaths. The absurd attack by the police on the island that harbors the fugitives, though staged in a highly theatrical, fanciful manner, recalls the Spaniards' siege of the island of Tenochtitlán, approximately on the same spot, in 1521. It recalls the bitter "Battle of Chapultepec" in 1847, when school-aged children—military cadets like the children in Carballido's play—died defending Chapultepec hill from the invading United States army (a statue commemorating the "Boy Heroes" stands in the park today). Moreover, Chapultepec Castle, overlooking the park, symbolizes the French domination of Mexico, inhabited as it was by the French-appointed imperial couple, Maximilian and Carlota, in 1864.

The domination of Ana by her Aunt and the violence suffered by the Neighbor's child do not constitute isolated acts of silencing and annihilation; rather, they indicate the perennial sacrifice of individuals trapped in a violent history. Yet this history is justified in the name of future rewards. Ana recalls her mother's saying before she died in 1899 that the "twentieth century was going to be marvellous!" (29). The Aunt justifies exploiting her niece by telling her that a "young girl's future is simply charged with promises" (31), and after all, she will inherit the house. The Man clings to the belief that his present hunger and misfortune somehow make sense in the cosmic order of things: "There are millions of people who sacrifice everything, and carefully construct the future of mankind, which others will enjoy two hundred years from now" (38). In pre-Hispanic times the shedding of human blood was considered necessary to keep the universe functioning by ensuring that the god Huitzilopchtli would have the strength to conquer the stars and usher in the new day. In present-day Mexico, where the government's austerity programs rest exclusively on the backs of the middle and poor classes, the notion of sacrifice expands to keep the many suffering to protect the few.

But power does not simply lie in the hands of the few; it is supported by ideologies. In this play, Carballido clearly refers to the positivist and evolutionary theories that have shaped Mexican thought since the end of the nineteenth century. His portrayal of the Teacher parodies the *científicos* or "scientists" under Porfirio Díaz, who argued that social institutions were fundamental in obtaining and maintaining the social order needed for progress.[8] Like the positivists in general, the Teacher emphasizes the importance of education by dutifully drilling his pupils. He echoes the belief in evolutionary (rather than revolutionary) change, in rationality, in social progress: "The zoological scale is perfectly graduated and it ends with the rational animals—men" (14). The irony, of course, is that the education he imparts to his pupils is not the kind that broadens their intellectual scope and sharpens their critical awareness. On the contrary, he insists that there is only one right answer to every question—his. When a student offers another answer, one given him by his father, the Teacher responds: "Would you kindly tell your father that he's talking nonsense" (15). He has the correct words to supplant the children's faulty vocabulary, preferably in Latin or Greek. And though he speaks of an evolutionary, zoological scale, it is clearly a finite, totalizing system; it ends with "man."

It becomes increasingly clear that this "scientific" education serves to elevate the foreign over the local and the "cultured" over the "primitive" in a manner characteristic of colonialism. It controls the children by objectifying and reducing them to dots on an evolutionary scale; further, it consolidates a political system based on centralized knowledge and surveillance of the population. "You are a homo sapiens," the Teacher tells his pupil, "a mammiferous vertibrate. The particular facts of your life are on file in the civil register and the archives of the school. At this moment you are undergoing a process of domestication but you will be locked up in a cage at the first sign of bestiality" (14). Knowledge is certainly power, not the knowledge ostensibly being passed from Teacher to pupil but the real political power exerted by identifying, locating, classifying, and "domesticating" a population. It is a process that objectifies the individual, and although it differs radically from the persecution analyzed by Griselda Gambaro's work, this too is the antithesis of individuation. It is an education that empowers the political system rather than the individual. The Teacher notes that "the more people know, the harder it is to control them. . . . The ideal system would be: nobody learns things they don't have to know."[9]

The education imposed by the Teacher is not only alien to the children's backgrounds but hostile to it. The extent to which positivist thinking has molded modern Mexican thought (more fully developed by Carballido in *Rose*) can be briefly summed up here. By basing itself on "scientific" and, more specifically, biological premises, positivism can treat racial and sexual prejudices as fact. The effects of Darwinism and theories of natural selection in Latin America, Harold Davis explains in his *Latin American Thought* (104), led to the development of theories of superior races: "The superior 'race' was often thought of as Portuguese or Spanish." Given the fact that 80 percent of Mexico's population is of mixed race, predominantly a mixture of indigenous and Hispanic peoples, the results of these theories on the nation's population are devastating. Moreover, combined with the *malinchismo* I noted in chapter 1, whereby racial self-hatred is conflated with a hatred of women (symbolized by Cortés's lover/translator Malinche), these racial theories have particularly damaging effects on the female population—doubly despised as women and as *mestizas*. When Carballido, in *Rose,* centers Mexican self-knowledge and identity in the person of a *mestizo* woman, a *mujer de pueblo,* he is fighting the sexism and racism pseudoscientifically grounded in the positivist theories.

Positivist theories also intensified the Mexican feeling of inferiority in other areas, specifically politics and economy. Positivism emphasizes institutions as central to social development and progress. The Teacher inanely confesses to his girlfriend: "It's nice working for an institution like this. Everything one could need—and discipline to boot! " (16). However, as Davis points out, the "Latin American sense of political inferiority" derives "from the failure to develop institutions of constitutional democratic government"; he concludes that a "sense of failure to achieve the economic prosperity promised by independence leaders increased the poignancy of political failure" (104-5). The theories offered by positivism, as applied in Latin America, legitimated conservative, elitist policies, the "evolutionary" rather than "revolutionary" answers to political, social, and economic problems.

It is important to indicate that Carballido also recognizes the dangers of the seductive, "positive" aspects of power, not just of its negative and oppressive ones. As Foucault notes in *Power/Knowledge* (59), "Power would be a fragile thing if its only function were to repress, if it worked only through the mode of censorship, exclusion, blockage and repression . . . exercising itself only in a negative way." The "knowledge" generated by the *científicos* in Mexico is a product of and in turn reproduces systems of power. The arts too, Carballido points out, function largely to celebrate power. In *Lions,* the tune the Man whistles changes from an expression of spontaneity and liberty when it becomes the background music for the "Intermission with Music," which in turn (and without interruption) flows directly into the "music of persecution" that opens Act 2[10] and intensifies into the "Prelude to the Nautical Battle" in Act 3 (41). Likewise, the lions' dance of liberty in Act 1 evolves into the dance between the Man and the Woman in Act 2, and later the police dance as they circle in on their fugitives. The persecution scene closes triumphantly with the "March of the Captured Lions" (44). (The representation of dramatic conflict through dance echos pre-Hispanic forms, the combined spectacle made up of dance, song, and representation.) Poetry, too, has been co-opted. As the Man relates, he himself is a poet who composed verses for the September 15 independence celebrations, yet he distinguishes himself from the "immortal bards" who serve another purpose, metamorphosed as they are into public figures, frozen as objects in the famous busts that line the Avenue of the Poets in Chapultepec Park. Finally, photography, as Carballido represents it, has ceased being an art form altogether and merely serves as an instrument of state disinformation. A newspaper photographer who covers the confrontation between the authorities and society's "bestial" elements (Ana, the Man, the lions) photographs the Teacher's corpse, and the official version of the Teacher's death—summed up in the caption to the photograph—demonstrates the complicity of art and power: although the bullet wounds suggest otherwise, the Chief, the Policeman, and the Photographer concur: "He was killed by the lions" (35).

Perhaps the appealing aspects of power are ultimately more dangerous than the oppressive ones. Fame and glory are seductive. The Man quotes one of the immortal poets, boasting of "certain birds that can cross the swamp and never soil their feathers" (11), but he is not one of them. At the end of the play he locks himself out of the natural cycle by trying to cash in on the economically and spiritually bankrupt system. Wearing a uniform, he waits for the authorities to honor their promise of a salary and prize money. He confesses to Ana: "I used to feel the seasons change in my veins—but not any longer" (46). Ana, through the bars of her cage, gently warns him to "beware" (45). The same seduction of heroism wins the young boy, López Vélez, back to the system. He alone was capable of defying the Teacher, but he becomes submissive under the glory showered on him for rescuing the Woman from drowning. Even though the Woman was not in fact in danger of her life, the young boy is photographed and turned into a *Niño Heroe* like the ones already honored in the park. The irony is not only that concepts of "heroism" and "honor" are now as worn and worthless as the Man's uniform but that one of the few named characters loses his name, becoming an anonymous, albeit prestigious, Boy Hero.

The world that Carballido depicts in *Lions* is the same lethal world I explore throughout this study. Like Buenaventura's inferno and Gambaro's terrorized state, this world also offers its members two choices, death or oppression—which, of course, is no choice, since choosing the first precludes life altogether and the second also leads to annihilation. For Carballido the problem lies in the contradiction that power systems can be seductive, fraudulent, corrupting, oppressive, and lethal, yet people cannot find "truth" and "reality" or sustain a viable existence outside them. Life in a cage, shouting insults at children "so they'll learn" (46), hardly seems the answer to Mexico's problems. And Ana's appeals to justice in some nebulous future—"One of these days you'll all be in cages while we lions run around loose, roaring through the streets"—only reactivate the utopian solutions that we have seen fail throughout the course of the play. Her inability to come up with a different response only accentuates the lack of real options, the absence of viable, life-affirming spaces. These are felt only as absence, as lack, in the totalizing structure. What I believe Carballido is saying about power, truth, reality, and self-determination is that they cannot be understood as lying outside or beyond the realms of social systems; it is within social systems on all their many levels that these issues must be fought out. There is no elsewhere, no outside, no beyond, no place free of political exigencies where truth and freedom can be found. Again, this is an idea that was later theorized by Foucault: "Truth isn't outside power, or lacking in power . . . truth isn't the reward of free spirits, the child of protracted solitude, nor the privilege of those who have liberated themselves. . . . Truth is a thing of this world" (*Power/Knowledge*, 131). The hope, then, lies not in Ana's distant "one day" but precisely in the title, "the day they let the lions loose." On that day Ana chose an authentic (and thus liberating) action over her previous acts of subjugation, thereby rupturing her restrictive world: she said no to her Aunt, recognizing that "I've lost so much always saying yes" (39). For Ana, that day becomes important not in historic terms but within her personal context. The oppressed must change their position within the system, even if that means becoming marginals, like Ana. We are all involved in the network of power—not just the police, the government officials, the Teacher but also the oppressed themselves. As Ana finally realizes, she has allowed herself to be used: "Right now I feel responsible for everything" (39). The Man says, "We're all of us responsible for our parents, our relatives, and our leaders" (39). Aunts, governments, bosses, theories—"they're all surgeons, butchers, amputating parts of our bodies, our minds, our actions."[11]

In *Lions*, Carballido only indirectly points to what will become the dominant theme of *Rose:* the epistemic grids determining the relationship between the world and the consciousness perceiving it. The dialogues between Ana and the Man pose epistemological questions about knowing in "totalities" of holistic thinking as opposed to knowing in parts or "details" (31) of pluralistic thought. The fashion in which the characters present the subject is straightforward. Ana believes that the "natural" way of perceiving experience lies in pluralistic thought, knowing in parts. The lions, like all cats, Ana tells the Man, "look at me as a combination of smells and sizes and feelings." Her cat, she says, "used to look at me in little bits, never all at once" (31). The Man claims that humans also know in parts. The multiple perspectives, however, never add up to any knowable, totalizable whole. Those who claim to know it all and submit, as the Teacher does, that "everything is known" (15) are in fact supporting totalizing structures and, as in this case, authoritarian institutions. Carballido here, and more directly in his depiction of orality in *Rose*, seems to propose the opposite of Claude Lévi-Strauss's "the savage mind totalizes"

(*The Savage Mind*, 245) or Walter Ong's more polite "the oral mind total-izes" (175). For Carballido, the officials representing government and educational institutions are the ones who impose totalizing world views. This totalizing, from Carballido's perspective, characterizes hegemonic thought more than it does the so-called primitivism of savages (whether felines or semiliterate populations). Neither the animals nor the Poet nor Ana herself thinks in terms of totalities.

There are two points worth noting in regard to Carballido's epis-temology, one political, one philosophical. Totalizing or universalizing is not only a hegemonic practice but is key to maintaining the hegemonic culture as central, as exemplary, as the model to be emulated. In order to escape Western hegemony, Carballido proposes a nonhegemonic approach to cultural activity. His aim is not to fight hegemonic practices by replacing one universalizing system with another but to find a way of thinking that does not ape or parody Western thought. Hence, he proposes that people know in parts, which make up a plurality of experiences that will forever elude closure or finality. Throughout *Lions*, he progresses from the par-ticular (Ana, cat, cage) to the social (oppression); in this way he combats the hegemonic propensity of "imposing universals of whatever kind upon the particular" (Dirlik, 50). Moreover, I think Carballido's philosophical as well as political views reflect the inductive method: no matter what the Teacher claims, we cannot know everything, we do not have answers to all questions. Even the Teacher, as he lies dying, admits that his theories did not prepare him for life's many mysteries: "I don't understand anything. Everything seems so strange" (28). *Lions* points to an infinitely more complex concept of existence than any theory or perspective can compre-hend, to dimensions of reality which, as the Medium warns us later in *Rose*, "we cannot even begin to suspect." A totalizing approach to thought, like the discourse that maintains it, tries to absorb and classify knowledge to sustain itself. The attempt to reduce the infinite to the finite explains not only the intellectual subjugation we see throughout the play but also the distortion of reality required to support the fictitious framework. Car-ballido humorously underlines the arrogance of, and ultimately the danger posed by, those who pretend to understand existence "in totality" and maintain that "everything that happens in the world is clear and intelligi-ble" (15).

## *I Too Speak of the Rose:* A Discourse on Discourse

Carballido's *I Too Speak of the Rose* (1965) probes the role of theatre, in itself a cultural activity and an instrument of communication, in a totalizing political system. Theatre, as Austin E. Quigley points out in *The Modern*

*Stage and Other Worlds* (53), "invites audiences not just to receive entertainment and instruction but to participate in an inquiry that questions both what we know and how we know it—an inquiry that also helps us recognize the complex dependence of our knowledge on our ways of knowing both in the world of the theatre and in the worlds beyond it." *Rose* focuses on the convergence of different, and changing, modes of perception. Carballido is not interested so much in events (plot) as in the discourses that shape those events and endow them with meaning.

*Rose* opens with a peasant woman, the Medium, sitting downstage center, talking in a quiet, introspective voice about knowledge. Her opening speech establishes that she is a *mestiza*, physically and ideologically a mix of indigenous and Spanish elements. She speaks Spanish, but her language conveys the poetic accumulation of images and the repetitive singsong quality of oral languages that rely on poetic devices for recalling information. Her particular use of Spanish, then, bespeaks the coexistence of another language alive within it; it is an odd, poetic bilingualism that simultaneously transmits two cultural codes. She retains oral sources of knowledge; she remembers stories handed down to her by word of mouth. But her oral knowledge is mixed with her knowledge of books and texts; both traditions come together in her, and her heart, that potent "central ventrical" (47), commingles them and pumps new life throughout the complex, hybrid organism. Her imagery identifies her as a Mexican from Mexico City: old Tenochtitlán. The allusions she makes to the city's pre-Columbian network of channels also describes modern Mexico City with its intricate freeways and *vías*. Only after she locates herself within an oral network of communication whereby she receives, stores, contemplates, and transmits information does Carballido proceed with the action.

The events, in fact, are minimal. Throughout the play only one thing happens: two lower-class children (Polo, aged twelve, and Toña, fourteen), who are playing in a garbage dump, derail a passing train. The antecedents as well are few. Polo is not in school because he does not have any shoes, and his mother cannot afford to buy them until the following week; children are not allowed into his classroom without shoes. Toña has decided not to go to school because she has not done her homework. They tamper with the public telephones looking for change; they flip the coins they find with a candy vendor, lose the coins, win them back, buy some candy, and give a few pennies to a passing vagrant. They meet their friend Maximino, who offers them money for school, but they turn it down to play by the dump: "We might find something. You can see the train go by" (49). The children dance around, joke, and pick things up. One of the things they find is a tub full of cement, used and discarded by some builders. On impulse, they roll the tub onto the tracks as the train approaches. The stage lights flash frantically as the audience hears a thundering crash. The lights go out, and in a second we hear the newsboy running through the theatre, crying out the headlines.

The newsboy reappears several times as the headlines change, alternately casting the children as vagrants, as schizophrenics, as proletarians. Throughout, the play juxtaposes interpretations of the crash, offering only a few hints regarding the fate of the characters. After the derailment, the terrified children stay where they are; the police take them to jail, where Polo's mother visits him and Maximino visits Toña. The play suggests that Maximino and Toña become romantically attached. At the end, the Medium asks us enigmatically: "Do you know how Polo came to own his own garage? And what Toña's marriage was like? . . . that's another story." [12]

The rest of the twenty-one scenes focus on the process and significance of interpretation, on the construction of meaning, on discourses. Four times, beginning with the first scene and ending with the last, the Medium speaks about knowledge and ways of knowing. The play's twenty-eight characters comment on the derailment in scattered scenes. Toña and Polo's school Teacher refers to her pupils as truants and blames their parents. The university students applaud what they view as an anarchistic act. The Emcee discusses three representations of the rose—the petal, the whole flower, and the microscopic fiber—and asks the audience to identify the "correct" image of the rose.

Carballido's *Rose* undertakes an examination of various discourses in relation to the various world views they propose. Like the rose of the title, which Carballido depicts as a complicated and interconnected conglomeration, inextricable from (and inconceivable without) its multiple parts (stalk, petals, fibers), the play is made up of numerous yet irreducible viewpoints and interpretations. Each ties into the creation of a new subject. Like the Emcee (or Locutor) who playfully separates the rose into three isolated images or "parts"—the rosebud, the petal, the microscopic view of the petal's tissue—the end product or composition of the subject matter under discussion is in part shaped by the discursive enunciation of it. We might well ask, looking at the Emcee's three illustrations, whether in fact we are looking at the same subject matter at all. The way the question is framed in a sense determines what we see and, hence, the "answer."

Because *Rose* raises so many issues, many of which exceed the scope of my particular analysis, it may be helpful to indicate what I am looking at. First, I examine the several interpretations and what they say about the speakers/knowers and about their relationship to the known and to their world. Then I focus on the politics and power of the various discourses in

structuring and legitimating world views, in defining culture, in privileging perspectives, in imposing distinctions between the so-called First
World producers of culture and cultural products and Third World impor-
ters, "imitators," and recipients of theories. Last, I signal the extent to
which these distinctions are misleading, not so much because they are
wrong as because they are reductive. Instead of a simple, one-directional
process by which dependent countries "import" cultural *products* (that is,
static objects) from First World nations, Carballido shows the ongoing,
vital activity of transculturation. Unlike the Emcee, I do not suggest that
we choose or privilege one view, dismissing all others as "false." On the
contrary, the artificial rupture of the multifaceted into isolated parts only
proves that no one of them can exist in isolation. While *Lions* calls attention
to false totalities, *Rose* cautions against radical separations. In both, Carballido suggests that the multiple parts coexist and together give a far more
complete outlook on reality. The microscopic closeup of the tissue is
unrecognizable as a rose. And who, as the Emcee himself suggests, can
conceive of a rose without its petals?

First, then, I turn to the various epistemic grids presented in *Rose*, the
"what we know and how we know it" (as posited by Quigley). The
differences in perception, culminating in the play's conflicting interpretations, is the aspect most studied by the various commentators. Sandra
Cypess has studied the patterns of "male" and "female" discourse in *Rose*,
emphasizing the relationship between power and discursive practice in a
patriarchal society such as Mexico ("I, Too, Speak," 45). For George
Woodyard (1976, quoted by R.A. Kerr, 57), the Medium, the play's central
figure, "is always the link between the rational and the irrational." However, an important dimension that has not been discussed, which I think is
fundamental to our understanding of the cultural specificity and the
political repercussions of the play, involves the distinct discursive and
perceptual modes stemming from different epistemic grids—orality and
literacy. Carballido presents a double confrontation of the literate and oral
spheres. The two first come together *horizontally* in the original conquest
and colonization of Mexico, when the literate, foreign culture imposed
itself on the oral, indigenous one. Here, we can see the impact of one
culture on another as an example of transculturation whereby cultural
material passes from one society to another. However, Carballido also
presents the confrontation *vertically*, as the literate culture cements its
domination to produce a stratified society in which the lower classes are
either semiliterate or illiterate.[13]

In *Rose*, Carballido explicitly links discourse to perception: we talk
about what we know, and what we know depends to a large extent on our
experience within language. In opposition to the play's two professors,

who use Cartesian logic to expound European theories of consciousness and being-in-the-world, Carballido presents the Medium, wearing a rebozo "like a peasant woman" and telling story after story. The philosophical schools that shape the professors' perception and the literacy that maintains it do not by and large form the traditions within which most Mexicans have lived and, to different degrees, continue to live. In a country like Mexico, characterized by the coexistence of literate and primary oral cultures, consciousness and discourse change according to how people receive, store, and transmit information and knowledge.[14] As the play begins, the audience, sitting in almost total darkness, listens to the Medium relating the things she knows: "I know many things!" She receives information and transmits it; knowledge is a fluid, ongoing, reciprocal exchange. She compares knowledge to her heart, which pumps blood through channels, each somehow connected to another. As she narrates what she knows—herbs, faces, crowds, rocks, books, pages, illusions, roads, events—it becomes clear that her source is the collective, orally transmitted knowledge handed down from generation to generation. The Medium gives special importance to the two major kinds of messages, news and interpretation, that Jan Vansina, in *Oral Tradition as History*, considers central to oral transmission. The Medium passes on "news," a word that she shouts out at the end of her first monologue, ushering in the thunderous crash of the train accident. The word "news" also introduces the newsboy shouting the headlines immediately following the crash. But while she is directly tied into the immediate, sensational world of "news," the Medium is far more concerned with the interpretation and meaning of the events she transmits. Following her opening monologue, the sound of the crash, and the newsboy's shouts, the play proceeds with the scene leading up to the derailment of the train and the multiple interpretations that follow.

The play flashes a series of interpretations past the audience, only a few of which can briefly be summed up here. For the Freudian professor (55-57), the derailment is symptomatic of the children's repressed sexuality, which culminates in destructive impulses. A psychologist's job, he says, is one of decoding the unconscious in order to render it conscious: "It is our duty to make the patient aware of them [traumatic nuclei] and thus guide him until he discovers for himself the secret reasons which lie hidden behind his impulses, the unconscious controls, the frustration of our acts, very much in the manner of some sort of explicit formulation. . . . Let us take, for example, this terrible act, difficult to understand, when one tries to explain it as a conscious and rational deed. Two adolescents derail a train. Well, it just so happens that there are certain antecedent factors which will permit us to explain concretely the hidden,

submerged impulses. . . . we will see how the *whole* matter becomes
logical and coherent." He then steps aside as the children act through their
original scenario again, but this time according to his direction. "Now," he
tells the audience as the children speak new words only vaguely similar to
their original dialogue, "I want you to observe the symbolic content of that
phrase." The entire scene changes, including the dump and the garbage.
As the stage directions indicate, "now in the various plants and objects are
distinct sexual configurations. . . . Polo picks up the broken piece of the
engine. It now has a very suspicious shape." While the children push the
tub of cement onto the railroad tracks, the Freudian has them chanting.

Polo:    Incest! Libido! Maximino!
Toña:    Defloration! Maximino! Father!
Polo and Toña: Womb! Jealousy! Crime!

The psychologist concludes his presentation with a self-satisfied "Psychology! Whenever a man's conduct appears to be inexplicable . . . psychology will lay it bare!"

For the Marxist professor (57), the act bespeaks the "extreme results"
of extreme economic contradictions: "We are all of us witnesses of the
event commented upon so extensively in the press. It is without any
question a clear expression of class struggle. Protagonists: two children of
the proletariat." He too directs the entire scene again. He emphasizes that
the children are not in school, that they are undernourished, badly
dressed, barefoot victims of all the social ills "typical" of "underdeveloped
countries." The "answer" to the children's almost hopeless predicament,
for the Marxist, lies in their hero worship of their friend and role model
Maximino, "an authentic representative of his class: exploited, socially
responsible, self-sacrificing, incorruptible, fraternal, vigorous, alert. By
his example, he plants within these children the highest ideals and principles." This too, however, involves an act of decoding; Maximino's face is
frozen in ideology and in his "expression the children can read his disap-
pointment at how corrupt syndicalism has betrayed the workers to the
power of capitalism." As the children push the tub of cement onto the
tracks, the Marxist has them declaiming.

Polo:    Fear is the springboard of all revolutions.
Toña:    One must fell a certain number of trees in order to preserve the forest.

For the university students reading the newspaper, the derailment
constitutes a gratuitous, anarchistic, and hence "inspired" act. For the
Señor and Señora waiting for the bus (52), the derailment only substanti-

ates what they think already: "Little savages, that's what they are. All of them. They're all a bunch of savages." This *malinchismo* or self-hatred substitutes for any insightful social critique. After concluding that "these people are criminal from the day they are born" and that they look forty years old, the Señor and Señora dismiss the children as barbaric and misery as "awful." They are more interested in the grisly and sensational news of a "trunk murder." For Polo's schoolteacher (52), the crime is due to "idleness," "stupidity," and "lack of civil spirit." For the owner of the train, the vandalism represents a loss of five million pesos. For Polo's mother, the whole thing is the fault of the father's alcoholism, child beating, and irresponsibility. For Toña's mother (54), the death of Toña's father is the cause of her actions. The derailment itself and the children's role in it are completely incomprehensible to her; it is all an economic nightmare: "I mean, why would they keep her locked up? Fat chance she'll ever pay for that train." And upon hearing that Toña *is* locked up, presumably "to keep her from doing it again," the mother responds, "As if she were going to go around derailing trains."[15] For the hungry scavengers who pick up food from the overturned train, the accident is a miracle of good fortune. All these perspectives fit together like petals on a rose, orchestrated by Carballido's other central image, the beating heart. There are no breaks in the action; the scenes pulse by the audience at a rhythmic pace.

In terms of time and staging devices, however, three perspectives claim preeminence. They are juxtaposed as three perceptual hypotheses during the Emcee's game show, and they correspond to the epistemic positions of the Freudian, the Marxist, and the Medium respectively. For the professor of psychology only the individual, the petal, matters. For the professor of economy only the collective totality, the rose, has significance. The Medium's "interpretation" (if we can even call it that) defies all pretense of objectivity: the children, she says, turn into "everything that surrounds them: they *become* the dump, the flowers, the clouds, amazement, joy. . . . and they understand. . . . they see! That's what happened" (60). But the play not only depicts different modes of perception in isolation and conjunction; it also refers us to the sources and traditions that make such modes of perception possible, and it points to the sociopolitical implications of the different positions.

The Medium's knowledge, we come to understand, represents a mode of perception different in kind and origin from the "scientific," objective knowledge posited by the professors. Her epistemological framework is primarily oral. Much of what she knows springs from an unwritten tradition, conserved by memory and passed on by word of mouth: "I also retain memories, memories which once belonged to my grandmother, my mother or my friends. . . . many of which they, in turn, heard from friends and old, old people" (47).[16] Yet she is a transcultured being, a hybrid of two cultural traditions. She also knows books and pages "in the style of Dürer, or of certain botanical and zoological illustrations of the German school of the nineteenth century, or of any old Mexican codices—perhaps all three" (51). Her mixture of orality and borderline literacy is a product of the history of conquest, and in turn it produces and feeds into a wide social network of cultural *mestizaje* (or hybridization), establishing her central position in it as much as literacy shapes that of the professors.

The play's most immediate distinction between oral and literate cultures lies in the relationship between knower and objects of knowledge. The Medium's knowledge cannot be called "objective"—empirically verifiable or *out there* in the world, outside or disconnected from herself as knower. Unlike the professors with their methodological and causal framework, she does not aspire to the Cartesian ideal of objectivity. From her first line in her first speech, the Medium approaches knowledge reflexively, comparing it to her heart, which, with its "canals that flow back and forth" (47), connects her with the rest of the world. As the fluidity of her speech shows, her way of knowing is anything but isolating or reductive; each idea opens a way to another, defying the possibility of conclusion. Her thinking progresses not systematically or linearly but rather through association; hence, she is incapable of interpretation in its strictest sense of formulating facts, ideas, impressions into a systematic whole.[17] She receives information; she contemplates and assimilates it; she stores knowledge in her memory; she comments on it and transmits it verbally.

Because she is not separate from what she knows, she is a subject, not an object, in a world of other subjects. The professors' way of knowing is eccentric in that they stand outside and removed from the source of their knowledge and information, which now in the literate society lies out there, in books and newspapers. Writing stores knowledge, and people write books in isolation. In contrast, we witness in the Medium's role the supreme importance of the speaker in an oral culture: if either the speaker or the audience is not present, there is no communication. Knowledge, kept alive by storytelling, avoids the dangers of reification. It is always fresh, its relevance assured by the presence of the speaker and the audience. If the subject were not of interest, they would not be listening. The physical presence of the professors is gratuitous in that they only read or speak what has already been prepared in writing. Individual scholars do not have to be together with their readers in order for the material to be communicated. They maintain a peripheral, alienated position in both the acquisition and transmission of their knowledge.

It is important to recognize the degree to which individuals' experience of themselves as knowing subjects or, conversely, as known objects, affects their experience of the world. Marx used the term "alienation" to describe the plight of the individual as subject in an objective and objectifying system. Alienation, then, is not an existential given but a product of the relationship between knower and known. Freud's theories challenge the individual's capacity to know, particularly to know her- or himself. He divides experience into several psychic structures—id, ego, superego— with unconscious and often unknowable links between them. The way we know affects the way we are. It need not surprise us that terms like the "divided self" and "alienation" have become commonplace in the twentieth century. The separation between knower and known, coupled with the inordinate value granted to the known over the knower, changes and reduces and fragments human experience. What Donald M. Lowe points out in *History of Bourgeois Perception* (105) about a bourgeois, literate society becomes even more acute in the era of rapidly advancing technology: "Being-in-the-world, under the pressure of visuality and objective reason, divided and turned in upon itself. Bourgeois society was highly compartmentalized; thus the articulation of the self took place in all the many spaces and times of that world. However, there was always more of the self than what could be realized in all those compartmentalized experiences. As a result, the person was disembodied into mind, body, emotion and sexuality. Each was a part of the person; but together they did not constitute a whole being."

Ironically, then, while literacy allows us to know more as well as more accurately, with greater abstraction and sophistication, it simultaneously widens the gap between knower and known.[18] The professors see the children as alienated, estranged from their "true" libidinal or proletarian "reality." But I maintain that Toña and Polo, chosen to illustrate theories, are frozen into the Sartrean "being-as-object"—alienated not in their lived experience as the professors argue but in the very act of "being-looked-at" (Sartre, *Being*, 344, 353). Discourse creates its own reality in the very act of framing the subject matter. This is not to suggest that the professors do not offer important readings of the situation. As Toña's crush on Maximino shows us, her adolescent sexual fantasies are revved up (to echo the Freudian professor's motorcycle analogy). And no one would dispute or underemphasize the poverty or the educational, economic, and social disadvantage of these children. However, the children are neither "neurotic" nor "alienated." They would not recognize themselves or what occurred at the dump in the professors' representations any more than they recognize themselves in the mug shots that make them look like forty-year-old hardened criminals. The problem arises because each professor, in his own way, "universalizes the self-conscious dissolution of the bourgeois subject" (Sangari, 157), creating an idiosyncratic reality and a meaning more in keeping with their society than with the children's situation. Hence, the political repercussions of discursive framing are multiple and long-term: the intellectuals, represented here as professors of psychology and economy, are alienated from the situation they are supposed to illuminate. Their alienation results in their distortion of reality, a misrepresentation of themselves and others that justifies or complies with oppression. As Edward Said (25) notes, the rift between intellectuals and society can result in "the regulated, not to say calculated, irrelevance of criticism." Yet the irrelevance of discourses does not mean they are dismissible or *benign*. They contribute to the marginalization and objectification of their subject—in this case the children. The ministers of education, Carballido makes clear enough in *Lions* and *Rose,* can intellectualize and legitimize hegemony.

The fact that reality—even the professors' so-called "objective" reality—is idiosyncratic indicates that all realities, as constructs, are in some way a product of our way of knowing, even when we become victims in our objectifying system. While the professors speak as if there were one "Truth" (a different one for each, of course) and claim "objectivity" in analyzing it, the play repeatedly reminds us to beware of the very idea of objectivity. The concept describes a particular system of human interactions both with others and with the world around them—but that system, like all others, changes and evolves. There is not one truth but many, with many centers. The newspapers reflect the changing perception of reality in a literate culture; the notion of objectivity quickly disappears. Even though the words on the paper are forever fixed—"objects" imbued with a certain authority because they are there, on the page—the many versions, each claiming truth, one replacing another in rapid succession, show the plurality of experience. The problem with written words is that they can outlive their context; they can become wrong, not in themselves but when they no longer speak to lived experience.

The Medium's perspective, in contrast with the professors', allows for change. The Freudian professor speaks of the children's "hidden guilt and desires for self-punishment" (55), which ultimately could be used to explain or justify whatever violent things befall them. Who can argue with self-destruction? (Then, of course, we remember that they are children in the hands of the Mexican police.) He compares the dump to human nature: "I don't believe that it is necessary to point out that by nature there exists within each and every one of us a veritable garbage dump!" (56). Again, who can argue with nature? The Marxist professor is also totalizing and essentialist: he says that "man is Economy. . . . There is nothing inexplicable in this act. It is typical of its class" (57).[19] The Medium's explanation, however enigmatic or inadequate, includes the vital concept of change: the children were *turning into* everything around them, they *became* part of it all. Her interpretation may elude us, but therein lies its power. The professors fix and objectify the children; they use them as examples to show the profundity of their thought and the strength of their theories and tradition. But as long as the children can evade being "classified" on a psychological, economic, or zoological scale, they maintain their identity as living subjects, active players in their continuing *historia*—as story, as history.

The Medium's subjective or reflexive relationship to knowledge, as opposed to the professors' "objective" approach, poses a question of sources of knowledge as well. The authority substantiating the Medium's position stems primarily from an internalized oral tradition, while the professors rely on external material: ongoing research and book learning. This does not imply that the Medium (any more than the professors) represents the original sources of knowledge. She, as Medium (mediator), functions as a vehicle or channel (*vía*) of thought as much as they. Her source does differ, however; her information is founded in collective wisdom, old wives' tales, "common knowledge" handed down through the generations.[20] The information passed on by the professors has individual sources, as demonstrated by the very terms "Freudian" psychologist and "Marxist" economist. The Medium's knowledge is unspecialized, though broader in scope. While she knows "books, pages, illusions," she also understands little-known aspects of popular culture such as herbal healing. Unfettered by the limitations of objectivity, she freely moves in realms of belief—the healer's "cure" or *limpia*, for example—that scientific thought would discard as manifestations of the occult or magic. This freedom, in turn, animates the world and the universe, which she approaches anagogically, through the mystical reading of signs that only superficially resembles literacy: "They are looking at signs like children learning the alphabet. They are looking at arrows that point out directions, paths. They are searching for crossroad signs,"(60). I say "superficially" because the signs-as-signifiers do not correspond to specific sounds or objects. The children are free to interpret them as they like.

Faced with such radically diverse world views and ontologies, our awareness of the implications of the differences in perception becomes key. It is not a question of choosing between perceptions, as the Emcee proposes, or privileging orality over literacy. The point is not to add the widespread misrepresentation or mystification of Third World subjects. Rather, it becomes critical to understand how our experience changes according to what and how we know, so that we can in turn change or modify that experience. "Each head is a universe" says the motto, and if Carballido rejects anything at all, it is only the arrogance and ignorance in those who presume that "whatever seems inexplicable in human behavior . . . can be explained!" [21] Framed as they are in the world of the play, the professors' worlds seem small and static. Carballido depicts them in a humorous, almost farcical manner, and we laugh not because they are wrong but because they are reductive. Everything that is unique and individual about people and situations is boiled down to the lowest common denominator. The Freudian uses language not to open up channels of communication, as the Medium does, but to obliterate distinctions. Telephones, motorcycles, horses, dreams of flight, he tells us, are all sexual symbols, all signs of the same signifier. The Marxist too equates man (with a small *m*) to Economy (with a capital *E*) as though they were the same thing. Both professors are incapable of addressing individuality and lived experience. Their use of interpretation recalls Sontag's argument that "the task of interpretation is virtually one of translation. The interpreter says, Look, don't you see that X is really—or, really means—A? That Y is really B? That Z is really C?" (*Interpretation*, 15). Though Carballido's Freudian claims to focus on the individual, he objectifies the "common man" into the "common patient." For Carballido's Marxist, the human face freezes into a text reflecting ideology. Neither of them satisfactorily explains the accident or proposes solutions to the problems they have identified.

But what about the Medium? Does she explain the derailment? Why the special authority Carballido seems to grant her, and what does it consist of? Her speech may be ambiguous or mysterious but never farcical. The cosmos illuminated by the Medium is more miraculous and inclusive and yet certainly no more *real* or *true* than the world of the professors. The brevity and opacity of her "interpretation" of the accident, along with her peremptory dismissal of the question—"that was all" (172)—does not "answer" any questions. On the contrary, it dissuades us from privileging her explanation over the professors'. She refuses to give answers, to say the last word, to anticipate or precipitate an ending to the stories. She commands such a substantial amount of stage time not because she is right but because she is vital, not objectively as an answer but subjectively as a presence. She tells stories in both meanings of the word *historia*, story and history. She represents the consciousness and memory of a race—its history—kept alive by the very act of speaking. As such, she commands all our attention because, in an oral tradition, when the speaker stops, the *historia* ends. This double dimension lends her her paradoxical character: she is firmly planted in the soil but also transcends it. Within the dramatic structure, she is central to the workings of the play. Metaphorically, her consciousness is central to Mexican thought if Mexico is to avoid aping modern European thinking.

Rooted in orality, the Medium's vision encompasses past, present, and future. While oral tradition as defined by Vansina (27) refers to "oral statements spoken, sung or called out on musical instruments" for more than one generation, Vansina also specifies that oral statements are not necessarily about the past. This is important to note, given that oral traditions are generally considered (by Ong and others) "conservative." While orality is necessarily "conservative"—if by that word we mean "conserving in memory"—it is a mistake to think of these societies as politically conservative. Jean Franco has stressed that "the secret weapon of the Indian group [during the colonial period] was the oral tradition in the native language. Indeed the most significant feature of colonial culture is this differentiation within the production process itself, between an oral culture dependent on community and a written culture, which was over-whelmingly associated with domination" ("Dependency Theory," 68). The Medium draws from that independent heritage and combines the stories from the past with her recently acquired knowledge. Her perspective cannot be viewed as regressive or nostalgic for two main reasons. First, the word "nostalgia" suggests a discontinuity, a break between past and present, which we do not have in the play. Second, there is no backward impetus, no archaeological intent to recuperate a lost past. It is crucial to recognize that the Medium, then, does not represent an escape from the present into Mexico's pre-Hispanic traditions. Such a move would be as suicidal—politically and culturally—as surrendering to the First World. Fortunately, as Carballido illustrates, the choice goes beyond those two options. The story the Medium narrates about the "two who dreamed," her third monologue in the play, illustrates how Mexico's indigenous past flows into and is part of its contemporary situation.

It is the story of two men who lived in different villages, Chalco and Chalma. One version, the Medium tells us, says they were twins, another that they were brothers, another that they were friends; we as audience have no way of knowing for certain. Be that as it may, each of them, in their separate villages and at exactly the same time, dreamed of a prodigious figure instructing him to go to the other's town and, together with the other, pray before the sanctuary next to his house. Both men awoke, walked toward the other town, and met halfway. "Each in turn told the other his dream and they were identical . . . like a mirror with two contradictory images." They do not know how to interpret the dream, or which town to go to. They flip a coin (much like the children in the play), which falls in a crack: "'It is a sign,' they said, and so they made camp on the very spot and waited for another sign . . . another dream. . . . The sign never came, and so they decided to fulfill their command right there where they were. It was a barren place covered with weeds and rocks" (the dump?), which they cleared and on which they built a "very small church."

The men, wearing the garments of their pre-Hispanic ancestors, "had a few drinks of mescal and then they danced and prayed. They danced in that complicated rhythm that had been passed down to them from their fathers. They prayed the prayers they had learnt from childhood. Two tired, dirty men decorated with feathers and mirrors danced and prayed in the nocturnal ambiguity of that wilderness without answers. . . . Their time was up and they knew no better way of satisfying the whims of the arbitrary being that had spoken to them in their dreams" (54).

The story of the two who dreamed spans from the ritualistic sung-dance of Mexico's pre-Hispanic past to the contemporary scene—the dump where the children dance, play, and flip their coins, the dump where the scavengers drink their tequila at night and sing their songs about yet another rose, the rose of Castille. The ritual the men perform recalls Mircea Eliade's description (*Sacred*, 27-28) of the archaic practice of invoking divine or supernatural guidance: "some *sign* suffices to indicate the sacredness of a place. . . . When no sign manifests itself, it is *provoked*" to "*show* what place is fit to receive the sanctuary or the village" (Eliade's emphasis). However, this in no way suggests that pre-Hispanic ritual can somehow solve the present situation in which the men find themselves.[22] What the play suggests, rather, is that generation after generation, people have tried to interpret the inexplicable—what the ancients would call the sacred; most 20th-century people, the "arbitrary." The dance the men perform as part of a holy rite resembles yet differs from the children's dance, and differs too from the professors' "explanation" of the dance. To the Freudian the dance represents "the mutual release and discharge of libido" (56); to the Marxist it is an example of "those dances with which capitalism manages to corrupt the true spirit of the people" (57). Carballido juxtaposes the various forms of dance to illustrate how the very concept and meaning of the activity changes according to the context. In *Rose*, the past forms a part of the present which opens up into some unknown, unforetold future. Through memory and imagination the Medium spans past and present. She holds, too, a promise for the future: more stories will be revealed; more will be known in the telling. Her sense of lived time—as opposed to chronological, "objective" time—is both retrospective and prospective. The past is incorporated into a lived present both in her memory and in the blood that flows through her veins that resemble the pre-Hispanic waterways of Tenochtitlán. By means of images and allusions she integrates the pre-Columbian past with modern Mexico in each of her four speeches. Her narration, the act of speaking itself, situates her as the living link in an ongoing series of *historias*. She does not allude to the concept of progress or to future fulfillment, the triumphalist reading of history offered by the Man in *The Day They Let the Lions Loose*. Rather, time unfolds story after story.

## Transculturation

The story of the "two who dreamed" provides Carballido with a framework within which to examine the concept of tradition, hegemonically and counterhegemonically. The men's feathers and mirrors, like the Medium's rebozo, dangerously border on the folkloric. As I noted in chapter 1, perpetuating a dead or dying tradition as a museum piece or a tourist attraction, often under the auspices of a Ministry of Culture, proves as artificial and alienating as imposing totally foreign cultures. It also contributes to what Dirlik (26) calls "hegemonic culturalism," a way of seeing culture as a "thing," autonomous from social activity and lived experiences: "An irrefutable tradition that defines the center of history is crucial to ruling-class history, and so is the presentation of that tradition as prior to everyday life." If culture in the Third World could be reduced to feathers and mirrors, mariachi bands and magic realism, the hegemonic cultures would not need to emphasize and fight for the centrality of a Western canon. The point, as Carballido illustrates, is that while the pre-Hispanic world is dead and buried, the traditions that have grown out of it are neither dead nor reified; they have survived by transforming and adapting to living societies. In the image offered by the play, the light from the star shining on the cavemen reaches our telescopes and illuminates our present, even though the star itself may be dead. The difference would be that while the starlight remains in its "pure" or unadulterated essence, culture survives by adulteration, by "impurely" mixing with other cultural elements. The dances, the songs, the prayers inherited from pre-Hispanic times change as the society does. The divine being is now an arbitrary being. The barren ground is now a dump; the garbage once had a use, and the children (much to everyone's shock) find new uses for things. The scavenger's house is constructed of some boards he found, some broken boxes, and "sheet metal I stole from the chicken coop over there." "It may be poor and rickety," he admits, "but I'll tell you one thing about my house, it's warm" (59). These useless, displaced remnants of past structures undergo change as they become part of a new, useful structure. Carballido does not depict this changing tradition and culture romantically; he shows dumps, derailments, and thefts as well as song and dance. Again, the point is not that culture is a museum piece of "folklore" but that it is vital. The process of cultural change, as the garbage humorously illustrates, is one of loss, selection, recuperation, recycling. Cultural products, like garbage, are the byproducts of living, changing societies: products are tried out, discarded, added to, displaced, replaced, rediscovered, and made over by combining the new with the old.

In short, what Carballido demonstrates in *Rose* is the process of cultural change, loss, and rejuvenation that Fernando Ortiz, in the 1940s, called "transculturation," a three-stage process consisting of the acquisition of new cultural material from a foreign culture, the loss or displacement of one's own, and the creation of new cultural phenomena. Angel Rama, in *Transculturación narrativa en América Látina* (33), points out in his commentary on Ortiz's theory that his is very much a Latin American perspective in that "it reveals the resistance to considering one's traditional culture, receiving the impact of the foreign culture that will modify it, as merely a passive or even inferior entity, destined to major losses without the possibility of creative response." For Rama, expanding on the three-step process, Ortiz does not sufficiently emphasize selectivity and inventiveness in transculturation. After all, cultures do not borrow indiscriminately; like the scavenger, one takes only what one needs. Latin American theatre, Rama notes, did not appropriate the Broadway musical. What it did appropriate were the absurdist, grotesque, and fragmented techniques that reflect a sense of Latin America's chaotic reality as well as more socially oriented dramatic techniques, associated with Piscator and Brecht, to help change the sociopolitical situations. Moreover, when these techniques were borrowed, they were radically altered by their new context. *Rose* is a fine example of the selectivity and inventiveness that Rama writes of, as well as what he calls the "rediscovery" of "primitive values almost forgotten within one's own cultural system that are capable of standing up to the erosion of transculturation" (39). Rama, then, speaks of four stages in the process—loss, selectivity, rediscovery, and incorporation—all of which take place simultaneously.[23]

Let us briefly look at *I Too Speak of the Rose* from the perspective of transculturation. The "borrowings" are obvious, and not just in terms of the Freudian pyschology and the Marxist economic theories so prevalent in Mexico around the time the play appeared. There are theatrical borrowings as well. Carballido himself calls the play a *loa*, which is both a short piece (usually one act) presented before a full-length play and a "hymn of praise" (47), a genre which, though common from the Golden Age to the nineteenth century, gradually went out of fashion in the twentieth. The narrator and the episodic structure seem Brechtian; the ritualistic elements, including the final scene, Artaudian. However, looking at the parts separately is misleading. Although *Rose* has Brechtian elements, this is no Brechtian play, as some commentators claim.[24] Looking at the Medium in the light of her own tradition, rather than through Western theories, we see that her role as narrator stems from her experience in an oral culture. Speaking rhythmically in the darkness, the Medium tells us, she can hear her heart, though her sense of sight is blurred. Moreover, we as audience experience that tradition in *her* terms, not ours. Like the Medium, we sit in darkness; we hear, but we can hardly see. Her speech draws us in, enveloping rather than distancing us, awakening us to the beauty and fluidity of her language. Carballido places us in the same physical position before her as we would assume before a bard; her scenes are intimate, quiet, introspective, or reflective. As Walter Ong (73) states: "The way in which the word is experienced is always momentous in psychic life. The centering action of sound (the field of sound is not spread out before me but is all around me) affects man's sense of the cosmos. For oral cultures, the cosmos is an ongoing event with man at its center." This experience, then, is profoundly different from that of the audience in Brecht's theatre. Brecht advocates leaving the house lights up to create an informal music-hall atmosphere in which people feel comfortable smoking, laughing, and commenting on the action.

The oral tradition also explains the episodic plot in *Rose*. As in Brechtian theatre, some of the twenty-one scenes seem strung together arbitrarily; one could change the order without significantly changing our experience of the play. However, the episodes are not Brechtian if we accept Brecht's own description (201) of episodic plots: "The individual episodes have to be knotted together in such a way that the knots are easily noticed. The episodes must not succeed one another indistinguishably but must give a chance to interpose our judgment. . . . To this end it is best to agree to use titles." The episodic structure in *Rose* is not meant to distance us. Though episodic, the scenes derive their structure from the narrative sequence characteristic of the oral tradition. The Medium is telling us the story; from her opening monologue, she knows how Toña and Polo's particular story unravels—"but more of that later" (47), she tells us, or "that's another story" (54). The misreading of the episodic plot lies in the insistence on labeling the episodic "Brechtian" rather than recognizing that Brecht's "epic" theatre picks up ("borrows") from the oral tradition. As Ong (144) states: "What made a good epic poet was, among other things of course, first, tacit acceptance of the fact that episodic structure was the only way and the totally natural way of imagining and handling lengthy narrative. . . . Strict plot for lengthy narrative comes with writing." Brecht himself was the first to admit that "stylistically speaking, there is nothing at all new about the epic theatre" (75), that he had used techniques and ideas from Asiatic theatre, medieval mystery plays, Spanish classical theatre, Jesuit theatre, and many more sources. Brecht, in fact, is one of the greatest examples of the vitality, selection, and innovation associated with intercultural exchange. However, what makes him *Brechtian* is his particular use of the acquired materials. What makes Carballido *non-Brechtian* is his particular use of *his*.

The same applies to the play's ritual elements. The story of "the two who dreamed" and the final scene of the play are not Artaudian because they invoke ritual; rather, Artaud is "ritualistic" because he invokes, even mystifies, Mexican indigenous rites. For Artaud the non-Western is the "true culture [that] operates exaltation and force. . . . In Mexico, since we were talking about Mexico, there is no art: things are made for use. And the world is in perpetual exaltation" (*Double*, 10-11). Carballido, on the other hand, does not mystify Mexico's past or, like Artaud, take suicidal risks to recuperate it.[25] Rather, more in the manner we have associated with transculturation, he "rediscovers" (Rama's term) and incorporates the past into the present. The ritual, we noted, does not point toward the past; it relates the experience of two men trying to function appropriately in an inexplicable wilderness devoid of supernatural or divine guidance, drawing from the traditions they have at hand. Moreover, Carballido's ritual dance linking the characters at the end of the play is not an ahistorical or nostalgic return to ritual community. It is a historically accurate depiction of what Kumkum Sangari (158) calls the cultural heterogeneity of Latin America: "The simultaneity of the heterogeneous is a matter of historical sedimentation that results from the physical coexistence over time of different ethnic groups. . . . Simultaneity is the restless product of a long history of miscegenation, assimilation, and syncretization *as well as* of conflict, contradiction, and cultural violence" (Sangari's emphasis).

Carballido's conscious use of foreign material is evident in *Rose*. As we have seen, he juxtaposes two traditions, two ways of knowing: orality and literacy. The theatrical techniques he uses to depict those two epistemic grids are also different, necessarily different, for what we know depends on how we know it. We would not understand what an oral tradition consists of if we only listened to the Freudian or Marxist expounding on it. Carballido, in the darkened theatre, recreates the situation in which an audience depends on its sense of hearing for its information and knowledge. The Medium, sitting quietly, relates. The literate world is portrayed through representation (rather than narration), emphasizing our visual sense by means of more openly theatrical scenes involving the professors, the Teacher, the Emcee. The action is fast paced, noisy, full of children's antics, bombast, pomposity—wonderfully visual and humorous as the stage becomes full of sexual shapes and revolutionary slogans. These theatrical scenes can be described in terms of Brechtian distanciation, for the stereotypical situations and the caricatured figures keep us out. They depict the alienation produced and reproduced by the theories themselves, and what better way to depict alienation than through Brecht's alienating techniques or "A-effect"? Carballido's use of distanciation in these particular scenes serves Brecht's original intention of sharpening our critical awareness. In opposition to the way we perceive in the Medium's company, these scenes are asking us to know something different, and in a different manner. What do we learn from the theatrical juxtaposition of these two worlds? Through the professors and the Teacher (endorsed ministers of education), through all their rhetoric and manipulation, we see the grim socioeconomic context in which the children live. The children grow up in poor, single-mother homes; they play in garbage, miss school, and seem destined at best to borderline literacy. To paraphrase the Marxist, this is unfortunately "typical" of the class that Carballido portrays. While the professors and the Teacher notice the problem and paint it in the darkest, most hopeless light, they seem unable to improve the situation. Their attitudes, instead of helping the children, only subject them to further violence, the violence of misinterpretation and reification. The children clearly do not recognize themselves in the professors' depictions, the Teacher's harangue, the newspaper headlines and photographs. They, as individuals, become "objects" of interpretation in a larger scheme of things, pawns to be pushed and pulled in political debate. Public attention focuses not on them but on the "event," the sensational derailment, in order to ignore what Paul Ricoeur in *History and Truth* (226) calls "the violence of exploitation." As Ricoeur makes clear, "battles are events, so are riots; but poverty and the dying poor are not events."

The Medium, on the other hand, never once alludes to the children's poverty. She is not insensitive to their poor living conditions; she too lives in an environment pervaded by smells of "smoke and stale food" (47), but she does not turn it into a metaphor to explain something else—repressed unconscious thoughts or a capitalist economy of waste. Through her vision, we understand the relativity of the junkyard. It is not only an unmitigated disaster of filth and trash, as the professors see it, equated by the Freudian with human nature and by the Marxist with capitalism. The children go there because it is fun; they find things. The Medium neither equates nor interprets; she simply places the issue in a broader context. By means of her consciousness, past flows into present. What we regarded as junk when it lay on the ground out of context now regains meaning. The piece of metal Polo picks up has a history: "This came out of a mine. . . . It formed part of a machine" (172). Toña and Polo are poor, but as they realize, they are healthy, productive, and capable of love. The Medium does not lock them into a theory; she opens up the realms of possibility, indicating more and more stories: "And do you know how Polo came to own his own garage? And what Toña's marriage was like? Well . . . that's another story" (153). For her, then, the catastrophic derailment is not a cause for alarm but an opportunity for rethinking history—past, present, and future—and for repositioning the hitherto marginalized both outside and within society.

Perhaps Carballido's most important political insight in *Rose*, however, is not his recognition of diversity or of cultural heterogeneity and simultaneity. Clearly, there are many different ways of seeing the world. Carballido's central image of the rose is itself the most obvious example of the plurality of interpretation. The rose appears in the title, in the scavenger's love song, in the play's enveloping structure, in the psychologist's description of the self. In the epigram, Carballido quotes lines from two Mexican poet-playwrights, Xavier Villaurrutia's "But mine is not the frigid rose," and Sor Juana Inés de la Cruz's "Portent of our human architecture." In the Emcee's game show the rose is portrayed from three representative perspectives: rose, petal, tissue, and the Emcee asks his audience if they are looking at "the image of a flower of the dicotyledonous bush of the rosaceous family" or "one of those divine roses which, among cultured and refined people, is taken as the favorite symbol of the human architecture. . . . Our job here is to reject quite definitely and conclusively all false images" (59). Clearly, however, the rose is one of the most complex and ambiguous of images; it stands for both "heavenly perfection and earthly passion; the flower is both Time and Eternity, life and death, fertility and virginity" (Cooper, 141). The rose heart is also an important pre-Columbian symbol of life in the Nahua tradition (Amaral, 155). What needs stressing, however, is that aside from the fascinating diversity, the rival and conflicting versions struggle to win out. For all his facetiousness, the Emcee is not just joking when he says that "there are three [images] and only one is authentic. The other two should be stricken from the books so that they will be forgotten forever. And any person who divulges them should be pursued by law. All those who believe in these false images should be suppressed and isolated! Kept under constant surveillance" (59). In the context of the game show, with its promise of a "magnificent prize" to the person who identifies the one true image, the Emcee's words are humorous. When placed in the context of Mexican history, however, the hegemonic discourse and its articulation and valorization of the "true" did in fact result in the isolation, suppression, and erasure of the "barbaric."

Carballido's strategy in this play (and others) lies not in replacing but in displacing the hegemonic discourse. He inverts the practice that has so long marginalized the *mestizo*, the female, the indigenous, the non-Castilian, and the non-Western in Mexico. In terms of stage time, the Medium dominates the action; she is central to the workings of the play. By making her central, Carballido not only legitimates the indigenous, oral traditions of Mexico but also situates woman as a positive, life-giving, and liberating force in the nation's history—a move that openly defies Mexico's *malinchismo*, or self-hatred, and misogyny. Women, even more than men, have been associated with the oral tradition because they have been denied access to education and positions of *author*ity considerably longer than indigenous males. [26]

Carballido also gives Mexicans back their own language. Instead of Castilian Spanish the children's expressions *órale, no se me raje, re fácil, ¡Quihubo!, cuate* situate us firmly in the streets of Mexico City. Mexicans, too, speak of the rose, in their own way.

Moving the marginalized from the periphery of the known universe to its center in itself constitutes an important, liberating, historical *act*, for by the same move the Eurocentric (the professors) recedes, reduced in importance. [27] Changing the relationship between the marginal and the dominant changes history, for as Hayden White points out in *Tropics of Discourse* (94), histories "are not only about events but also about the possible set of relationships that those events can be demonstrated to figure." I go into the subject of the struggle for history in the next chapter; here it is sufficient to note that Carballido depicts the derailment in order to propose various ways that the event figures in divergent discourses. Framing the derailment in different ways, gives it different meanings, which then become the basis for different world views. Reclaiming the events in an indigenous discourse makes the articulating, speaking self central to history. This move becomes obvious in any theatrical production of the play—quite simply, the more time the Medium is onstage, the less time there is for the professors. Clearly, in *Rose* the Medium "steals the show." Dominating our attention, she is the presence that was perceived as absence in *Lions*. Here, right in the center of Mexico's systems and traditions, is the spirit and language of a people that has managed to survive both the cages and the hegemonic system. But the political repercussions of the displacement of Western thought to the periphery, where it is allowed to coexist and intermingle with the non-Western traditions without eclipsing them, is truly significant. Perhaps it surprises no one that the Medium's interpretations are no more valid or correct than those of the professors; no one would expect them to be. But to maintain that the most advanced Western theories of individual and economic development are no more real or valid than those of the Medium is indeed extraordinary. The professors' theories appear irrelevant, if not downright hostile, to the reality they are supposed to be illuminating. By making the Medium central, the play makes them marginal to Mexican reality. Marginality, I stated in chapter 1, is *positional*. Now the professors are irrelevant *and* marginal. And although the *científicos* have long dominated the Mexican scene, *Rose* illustrates that the professors are no more correct than the Medium. However, as Carballido stresses by introducing the story of the "two who dreamed," life in Mexico did not start with the Conquest, nor did it end there. Although the professors seemingly deny the possibility of change, Mexico is changing. What seems static, fixed, hopeless (a single petal of the rose) must be understood as part of a larger, multifaceted conglomerate. The liberating strategy does not lie only in military prowess; perhaps more urgently, it lies in reclaiming center stage in one's own culture, one's traditions, one's history.

What will come of Carballido's political vision? Can it ever be more than a vision? Can it help Mexico and Mexicans find nonviolent ways out of their political and social chaos? The "two who dreamed" would tell us from their experience that it is impossible to know the results of one's action. The Freudian professor (like the Octavio Paz of *The Labyrinth of Solitude*) would call Mexico a hopelessly schizophrenic country: mother Malinche's seduction by father Cortés has created a traumatized, self-hating brood. For the Marxist, Mexico is an underdeveloped country on the brink of open class warfare. For the Medium, Mexico is a miracle of creative energy that has survived centuries of oppression and kleptocracy. Carballido's vision, like the Medium's, transforms the discordant notes of Mexico's many dissonances into a *loa*, a hymn of praise.

# 5

# DESTROYING
# THE EVIDENCE:
# ENRIQUE
# BUENAVENTURA

ENRIQUE BUENAVENTURA (b. 1925 in Colombia), playwright, actor, director, and theorist, is one of the most important and respected theatre practitioners to come out of Latin America since the 1960s and, paradoxically, one of the least analyzed and understood.[1] Commentators cannot speak highly enough of Buenaventura or overemphasize the importance of his dramatic production. They situate him next to Brecht and Piscator in the European tradition of political theatre and interpret his plays in accordance with Brechtian models.[2] They emphasize his preoccupation with history, note his use of historical figures as central characters (Rey Christophe and Bartolomé de Las Casas), and his theatrical technique of "documentation."[3] It is a critical commonplace that Buenaventura is one of the finest "popular" theatre practitioners to come out of Latin America, and his work epitomizes and in fact has almost become synonymous with "new theatre."[4] Moreover, these views are usually advanced simultaneously; the words "Brecht," "history," and "popular" appear in tandem in most studies.

Buenaventura's theatre certainly deserves all the praise it receives, and all the usual observations are in some way "true." He repeatedly acknowledges his admiration of and indebtedness to Brecht. From his earliest pieces onward we can discern Brechtian motifs and techniques: *A la diestra de Dios Padre* (*On the Right Hand of God the Father,* 1960) recalls moments of *The Good Woman of Setzuan*; and his cycle of plays *Los papeles del infierno* (*Documents from Hell*, 1968) is based on Brecht's collection of short pieces,

To the memory of Stacey Coverdale, my student, whose rendition of *La orgía* comes to mind every time I read the play.

*Fears and Miseries of the Third Reich*. Buenaventura's concern with history, too, is evident throughout. *Los papeles*, as he announces explicitly in the prologue, "is a testimony of twenty years of violence and undeclared civil war," the period in Colombian history known simply as *La Violencia*, which began in the mid-1940s.[5] Furthermore, Buenaventura is certainly a "popular" theatre practitioner. He is committed to social change, even revolutionary change.[6] In 1962 he founded Colombia's first professional theatre and repertory company, the TEC (Teatro Escuela de Calí; from 1970, the Teatro Experimental de Cali) and wrote single-author plays for that group until the late 1960s, when he began experimenting with collaborative playwriting. The texts of collective pieces emerged after a rehearsal process in which he and other TEC members devised, researched, and shaped a topic.[7] In addition to his popular political perspective, Buenaventura addresses a "popular" audience, traveling with his shows to rural areas where people have never seen theatre before. Aesthetically, these activities imply radical departures from traditional and hegemonic concepts of "text," "author," and "culture." Politically, these departures have cost Buenaventura his teaching position at the Escuela Departamental de Teatro del Valle and resulted in the loss of all governmental recognition and support for the TEC (see Risk, 21).

All this information is important, but the standard interpretation of it has resulted, inadvertently, in obscuring rather than illuminating Buenaventura's importance and his position vis-à-vis his country's crisis. A brief look at the assumptions behind the different critical postures will show why they have failed to touch on what is most innovative and radical about Buenaventura's dramaturgy.

The most obvious limitation of the view that Buenaventura is Brechtian, historical, and popular is that those particular terms are themselves problematic and essentialist; they mean different things to different people, and they suggest that there is *one* Brecht, *one* Buenaventura. The case for Brechtian "influence," to be meaningful, would require a host of considerations, perhaps principally of periodization (early Brecht? late Brecht? early Buenaventura? late Buenaventura?), which are not addressed in these studies. What do we mean by Brechtian? Are we referring to a political, dialectical theatre? To theatrical techniques such as having women act men's roles and vice versa? To distanciation? To epic narration? Finding answers would involve an examination of transcultural trends, the process by means of which Buenaventura selects and adapts Brechtian themes and strategies to construct "meaning" in relation to his own specific spectators, many of whom have never heard of Brecht. The Brechtian elements are not popularly known "pretexts" for spontaneous improvisation, as the commedia dell'arte plots and characters were for its audience; nor do they constitute a shared belief or tradition, as biblical stories do for some groups and mythological ones for others. What, then, is the point of introducing these elements? How do these adapted features "read" or "play" when Buenaventura's theatre, in turn, is transplanted to another culture?[8] Moreover, to argue simultaneously that Buenaventura is a Brechtian and a "collective" playwright poses the problem of what we mean by *author* and *oeuvre*.[9] Single-author "works" are difficult enough to establish, let alone compare with texts by other authors. The issue becomes even more troublesome with reference either to Brecht or to Buenaventura as "author": the former collaborated with Ruth Berlau, Elisabeth Hauptmann, and Margarete Steffin, for example, not to mention musicians such as Kurt Weill; the latter gradually became a collaborator in a collective creation. Which Brecht or which Buenaventura are we thinking of? Can we even think of Buenaventura's later works as part of his *oeuvre* in the same way as we do his single-author plays?

Clearly, too, an emphasis on the Brechtian elements clouds the many important Latin American components of his work. His *A la diestra de Dios Padre*, much like Brecht's *Good Woman*, represents multiple "gods": Jesus and St. Peter try to find and help a good person. What are rarely discussed, however, are the other traditions feeding into this drama, from Spanish mystery plays or *autos sacramentales* to the grotesque humor of Ramón del Valle Inclán's (1866-1936) *esperpentos*, to the farcical, masked *festivales* such as the *mojiganga*. Moreover the different representation of the gods bespeaks different world views and hence radically different "solutions" for surviving in the face of formidable odds.

We could argue that Buenaventura's appropriation of foreign cultural material is Brechtian in spirit. After all, as I pointed out in discussing transculturation (chapter 4), Brecht was one of theatre's most avid borrowers. Even here, however, the emphasis on Brecht is misleading; what we should be looking at is the process of transculturation itself. Just as Brecht's specific use of the elements he borrows makes him Brechtian, so does Buenaventura's use of his make him a new original. Buenaventura himself, from *A la diestra de Dios Padre* onward, calls attention to the process of transculturation by means of which marginalized people absorb foreign models and use them for their liberation: Jesus and St. Peter are furious because their designated "good man," Peralta, has misused his powers, but Jesus acknowledges that he has been outsmarted, that in fact Peralta "has done nothing more than use the powers that I gave him" (240).[10] Peralta will not be easily defeated or excluded; in the final scene, using the very wishes Jesus granted him, he jumps into the right hand of God, determined, as William Oliver (174) puts it, to "plague God's own creativity" for eternity. This, then, is a counterhegemonic strategy that

Buenaventura proposes for his audiences; they are directed not to imitate the West but rather to appropriate the weapons of the powerful and use them for their own decolonization. Moreover, he explicitly refers to this strategy in his theoretical papers; he explains that he and his group purposely chose for production foreign plays that illuminated their own specific problems, notably colonization and dependency: "We knew that the colonizer that imposed his culture was also giving us the instruments of liberation. But we can only use those instruments if we apply them to our concrete reality." [11]

In short, to emphasize the Brechtian elements is misleading. Though it is laudable on the part of the commentators to want to stress the quality and importance of Buenaventura's work by situating him next to Brecht, this emphasis leads us away from those characteristics (by and large non-Brechtian) that most contribute to Buenaventura's importance. Ironically, scholars who stress Buenaventura's relationship to Brecht fail to mention what I consider its single most important feature: that Brecht, as an openly political dramatist, has become a common source of inspiration to dramatists from many colonized and marginalized societies, indirectly introducing them to each other. [12]

Similarly, we contribute to the critical obfuscation of Brecht's work by simply stating that he is one of Latin America's foremost "popular" theatre practitioners, since no one quite agrees on what "popular theatre" means. Rather than allowing for differentiation between many kinds of "popular" or "people's" theatre—Chicano theatre, Piscator's "epic" theatre, Boal's theatre of the oppressed, and others—the term "popular" tends to group them all together, despite their important differences. What does the label "popular" tell us about Buenaventura's own production? That it is *for* the "people"? Yes, if by that we mean rural and semiliterate audiences along with urban and literate (university student) ones. That is is *by* the "people"? Buenaventura is a self-taught, highly knowledgeable, articulate intellectual, not a man of the semiliterate circles he wants to incorporate in theatrical activity. That this theatre privileges political over aesthetic effects—that is, focuses specifically on a given set of social problems? Buenaventura has adamantly denied that theatre must sacrifice aesthetics to politics, differing radically in this respect both from Piscator and from many practitioners of the Chicano theatre. [13] "'Popular theatre,' or a 'theatre for the masses,' a theatre for a fixed audience and about a specific set of problems," he says, is "just another trick of the system, as elementary as nationalism, folklore, or agitprop. Because the system has cast out the exploited, should you create a product for them that is no more nutritious than the food surpluses it leaves them? Some maintain that the exploited don't want anything else, that they don't have the capacity to participate in the full and complex diversion of a real theatrical production. . . . To accept that we must do low-quality theatre at the outset to 'elevate' the level of the people is to enter wholly into the system" ("Theater and Culture," 154). The issue of "popular theatre," then, is disorienting; it draws attention away from what Buenaventura actually does, away from the artistic and technical strategies he devises to communicate with disparate audiences and to continue producing outstanding theatre in the face of overwhelming difficulties—traveling to rural areas that lack traditional theatre spaces, working with minimum financial and technical resources, dealing with political ostracism and harassment. His is truly a "poor" theatre in the economic sense of the word.

More important, however, is the fact that Buenaventura does not follow the path of consciousness raising normally associated with popular theatre. Rather than propose a vision or communicate a message associated with a specific ideology, he subverts dominant ideology through a process he calls "deconscientization" (*deconcienciación*) or "demystification." For Buenaventura, this means seeing through the concepts of "tradition," "history," and race, class, and gender "difference" which sustain the power elite. He undermines the boundaries—social, political, economic, cultural, and historical—by means of which the system excludes a substantial portion of its population as grotesque, poor, dirty, infirm *others*. He does not simply propose overthrowing the oppressors and grabbing their power, however, perpetuating thus the binary system of oppressed and oppressor. He has no intention of substituting one form of violence for another, or "one set of illusions for another" (Reyes, 22). Rather, Buenaventura questions the entire system, including the role of the oppressed themselves within it. The sociopolitical demystification proposed by Buenaventura strives toward the same political ends as do consciousness-raising theatres, but the difference is an important one that accounts for the subtle, nondidactic nature of Buenaventura's drama: it exposes, rather than imposes, ideology.

Likewise, the use of the term "historical" in describing Buenaventura's work is not only ambiguous (what does *historical* mean?) but again misleading. The general idea seems to be that Buenaventura stresses the importance of understanding Colombia's past in order to forge a more productive and equitable future. This is absolutely true. What has not been pointed out in Buenaventura studies, however, is that Colombia's actual past, with its innumerable "events" and "facts," is not the same thing as the selection, arrangement, and interpretation of those facts by historians in a narrative commonly known as History, which for the sake of clarity I will continue to designate by a capital H. In *Metahistory* and in *Tropics of Discourse* (84), Hayden White has called our attention to an age-old insight: namely, that historical facts or events alone do not "constitute a story; the most they offer the historian are story elements. The events are *made* into a story by the suppression or subordination of certain of them and the highlighting of others, by characterization, motific repetition, variation of tone and point of view, alternate descriptive strategies, and the like—in short, all of the techniques that we normally expect to find in the emplotment of a novel or a play" (White's emphasis).[14] Buenaventura does not deny the importance of history. On the contrary, the struggle for history is central in empowering the dispossessed. What he challenges is the fictionalized History bolstering the position of those who control the record. He wants to point to the heterogeneity of perspectives, events, facts, and experiences that are generally *off the record*. Rather than presenting a coherent vision of Colombia's past he uses elements from it to show that the history of Colombia is *not* a coherent, comprehensible unity, not an encompassing vew of collective peoples living and working together; it does not include all the facts; it is not based on Christian or democratic traditions as it claims. The history of Colombia bespeaks rupture, exclusion, ongoing civil warfare, political obfuscation, foreign colonization and exploitation.

The demystification of hegemonic History that Buenaventura undertakes does not question the validity of actual events or of what we normally think of as historical context. It is not an example of the worst kind of historical revisionism, which denies the events themselves (the "holohoax" denying the Holocaust, for example). This alone would push the oppressed further into oblivion. Buenaventura attempts the opposite: to inscribe and make audible the voices that have traditionally been kept out of Colombian History, voices of the victims, the victimizers, the participants or collaborators who make up the infernal world of his plays.

The crisis reflected in *Los papeles* directly refers to the chronic Colombian sociopolitical conflict culminating in the virulence of *La Violencia*, which left 300,000 dead between 1948 and 1964-65. The causes of the violence, though multiple, can be reduced to a few key ones for our purposes here. Colombia has been torn asunder by a fiercely antagonistic two-party system—Liberals (anti-Church federalists) versus Conservatives (pro-Church centralists)—which dates back to 1849. There have been numerous bitter civil wars and nine constitutions, byproducts of the ongoing factionalism. Moreover, party politics and divisions have tended to obfuscate what is also a deeply rooted class conflict; the rulers (whether Liberal or Conservative) belong to the highest social echelons and hence have common financial interests, allowing them to reach compromises that exclude the poorer sectors of the country. Thus, the middle and lower classes are oppressed by the ruling class and, at the same time, profoundly split into uncompromising (at this socioeconomic level) oppositional political factions. As Harvey F. Kline notes in *Colombia: Portrait of Unity and Diversity* (51), political reconciliation has been difficult if not impossible because *noncooperation* was preached from the pulpits, and everyone had a martyr in the family. Eventually, the spreading violence led to systemic crisis, what Paul Oquist (9) calls the "partial breakdown of the state." However, "the blame for what has happened" does not—as W.O. Galbraith (v) would have us believe,—lie "squarely on the shoulders of a relatively small number of politicians, both Liberal and Conservative, who have brought Colombia to the brink of ruin and anarchy." Colombia has also been victimized by foreign powers since its independence in 1819, especially by the United States, which took Panama from Colombia in 1903. As a passing example of the ideological slant in the historical representation and interpretation of "facts," Kline (42) calls this act the "rape of Panama," whereas Galbraith (15) describes it as an act of American duty "to protect the life and property" of a then nonexistent group, the Panamanians. The United Fruit Company entered Colombia during the first decade of the twentieth century, buying up land and setting up "banana enclaves" (Kline, 42). Colombia entered into financial dependency on the United States, and from the 1920s onward Colombian troops have defended U.S. interests over those of Colombians. Perhaps the most notable example was the massacre of Colombian workers striking against the United Fruit Company in 1928, which Buenaventura and his group chose as a theme for their collective work *La denuncia* (1973). The current sociopolitical situation in Colombia is disastrous; as a result of drug-related conflicts, murder is the leading cause of death for males between the ages of fifteen and forty-four (Lernoux, 512).

## *Los papeles del infierno:* The Nature of the "Documents"

*Los papeles del infierno* is a cycle of one-act plays through which Buenaventura explores a society in crisis and illustrates just how difficult and dangerous it is to accept encompassing, harmonizing terms such as "tradition" and "History" in societies undone by violence. The very structural makeup of the cycle in itself reflects rupture and discontinuity. The short vignettes are shards, bits and pieces of a mosaic. No one agrees on which, or how many, plays make up the cycle or in which order the plays should appear. The journal *Tramoya* published nine in 1979; Fernando de Toro refers to four;[15] Penny Wallace lists *La maestra* (*The Teacher*), *La autopsia* (*The Autopsy*), *La requisa* (*The Requisition*), *La tortura* (*Torture*, translated as *The Twisted State*), *El entierro* (*The Funeral*), *La orgía* (*The Orgy*), *El menú* (*The Menu*), and *The Dream* (apparently available only in the English typescript called "Leave from Hell," translated by José Barba-Martin and Robert E. Louis). Only one source (Collazos, 9) associates *El menú* with the original cycle.[16] Errol Hill's anthology *A Time and a Season: Eight Caribbean Plays* includes *The Orgy* as well as a piece not listed elsewhere, *The Funeral*, as representative of the cycle. The 1977 collection of Buenaventura's work, *Teatro*, lists five as constituting the cycle: *La maestra, La tortura, La autopsia, La audiencia* (*The Hearing*), and *La requisa*, although the volume includes also *El menú* and *La orgía*, which according to Carlos José Reyes's introduction (8) also form part of the cycle. To complicate matters further, there are several (sometimes as many as four) versions of the same play—the result of its having incorporated changes suggested by the actors and even, at times, the audience during rehearsal or production.

The fragmentation of the cycle, although a source of frustration to commentators, underlines its thematic concern with Colombia's ongoing history of crisis, rupture and fragmentation. As the word "documents" (*papeles*, papers) suggests, the work is about history, a series of disconnected pieces of information without beginning or closure. The cycle forces us, as literary critics, to take the place traditionally reserved for historians. It presents us with "documents" and asks us to interpret them on the basis of questionable facts and nondefinitive texts. But whereas legal or official documents purport to present raw material as a basis for further interpretation or action, these vignettes, however simple and straightforward they appear, clearly are highly elaborate pieces. Legal documents aspire to disinterested objectivity by recording facts; these plays are personal, interested representations of those facts. Rather than discrediting the validity of the cycle, the dubious objectivity of the documents makes us question the veracity of documents in general. No documents, however legal and official, are innocent; they just seem so. They are created to serve a specific function and to further specific interests. They are the bricks out of which History is constructed. Hence, the cycle raises questions about documents in general and about these in particular. How do we decide which plays to include, which to exclude? How do we select between the various versions or agree upon their order? Evidence that might give us a "definitive" grasp eludes us. We must chart our own course and bring our own direction to this extremely complex, interwoven material. Given the elusiveness of the facts, we need to rely heavily on interpretation.

The same challenge faces the director. Some of the plays are very short; *The Teacher, Torture* and *The Autopsy* run less then ten minutes each; even the longest, *The Menu* and *The Orgy,* run less than an hour. Several plays (though not all) could be staged as one production—but how to select? On what basis does one arrange or impose an order on this disordered material? It is the director's selection, arrangement, and decisions, more than in most plays, that will create the production the audience sees. The audience too is called upon to provide missing links between the pieces. How do they fit together? The abrupt starts and stops of the short pieces undermine all Aristotelian notions of a continuous performance as an integrated aesthetic universe with a beginning, middle, and end. The fragmentation reinforces the audience's feeling that it is seeing only a part of some larger whole, that something is always being left out, that we do not have access to that which would make it all familiar, comprehensible, or complete. The texts, scripts, and documents are evidence of what we know and, simultaneously, reminders of what History leaves out.

While there is clearly no rigid pattern, as I see the makeup of and relationship between the documents, the plays seem to gyrate in ever widening spirals. The first turn consists of at least three perspectives: those of the victim (*The Teacher*), the victimizer (*Torture*), and the collaborator (*Autopsy*). The figures seem to exist in isolation, each in her or his own play, but strong echoes link them together. In *The Teacher*, the soldier who kills the father and rapes the teacher insists that he, personally, is not to blame. He is following the orders of those who want to remove the "*caciques* and hanger-ons of the old regime" (28).[17] The torturer, in the next play, also emphasizes that being a torturer is just a job like any other, "like being a doctor or a butcher. Have you ever seen a doctor or an honest butcher sick from scruples?" (35). When his wife complains about his occupation, he accuses her of hypocrisy because she benefits from what he does: for every nail he tears from a victim's fingers she gets a new pair of stockings; her new dress was bought with the money he earned by burning the soles of a victim's feet. The physician in *The Autopsy* also claims to be doing his job; if he "doctors" the evidence to prove that brutalized victims died natural deaths, well, "that's because the world is a slaughterhouse" (41). Even when he must finally perform an autopsy on his own son, murdered at the hands of the police, what can he say? As he asks his wife, "Do you want me to bring the world down around us? Do you want them to take me away to the slaughterhouse and fire a bullet into my neck?" (39). Besides, as he reminds her, she too has been complicitous: "When I said I would have to invent something if I wanted to hang onto my job, you said, 'It's not easy getting another job'"(41).

Though they explore the theme of complicity with a brutal regime from three perspectives, the three vignettes are not intricately connected from an aesthetic point of view. As short, one- or two-character plays that introduce the main players in Colombia's violent drama, they seem to belong together, but their arrangement in this order is not an artistic necessity. The sequence could be altered or other short vignettes added without altering the basic picture. What the structural fragmentation underlines, however, is that the pieces are not totally separate; victim, victimizer, and collaborator all make up the larger picture. The interconnections belie the notion that violence is an isolated affair or "a marginal phenomenon in the political realm" (Arendt, *Revolution*, 19). Violence, within this context, is central to every action and interaction. And although criminal societies may try to keep violence separate (torture chamber) and compartmentalized (legal system), it threatens to undermine all distinctions between private and public, justice and atrocity. The soldiers target those they consider pillars of the old society, but that essentially means everyone in the society. The teacher describes how death struck indiscriminately like lightning from the sky. The torturer, unable to break his victim, turns on his wife. Her eyes remind him of the prisoner's eyes; he tears them out as he kills her. The physician and his wife discuss their predicament in the "privacy" of their home though they are painfully aware that the neighbors are listening, and they cringe when someone from headquarters calls him on the phone.

The second gyration of the spiral includes at least two plays, *La audiencia* (*The Hearing*) and *La requisa* (*The Requisition*). These longer pieces with larger casts illustrate how violence has undermined all the barriers devised by society to contain it. *The Hearing* brings together the victims, victimizers, and collaborators, hiding behind their robes, masks, and jargon, who make up a judicial farce. The sham trial legitimizes the process of extermination. But although the victimizers try to focus violence on their chosen victim, violence is rampant. All the characters suspect and fear one another. The henchmen (like the torturer) feel underpaid and maligned; the professionals (like the doctor) fear for their lives or their positions; the victim is a silent, anonymous player whose presence is necessary primarily to keep the sham functioning. The unchanneled hostility onstage alerts us that the crisis far exceeds the alleged misdeeds attributed to the accused—a naked, bound man who does not utter a word throughout the entire proceeding. As in other examples of the theatre of crisis, here too the mechanics of persecution invert the cause and nature of the violence: the victim, as perceived *cause* of the crisis (he is a "Communist") is in fact the *result* of crisis. By sacrificing the accused, the accusers win a moment of respite, diverting their attention and hostility from each other in much the way as René Girard describes the process in *Violence and the Sacred*.

*The Requisition* is a companion piece to *The Hearing*. It too accentuates the role playing, the anonymity, the bad faith, the personal rivalries, the myths of self-sacrifice, and the reality of betrayal that make up social interaction. But this time Buenaventura concentrates on the "good guys," the revolutionary group, stripping the players to their most elemental roles: "I am She"; "I am He." *One* "is in charge of maintaining order." *Two* "in the midst of disorder, collaborates with order." Members of the Chorus "fight against an order that maintains chaos, violence, and poverty" (65). Buenaventura indicates that the revolutionaries struggling so hard to survive in a criminalized society are not automatically "heroes"; they are also products of a society in crisis, victims of internal squabblings, ideological contradictions (sexism specifically here), and blind spots. It would be naive to suppose otherwise and dangerous to mythify one's revolutionary role. Rather, the whole concept of heroism must also be examined. The revolutionary hero has close financial ties to his antirevolutionary father; he lies to his wife and infantilizes her as much as his antirevolutionary brother-in-law cheats on his. The oppressed are not free of their oppressors. "What gives birth to the torturer, to the accomplice or collaborator? What circumstances produce the traitor? We know, of course, that it is precisely the same situation that produces the victim, the same circumstances that produce the heroic resister" (Soyinka, x). The hope for decolonization, Buenaventura stresses throughout the cycle, does not lie in the oppressed's assuring themselves that they are different from their oppressors but in their scrutinizing what makes them the same and to what degree they have internalized their oppressors. In the end, "He" is murdered by the police, and his wife and companions glorify his martyrdom. In a disturbing irony, those who side with the oppressed hit upon sacrifice as a solution in much the same way as the oppressors do: for both, "He died so that we might live."

*The Menu* and *The Orgy* make up the third and widest gyration of the cycle. These are much longer plays with complicated plots, large casts, and wonderfully theatrical scenarios. Both are complex, funny, and grotesque works that reunite victims, victimizers, and collaborators in representations of oppression and colonialism. *The Menu* depicts a banquet organized by a social "circle" of charitable Ladies (*Señoritas*) to launch a candidate into society's highest spheres. The Secretary emphasizes the supreme honor of the annual event: "To be launched by the circle, following the customary banquet, has been the aspiration of ministers, professors, in short, of public figures" (94). A few select beggars, a blind man, a "half man" (without use of his legs), a circus guru, the Fakir, and a soothsayer called the Initiated One are allowed to participate because they somehow amuse the Ladies. The Secretary and his henchmen strip, fumigate, and dress the poor in clothes that do not fit them and make them look grotesque. Only then are the paupers allowed into the space designated by different colored circles representing the hierarchies of social grace. They cannot reach the inner circles, of course, but they join in the ritual by eating the leftovers. The presence of the beggars—though they are rigorously controlled and basically "symbolic," as the Secretary points out (99)—is indispensable in a farce dedicated to democracy and social integration. This year's banquet, the Secretary complains, is an aberration owing to the outright unworthiness of the Candidate. Not only does he come from society's lower stratum, but hearsay has it that he is "colored"— though no one knows for certain whether he is black, blue "like the corpses that stay too long at the morgue," purplish "like hanged men left exposed to the air," or green "like the cadavers that turn up after days in the grass" (92). The candidate, "totally susdevelopé [*sic*]" according to the Maître d' (called Metre), reduces the entire process of exaltation to a parody. As the Secretary states: "You can't just take a monkey and crown him" (93). But then, what can one expect of a candidate chosen by women: "Have you ever known a woman to think?" (92). All that this can possibly lead to, the Secretary insists, is a degrading level of "equality that will sink us all" (95). The Ladies enter, a collection of freaks and hybrids—the WoMan, the Fatso, the One-Eyed, the One-Handed, the Dwarf—as deformed and incomplete as the beggars. Then the Candidate arrives, a puppetlike creation shrinking behind a mask, a blond curly wig, and white gloves. Throughout the play he never says a word, submitting passively to violent force-feeding. What looks like a high mass (the table is set like an altar, and the Ladies drink from their chalices) is in fact "the sacrifice of the Candidate" (119). At the end of the ordeal he is left broken, retching, and abandoned by those who used and abused him. The beggars further victimize him, imitating the insults of the mighty, stealing his clothes and attacking him. Then the Ladies' henchmen come back for the forgotten Candidate: "They reconstruct him quickly and carry him out on their shoulders. The Candidate comes back to life and greets the public with the large gestures of a professional politician" (133).

*The Orgy* again presents victims participating in the drama of their own humiliation and destruction. The Old Woman, ugly, degenerate, impoverished, wants to relive a glorious moment in her past when the Prince of Wales, on his first and only visit to South America, kissed her hand. She hires beggars at a miserable wage to dress in the fine though threadbare garments of her late lovers—a colonel, an ambassador, a bishop—and pay homage to her. She steals money from her son, the Mute, who scrapes a living shining shoes. The beggars—hungry, worked up by their roles, and fed up with the Old Woman's miserliness—kill her, eat the food, and steal the Mute's money. The Mute, arriving just as the beggars have left, turns to the audience and signs "Why?"

As this sketch indicates, more and more plays could be added to the cycle without disrupting its basic movement. Perhaps what needs mentioning, however, is that the movement from one play to another is not dialectic—there is no *other.* All we have is an intensification of the same, a *spirale du pire* encompassing more and more violence and desolation. On and on, worse and worse—this for Buenaventura is the history of Colombia.

## History as Erasure

The plays in the cycle show how Buenaventura emplots the history of Colombia, how he asks us to read History as fiction and fiction as history. Beginning with *The Teacher,* he situates us in the lacuna, the dead space created by the violent (Donald Lowe's word is "seismic") confrontation *between,* rather than *within,* changing sociopolitical orders.[18] Sitting alone onstage, the teacher, a young woman, informs us that she is dead; she let herself die by refusing to eat and drink after her father, who founded the town, was shot by incoming military soldiers, who later raped her. "Why eat?" she asks. "One eats to live and I didn't want to live. It didn't make any sense to keep on living" (26). The acts she describes are all too common and concur with the facts of violence and gender in Latin America: death (usually inflicted nonsexually) for the men, sexual violence (usually rape or including rape) for the women.[19]

The date of the event is unspecified: "It's been some time now since fear came to the town and hung over it like an immense thunder cloud. The air smells of fear; voices dissolve in the bitter saliva of fear and people swallow their voices. One day, the cloud ripped open and the lightning struck us" (27). This unspecified "one day" is not Pozzo's nightmare of undifferentiation—"one day we were born, one day we shall die, the same day, the same second"—in Beckett's *Waiting for Godot* (58). Although unlocalizable on a chronological chart, this day marks the dead space, the void in the "seismic" shift, the suspended, terrifying moment between the breaking and the making of a world best summed up by Anthony Kubiak (82): "The moment of terror, like the instant of pain, is a moment of zero time and infinite duration. Although terror can only occur in history, it is felt as naked singularity, existing outside all possible representation." What we have to examine in order to understand her story then, is not History as an evolutionary, unifying narrative but historic events as discontinuity, producing ruptures so profound that they affect language, discourse, epistemic grids—in short, not only the victim's experience of the world but the social configuration of the world itself.

From the graveyard, beyond space and time, beyond conflict even, the teacher recalls the loss of her world. She speaks of a distant past, an almost ahistoric time dating back to Christian myths of creation. Like

God, her father created order out of chaos, founding a town in the jungle. Like Adam, he named the town—ironically, *La esperanza*, Hope. She was born in the town, in the little house on the edge of the dusty red road that leads to the cemetery. Time, for her, is the natural time of the year's two seasons: the rainy season, when the thick, flowing red mud devours the peasants' sandals and splatters the mules and horses with red, wet earth; the dry season, which disgorges the sandals and covers the town and townspeople with a fine red dust. Time is also the dust-to-dust movement of the life cycle, although as the road images indicate, Colombia's earth has been blood red from time immemorial, and people are never quite free of the dust. The cycle, for her, is one of cosmic balance based on perpetual loss and restoration. The river of mud takes the sandals but it also gives them back; the Lord giveth and the Lord taketh away.

The crisis in the play reflects the transformation from the teacher's past to a present that introduces a new economic structure and a new vocabulary of power. Instead of a "founding father" who accepts rights along with responsibility—"as the founder he got the house on the road and the farm land" (27)—we have "political bosses," "legitimate owners," "elections," and "jobs." The shift in terminology signals the struggle to control the "record" and, thus, history. The written word dispossesses those who live within the oral tradition. The process of codification and legalization legitimates violence, for even as it records and validates one system of rights (in terms of both power and ethics), it erases and invalidates another. "Legitimate" owners render all others illegitimate in the very act of naming. What democratically minded person would argue against elections, jobs, and legitimacy? It almost makes us overlook the relationship between legalization and oppression; we forget that the conquerors' *pronunciamientos* (written decrees) deprived the conquered of their lands much as the soldiers' "due process" annihilates the teacher and her world. The terminology effectively eclipses the very world it is destroying; possession and dispossession are two sides of the same coin. Moreover, the obliteration is built into the historical enterprise itself. Hayden White (98) specifies that history, like all narrative, "is not simply a recording of 'what happened' in the transaction from one state of affairs to another, but a progressive *redescription* of sets of events in such a way as to dismantle a structure encoded in one verbal mode in the beginning so as to justify a recoding of it in another mode at the end" (White's emphasis). What we as spectators see as devastation is subsequently woven into Colombia's historical narrative as supposedly democratic "development," supplanting archaic social structures with democratic ones. In fact, the codification is the authoritarian discourse of "the Law," a law controlled by the interests of the oligarchy.

There is no room for the teacher or her experience in either the new political language or the power structures that the language maintains. It is not simply that the teacher, born into a patriarchal, predominantly oral culture in which knowledge and social responsibilities pass from one generation to another, conceives of no other way of living: "My mother was the first teacher the town had. She taught me and when she died, I became the teacher" (28). She has no access to the new language or reality; it makes "no sense" to her. The shift in meaning renders her perspective meaningless. Her conservative (that is, conserving) epistemic grid translates into naive, almost infantile political conservatism in the new lexicon: "I taught reading and writing, the catechism and love for one's country and flag" (28). Like her father before her, she knew "little about politics." The abrupt transformation of one way of life to another deterritorializes her; she is an outsider in her own town; she cannot make sense of the language spoken around her. This deterritorialization exemplifies the internal exile so prevalent in Latin America. People do not have to leave their countries to see their surroundings as suddenly strange and hostile.

As victim, the teacher exists outside the boundaries of representation. In the oral tradition, witnesses represented a major source of historical knowledge.[20] Now, in the new military (and written) culture, she stands outside, both as known object and as knowing subject. Donald Lowe's (basically *un*-Whitean) position in *History of Bourgeois Perception* (174) is that "there can be no history without evidence, for history is neither memory nor fiction. The vestiges, monuments, and legacies from a past necessarily prescribe the boundary of its presentation." The teacher's experience of victimization, however, is not "evidence." Rape, when it is even considered a crime, is hard to prove. And she admits that she let herself die. Nothing attests to her ordeal, yet she as victim is incontestably real, the *only* reality within the world of the play. Buenaventura simultaneously depicts both her powerful presence and her exclusion. Spatially, she sits downstage-center, separate and completely disconnected from the representations taking place behind her; temporally, she is beyond time, dead, and yet she speaks in the eternal present characteristic of dramatic speech. Two stories are taking place concurrently: the teacher, as victim, suffers the annulment of her personal "story" (her *historia*) by a History that is being rewritten, formulated in words and systems she cannot understand. History must erase her in order not to incriminate those in power. The new order does not record the victims. Either these are transformed into "enemies" (and shot, like the father) or "numbers" (and tallied), or they disappear, like the teacher. Yet in Buenaventura's play, she claims center stage, the present as absence, an absence that forces us to reexamine our way of recording presence as well as the present.

History may not be *simply* memory or fiction, but within the context of these plays (and of Colombia itself) Buenaventura asks us to consider to what degree History is a fiction based on manufactured or suppressed facts and evidence. No monuments or vestiges bespeak the teacher's victimization. The "He" of *The Requisition* "lies in the ground anonymous as the seeds" (84). The process of suppressing reality proceeds simultaneously with the inscription (creation) of the new narrative. The torturer's "job" is to acquire evidence. He must make the accused sign a document; the military must have "proof" of antisocial behavior. In *The Autopsy* the physician must alter the evidence to show that his son was a criminal rather than a victim; he was not brutally assassinated by the military, "who put a machine gun in his mouth and shot him" (40), but rather provoked his own death "in a confrontation with the army." Evidence is concocted and manipulated in judicial trials, as in *The Hearing,* converting the naked, powerless victim we see before us into the most dangerous perpetrator of heinous crimes, capable single-handedly of toppling the state. As the lawyers realize, creating evidence is not simply writing fiction; it is more difficult: "Inventing a criminal is easy in detective books, in real life it's much harder" (47). The lawyers have to be careful, they do not want "to create another hero. There are too many already. . . . They want to discredit him" (47). They must be careful, too, not to generate evidence of foul play by leaving traces of torture on the prisoner's body. The lawyers remind the henchmen that electrodes (*picana eléctrica*) produce lesions on the testicles.

History, since the time of Aristotle, has been differentiated from drama in that the former "report[s] what has happened," the latter "what is likely to happen" (*Poetics* 9.37). Buenaventura presents dramatic documents to undermine our reassuring distinctions between fact and fiction. If society creates its own facts, with the evidence to prove it, the history of Colombia becomes a fiction, a drama. The idea of History as drama is not a new one. Hegel, in "Die Poesie" insists that "the principles of history writing are precisely the same as those informing the drama, and tragic drama specifically" (qtd. in White, 76). Nietzsche in *The Use and Abuse of History,* speaks of the historian, like the dramatist, weaving "elements into a single whole" (qtd. in White, 53). White (85) states that the "emplotment," or literary arrangement, of facts and events gives them their particular tone and quality: "Historical situations are not *inherently* tragic, comic or romantic. . . . All the historian needs to do to transform a tragic into a comic situation is to shift his point of view or change the scope of his perceptions." 21

Clearly, Buenaventura indicates, the Colombian elite wants to present its History as high drama (if not quite tragedy) dealing with the trials and tribulations of those in power, the humble participate tangentially as audience and chorus.[22] If we set aside for a moment the indisputably *tragic* "facts" of Colombia's perpetual crisis and shift to the interpretation or "emplotment" of those facts, it becomes easier to see that these noble shams serve the interests of those in power. According to the charitable Ladies of *The Menu*, the Old Woman in *The Orgy*, and the lawyers in *The Hearing*, the drama they perpetuate is one of utmost magnitude and solemnity. The banquet, the orgy, and the trial are clearly conceived theatrically. The pomp and formality of ceremony legitimate the proceedings. Those in power dress their parts, force the victims and underlings to assume theirs; the powerful demarcate the space, choose the plot, and carry out the action with all the precision of a performance. The Ladies' banquets always have some culturally legitimating theme chosen from Greek and Roman antiquity or from European *haute culture*. Although the decor looks "totally fake" (90) and the actors set the stage themselves, balancing the hollow Corinthian pillars and hanging up the emblems as they go along, nobody is supposed to recognize them as anything less than the "real thing." The show asks to be appreciated aesthetically, as form rather than function.

Mighty and weighty proceedings occur in these lofty circles. As the public prosecutor reminds the judge in *The Hearing*, all this is highly serious: "We can't participate in a farce. Hearings should maintain the strictest *appearance* of reality" (61; my emphasis). The Ladies' ceremonies launch Candidates into the highest political stratosphere; an apotheosis of integration and democracy. Theirs is a banquet of transformation, from the lowly to the great, from the material to the spiritual. The poor have needs; they are hungry and sick, hence *lowly*, material beings. By force-feeding the Candidate, the Ladies place him above need. The Queen of England, the Metre informs us, lives off a drop of "butterfly wings consommé" (124). As in religious communion, where the wafer links the human to the divine, here too food raises the lowly to awesome heights; it serves as the inverse barometer of social and spiritual well-being: less is more. The Old Woman in *The Orgy* also belabors the spirituality of her orgies: "They are spiritual *soirées*, consecrated to memory. I refuse to let them be tarnished by the materialism of the times" (141). She derides the beggars for being hungry, sick, arthritic; she forces them to decline the food in front of them because her lovers, whose roles the beggars play, were refined and delicate creatures who hardly touched food. She throws away food to substantiate the myth of wealth and abundance. The beggars, according to her, stubbornly refuse to be transformed: one cannot squeeze his twisted arthritic fingers into the lace gloves; another cannot sublimate his hunger.

By means of these dramas, the powerful flaunt their fantasies, which become in a real way the History of Colombia. Authority figures—the general, the bishop, the diplomat, foreign dignitaries—strut across this grotesque stage. While they mutually support each other, as their tableau pose in *Orgy* illustrates, they have the power to turn the lower classes against each other. The general's story exemplifies the History-making power of his narration. The one-Legged beggar playing the general hero-ically recounts how he lost his leg in the "War of the Thousand Days." He rides, leading his troops; the flags are waving! The Old Woman reminds him not to leave out the part about his leg, enshrined on the national altar. But the war between Liberals and Conservatives, which lasted from 1899 to 1902, was anything but a glorious display of heroism. As Kline (38) observes, "The balance sheet included more than 100,000 men dead, more with disabling injuries, commerce ruined, difficult communications, economic production almost nil, and a paper currency (used by the govern-ment to finance the war) that had a paper peso that was worth less than a gold centavo." Yet politicians continue to tap into Colombia's historical conflicts to mobilize the population. The beggar, in his role as general, makes a nasty remark about the Conservatives that throws the rest of the beggars into turmoil and provokes a fight onstage. The Old Woman is thrilled and excited: "I adore military battles!" (151). Like the Old Wo-man, those who produce the show can choose the script, set the players against each other, and enjoy the spectacle the underclasses make of themselves.

Buenaventura, of course, emplots Colombian history otherwise. The heroic History of the powerful has been the never-ending nightmare of the poor. The events and facts are tragic, but they were neither destined nor inevitable. Rather, the manner in which they have been manipulated situates them closer to farce—unbelievable, grotesque, violent, and "hid-eously true."[23] If farce is a lowly, anarchistic genre, full of stops and starts, that cleverly exploits all the possibilities of the plot, it aptly represents the catastrophic history of the country, its colonization, turbulent indepen-dence, neocolonialism. Instead of quasi-religious ceremonies dedicated to social integration and national improvement (*superación*), the banquet is what Memmi (91) calls "the colonialist's hoax," the scene of segregation and degradation. *The Menu* is literally a farce (*farci* = to stuff) in that the Candidate is brutally stuffed until he almost chokes on the demonstration of "equality" that is being forced down his throat. While staging celebra-tions to democracy and endorsing "the liberal fantasy that anyone is welcome to share in the power of the reference group if he abides by the rules" (Gilman, *Self-Hatred*, 2),[24] the Ladies do not allow their Candi-date—much less the poor—free access to the circle. The underlings are kept spatially and temporally apart. The circles on the floor indicate where they can step; the Candidate eats by himself, and the poor get the leftovers after he has finished; their behavior is graded. The real purpose behind the banquet belies its proclaimed function. It pays lip service to equality while ossifying inequality; it congratulates itself on bringing the "high" and "low" together while rigorously differentiating between them. The "wretched of the earth" must be kept separate, even as the Ladies proclaim their compassion. In fact, as the Secretary explains, the Ladies have hit upon a brilliant strategy to do both at the same time: "The Circle has decided to consecrate this day of the year to distinct acts of solidarity. In the morning, [the Ladies] have breakfast with tuberculosis victims." This is followed by a fraternal banquet dedicated "to the children drowned in the last flood and the children carbonized in the last fire. . . . It's very practical," he adds. "That way people can forget about these things for the rest of the year because they know there is a day especially set aside for them" (98).

The poor are expected to participate in the annihilating fictions of the powerful. Not only have they been the cannon fodder for war, but they have to star in dramas of their own oppression. In *The Menu*, the borrowed clothes make the beggars look like clowns; they trip in the ill-fitting shoes. The beggars in *The Orgy* dress in the cast-off clothes of the mighty; they have to play the roles of bankers, diplomats, and generals expressing their contempt for the underclasses. The one-legged beggar even tries to capitalize on the fact that his handicap makes him especially valuable to the fantasy; because he can convincingly play the general, he demands more pay than the other beggars. The underclasses, by playing along with this History, are co-opted into roles that only further divide and degrade them.

Behind this enforced separation the powerful *need* the lowly. There exists a mutual dependency between oppressors and oppressed: the oppressed hope to be fed and cared for; the oppressors want to differentiate themselves as "high." Not only does a high need a low as comparison, but the outcasts must also absorb all the negative characteristics that the defining group attempts to distance from itself. The underclasses, then, can be safely marginalized, infantilized, and controlled because they are "dirty," "sick," and troublesome. Systems must be set up to "keep them in their place" (124). Rules and handbooks are devised; the Secretary keeps reminding the beggars that the handbook prohibits protest. Circles are painted on the floor; middlemen like the Secretary and his musclemen make the stage safe for the Ladies' charity.

The narrative the Ladies act out is the story of colonization complete with its secondary manifestations: internalized colonization and self-hatred. These hybrids and freaks (I mean these *Ladies*) associate with

Queens and Crown Princes; they derive their original sense of worth or dignity from their foreign patrons. In *The Orgy*, the Old Woman's glory resides in the fact that the Prince of Wales kissed her hand and said "I love you. . . . You mucha mujer, muchísima mujer. . . . You very good" (153). Her entire life is built around the quasi-religious observance of this glorious moment, when she was in her prime and South America still seemed exotic. Now she is an old hag who has come down in the world, who is forced to pay for the attentions she used to charge for. And why, she asks, would royalty "want to visit the horrible South America of nowadays?" (140). She needs her beggars to keep what she repeatedly refers to as her "history" alive, although she is decrepit and impoverished, hard put to pay for the extravagance.

However, the colonized who have internalized the colonizer have more than simply *access* to power. Within their circle they have the power to decide what power is or should be—they legitimate. They borrow the trappings of foreign culture (the Corinthian columns and the French food in *Menu*, for example) and use them as proof of a taste and distinction that necessarily separate them from the "masses," the undiscerning, the non-connoisseurs. What is essentially a class conflict is transposed from the material to the cultural field, much as the banquets transpose the material to the spiritual realm. This transposition can be studied along the line of cultural critique proposed by Pierre Bourdieu in his study *Distinction*. While he does not extend his examination of culture-as-politics to situations of oppression, I believe that his analysis of culture as a mechanism for excluding the underclasses on matters of "taste" is doubly pertinent to colonization in general and to our understanding of *The Menu* in particular. On the first level, the foreign colonizer can always differentiate from the colonized on the basis of "taste," manners, and the familiarity with culture which alone communicates class. For the colonizer, these are "natural" attributes born of cultured environments; for the colonized, they are acquired. As Bourdieu (4) states, tastes—including artistic tastes—are not universal: "A work of art has meaning and interest only for someone who possesses the cultural competence, that is, the code, into which it is encoded." Cultural competence in itself is sufficient to set colonizers and colonized apart. The colonizers control the cultural field; the colonized, in an attempt to be accepted into these upper spheres, compete for legitimacy.

The phenomenon of "raising" class conflicts to the field of culture, we see in *The Menu*, works in the same way on the second level: the colonized who have enjoyed a certain proximity with the colonizer adopt some of the high-class tastes and manners; some of the distinction of the latter rubs off on the former. The colonizer accumulates a certain amount of "symbolic capital." In turn, like the Ladies, these hybrids differentiate between themselves as "high" and their countrymen as "low" by means of the same taste tests formerly imposed on them. The Candidate's poor table manners are a source of constant irritation to the WoMan, who rudely, sternly, and even violently corrects him. The beggars admit they have no taste for champagne—"It tastes like cork" (117)—and they dislike crawfish. They would trade all that, they confess, for some milk and eggs (121). Yet even among themselves they vie for distinction. The Half-Man complains that the Ladies are "throwing pearls before swine" (120); his fellow beggars will "never learn how to eat" (121).

The Ladies, through their charitable banquet and manners, impose hegemony. They define the cultural field and set the rules of conduct. They decide that hunger is "materialistic" and "sousdevelopé." They force others to compete for food or validation. This force can manifest itself either as direct violence, as when the Secretary warns the beggars, "Stay in your place if you want to stay alive!" (124), or as indirect, unspoken violence, as when the Ladies teach the Candidate "good manners." The treatment to which they subject the Candidate, they would argue, is not violence but, on the contrary, a *privilege*.

The irony, of course, is that the Ladies are even more grotesque than the beggars they try to control and keep separate. Though the latter are maimed (blind, paralyzed), they are not deformed (WoMan, Dwarf). As Albert Memmi (119) observes, the "body and face of the colonized are not a pretty sight." Furthermore, the aristocrats are self-deceived: they impose ridiculous costumes on the beggars but do not recognize their own fantastic outfits as *disguise*. While the poor fight among themselves, the Ladies too bicker and compete for attention. The poor are hungry and fight for the leftovers; the Ladies, too refined to need food, gradually get drunk on their imported liquor. They are essentially no different from the lowly, although their identity depends on radical differentiation. The Circle, then, provides the arena for identity formation. The operation is a double one: it separates and differentiates the "high" from the "low," yet it joins them in symbiosis—the "high" need the "low" to validate their presumed superior identity.

The beggars in *The Menu* and *The Orgy* participate in roles that reinforce their positional disadvantage in the oppressed/oppressor binary. The only means of escape they see is to attack the oppressor in person or in proxy. The beggars in *The Menu* turn on the abandoned Candidate at the end of the play; the beggars in *The Orgy* kill the Old Woman. They never leave the field defined by the Ladies; they are very much part of it; they make up "the circle of misery," as the WoMan says (*Menu*, 130). Rather than break the circle, they merely want to change their places within it. They do not condemn their oppression; they just want to exchange places with their oppressors. At the end of *The Menu*, the beggars simply appropriate the words of the powerful to further humiliate the now powerless Candidate— he is blue like the hanged man, green like a cadaver found in the fields. Both plays suggest that Frantz Fanon is correct when he asserts in *The Wretched of the Earth* (39, 45) that the colonized person "dreams of posses- sion. . . . [He] dreams at least once a day of setting himself up in the settler's place"; only through *decolonization* does this person understand that "my life is worth as much as the settler's, his glance no longer shrivels me up nor freezes me, and his voice no longer turns me into stone." The beggars' ironic march for liberation at the end of *The Menu*, in which the Fakir jumps on the Half-Man's little cart and the Initiated One leads them around the circles, guided by her intuition and protected by her umbrella, illustrates that they have a long way to go. The murder of the Old Woman in *Orgy* is also a futile act; we wonder whether it gets the beggars more than a hurried meal. Buenaventura explodes the myths of vengeance.

Decolonization, then, requires a struggle for history, for culture, the telling of one's own stories in one's own voice. The fight to produce and control the "record" is as vital as armed warfare.[25] The nature of Buena- ventura's participation in the conflict tells us something important both about him and about the *Documents*. For Buenaventura, the struggle cannot be fought from abroad. Although he says he sympathizes with Latin American intellectuals who "live in Europe and support Cuba" and stresses that he considers "that position deeply honest," he personally cannot do it. As a playwright, he has to be close to his audience. Together they produce an "event" and the "documents" that challenge Colombia's History. A "director-actor-playwright" depends on his audience; "he can- not pack up his way of life and memories and go off to set them down in a tranquil place without soldiers, without guerrillas, without starving pro- letarian masses, without students. I confess I regret very much that I am unable to escape, that every day I have to make an almost mystical effort not to run away" ("Theater and Culture," 152-53).

This also tells us something about the nature of these "documents." The fragmentation reflects the vital character of the pieces. Their identity is completely tied into the rehearsal or production process. The changes in them reflect the shifting concerns or priorities of audience, actors, and playwright. The various vignettes, then, are evidence of the changing history of their production, productions that in turn reflect the History of Colombia. The documents become a history much as History becomes a drama with its fictions of power (*Torture*), fictions of justice (*The Hearing*), fictions of democracy and charity (*The Menu*). Does the issue of "truth" or "reality" in fact differentiate these dramatic accounts from official records? Who writes those records? Certainly not the victims, and probably no one who admits to being a victimizer or a collaborator. Those who have a "legitimate" right to discourse do not associate with the protagonists of Buenaventura's fiction. Are these stories "true"? Do physicians doctor autopsy reports? Do soldiers blow people's heads off on a whim? The records of Amnesty International and similar organizations show that this information is undoubtedly "true." What Elaine Scarry (42) points out in regard to Uruguay holds for other terrorized countries throughout Latin America: physicians "who refused to assist the torturers disappeared at such a rate that Uruguay's medical and health care programs entered a state of crisis."

If the History of Colombia is a collection of fictions, as the cycle suggests, who will speak for the victims? Buenaventura demonstrates that memory and fiction (Lowe notwithstanding) can speak to what History leaves out. We have "proof" of this kind of evidence, from the Aztec versions of the Conquest of Mexico compiled by Miguel León-Portilla in *The Broken Spears*, to Jacobo Timerman's testimonial writing, from Anne Frank to Elie Wiesel. The fragmentary vignettes need not gloss over the lacunae, the ruptures and contradictions incompatible with totalizing and coherent narratives. Buenaventura focuses his inquiry precisely on the breaks, the dead spaces, the meaningless voids—"meaningless" insofar as they have not been officially inscribed. Memory recalls the many voices; fiction makes visible the absence that History has not validated as presence or present. By inscribing, or documenting, that which otherwise would disappear without a trace, without evidence, Buenaventura's cycle calls attention to the limitations inherent in Colombia's major narrative. History, then, is redefined; its validity is tested as much by what it leaves out as by what it records. *Documents from Hell* challenges the possession of History by those in power, the particular emplotment of events that assures them their place in the center of things. The fragmented cycle allows for no center; it decenters the narrative and opens the material to other interpretations. Now, others have a bid in the struggle for history; this, I would argue, is Buenaventura's concern with the "historical" framework.

What the *Documents* inscribe is not just the History *of* erasure, or even history *as* erasure. The void, the crisis, the collapse of moral, judicial, and ideological frameworks shows erasure as the history of Colombia. Behind the fictions, the cycle shows a world undone by violence. The *Documents* address the problem of social crisis in the language of crisis—fragmentation, ambiguity, spatial and temporal suspension. The cycle has no agenda, no "solution." In fact, it challenges all myths of liberation, including the revolutionary. The road that the beggars embark on is long, difficult, and relatively unexplored. Who has the answers? Where will the crisis end? These vignettes promise no closure. The *spirale du pire* continues its infernal trajectory, on and on, worse and worse.

# 6

# CONFLATION
# AND CRISIS:
# EGON WOLFF

*FLORES DE PAPEL* (*Paper Flowers*) by Egon Wolff (born 1926 in Chile), like all the examples of theatre of crisis examined in this study, dismantles the known universe.[1] Unlike the other plays presented here, however, this one decomposes itself in the process. As in the other plays, we see the socioeconomically marginal protagonist (the Hake) moving toward center stage; both systemic and personal boundaries are suspended as forces previously considered *outer* penetrate the domain of the *inner.* Traditional notions of identity crumble; ideologies disintegrate. Here, too, the crisis provokes a violent response of persecution and scapegoating. The difference between this play and the others, and the reason it is important to our purposes here, is that *Paper Flowers* falls victim to the crisis. While the other plays under discussion point to the multiple ideological blind spots and contradictions that we must acknowledge in order to change the participation of the oppressed in the social system, *Flores* cannot see its way out of them. In fact, it cannot even recognize the dangers for what they are. Like Triana, Gambaro, Carballido, and Buenaventura, Wolff is acutely aware that the entire social structure, with the pillars sustaining it, must be radically transformed if oppression is to end. But *Flores* has no perspective on its own discourse; it simply replaces one kind of blindness with another, one form of oppression with the one it ostensibly sets out to overcome. As such, the play *reflects* rather than *represents* crisis.

In *Paper Flowers* (1968),[2] Wolff confronts two clearly defined worlds, two antagonistic spaces—the *inner* world traditionally associated with woman, home, creation, middle-class stability, health, order (to name its most salient features) and its antithesis, the *outer,* the marginal "riverbank" (220)[3] that in this play represents the world of the man, the economically dispossessed, the physically and mentally infirm, the dark and dangerous universe of the have-nots. The conflict in the play is as straightforward as the spatial opposition itself. The lights come up on a tidy, comfortable, and conventional apartment. It is empty except for a canary in a cage. Eva, fortyish, a middle-class divorced woman (who repeatedly refers to herself as an "old maid"), returns from her shopping with a man who is carrying her groceries. She is decisive and well-dressed; he is uncombed, dirty, thin, pale, sickly, given to severe tremors. The thirty-year-old man, called "the Hake," flatters Eva by telling her that he remembers seeing her a year ago at the Botanical Gardens where she was painting flowers. He rejects her offer of a tip and asks instead that she give him a cup of tea. The Hake convinces her that a couple of his ruffian friends, whom he beat at cards, are positioned outside her apartment, ready to kill him as soon as he leaves her place. She looks out the window, and sure enough, there they are. Flustered and obviously flattered that he has taken notice of her, she gives him some soup and allows him to stay in the apartment while she goes to work on the condition that she can lock him in.

During the play's six scenes, the Hake wins Eva's love and takes over her home. In the first, he talks in an ugly, menacing fashion to the canary as Eva leaves for work; in the second, after her return from work, he tears newspapers to shreds in a maniacal fashion as he professes to teach her to make paper flowers; in the third, installed comfortably in the house and wearing Eva's robe, he destroys all the wicker figures she has made and replaces them with his paper figures; in the fourth, he kills the canary; in the fifth, he destroys Eva's furniture; in the sixth, he annihilates her features. Finally, in a grotesque parody of the happy ending in comedies, he marries the now faceless Eva. As she stands almost senseless in her old wedding gown, the Hake shreds it to pieces on her body and covers her face with a huge paper flower. He too is almost naked, wearing only a train made of paper strips. To the triumphant notes of Mendelssohn's wedding march, the groom leads his bride out of the ravaged apartment to their new abode—the outer, *other* world of the dark and dangerous riverbank.

The blind spot in the play is that it presents the confrontation as a quasi-justified attack on class. The action so forcefully directs us to see the Hake as a victim of class oppression that commentators have been blinded to the play's misogyny. It may even appear that I am seriously misreading the play and its reception by noting that though *Paper Flowers* is one of the best known and most produced plays from Latin America, no one has yet commented on the fact that the political battle takes place on a woman's body—and not just any woman but "Eva," Eve herself, Woman. What passes as an inevitable attack on a complacent, unrealistic middle class completely obscures what is also one more attack on women, the relatively undiscovered oppressed group in Latin America.[4]

Commentaries on *Paper Flowers* have tended to fall into the two critical camps I pointed out at the beginning of this study. The first decontextualizes the work and compares it with Western masterpieces: Strindberg's *Miss Julie*, it has been noted, shares a similar theme (class and gender tension) and imagery (the dead bird).5 The second, best expressed by Juan Villegas in "Los marginados como personajes," contextualizes the play and refers specifically to the sociopolitical struggle producing it.6 Clearly, both perspectives are important and have contributed to our understanding of the play. The first has been well expounded; I will only add briefly to the second before moving on to my own, a third, interpretation.

The Hake, an outsider who scrapes a living doing odd jobs, does in fact represent a whole new Chilean underclass that migrated from the countryside to the cities, desperate for work, during the 1960s. As Thomas Skidmore and Peter Smith point out in *Modern Latin America* (130), not only was there little work, but these people were "ill-housed, ill-fed, and ill-educated. . . . These 'marginals' were the tragic underside of capitalist urbanization in a Third World country. By the end of the 1960s about 60 percent of the Chilean population lived in urban areas." Moreover, of course, the late 1960s and early 1970s were times of intense political confrontation between capitalist and socialist factions in Chile. The Christian Democrats under Eduardo Frei (strongly supported by the United States), who won power in 1964, had promised a "Revolution in Liberty." By the time of the 1970 election, their "revolution" no longer convinced the population, and the vote split three ways: Salvador Allende's Unidad Popular (UP) won with a narrow lead of 36.3 percent of the vote, followed closely by the right with 34.9 and the Christian Democrats with 27.8 percent. This was indeed a shaky political base from which to undertake a program of socialist socioeconomic change, especially with such a formidable opponent as the United States government ready to abort the democratic process in the name of democracy.7

As Juan Villegas rightly notes, the explosive background to the play has rarely figured in scholarly discussions of it. Villegas stresses that Chilean theatre in the 1960s was predominantly a middle-class monologue, written and produced by and for the middle class. There were no really marginal or outside voices. Hence, the marginal characters who appear onstage incarnate either the fears or the myths of the middle class. This, I think, is absolutely true. Where we disagree is, to a degree, in our reading of Wolff's portrayal of the outcast and, more significantly, I would emphasize that the discourse in *Paper Flowers* is both middle-class and *male* discourse. For Villegas, Wolff presents the underclass as a threat to the middle class, which shows up the weakness of the latter's ideological system. Self-serving charity is no longer enough; the middle class needs new strategies for dealing with the underprivileged. Villegas sees the differences between Wolff's earlier work, *Los invasores* (*The Invaders*, 1963), and *Paper Flowers* as a reflection on the growing power of the representatives of these underclasses. In "Los marginados" (93) he calls attention to what Wolff depicts as the progressively intrusive move of the oppressed to the center of Chilean life: "In 1963, *The Invaders* signals the danger of the *other*, his potential danger and the diverse responses toward it on the part of different generations. . . . In 1971, the other, the one who comes in from the street and takes over the house, is a reality confronting the protagonist [Eva], whose inherent weakness makes her submissive and impotent in defending her own domain. It is no longer a threat, it is a reality" (Villegas's emphasis).

Though Wolff no doubt presents the Hake as a threat, he is not *only* a threat; there is something fascinating about him which, however disturbing, must be accounted for. If Wolff wants to decry the invasion of the middle classes by dangerous outsiders, his mythification of the Hake subverts the enterprise. If, on the contrary, he wants to support the lower classes in their struggle for empowerment, his depiction of their representative as a crazed maniac subverts that too. Villegas is correct in calling Wolff's a middle-class perspective, but there is such a potent dose of middle-class self-hatred, mixed with a profound hatred of the *other* (both lower class and female), that Wolff continually undermines his own discourse. He seems to mean one thing and say another. While he would adamantly defend his egalitarian political views, the play itself reveals his gender and class biases.[8] This is a play that does not recognize its boundaries or identity, a play undone by the very contradictions it proposes to illuminate.

There is no doubt that the Hake is threatening. He is violent, destructive, and full of rage. Yet he seems the opposite also, resourceful, full of energy, and at times almost endearing. Like the other monstrous characters we have encountered, Buenaventura's perhaps most of all, he seems deformed by oppression. When we first see him carrying Eva's packages, it is almost as if he were shouldering the so-called white man's burden. When she asks how he manages financially, he responds: "There's always someone whose bags are too heavy for them" (154). Her abundance and comfort only accentuate his poverty and misery. Her incessant movement and conversation emphasize his awkwardness and reticence.

Like most of the other characters in this study, he essentially has no name. "The Hake," he explains to Eva, is a nickname he picked up in the slums. When she asks his "Christian" name, he replies enigmatically that he does not have one: "Names get lost in the alleyways and down the gutters" (171). Finally he says that his mother called him "Roberto," "Beto" for short, and "bastard"—"bastard before eating, Beto afterward. I had two mothers, one before and one after" (171). At the end of the play he calls himself "Ukelele," the Simba warrior. Again, his lack of a name, which later in the play is presented almost as a lack of identity, reflects more on others than on himself. We are tempted to feel compassion for the Hake as victim, product of a schizophrenic mother and a hostile social environment.

The Hake's misery in *Paper Flowers* is depicted more as an incrimination of others than a reflection on self. When out of compassion or vanity (more of this later) Eva offers him a bowl of soup, his body shakes from malnutrition. She, on the other hand, is on a diet and can eat only a boiled egg: "I have a terrible tendency to gain weight" she confesses, apparently oblivious to the political, rather than aesthetic, nature of his emaciation: "If I didn't diet, I'd be as round as a balloon" (155). In scene 2, when she returns with food for him to take back to the riverbank—salami, cheese, and wine—he turns it down, explaining that his stomach cannot tolerate heavy food after a meager diet of broth and rice. Eva, embarrassed, only talks more, admitting that she has nothing in her life but food: "That's all I ever do. Eat and eat. Eat in the morning, eat at noon, eat at evening" (166). Again, Eva's privilege and compassion somehow seem to account for the Hake's dispossession, as if there were a cause-and-effect relationship between the two.

The interconnected economy between the haves and the have-nots is one we associate with oppression. What we see here is the same kind of "scale" that Albert Memmi refers to in *The Colonizer and the Colonized* (8): the colonizer, like the oppressive middle class in *Flowers*, "finds himself on one side of the scale, the other side of which bears the colonized man. . . . If [the colonizer's] standard of living is high, it is because those of the colonized are low. . . . the more freely he breathes, the more the colonized are choked." If what we are indeed witnessing in *Flowers* is the representation of oppression, then the play reads in a way that strongly resembles Buenaventura's *The Menu*. Eva, like the charitable Ladies, offers the down-and-outer the leftovers; *Paper Flowers* explicitly calls attention to the fact that Eva warms up leftover soup for the Hake. She, like the Ladies, decides to help him, but not because he needs help in what he insists is a life-threatening situation. Rather, she helps him because he flatters and amuses her; she even confesses as much: "If you were only the poor vagabond you appear to be, we couldn't even be having this conversation. . . . After giving you the soup, I would have got rid of you because I'm sure you would have ended up . . . boring me" (195). Like the Ladies, Eva suspends the inequality between the upper classes and lower classes.

She asks the Hake to address her in the familiar form *tu* (193); she stresses repeatedly that she does not acknowledge any difference between them, that she does not want to place "false barriers" between them (196). However, as the Hake points out, everything is a barrier. He measures the distance between them in meters, language, clothes, and taste: "There is an abyss between us, as wide as the distance around the entire earth" (210).

Surely, if this is a play about oppression, we must agree with him and admit that Eva is self-indulgent and self-deceiving, much like Buenaventura's Ladies. Her compassion, as Pascal Bruckner would argue in *The Tears of the White Man,* is another form of contempt. Such notions as "equality" and "heroism" are luxuries reserved for the wealthy. Eva enjoys thinking of herself as magnanimous; she can indulge her "obsession with heroic acts" (158). But as the Hake reminds her, "you have your fantasies and I have only my reality, which is much poorer, much sadder, much more disillusioning" (195). We understand why he interprets her talk of equality as a cruel joke, and why it only provokes greater distancing and rage on his part. His refusal to accept what she considers generosity seems the inevitable result of his life of deprivation and disease. When he begs her for blue pin-striped pants to replace his rags, it appears that he too hopes to bridge the gap between them. When he throws them on the floor and insults her (because she could not find blue ones and bought gray ones instead), it reminds us that the consequences of dispossession far exceed the material question of possession itself. When he smashes her wicker animals and substitutes figures made from newspaper in their place, the destruction tries to pass as an assault on kitsch and, as such, an attack on middle-class sensibilities and bourgeois "respect for beauty and for the order of things—for the established order and things as they are" (Friedländer, 25).[9] After all, this is the cultural order that has excluded him. "Nobody wants filthy newspaper butterflies," the Hake stammers. "Nobody wants to get their temples filthy from putting filthy paper flowers in their hair— at least, that's what the bourgeois say—and they are the arbitrators of fashion—in everything—including in how one works with—news—paper" (170). He ironically sings a jingle praising the consumer society to which he does not belong: "For those who cannot buy, all that is left is to die. (He laughs) I'm a poet and didn't know it" (208). In all this, the Hake's violence ties into his socioeconomic destitution. He repeatedly identifies himself as a man of the lower classes, a man full of "rage and stupor" (173). He, unlike Eva, has nothing—no home, no name, no pets.

It is clear, however, that the depiction of the Hake as oppressed victim is extremely problematic. He seems more like a madman playing victim. Moreover, he is the stereotypical madman. He refers to himself as a "crazy maniac" (209); he makes allusions to a hospital with male nurses where he was not allowed to have scissors. He confesses that when he becomes obsessed with things, he "sees double" (203). His physical tremors suggest that he is out of control. He is paranoid of, or obsesses on, what others will think of him, because there "are suspicious characters out there. . . . They suspect that people are what they aren't, that they aren't what they are, just by glancing at them—they have radar in their noses—they see a person in rags and they deduce a world of things—they deduce that one is a drunk, a drug-addict, a pederast, a thief, a con man, a pimp, an exhibitionist, a sodomist, an infanticide, a narcissist, a necrophiliac, a prostitute with the same facility with which they would place a camelia in their buttonhole. The simple presence of rags wakens in them a fantastic mythology" (199). It is evident that his language alone bespeaks a dangerously borderline personality—and this is one of his more balanced monologues. They become increasingly long and fragmented as the play progresses.

The Hake's insanity, if we call it that, displaces the question of oppression; he sees his rags through the eyes of the defining group. It is that group's fear of the outcast, rather than the reality of the outcast, that looms large. Sander Gilman, in *Disease and Representation* (1), writes of the projection of *dis*ease onto the other as a way of localizing and controlling it: "The fear of collapse, the sense of dissolution," he observes, "contaminates the Western image of all diseases, including elusive ones such as schizophrenia. But the fear we have of our own collapse does not remain internalized. Rather, we project this fear onto the world in order to localize it and, indeed, to domesticate it. For once we locate it, the fear of our own dissolution is removed". The middle class's fear, as Villegas noted, creates this infirm other. *Paper Flowers*, as he states, is a middle-class monologue; the Hake is a middle-class creation, the maniacal madman as "one of the most common focuses for the general anxiety felt by all members of society" (Gilman, *Disease*, 11). He is conceived as the negation or absence of "the haves," the outsider from the riverbank who insinuates himself into the "the pretty apartment on Plaza España" (210). The Hake embodies the insider's nightmare of the outsider as excentric, as crazed, diseased, cunning, and cruel. He lacks personal substance; his smile is always described as "empty"; his expression is "open, but does not say a thing" (159). His reality, like the hand shadows he projects on the wall, seems to reside elsewhere, beyond our realm of vision. The issue of oppression, then, is pushed aside as it is in all overtly "antipopular" theatre. If we do not want to associate the oppressed with insane criminals, we must conclude that the play is not about oppression but about something else—say, madness as the displacement of middle-class fear. The subject of oppression serves to distract us from the real issue.

Moreover, we notice that the Hake also sees himself as a middle-class creation. He always defines himself from the point of view of the other: "They call me 'the Hake'" (171). He visualizes himself as other; what will *they* think of him, dressed as he is? He places himself in the position both of *see-er* and *seen*. He thinks of himself as a loathsome other and forces Eva to treat him with the contempt he thinks she must feel toward him: "I want to hear you say it! 'It would be better if you took a bath, Beto, because the way you look, with those clothes and that dirt—' Let's hear it" (173). He describes his work with newspaper not from *his* position but refracted from what he considers the prevailing social norm. From the vantage point of "the bourgeois" (170), *he* represents lack and inadequacy. The chair he hammers together, according to him, reflects "the hand *without* class—*without* refinement—made by a man from the—lower classes!" (210; my emphasis). He forces Eva to play the condescending oppressor vis-à-vis his rendition of the oppressed.

Hake: Say it, let's see— 'I like your chair—'
Eva:   I like your chair—
Hake: No, no! Not like that. A longer *i*. Like this, you see? 'I liiike your chair—'
Eva:   I liiike your chair!
Hake: (Shouts triumphantly) There! You see! Hear that tone in your voice? That uneasy quiver! That painful trill!—You pity me! (209)

The Hake, then, seems to support the image of himself as other, an image founded on middle-class fears and projections. The issue is confused, however, by our impression that he seems to be doing the controlling and the projecting. Like Eva, we wonder who this man is and where he is coming from.

The negative representation of the Hake as a demented other is further obscured by the alarming mythification of that same madness. In contrast to the lethargic banality of Eva-as-middle-class, he has an enviable vitality. He is Dionysian, the creator and destroyer, closely associated with wine throughout the play. He takes all forms: the Hake, Beto, Roberto, Ukelele, bastard. He dresses in multiple garbs, from Eva's ex-husband's tennis outfit to her dressing gown: "You're multiple," Eva tells him, "absolutely multiple" (180). He speaks different languages. He has prodigious energy; a "fever" comes over him as he takes apart all her furniture in one night and puts it together again following his own wild specifications (203).

The Hake's passionate unmaking of the world is meant to conjure up some of the positive attributes of the Dionysiac prototype he is modeled on. The Bacchic rite implies not only danger and excess but also creativity and insight. Throughout this "orgy of destruction," to borrow Pedro Bravo Elizondo's phrase (20), the Hake relates destruction to knowledge, justifying violence in the name of "Truth" much as Euripides' Dionysus does in *The Bacchae*: "You do not know what life you live, or what you do, or who you are" (197). The Hake pretends to possess a higher authenticity that justifies his bullying Eva and rejecting her love as somehow dishonest: "I don't want that! I want the truth. . . . the pure, holy, whole and absolute truth!" (208). He destroys everything he touches, both the malleable things he can control (newspaper) and those that exceed his grasp (the bird), but blurs the chaos by stating that he is in fact creating something superior, more inspired. He does not like her furniture; it is common, it has "no imagination, no fantasy, no illusion of any kind. . . . You have to be a poet to choose furniture" (196). He kills the bird, but then, death is preferable to lack of liberty. If the Hake leaves nothing standing, the play almost encourages us to conclude that the bourgeois, stale existence of a middle-aged, middle-class woman who lives in an apartment as empty and conventional as herself, who paints flowers in the Botanical Gardens and makes wicker animals, was not worth much anyway. He may be destructive, but she is a fool; she tries to understand "Beto," while ignoring "the Hake," "Roberto," and the "bastard."

The lights go down on the wrecked set; the furniture and even the walls themselves have disappeared. Now, filled with grotesque paper flowers described as "clumsy, huge, and ravaged," the set acquires "a new beauty" (221). Wolff glorifies his protagonist's insane unmaking with the redemptive insight sometimes associated with madness: "I look for the nucleus of things, their essence. It's like children who break their toys or destroy their dolls to see what's inside them. . . . 'The Hake' destroys the furniture and furnishings. That expresses the deepest desire of my life: to get to the bottom of things" (quoted in Otano, 18-19). However, the insight or "truth" that the Hake aspires to is a misnomer for the deep, prevailing hatred and need for control evidenced by his actions.

The Hake's penetrating gaze reflects the violence of violation more than the insight associated with revelation—although his Dionysiac quality would have us believe otherwise. He stands outside in a way that expresses the critical distancing of not being "taken in." Observing, he resists absorption and clings to difference, measuring it in terms of meters (198), of vocabulary, of clothes. He speaks of different worlds, of the abysmal gap between him and Eva. His approach to every thing and being throughout the play remains consistent: he stands back, regards "it" as an autonomous creation, and destroys it in order to recreate it. He constructs a totalizing system; he rearranges all the parts; he replaces everything he sees with his own reality. He controls the fiction by redirecting Eva to speak "with a very special emphasis" (209).

Yet the process conveys violation rather than revelation in that nothing new comes from it. As I argue elsewhere (Taylor, "Art and Anti-Art"), he destroys but he cannot create. Unlike the Dionysiac myths in which, as Lillian Feder (43) points out, "self-knowledge emerges through violence and destruction, reason through madness," the penetration in *Paper Flowers* has no generative power. The Hake functions as an exteriorizing pressure that tears to pieces the hermetic social and theatrical system originally introduced onstage. Eva acts out a predictable part in a conventional "well-made play." The Hake's role changes all that. He sets the stage, puts on a performance, and simultaneously participates in and controls the action. He disfigures Eva and dismantles her world; the well-made play dissolves into a demented monologue. The dramatic discourse of *Paper Flowers* shatters the "inner" world, and the Hake, as destruction personified, nullifies the landscape and language of interiority. At the end, playing the Simba warrior Ukelele, the Hake confesses: "Ukelele has your guts in his hands and he does not know what to do with them" (220). When they step out of the room, out of drama, they disappear into the realm of death and desolation.

Nobody, however, has objected that Eva is not an object, a "doll," and that annihilating her in the name of hidden truths only perpetuates the age-old violence and suppression of women. On the contrary, Eva is said to represent only the middle class, and we are led to believe that as such she deserves all the violence coming to her. Wolff himself stresses this interpretation: "The absurd act of encaging a beautiful bird for one's own enjoyment seems absolutely appropriate for bourgeois women such as Eva." [10] But there is something profoundly disturbing, almost fascistic, in the play's staging of the infirm, diseased outsider who penetrates and undoes the "body" politic. The enfeebled social body cannot stave off infection. The Hake's illness is "experienced as a ruthless, secret invasion" connoting the "other place," the "night-side of life, a more onerous citizenship" (Sontag, *Illness*, 5, 3). The insistence on images of disease throughout the play, combined with the thematic undercurrent that the debilitated bourgeoisie almost provokes and merits its own annihilation, exemplifies the circle of hatred and self-hatred best summed up in Hitler's *Mein Kampf* (229-30): "We more than deserve this defeat. It is only the greatest outward symptom of decay amid a whole series of inner symptoms. . . . defeat is the payment meted out to peoples for their inner rottenness, cowardice, lack of character, in short, unworthiness." Eva, blind, weak, well-meaning, seduced by her own desire, precipitates the "fall." History repeats itself, and Eva, the bad woman, once again causes human misfortune and the loss of a world.

In opposition to the middle-class creation of the underclass as grotesque other, we have also the male discourse creating Eva and distancing her as grotesque other: woman. Nor is she just any woman. The specific representation of woman-as-Eve in itself connotes a negative view of women: "In her baser forms as Eve or as Helen—the instinctive and emotional aspects—Woman is on a lower level than the man. It is here, perhaps, that she appears at her most characteristic—a temptress . . . who drags everything down with her" (Cirlot, 356). Eva as the male creation of quintessential woman reflects all the stereotypes. She herself embodies *bad* Eve, but the play suggests that there are no *good* women; some are simply worse than others. Even the images associating her with the traditionally more positive or neutral images of woman (as Virgin Mother or Mother Earth) are ridiculed. Eva speaks of herself as round like a balloon, in the tradition of Mother Earth or the pregnant womb, but she has no children. Again, the absence of children signals the *bad* woman.[11] Her roundness is associated not with reproductive functions but with unproductive overindulgence. Eva is the very image of interiority; she contains, she encloses, she inhabits the home, she connotes intimacy.[12] However, these qualities too are perceived as threatening: Eva cages the bird; she locks the Hake into her apartment. She wants to embrace the Hake; she puts her arms around him, but her interiorizing nature as woman threatens the male with the possibility of absorption and castration. When he pulls back, she reassures him that she is not going to "eat" him (182); she is not the witch of fairytales. Still, she is obviously perceived as a menace, not only by the Hake but by commentators such as Myra S. Gann, who as recently as 1989 called the Hake a "victimized" man "now in danger of being entrapped by Eva" (31).

*Paper Flowers* reads like a textbook parody of Freud's opinion of women as unknowing and unknowable: "Throughout history people have knocked their heads against the riddle of the nature of femininity. . . . Nor will you have escaped worrying over this problem—those of you who are men; to those of you who are women this will not apply—you are yourselves the problem" (Freud, qtd. in Murray, 272). Eva, like the circular image used to describe her, is also a *lack*. A circle is no thing in itself; it engulfs, exists in relation to, something else. If we say a woman contains and encloses, that alone defines her in relation to that contained other—the fetus, the enclosed penis. Woman equals Mother and Lover; her very essence is tied into what her man gives her, be it himself or his child. The woman herself is nothing but a lack of maleness in the Freudian world view that Luce Irigaray undertakes to decode: "The woman, supposedly, has *nothing* you can see. She exposes, exhibits the possibility of a *nothing to see*. . . . Woman's castration is defined as her having nothing you can see, as her *having* nothing. In her having nothing penile, in seeing she has No Thing. Nothing *like* man. That is to say, *no sex/organ* that can be seen in a form capable of founding its reality" (*Speculum*, 48; Irigaray's emphasis). Thus, woman is defined according to male models by which she is judged lacking and therefore needy and weak. Eva repeatedly states that she is alone and lonely, desperate for affection. All her activities are merely a substitute for the missing man. She is an "old maid" who paints out of "desperation" and "clings, out of nostalgia, to the clothes of the man who left the nest centuries ago" (200). Eva holds on to the only roles society allows her, mother and lover. She calls the Hake a "spoiled boy" and "pampered boy" (193). She encourages him to imagine that she is a sensuous woman capable of loving. While he hesitantly tolerates her maternal indulgence, he rejects her as a woman. He turns his back on her and humiliates her, no doubt frightened at the thought of losing his *thing* in her *no-thing-ness*.

The stereotypes have obfuscated the very real sexual violence that the Hake inflicts on Eva. The first link between the two protagonists, we remember, is the detail that the Hake observed her as she painted at the Botanical Gardens. While Eva is flattered by what she supposes is proof of his interest in her, she in fact has stepped into his trap, for, as Foucault points out, "visibility is a trap" (*Discipline*, 200-201). He watches her while she does not perceive his presence; he catches her unaware; he has the advantage over her. Nor is this an isolated example: once inside the apartment, the stage directions indicate, "he never takes his eyes off her" (155). The insistence on sight throughout the play should alert us to the Hake's voyeurism, his sexual perversion, defined by Robert Stoller (*Perversion*, 4) as the "erotic form of hatred." Throughout, Eva is the object of the Hake's merciless gaze. She cringes from it time and time again: "Don't look at me like that. Don't look at me so much!" (168). She is a seen object rather than a seeing subject. As her reiterated reassurances to him manifest, she does not look; she accepts: "No me fijo en eso"— "I don't *look at* those things," equivalent in English to "I don't *care* about those things" (184). What appears in scene 1 as a relatively innocent remark about the Hake watching Eva takes on its full, horrifying significance in scene 6. While she stands, annihilated, letting him rip off and tack on shreds of her wedding gown, he confesses in a frenzied, orgiastic manner: "The little brides!— I've seen them!— Hidden under the bushes in the park. . . . I've seen them, I've looked at them. It's not that I have twisted feelings— no! . . . There, right there, at that very moment, under the lascivious gaze of all the horrible dwarves, hidden behind the bricks of the walls, under the canopy of shade, I've seen them!— (He chokes. Trembling) I've seen them—open—the petals of their bodies—and offer! Can you imagine? Offer!— (He screams) Offer! (He calms down) their virgin corollas to the consummation of love!— (A stifled scream) Oh God! " (217).

The Hake's voyeurism changes the entire meaning and function of his distancing. It is not, as in the case of oppression, a real barrier that has been erected between classes and cemented by hegemony. Rather, distance is necessary in maintaining his sexual excitement and his sense of power. Voyeurism, as I noted in relation to the scopic drive that Gambaro calls into question, "always keeps apart from the object and source of the drive" (Metz, 59). The Hake's gaze implies both distance and power. He acts not like the lover in Eva's fantasy but as the moon-eye, the "intrusive moon—watching—our passion" (206), the "moon as witness" that she remembers from a far-off night of lovemaking. He watches; he withholds. His gaze involves secrecy and triumph. The voyeuristic transgression through the gaze in itself violates the woman's intimacy, for what she thinks is a private act (be it painting or intercourse) has in fact been opened to scrutiny. The "man's eye—understood as substitute for the penis—will be able to prospect woman's sexual parts" (Irigaray, *Speculum*, 145). While piercing her with his gaze and invading her space, the Hake remains outside, never aspiring to intimacy or inhabiting her world of interiority. He attacks the circle without filling the void. He stands outside, manipulating, dominating, shattering her world. As he wrenches power by objectifying her, the relationship becomes a parody of the loving reciprocity between "two equals" (193) that she had envisioned.

Voyeurism, studies indicate, always involves a certain degree of sadism (see Metz, 62), and the excessive sadism evident in *Paper Flowers* recalls scenarios of torture. Like torturers forcing victims to confess their crimes, the Hake insists that Eva "confess" and "say" (173) the words he puts in her mouth. He attacks her where she is most vulnerable, in her self-image as a woman. Although he rejects her sexual overtures, he suggests that she is a whore by referring to himself as a "gigolo—only good for warming his bitch's bed" (190). Everything she values—her feelings, her bird—the Hake turns into an instrument to hurt her. Like torture victims, whose world becomes gradually reduced to the site of pain, Eva finds her world shrinking around her. Much like the Young Man's room in Gambaro's *The Walls*, Eva's living space becomes smaller and smaller. At first she has the run of the apartment; by scene 3 the Hake is installed in her living room; by scene 5 he has destroyed all but one chair; by scene 6 there is nothing left. Unlike the walls that crush the Young Man, these walls give way altogether. Nothing protects Eva from the exterior "geography of the river" that the Hake describes: "a river clotted with broken furniture; many people, falling in it, break their spines" (221).

Also, like torture, *Paper Flowers* directs our (the public's) response to the action. How can commentators witness Eva's destruction and still consider the Hake the victim? By participating in the crisis we have analyzed thus far. As both Elaine Scarry (35) and René Girard observe, the persecutor will always try to persuade the public that the undeniable violence they see before their eyes is really something else—self-defense, or justice, or justified retribution. The victim, rather than the victimizer, is guilty of enormous crimes; the victimizer, rather than the victim, is to be pitied. Girard adds: "Those who make up the crowd are always potential persecutors, for they dream of purging the community of the impure elements that corrupt it, the traitors who undermine it" (*Scapegoat*, 16).

No matter how perverse the Hake's behavior is, we must recognize that we cannot dismiss it merely as an individual aberration, excentric to our field of inquiry. While his onslaught goes to dramatic extremes, the way he controls Eva is typical, not atypical, of the historical domination of women. It is through the male gaze that women have been defined and subjugated. Societies in Latin America and elsewhere have physically constructed their cities, houses, institutions, and conventions in ways that keep women within a tightly focused scopic field. Jean Franco explains that "to describe someone as a 'public woman' in Latin America is simply not the same as describing someone as a public man. . . . The public woman is a prostitute, the public man a prominent citizen. When a woman goes public, she leaves the protected spaces of home and convent and exposes her body" ("Self-Destructing Heroines," 105). Needless to add, the reason behind such a radical separation of spaces is not to spare the woman an intrusive glance but to protect her man's honor.

Moreover, a woman's very identity has been tied into the defining gaze. Whoever controls the field of vision controls the nature of the participation of those in the field. As John Berger indicates in *Ways of Seeing* (45-46), "The social presence of a woman is different in kind from that of a man" because she is treated as a perceived object rather than a perceiving subject: "She has to survey everything she is and everything she does because how she appears to others, and ultimately how she appears to men, is of crucial importance for what is normally thought of as the success of her life. Her own sense of being in herself is supplanted by a sense of being appreciated as herself by another." Although individual women have been admired and loved, women in general have been looked down on as threatening and manipulative if they aspire to heights that men regard as their own. Men do not usually consider themselves phallocentric for excluding women, but women are frequently considered aggressive for wanting "male" privileges. Freud's "gaze" plays itself out in many arenas; it defines woman as "lack"; it reduces gender politics to penis envy; she wants what she does not have, that which man possesses as if by natural endowment.

*Paper Flowers*, to sum up, confronts discourses pertaining to class and to gender, and nullifies both. In attempting to unravel the dominant male discourse (in which the woman remains marginal, a male creation) from the middle-class discourse (in which, conversely, the borderline protagonist remains a middle-class fiction/nightmare), we can recognize the series of distortions, displacements, and projections that make us, like Eva, wonder where this violence is coming from. Self and other, the play shows, are slippery concepts indeed. Inner and outer fail to differentiate: the Hake has strayed from the riverbank; Eva no longer belongs in her home (207). The two characters function more as "signs," signaling positions that are not their own, than as psychologically individuated entities.

Read as a political allegory, *Paper Flowers* transposes Eva-as-Woman (Woman = lack, inadequacy) into middle-class degeneracy, effeteness, and weakness. This gendered representation of the middle class continues in the tradition of feminizing the political enemy. Joan Landes (47) observes the same phenomenon during the French Revolution, when the aristocracy was depicted as feminine, "frivolous," greedy, and depraved; "as the most egregious examples of aristocratic stylistic excess and imposture"; as the "violators of the order of nature in language, dress and society." The Hake signals the other as poor = lack = crazed revenge. Eva, an unseeing object under male gaze, becomes blind subject, the sheltered middle class unable to perceive the danger that threatens it. The combination of feminine stereotypes (nurturing, vain) that prompts her to offer the Hake a bowl of soup reads as a pathetic example of self-serving charity, similar to that of Buenaventura's Ladies, who pretend to solve the problem of human hunger and suffering by hosting a banquet. When Eva brings the Hake salami and cheese, the act is a variation of the unthinking, contemptuous "let them eat cake." Eva's need for love on a personal, human level becomes translated into a ridiculous political stance of the "why can't we all love one another" variety. She is weak, needy, and passive—guilty not only of misjudging him but of allowing her own destruction.

What we see in *Paper Flowers* is not so much the representation of violence but the violence of misrepresentation—the distorted, hateful depiction of the other that Klaus Theweleit describes so accurately in *Male Fantasies* (1:171): women are "evil and out to castrate and should be treated accordingly." Amoebalike, they will absorb men into their engulfing, gobbling mouths, vaginas, bodies. The poor are crazed, dangerous, infirm; they will attack the well-to-do and destroy everything they value. Both Eva and the Hake are violent caricatures. The Hake claims throughout that Eva fictionalizes him and, consequently, retains power over him: "You have your fantasy, I have only my reality" (195). But again, his objection holds only on one level while proving blatantly untrue on another. He, as the man, retains the power and advantage throughout the play. She, as object of his gaze, is perfectly transparent and predictable to him: "I knew, the thousands of times I have watched you, that you were what your eyes said you were" (160). He physically molds her, dresses and disfigures her. She, on the contrary, cannot "see" him or his reality. She can know what she wants him to be, his "potential," but that further exposes her rather than him.

Both depictions, based on negation, on sexual or social *lack*, obliterate the possibility of a real face behind the generic mask. Who creates whom? Whose madness is this anyway? The two characters incarnate the void (rather than the reality) of the other. They straddle the abyss repeatedly alluded to throughout the play, struggling with the gap, the lack of self-definition, the displacement of place. The abyss cannot be bridged in a world of broken values where "pity is a broken bridge" (210) and "love is like broken teeth in a hungry mouth" (212). As Foucault observes in *Madness and Civilization* (288), the discontinuity brought about by the discourse of madness "opens a void, a moment of silence, a question without answer, provokes a breach without reconciliation where the world is forced to question itself. . . . the world is made aware of its guilt."

But does the play incriminate us? Clearly, it wants to. The Hake's madness judges (and finds contemptible) the center that expels him as excentric. He moves from his position, which he defines as object of condemnation, to condemning subject. Lodged in her apartment, conquering her domain, he uses his position to attack those he feels judge him—the "fucking bird," "Miss Smiley-puss," "Mister Happy Face" (214), imaginary shopkeepers who "have radar in their noses" (199)—his depictions of "them." Are we, as Villegas's middle-class audience, guilty of oppressive exclusion? Does the Hake create us—as enemy? Did we create him—as enemy? Is Eva the enemy, as the play suggests? Or are we, watching it? "How, as women, can we go to the theatre without lending complicity to the sadism directed against women?" (Cixous, 546).

The oppositions in *Paper Flowers* are not—as in the other plays associated with the theatre of crisis—between self and other, inner and outer, creation and destruction, reason and madness. Rather, the play subverts all distinctions between them—self creates, and in turn is the creation of, other; the outer is lodged in the center of inner, and inner opens onto outer; reason is madness (bourgeois self-deception), and madness is the highest form of reason; destruction becomes the most authentic manifestation of creation.[13] At the end of the play, Eva can only whisper "I—" an echoed memory of self. The Hake, acting the Simba warrior, becomes trapped in his own monologue, which erases self and other, all possibility of meaning and differentiation: "To renounce one's own identity for the identity of the other, until one's own identity and the other's and one's own—own—identity—of the other's identity . . . own. . . . Don't you think?" (220).

*Paper Flowers* speaks not *of* crisis but *in* crisis, the breach, the void from which the discourse of the characters originates. Without realizing what he has done, Wolff has responded to crisis by reactivating the very mechanism of crisis—persecution and scapegoating. Unable to identify the cause of the social malaise, he sets in motion yet another "miniaturized ritual of subjugation" (Roach, 175). Eva is sacrificed so that the middle-class audience can displace the violence it sees coming to it. Wolff deflects real class confrontation onto an expendable victim—woman. Once again, the woman has been reduced to silence. This is pure scapegoatism: *she* dies because *they* fear they deserve to. Scapegoatism, we have seen throughout this study, is intricately connected with crisis. Unlike Wolff, the other playwrights presented here understand the connection between crisis and scapegoating and point it out to the audience through their plays. *Paper Flowers* is particularly interesting because, without understanding crisis, it reflects it. As Robert Jay Lifton notes in *Boundaries* (xii), one response to crisis is "to destroy, or seek to destroy, all boundaries in the name of an all-encompassing oneness. . . . The approach all too often collapses into a pseudo-instinctualism in which the only heroes are the infant, the pre-human animal, and the schizophrenic." Like the other plays analyzed here, *Paper Flowers* takes the world apart. Triana, Gambaro, Carballido, and Buenaventura dismantle their known world in order to put it back together in a more equitable manner. But Wolff, like Ukelele the Simba warrior, is left holding the pieces in his hands, and like Ukelele, he does not know what to do with them.

# CLOSING REMARKS

SEVERAL QUESTIONS have remained with me throughout my work on this study. Does the term "theatre of crisis" obfuscate more than it illuminates? No doubt there is such a thing as crisis. Latin America's history reveals one crisis after another. And there are crisis theatres; theatre of the absurd, theatre of the Holocaust, and protest theatre owe their very existence to sociopolitical crisis. The theatre of crisis that I have examined differs from these in concurrently reflecting systemic (objective) and personal (subjective) loss of identity, self-definition, and boundaries. Yet are all the works presented in this study alike? Are they all theatre of crisis in the same way, or does the term itself (as I argued in the case of popular theatre) obscure the very real, very important differences between these plays? Would it not perhaps be best to speak of theatres of crisis? And if discourse constitutes the subject under examination, as Carballido's *Rose* suggests, to what degree has my own discourse—as a bilingual, bicultural, middle-class, white Canadian-Mexican woman living in the United States—constituted this area of inquiry, characterized as it is by uneasy boundaries and blurred identities?

The term "theatre of crisis" is as problematic as any term; like "theatre of the absurd," it suggests false unities. Do Enrique Buenaventura and Egon Wolff have any more in common than Eugène Ionesco and Fernando Arrabal? I would answer in the affirmative: for all their individual and historical differences, the playwrights studied here share recognizable social, economic, historical, and cultural commonalities. Centuries of colonization, turbulent histories of independence, racial conflicts, *machismo*, the shaky sense of self-definition and identity, the pronounced self-hatred—all these factors enable us to speak of this theatre, however tentatively, as Latin American theatre. Moreover, the sociopolitical and ideological crisis that struck in the late 1960s, and early 1970s affected all of Latin America. The hopes for a freer, decolonized Latin America following the Cuban revolution in 1959 had swept from Mexico to Tierra del Fuego. By the late 1960s, however, these dreams could no longer compete with the grim reality; not only was Cuba not the free society observers had envisioned, but the counterrevolutionary backlash was devastating. Military dictatorships sprang up in a majority of Latin American countries. U.S.-backed counterinsurgency groups turned Central America into a battlefield. Military dictatorships dominated the Southern Cone. There was a heavy price to pay for dreams of nonoppression.

Not all the theatre that sprang up during this time was theatre of crisis as I use the term; some maintained a strict ideological program. Like the groups described by Rosa Ileana Boudet in *Teatro nuevo*, some practitioners clung to the belief that a Marxist-Leninist philosophy and a commitment to the Cuban revolution would see them through the stormy times. Others, comfortably lodged within the dominant classes, produced entertainment. Even within the circle of politically progressive playwrights who shatter the agit-prop monologue there are some who do not reflect the characteristics I associate with crisis. Most of these, my preliminary examination of their work indicates, were for various reasons more deeply rooted in European traditions and ideology than those playwrights more profoundly affected by the crisis. Practical limitations made it impossible for me to include all the writers within this last group. By the very selection of materials and by the perspectives I bring to them, my discourse shapes the subject matter. Throughout, I have tried to be conscious of my own ideological and discursive limitations. Therefore, I submit this study not as the last word (even if there were such a thing) on the subject but as one more perspective on a vital and dynamic theatre. I, too, speak . . .

But why the late 1960s? Surely people will argue that the crisis in Latin America became evident in the 1970s. The reason the period from the middle to late 1960s is so interesting for this study is that the crisis was perceived (as the plays themselves indicate) but not understood. While it was much easier to recognize the crisis in the 1970s—given the firmly installed military regimes, the torture chambers, the disappearances, and the atomized populations—the years before were the turningpoint, the crisis, between regeneration and repression.

The years from 1965 to 1970 mark the moment of limbo in the transformation, a loss of ideological certainties accompanied by a desperate search for values and ideas that might withstand the profound systemic shifts. Everything comes under scrutiny. The entire system of beliefs, we see in this body of works, is dismantled. Definitions are undone. The relationship between the individual and the system and the interrelationship between individuals, involving prejudices of gender, race, and class "difference," all come under examination. Clearly, concepts of selfhood are firmly tied into the existence of the other. But who is this other? Is the other the enemy, as Lorenzo believes in Gambaro's *Siamese Twins*? Is the self the creation of the other, as Triana's Lalo concludes in *Assassins*? Wolff's *Paper Flowers* makes us wonder who creates whom. Who is the enemy—oneself or the other? Does the danger lurk outside or inside? Is it foreign or familiar? Who are the oppressors, who the oppressed? It becomes increasingly apparent that everyone is involved, that the problems go much further than the facile ideology of separating the world into "false" consciousness and "right" consciousness.

Nor do the problems end here. The dismantling of the entire social apparatus proceeds; the question also becomes one of historical placement. Preparing for the future requires some understanding of history. But again, authors such as Buenaventura indicate that their countries' historical representations reveal more about present power structures than they do about the past. And the issue of history, as Carballido makes clear, is linked to discourse: those who control the power to articulate, to record, to define and represent the other are those who shape one's understanding of past, present, and future. The struggle, then, must also involve culture. If culture is to be more than a luxury item for the wealthy, reflecting First World fantasies more than Third World realities, it must represent local conditions and concerns. But again, who is entitled to speak for the dispossessed? How can "popular" interests best be served, and who can decide what those interest are without perpetuating the authoritarianism of elitist governments? In short, the problems multiply. When one identifies a certain problem, more spring up. All the issues are so intricately connected that the social fabric unravels in the inquiry.

This unraveling or dismantling, however, should not suggest that the theatre of crisis is a negative theatre. Usually, we have seen, it is not. The dismantling always presupposes the hope of a better system, even when the playwrights cannot bring it to being. Though there is a utopian dream in most of these works, the plays themselves are profoundly honest about the very concrete obstacles to any kind of social, racial, or sexual equality. They offer no simple answers or solutions, even though they long for them. This, then, is a *radical* theatre; it goes to the roots of the matter. It is a theatre that questions itself, its own ideology, its own blind spots. It is a theatre of crisis because it has not progressed beyond the dismantling to a remantling. That is not a weakness; one could argue that therein lies its strength, its sense of urgency, its complexity.

During the 1970s Latin American theatre revealed a firmer sense of direction and mission. The crisis was more visible than before. The limits of the systems had been tested. It became clear in most countries what governments would do to regain or retain control: Argentina, Brazil, Uruguay, Paraguay, Chile, Guatemala, El Salvador—to name only the most repressive—started terrorizing their populations. The theatre of this period no longer dwelt as much on oppression or colonization. The violence unleashed throughout these societies required strategies for immediate survival. The onstage worlds continued to reflect a grotesque, distorted reality, but there was no longer the same conflation of oppressor and oppressed. It had become easier to identify the enemy. The crisis was no longer experienced as a disorienting, suspended limbo. It was becoming obvious that crisis served a very real political function in the governments' destabilizing campaigns. The ability to recognize the concrete *causes* of crisis, rather than the multiple *effects* that we see in the theatre of the 1960s, enabled the playwrights of the 1970s to go beyond the crisis ideology. Their very different tactics for responding to violence await examination in another book.

# NOTES

## Introduction

1. Throughout this book, all translations from the Spanish are mine if not otherwise attributed in Notes or Bibliography.

2. The term "theatre of the oppressed" is associated with theatrical techniques and exercises developed by Augusto Boal in *Teatro del oprimido*. While these follow a specific model, in a general sense the term applies to all "committed" or oppositional Latin American theatre from the 1960s onward.

3. Clifford Geertz, in *Negara* (13), calls the nineteenth-century Balinese society a "theatre state" pointing "toward spectacle, toward ceremony, toward the public dramatization of the ruling obsessions of Balinese culture: social inequality and status pride." I discuss this concept in relation to pre-Hispanic ritual in chapter 1.

4. Among the major plays of the period in addition to those examined here are Virgilio Piñera's *Los dos viejos pánicos* (1968, Cuba); five plays by Eduardo Pavlovsky (Argentina), including *La cacería* (1969) and *La mueca* (1970); the first plays of Mexico's Vicente Leñero, including his famous *Los albañiles* (1969); Ricardo Talesnik's well-known work *La fiaca* (1967, Argentina).

5. See James O'Connor, *The Meaning of Crisis,* for a discussion of the modern capitalist crisis theory, the economic crisis theory, the social and political crisis theory, and the personality crisis theory. The concept of "crisis," as O'Connor (109) points out, is itself in crisis, and exact definitions are difficult to find. In the most general sense, the term has been used to denote "imperialist rivalries and world wars; national liberation struggles and counter-revolutions; dangerous moments in the Cold War; the transformation of race relations; the break-up of the modern family, and so on."

6. The terms "First World" and "Third World" are problematic. "Third World" was coined by the French demographer Alfred Sauvy in 1952—for me an ironic reminder that a Frenchman also coined *Amèrique Latine* in the nineteenth century; Latin America has always been named by the defining other. Moreover, as Régis Debray observes, the term itself was "a shapeless sack into which one could simply dump peoples, classes, races [let me add gender], civilizations and

continents so that they might more easily disappear" (qtd. in Barbara Harlow, *Resistance Literature*, 6; see Harlow's chap. 1 for background information on the use of the term). Pascal Bruckner, in *The Tears of the White Man* (79), writes of the "Third World as the Turd World," a term that radically separates the defining group from the defined: *"They are the masses; we are the individuals"* (Bruckner's emphasis). I continue to use the terms, much as I use "Western" and "non-Western," for lack of better ones, but I use them with a sense of irony and self-consciousness.

7. Columbus's *Diario de navegación* already refers to stories of monstrous cannibals.

8. Michael Foucault in *Discipline and Punish* (200) describes Jeremy Bentham's proposed "panopticon," a building constructed thus: "at the periphery, an annular building; at the center, a tower; this tower is pierced with wide windows that open onto the inner side of the ring; the peripheric building is divided into cells, each of which extends the whole width of the building; they have two windows, one on the inside, corresponding to the windows of the tower; the other, on the outside, allows the light to cross the cell from one end to the other. All that is needed, then, is to place a supervisor in a central tower and to shut up in each cell a madman, a patient, a condemned man, a worker or a schoolboy. By the effect of backlighting, one can observe from the tower, standing out precisely against the light, the small captive. . . . They are like so many cages, so many small theatres, in which the actor is alone, perfectly individualized and constantly visible."

9. Unpublished interview with Jorge Díaz, Madrid, May 1988.

10. See also Heilbroner's 1988 study, *Behind the Veil of Economics*.

11. One of the dangers Barbara Christian singles out (though perhaps in excessively schematic terms) in the "race" for literary theory is that "new emphasis on literary critical theory is as hegemonic as the world which it attacks . . . making it possible for a few people who know that particular language to control the critical scene—that language surfaced interestingly enough, just when the literature of peoples of color, of black women, of Latin Americans, of Africans began to move to 'the center'" (55).

12. The translation of "el pueblo es necio" to "people are fools" is my own.

13. Marvin Carlson, in his *Theories of the Theatre* (475), writes that Boal, like Brecht, "rejects 'Aristotelian' drama as an instrument of the established class structure, but he is far more detailed and explicit than Brecht as to how Aristotelian drama functions in this capacity." Ngugi wa Thiongo'o (Kenya), in his *Decolonising the Mind*, speaks of Boal's important work in theatre within oppressed societies. Boal is perhaps even more influential outside his native Brazil than in it. His workshops and techniques designed to change the nature of the audience's participation superficially resemble J.L. Moreno's psychodramas and sociodramas, developed in Vienna in the 1920s. What differentiates Boal's work is its noncathartic character. Moreno goes back to the original Greek meaning of catharsis as a purgative process; his psychodramas are theatrical exercises to provoke cathartic emotional release in his patients, who can then, he believes, better cope with reality. Boal's purpose is diametrically opposed. Catharsis, according to him, purges "antisocial elements" (*Oppressed*, 46); his theatre is anticathartic, intended to direct aggressive energy rather than diffuse it. By

rehearsing active political participation among the members of the audience, he encourages them to change (rather than adapt to) the social system.

## 1. Theatre and Crisis

1. See Hernán Cortés (1485-1547), *Cartas de relación de la Conquista de México*, 3d letter; Gonzalo Fernandéz de Oviedo (1478-1557), *Historia general y natural de las Indias*; Fernández de Alva Ixtlilxóchitl (c. 1568-c. 1648) *Historia chichimeca*; Diego Durán (†1588), *Historia de las Indias de Nueva España*; Bartolomé de Las Casas (1474-1566), *Apologética historia de las Indias*; "El Codice Ramírez"; Diego de Landa (1524-79), *Relación de las cosas de Yucatán*; Jerónimo de Mendieta (1525-1604), *Historia eclesiástica indiana*; Fray Toribio Motolinía, *Historia de los Indios de la Nueva España*; Fr. Bernardino de Sahagún (1499-1590), *Historia general de las cosas de Nueva España*.

2. Durán, *Historia de las Indias de Nueva España y Islas de Tierra Firme*, 2: 231; English version cited from Miguel León-Portilla's *Pre-Columbian Literatures of Mexico*, 98. For the English language reader, León-Portilla's book is the single most important work on this subject. It contains complete bibliographical entries for the texts dating from the early colonial period.

3. On one hand, the writings of these witnesses show a strong tendency to regard the indigenous people as barbarians. On the other, it remains unclear how much they actually knew about theatre, even though Sten (21) argues that "there are enough reasons to suppose that Cortés had seen numerous stages [*carros, tablados y carrillos*] in the representations associated with Corpus Christi in Spain to use the term [theatre] correctly." Moreover, as Francisco Monterde notes in his prologue to *Teatro indígena prehispánico*, the friars did not look sympathetically on profane theatre and ordered the abolishment of such representations due to their "obscene and idolatrous" nature (xii). Durán calls some dances "agile and dishonest" (230-31). Agustín del Saz (14) argues that "for the conquerors, the American landscape was a vast stage, and those who appeared on it acquired in their eyes the interest of a comedian or some outlandish actor type [*representante*]."

4. Wole Soyinka argues that "contemporary drama, as we experience it today, is a contraction of drama, necessitated by the productive order of society in other directions" ("Theatre, 241). Much twentieth-century theatre, from Artaud to Grotowski to Beck, to the Bread and Puppet group to Barba, attempts to expand its power to transform social and individual consciousness by becoming more ritualistic. In recording what I perceive as a Eurocentric bias in the dramatic theory and criticism of indigenous spectacle, I put the words "privilege" and "theatre" in quotations only to illustrate that other cultures do not necessarily rank theatre over ritual. Rather than valorizing one over another, it seems sufficient to point out that ritual and theatre serve different functions within different contexts. Ritual has a sacred component; people participate in an activity that they believe puts the community in harmony with the ancestors, or the gods, or whoever they perceive as the guides of human destiny. Theatre is a secular activity. The initial separation (the secular from the sacred) makes way for a

series of other separations (actors/audience), generic distinctions (tragedy/comedy), and aesthetic hierarchies (high comedy/low comedy). As society becomes more specialized and compartmentalized, so does theatre. The antiritual prejudice of scholars working on pre-Hispanic spectacle stems from their Eurocentric misinformation about the nature and function of ritual. The "embryonic" or biological metaphor suggests that theatre evolves out of or replaces ritual, which from this perspective would be the less developed form. But this evolutionary approach to theatre does not hold for all its manifestations; some dramatic forms evolve from ritual, some do not. Certain African societies—Nigeria, for example—currently have both active ritual and theatrical practices.

5. See "Túpac Amaru," in Rodríguez Monegal, *The Borzoi Anthology of Latin American Literature*, 1:169-70.

6. Some scholars use the examples of Alarcón and Sor Juana to argue that colonial dramatists were not excluded. Alarcón, Richard Reeve notes (Luzuriaga and Reeve, 9), competed with the Golden Age "masters" themselves, Lope de Vega and Calderón. This argument, however, fails to weigh the specifics of the situation; the most it proves is that those born in the colonized countries were not seen as inherently biologically inferior. Alarcón's move to Spain, the cultural "center," underlines, rather than dispels, the reality of colonial exclusion. And Sor Juana, writing within a male, Catholic, Eurocentric discourse, had to insinuate her views into its language. Perhaps more because of her brilliance than in spite of it, the system could not tolerate her; no editions of her works were published from 1725 until 1910. Now, finally, it appears that her work will attract the attention it deserves.

7. See Michael Taussig, *Shamanism, Colonialism and the Wild Man*, 240-41. Retamar (*Calibán*, 30) states that the Latin American "symbol is not [Shakespeare's] Ariel, as Rodó thought, but Caliban. This is something that we *mestizos*, who inhabit the same islands where Caliban lived, recognize with particular clarity: Prospero invaded the islands, killed our ancestors, enslaved Caliban and taught him his language in order to communicate with him: what else could Caliban do but use that same language—today he does not possess another—to curse him, to call the "red plague" down upon him?"

8. Gloria Anzaldua, "Speaking in Tongues: A Letter to Third World Women Writers" (qtd. in Kaplan, 190).

9. Caren Kaplan (188).

10. Although my two examples, Usigli and Gorostiza, both come from Mexico, the increasing rejection of the defining other's representation of the indignenous self, along with the growing awareness of the native's own self-hatred, has been presented by many dramatists throughout Latin America during this period, among them Francisco Arriví (Puerto Rico), Agustín Cuzzani (Argentina), Enrique Solari Swayne (Peru).

11. Within the Nigerian context, Karin Barber (433) argues, popular theatre means Yoruba theatre using the Yoruba language and reflecting the attitudes of ordinary people: "This theatre is genuinely popular in both senses of the word: it attracts large audiences, and they are not elite but farmers, workers, petty traders, minor public servants, drivers, schoolchildren, etcetera." However, the plays she provides as examples seem only to cover up existing sociopolitical corruption and domestic violence.

12. For Boal's comment on carnival, see his essay "Sobre teatro popular y antipopular" (32).

13. Etherton, in *The Development of African Drama* (314-15), gives a superb example of this phenomenon: the professionalization of the "Nyau" dance in Zambia. However, readily recognizable examples abound, among them the Mexican mariachis and hat dancers and the Yaqui Indian deer dance in Arizona (described by Schechner in *Between Theater and Anthroplogy*, chap. 1).

14. For analyses of popular theatre in Latin America, see the collections edited by Sonia Gutiérrez and Gerardo Luzuriaga. Boal's "Teatro popular" (in the latter) specifies: "A spectacle can be called 'popular' when it assumes the perspective of the popular class, within the social microcosm in which it appears—the characters' social relationships, etc.—, even if there is only one spectator, even if it is only a rehearsal in an empty theatre, even if its targeted audience is not a popular one. The presence of the popular classes does not necessarily determine the popular character of a spectacle. Often enough the popular classes are present as victims of the theatrical production" (33).

15. Rizk, 35; de Toro; Boudet, 24.

16. Pianca's first stage "is a period of consciousness-raising, a period in which one's historical conduct is very much in the forefront of theatrical activity. . . . During this period a process of structuring and generating theatrical activity is carried out on the *national* level"; her second "is characterized by the *internationalization* of this process and by the development of a theatre intimately linked to Latin America. There is a struggle for the integration of Latin America as the only vehicle for cultural and political self-determination. In 1968 the first versions of the international festivals appear for Latin American theatre" (8-14).

17. Qtd. in Stabb, 118. See also Mariátegui's *7 ensayos*.

18. Hannah Arendt's remarks are helpful in distinguishing the various meanings: "While the elements of novelty, beginning and violence, all intimately associated with our notion of revolution, are consciously absent from the original meaning of the word as well as from its metaphoric use in political language, there exists another connotation of the astronomic term . . . I mean the notion of irresistibility, the fact that the revolving motion of the stars follows a preordained path and is removed from all influence of human power. We know, or we believe we know, the exact date when the word 'revolution' was used for the first time (July 14, 1789, according to the Duc de la Rouchefoucauld—Liancourt, Paris) with an exclusive emphasis on irresistibility and without any connotation of a backward revolving movement; and so important does this emphasis appear to our own understanding of revolutions that it has become common practice to date the new political significance of the old astronomic term from the moment of this new usage" (*Revolution*, 47).

19. See Augusto Boal, *Theatre of the Oppressed*, ix, and "A Note on Brazilian Agitprop," 96.

20. Mitchell coins the word "hypericon" to denote "the way in which images (and ideas) double themselves: the way we depict the act of picturing, imagine the activity of imagination, figure the practice of figuration" (5-6).

21. Images, conversely, also detract from real accomplishments. Toril Moi argues in her study of Simone de Beauvoir that the French writer suffered

professionally, to a degree that threatens to undermine her status as a writer and thinker, because she did not look the part of a writer and philosopher in keeping with the dominant male model. In "Politics and the Intellectual Woman," Moi convincingly illustrates how Beauvoir's lack of "virility," "objectivity," and poise seemed sufficient basis for critical attack.

22. The Padilla affair involved the awarding of Cuba's Casa de las Américas prizes for poetry and theatre to Heberto Padilla and Antón Arrufat, respectively, in 1968. The awards created a conflict because some members of the Executive Committee (of which Triana was one) did not agree with the judges on political grounds. The former opposed awarding the prizes to Padilla and Arrufat because the authors' works were ideologically ambiguous and ahistorical. The awards were granted despite this opposition, but the dissenters expressed their objections in a preface to each volume, stating that they "would not surrender their right or their duty to watch for the adherence to the principles that informed our Revolution" (Arrufat, 8).

23. Murena (143) writes: "Within this imagined 'no man's land' of the person who has not been convinced by either of the two vociferous ideologies which have been saturating the world's atmosphere, one notices that after all, both sides are propagandistic, And propaganda—and by now this must be said openly—is essentially negative. For propaganda consists of malignant exploitation—be this done consciously or unconsciously—of man's 'openness' to the world, of that capacity for love which makes communication possible. It is evil since it opposes communication, and to this extent, it is contrary to the Revolution, to all revolution. . . . The Revolution wishes man to become once again completely his own master, while propaganda seeks to take full control of him. Propaganda proposes to change man, to alienate him from himself. Though it claims to be promoting the Revolution or defending liberty, its real effect is to paralyze him, and enslave him."

24. See Esslin's *Theater of the Absurd* for his analysis. I use "crisis ideology" here in the sense that Jürgen Habermas uses in *Legitimation Crisis* (4): "A contemporary consciousness of crisis often turns out afterwards to have been misleading. A society does not plunge into crisis when, and only when, its members so identify the situation. How could we distinguish such crisis ideologies from valid experiences of crisis if social crisis could be determined only on the basis of conscious phenomena?"

25. Langer (21) distinguishes between atrocity and other forms of violence: "The distinction is difficult and controversial, and must therefore remain tentative; yet Picasso's *Guernica*, perhaps the first valid example of an art of atrocity in our time, for all its roots in his earlier work, laid the foundations for a fresh way of perceiving—and conceiving—reality, as a direct result of the incomprehensible historical action of the decimating of a helpless town, the victimizing of its women and children, for no apparent reason other than the desire (and need?) to terrorize and destroy. As never before, the pressure of the *hideous* penetrated the consciousness of the literary imagination, forcing it to reconstitute reality in shapes and images that reflect a fundamental distortion in human nature, while compelling us to revise our conception of what is normal in human character and to see aberration and the grotesque as standards from which the rest of reality deviates. *No apparent reason*—doesn't the distinction between violence and

atrocity lie here?—for an act of violence, however unattractive to the civilized mind, however unjustifiable in its form or nature, is an explicable event, in the sense that a cause and effect exist, the connection between agent and victims is clear (though, as I say, it may horrify us, as Claudius's cold-blooded murder of Hamlet's father horrifies us), and suffering somehow seems to be a direct (though not necessarily equivalent) consequence of the impetus behind it."

26. The term *univers concentrationnaire* was coined by David Rousset; Langer uses it throughout *The Holocaust and the Literary Imagination*, as does Marrus in *The Holocaust in History*.

27. See Girard's discussion of parricide and incest as "contagious crimes" that destroy "difference" within communal and family circles (*Scapegoat*, 15). In *Violence and the Sacred* (74-75), Girard relates the idea of such crimes specifically to Oedipus, the "slayer of distinctions," who abolishes the father-son relationship by becoming his father's killer and his children's brother-father, the mother-son relationship by being simultaneously his mother's son and husband. It spreads to his children: "Oedipus' monstrosity is contagious; it infects first of all those beings engendered by him." And it spreads to Thebes, ravaged by disease.

28. Duque de Rivas's *Don Alvaro o la fuerza del sino* presents a confused, confusing, but nonetheless intriguing mixture of ideas (classical "inevitable" fatality versus Christian free will versus predestination), conflicts (Spain's loss of the colonies on the one hand and its inability to accept them as independent equals on another; Spain's invasion by Napoleonic forces and the growing Spanish nationalism coupled with an admiration of foreign literatures and ideas), styles (the uneasy, not to say unhappy, marriage between neoclassicism and romanticism—the latter with its own internal conflict between a nostalgia for Spanish values and religion on one hand and the attraction to foreign models, including Byronic satanism, on the other), which illustrate another "critical" rupture between ideologies, the breakdown of a social order that has not yet been replaced by a new one, clashing ideas that as yet do not form a cohesive ideology. Moreover, caught between political forces, Duque de Rivas also experienced the subjective threat of annihilation. After he fought against Napoleon and was wounded (almost mortally) in the service of his king, Ferdinand VII, the same king sentenced him to death for his liberal ideas. He escaped and went into exile in England. Following Ferdinand's death in 1833, he returned to Spain, reaped fame and fortune, and then once again was in danger of losing his life in 1836—this time for his conservative ideas—and again went into exile.

29. See Skidmore and Smith, *Modern Latin America*; Rock, *Argentina 1516-1987*; Rouquié, *The Military and the State in Latin America*; and Malloy and Seligson, *Authoritarians and Democrats*.

30. The "passivity" of the indigenous peoples of the Americas is a widespread cliché. Reports blame Moctezuma's passivity for the fall of the Aztec empire, rather than a host of very concrete factors: a raging epidemic of smallpox decimated a native population never before exposed to the disease; the Spanish capitalized on internal political rivalries and antagonisms to the extent that hostile indigenous groups were instrumental in conquering themselves; the native warriors had no horses, were unacquainted with firearms, and had radically different visions of warfare (e.g., they did not intend to kill their enemies in

war). Reports from the early twentieth century note that "the Indian is so humble
. . . he himself stretches out his hands and throws himself on the ground to
receive the punishment" (Taussig, 35). However, the same reports prove, although
without acknowledging the significance of the fact, that the Indians were deliberately starved and therefore weak and infirm. Moreover, when they did run away
to avoid being slaughtered, they were hounded down: "We had to go out on
expeditions and catch them" (46). Even natives who did not try to escape were
massacred. The colonizers "also tortured the Indians with fire, water, and upside-
down crucifixion. Company employees cut the Indians to pieces with machetes
and dashed out the brains of small children by hurling them against trees and
walls. The elderly were killed when they could no longer work, and to amuse
themselves the company officials practiced their marksmanship using Indians as
targets. On special occasions such as Easter Saturday, Saturday of Glory, they
shot them down in groups or, in preference, doused them with kerosene and set
them on fire to enjoy their agony" (34).

Similarly, as Michael R. Marrus in *The Holocaust in History* (108) notes:
"There are few more durable generalizations about the history of the Holocaust
than the characterization of Jewish passivity in the face of mortal threat. 'The
Jews,' it has often been said, 'went to their deaths like sheep to the slaughter.'"
Again, many contributing factors are left out, including "a dying population,
overcome by starvation, exhaustion and disease," the Jews' incomplete information about the mass exterminations, their geographical isolation, "the flood of
different emotions that various sources communicate to us—hope, demoralization, despair, bitterness at being abandoned, fear, anger, piety, and even a sense of
shame" (120-21).

31. In noncrisis situations we can sometimes make and uphold distinctions
between such concepts as power and force and violence. Hannah Arendt's
definitions *(Violence)* are helpful: *power* is "the human ability . . . to act in
concert. Power is never the property of an individual" (44); *strength* is "an
individual entity. . . . It is in the nature of a group and its power to turn against
independence, the property of individual strength" (44); *force*, "forces of
nature," indicates "the energy released by physical or social movements"
(44-45); *authority* "can be vested in persons . . . or in hierarchical offices. . . . Its
hallmark is unquestioning recognition by those who are asked to obey; neither
coercion nor persuasion is needed" (45); *violence* "is distinguished by its instrumental character. Phenomenologically, it is close to strength, since the implements of violence, like all other tools, are designed and used for the purpose of
multiplying natural strength until, in the last stage of their development, they
can substitute for it" (46). Arendt further differentiates between power and
violence by pointing out that "power always stands in need of numbers, whereas
violence up to a point can manage without them because it relies on implements"
(42). The opposite of violence, from her point of view, would be power rather than
nonviolence: "Power and violence are opposites; where one rules absolutely, the
other is absent. Violence appears where power is in jeopardy" (56). Nonetheless,
the distinction between violence and power, as Arendt herself concedes, is often
tenuous and all but nonexistent in times of crisis. Is slavery a manifestation of
power or of violence? Can we describe the deadly order maintained in Franco's
Spain or by Argentina's military or in Pinochet's government as the *absence* of

violence? Conversely, can we deny their power? Insofar as the power of these governments (no less *real* because they were not democratically elected or universally supported) is geared to engender fear and submission rather than consensus in the population, they are violent governments. Power, in this context, is inseparable from violence and relies on the constant exertion or threat of violence. The violence can lie either within or outside the boundaries of the law—executions as opposed to torture, for example—but the violent displays of power serve the purpose of disempowering the population, dispersing individuals, making them constantly afraid of each other, making them afraid of arbitrary attack or betrayal. Thus the government empowers itself.

The reluctance to talk about violence is evident in all the sources directly or indirectly confronting violence that I have consulted for this study, regardless of their many other differences. Sahagún, in *Historia general de las cosas de Nueva España*, begins his study of the Mesoamerican practice of human sacrifices by saying that he will keep his description simple, "for they are so cruel and inhuman that whosoever heard about them would be horrified and frightened" (2:xx). Marrus (126) notes that "historians have said remarkably little about the world of the Nazi camps, whose horrifying landscape has been mainly described in survivors' memoirs and by literary critics who have built upon these accounts." Barbara Ehrenreich (xi) observes that when faced with violence, the "reader's impulse is to engage in a kind of mental flight."

32. Set up in this have/have-not, active/passive opposition, which is also implicitly gendered, male/female, the oppressed's desire to become the persecutor (as described by Fanon) seems a variation on Freud's penis envy.

33. Many of the characters in these plays seem abnormal or pathological when viewed from a strictly personal perspective, but we will see that these mental deformities are products of an oppressive situation, the results of what Alice Miller, in *For Your Own Good: Hidden Cruelty in Child-Rearing and the Roots of Violence*, calls "poisonous pedagogy."

## 2. José Triana

1. Triana was born in Bayamo, Cuba ("the cradle of Independence") in 1932. He studied in Cuba, was inspired by Martí as a student. He became a friend of the writer Virgilio Piñera in 1952 and published some poems in the literary magazine *Ciclón*. He sympathized and participated with the incipient revolutionary movement and, after the attack on Moncada (1953), was warned to leave the country. He left for Spain in 1954, spent two years at the Universidad Autónoma de Madrid, and started attending and working in theatre. In order to have the opportunity to see actors and directors at work, he swept the stage for a theatre company. He saw plays by Beckett and Ionesco, which impressed him, and started writing plays: *Un incidente cotidiano* (which he destroyed) and *El Mayor General hablará de teogonía* (*The Major General Will Speak of Theogony*, 1957). He acted in Shakespeare's *A Comedy of Errors* and Piñera's *The Slaves*. Inspired by Piñera's *Electra Garrigó*, he wrote *Medea en el espejo* (*Medea in the Mirror*, 1960) upon his return to Cuba after the revolution. These plays were

followed by *Parque de la fraternidad (Fraternity Park*, 1962) and *Muerte de un ñeque (Death of a Thug)* in 1963. *La noche de los asesinos (Night of the Assassins*, published in English as *The Criminals)* was written in 1965 and won the Casa de las Américas award in 1966. *Ceremonial de guerra (War Ceremonial)* was written between 1968 and 1973 (recently published for the first time by Ediciones Persona). *Revolico en el campo de marte (Frolic in the Battle Field)*, written in 1971, premiered at the Bentley Theatre, Dartmouth College, in 1981. *Palabras comunes (Worlds Apart*, 1979-86) was staged by the Royal Shakespeare Company in Stratford-upon Avon in 1986. Triana lives in Paris with his wife, Chantal.

2. In Abelardo Estorino's interview with Triana and Vicente Revuelta, director of the award-winning production of *Assassins*, Triana claims he began a three-act version of the play in 1958 ("Destruir los fantasmas," 6). In an interview with Ramiro Fernández-Fernández, "José Triana habla de su teatro" (38-39), Triana states that a one-act version of *Assassins* began taking shape in his mind as early as 1957-58 and that it depicts the prerevolutionary miasma, the need to find a solution to national problems; he could complete the play only with the triumph of the revolution, with "the national consciousness that the revolution has given our people, that has allowed our people to move forward." Thus he was surprised that critics considered the play antirevolutionary. Fernández-Fernández (40) attributes the critical misunderstanding of the work to an "unfortunate distortion" on the part of bourgeois critics unable to comprehend the avantgarde, which is then appropriated by "reactionary critics, who impose an interpretation alien to the possibilities offered by the text."

3. Terry L. Palls, in *The Theatre in Revolutionary Cuba*, compares *Assassins* to theatre of the absurd, which poses existential rather than social problems. Frank Dauster ("Game of Chance," 168) stresses that Triana's works "are rooted in a critical sense of Cuban reality," and although he associates them with theatre of the absurd, he qualifies the term with a quote from Julio Miranda's article "José Triana o el conflicto": "The fact [is] that the absurd has not been utilized in Cuba as an instrument of metaphysical investigation, with reactionary results à la Ionesco and Beckett, in which the nothingness winds up filling the stage with its oppressive negativity, but rather [as] an effort at a sociopolitical search for a judgement of an antihuman order of things, absurdly sanctioned by law and custom and penetrated, as such, absurdly, by the new theatre."

4. Schechner's statement that the Cubans had no theatre was simply not true. George Woodyard, in "Perspectives on Cuban Theater," describes the intense theatrical activity in Cuba following the revolution: "In the five years preceding the Revolution, only 30 plays were staged, many of them because February of 1958 had been designated Cuban Theater Month" (42), but the political transformation was accompanied by a cultural one. Theatrical activities were organized by the National Council on Culture, which put playwrights, directors, actors, and technical and artistic staff on salary and funded productions. The Casa de las Américas and the Union de Escritores y Artistas de Cuba held competitions and festivals to encourage, stage, and publish theatrical works. Collective theatre groups *(creación colectiva)* such as the Conjunto Dramático del Oriente, founded in 1961, offered training in theatrical production, history, and analysis. Aside from producing international and Latin American plays, the group resuscitated the *teatro de relaciones*, "a dramatic form which

was developed in Cuba by the oppressed classes and used since colonial times until its disappearance in the early 1950's"; this theatre searched "for its roots in the past as a means of establishing direct communication with the people within the framework of the Revolution" (48). The Grupo Teatro Escambray, started in 1968, developed a Marxist-Leninist program consistent with the ideological aims of the revolution itself and traveled to rural areas to work on specific local issues and political problems. Many groups like this formed in the late 1960s and continued working into the 1970s—La Yaya, Grupo Teatrova, Grupo Teatro Estudio, Grupo Yarabey, etc. However, as Mario Benediti noted, theatre in Cuba was experiencing a "serious crisis. The first time I came to Cuba, in 1966, there was sustained theatrical activity, with various good quality companies. On my second visit, in 1967, I saw a couple of high-level shows, like, for example, *Unos hombres y otros*, an adaptation of stories by Jesús Díaz, and *La noche de los asesinos*, by José Triana . . . But then came the collapse" (qtd. in Woodyard, "Perspectives," 49; the suspension marks do not represent an omission from the text). Woodyard advances several hypotheses for the decline of theatre in Cuba, among them the intellectual intolerance (exemplified by the Padilla affair in 1968 and UNEAC's disagreement over Arrufat) and the gradual institutionalization of the Cuban revolution.

5. Triana and Taylor, "Entrevista," (in Taylor, *Imagen*, 116).

6. "Declaración de la UNEAC," in Arrufat, 11-12. A highly charged dialogue (in which Triana was directly involved) concerning "revolutionary" and "antirevolutionary" art took place in Cuba in the 1960s. The uproar surrounding the "José Antonio Ramos" (UNEAC) award to Arrufat's *Los siete contra Tebas* and Padilla's *Fuera del juego* in 1968 shows the political questions surrounding aesthetic representation of ambiguity and ahistoricity. Triana (who had already won Cuba's Casa de las Américas award with *La noche de los asesinos* in 1965) and two other members of the UNEAC committee supported the awards for Arrufat and Padilla, while the remaining two members denounced the works for ideological reasons that could also have been applied to Triana's *Asesinos*: "Its antihistoricism is expressed through the exaltation of individualism even in the face of the collective needs of the people in a period of historical development, as well as in its circular, repetitive—rather than linear, ascendent—concept of time. Both attitudes have always typified right-wing thinking and have traditionally been used as instruments of counter-revolution."

7. Page numbers for *Assassins* refer to Dauster, Lyday, and Woodyard, *9 dramaturgos hispanoamericanos*, vol 1. Again, translations are mine unless otherwise noted.

8. Turner (83) distinguishes between ritual and secular ritual or ceremony: Ritual "does not portray a dualistic, almost Manichean, struggle between order and void, cosmos and chaos, formed and indeterminate, with the former always triumphing in the end. Rather it is a transformative self-immolation of order as presently constituted, even sometimes a voluntary *sparagmos* or self-dismemberment of order in the subjunctive depths of liminality."

9. "Man grows through antistructure, and conserves through structure," 114. Turner (24-25), like the eminent anthropologist Arnold van Gennep (1873-1957), distinguishes three phases in the ritual process—separation, transition and incorporation. "The first phase of *separation* clearly demarcates sacred

space and time from profane or secular space and time. . . . It includes symbolic behavior—especially symbols of reversal or inversion of things, relationships. . . . During the intervening phase of *transition* . . . the ritual subjects pass through a period and area of ambiguity, a sort of social limbo which has few (though sometimes these are most crucial) of the attributes of either the preceding or subsequent profane social statuses or cultural states. . . . The passage from one social status to another is often accompanied by a parallel passage in space, a geographical movement from one place to another. This may take the form of a mere opening of doors or the literal crossing of a threshold which separates two distinct areas. . . . The third phase . . . 'incorporation' includes symbolic phenomena and actions which represent the return of the subjects to their new, relatively stable, well-defined position in the total society." Turner, *From Ritual to Theatre.*

10. From Adrian Mitchell's adaptation of Triana's *Assassins,* published as *The Criminals,* trans. Pablo Armando Fernández and Michael Kustow, *Drama Review* 14/2. (Winter 1970): 122.

11. See Hegel's "Lordship and Bondage," in *The Phenomenology of the Mind,* arguing that the bondsman derives his identity through the master. See too Alexandre Kojève's *Introduction to the Reading of Hegel* for a succinct summary of Hegel's master-slave relationship. To "speak of the 'origin' of Self-Consciousness is necessarily to speak of a fight to the death for 'recognition'"; the human being "is begotten only in and by the fight that ends in the relation between Master and Slave" (Kojève, 7, 9).

12. T. Philemon Wakashe, in "*Pula:* An Example of Black Protest Theatre in South Africa," describes a production of *Pula,* written by Matsemela Manaka, in which the actors call for solidarity in the blacks' struggle to repossess their land. Wakashe, as audience member, states that "if at that moment the actors had dared to call on the audience (at a black township hall in Soweto) to rise and repossess their lands, I believe all of us would have gone."

13. Pianca, in *Diogenes* (1:8), quotes Sergio Corrieri, director of Teatro del Escambray: "The whole generation was revolutionary; we were militant, we had fought at Girón, we were facing the most difficult transformations and the most serious problems of revolutionary change and . . . damn! then we'd go and rehearse Ionesco."

14. "Still about Avant-Garde Theatre," 8. Ionesco distinguishes between permanent and topical truths: "More of us die in wartime: topical truth. We die: permanent truth" (94); hence, he feels we can speak of some plays as being "more true, more universal" than others. In "Remarks on my Theatre and on the Remarks of Others" (98), he adds that a work of art "cannot have the same function as an ideology, for if it did it would be an ideology, it would no longer be a work of art, that is to say, an autonomous creation, an independent universe with its own life and its own laws. . . . A work of art is for me an expression of native intuition that owes almost nothing to other people."

15. References to *Ceremonial de guerra* and *Palabras comunes* are to Triana's unpublished typescripts of the plays.

16. The use of the map is problematic, and I deal with it as part of more detailed analysis of *Ceremonial* in Taylor, "Framing the Revolution."

## 3. Griselda Gambaro

1. Griselda Gambaro was born in Buenos Aires in 1928. Although she has always loved writing, she started writing seriously for the theatre when she was twenty-four. She has published award-winning novels and short stories as well as close to thirty plays, including *Las paredes* (*The Walls*, 1963), *El desatino* (*The Blunder*, 1965), *Los siameses* (*Siamese Twins*, 1965), *El campo* (*The Camp*, 1967), *Nada que ver* (*Nothing to Do*, 1972), *Decir sí* (*Saying Yes*, 1972), *Información para extranjeros* (*Information for Foreigners*, 1973), *La malasangre* (*Bitter Blood*, 1982), *Real envido* (*Royal Gambit*, 1983), *Del sol naciente* (*From the Rising Sun*, 1984), *Antigona furiosa* (*Furious Antigone*, 1986), *Morgan* (1988). Gambaro was in exile in Barcelona during the height of the Dirty War, and then she returned to Buenos Aires, where she continues to live with her husband, a sculptor, and her two children. Beginning with her first work, awarded the Fondo Nacional de las Artes prize, she has won numerous prestigious awards and is considered one of the most important writers in Argentina.

2. Aldo C. Vacs (15) describes a pattern of "spasmodic shifts": "suddenness, lack of control, unexpected outcomes, and discontinuity" caused by "the question of legitimacy; the dilemma of capital accumulation versus redistribution; the problem of hegemony; social characteristics, especially of political parties; the unstable nature of military-civilian alliances; and the corruption of the military."

3. Rock, chap. 7, "The Apogee of Perón, 1946-1955," details Peron's use of theatrical effect to control public perception and its relationship to the repressive measures needed to maintain public order. Rock notes the diversionary tactics and theatrics organized by Perón to divert attention from Argentina's economic crisis in the late 1940s and early 1950s: "But neither Perón's barrages of self-publicity nor political scapegoating could check the growing demoralization among his supporters" (312).

4. Elaine Scarry, in *The Body in Pain* (56), writes of torture as a "pathetic drama," a concept I develop later in the chapter.

5. See Daniel Zalacain, "El personaje 'fuera del juego'" (59); Tamara Holzapfel, "Griselda Gambaro's Theatre of the Absurd"; Teresa Mendez-Faith, "Sobre el uso y abuso de poder" (832).

6. This and all references to Gambaro's *Las paredes* and *El desatino* are from Griselda Gambaro, *Teatro*; references to *Los siameses*, however, are from *9 dramaturgos hispanoamericanos*, vol. 2 (my translations).

7. English translations from *The Camp* are from William I. Oliver's translation of the play in his anthology *Voices of Change*. I maintain the Spanish spelling of the names, however, because "Franco" has connotations accessible to English audiences that "Frank" does not convey.

8. Barbara Ehrenreich, in her foreword to Klaus Theweleit's *Male Fantasies* (1:xi), warns us against reading murder, specifically fascist murder, as "'something else'—a symbolic act, if not a variety of performance art."

9. The luxurious trappings of the room are characteristic of the torture rooms described by Scarry (40), which "are often given names that acknowledge and call attention to the generous, civilizing impulse normally present in the

human shelter ('guest rooms,' 'safe houses'). They call attention to this impulse only as prelude to announcing its annihilation."

10. See also Vivian M. Patraka's "Contemporary Drama, Fascism, and the Holocaust." Friedländer provides examples of the pacifying effect of images and language that bind kitsch or the mundane with the horrific reality of death. He cites the scene in Hans-Jürgen Syberberg's film *Hitler, a Film from Germany,* in which Hitler's valet discusses the problem of his master's socks: "With the stockings, he always had something to complain about, for they were usually too short, so they supposedly slid down his calves. He would then exclaim: 'Isn't it possible for the Führer of the German people to get a pair of decent socks?' Frau Kannenberg and I combed all the stores in Berlin. The black shoes with the colored suits were an atrocity." As Friedländer remarks, the innocuous detail almost makes Hitler seem innocuous: "This great man who made and unmade history, unable to match socks and suits! . . . Compassion is born here for the hero's vulnerability to the small things in life. The spectator identifies with what he sees, and feels superior, for he knows how to pick the right socks" (63).

The same binding operates on the level of language: by joining two sets of facts, the bureaucratic with the horrific, the first cancels out the second. Friedländer uses Martin Broszat's "Hitler and the Genesis of the 'Final Solution'" as an example of this discourse, of which I will quote only one sentence: "(A) The Jews of some transports that had been diverted to the Reichskommissariat Ostland, mainly to Riga, Minsk and Kovno, were not assigned to the local ghettos or camps, as were the majority of the later transports; (B) these Jews were shot upon arrival" Friedländer comments: "Here the unreality springs from an absolute disparity between the two halves of the phrases: The first half implies an ordinary administrative measure, and is put in totally normal speech: the second half accounts for the natural consequence, except that here, suddenly, the second half describes murder. The style doesn't change. It cannot change. It is in the nature of things that the second half of the text can only carry on the bureaucratic and detached tone of the first. That neutralizes the whole discussion and suddenly places each one of us, before we have had time to take hold of ourselves, in a situation not unrelated to the detached position of an administrator of extermination: Interest is fixed on the administrative process, an activity of building and transportation, words used for record-keeping. And that's all" (89, 91).

11. See Jean Baudrillard's *Simulations* (2): "Abstraction today is no longer that of the map, the double, the mirror or the concept. Simulation is no longer that of a territory, a referential being or a substance. It is the generation by models of a real without origin or reality: a hyperreal." It seems to me that *The Balcony,* written 1958 and revised in 1962, is more representative of what Baudrillard terms the "hyperreal" than are more contemporary Latin American plays in which the sociopolitical reality is reaffirmed rather than put in question.

12. Rock (368) cites the figures of *Latin America: Political Report* (London), 1976-1982 (weekly), (Jan. 1978) indicating that less than 20 percent of the victims of state terrorism were guerrillas.

13. Kirsten Nigro's point that the active/passive, powerful/powerless opposition reflects a gendered (masculine/feminine) opposition (although not a biological sexual difference) is important. I believe that the relationship between Lorenzo and Ignacio is more than a masculine/feminine opposition; it is also a

child/mother one. Ignacio, as the "feminine" one of the two, is also the nurturing one, the one that looks after helpless Lorenzo, the one who so anxiously desires to cut the cord.

14. See Elaine Scarry's *The Body in Pain*, 28, Edward Peters's *Torture*, Jacobo Timerman's *Prisoner without a Name, Cell without a Number*. The situation described in the prologue (xvi) to *Nunca más: The Report of the Argentine National Commission on the Disappeared* succinctly states a conclusion about the gratuitous nature of the interrogation which coincides with the findings reported in the different studies: "They were tortured, almost without exception, methodically, sadistically, sexually, with electric shocks and near-drownings and constant beatings, in the most humiliating possible way, not to discover information—very few had information to give—but just to break them spiritually as well as physically, and to give pleasure to their torturers. Most of those who survived the torture were killed."

15. See Sandra Messinger Cypess, "Physical Imagery in the Works of Griselda Gambaro," 359-60.

16. Twins suggest the danger of undifferentiation and are thus considered threatening and impure by some societies; e.g., the Nyakyusa leave newborn twins out to die (Girard, *Violence*, 57). Conversely, as in the black Caribbean culture of Alejo Carpentier's *The Kingdom of this World*, twins can be considered extremely lucky in an inversion of the same phenomenon. The image of the prodigious-monstrous twins relates to an entire group of images associated with crisis, images depicting nonhuman unions and natural aberrations of all kinds. Girard (*Scapegoat*, 30-31) notes the "catastrophic" association of "twins or fraternal enemies who illustrate the conflict between those who become undifferentiated in a particularly graphic fashion. No doubt this is why the theme provides the most classic beginning for myths everywhere."

17. See Dumouchel's introduction to his edition of critical essays on Girard, *Violence and Truth*, for a clear discussion of Girard's theory of mimetic desire and violence.

18. This is a Jungian definition of individuation. See C.G. Jung, *The Undiscovered Self*, or Jolande Jacobi, *The Psychology of C.G. Jung*, for an explanation of individuation.

19. Scarry (20) notes how the interrogation associated with torture "graphically objectifies the step-by-step backward movement along the path by which language comes into being and which is here being reversed or uncreated or deconstructed. We will see that this same mime of uncreating reappears consistently throughout all the random details of torture—not only in relation to verbal constructs (e.g., sentences, names) but also in relation to material artifacts (e.g., a chair, a cup) and mental objects (i.e., the objects of consciousness."

20. The appeal to national identity and destiny, rather than to class consciousness, is of course one of the distinctive features of fascism, making it by definition an anti-Marxist movement.

21. See chapter 1, n. 33, for a summary of Miller's theory in *For Your Own Good*.

22. General Jorge Rafael Videla, leader of the military junta that took power in 1976 (qtd. in Rock, 368).

23. Qtd. in "Griselda Gambaro: La ética de la confrontación," interview with Gambaro by Roster and Giella, in Gambaro, *Teatro* (15).

24. See Skidmore and Smith's *Modern Latin America* for a brief historical overview of this period. See too Anthony James Joes, *Fascism in the Contemporary World*, for an overview of fascism in Argentina.

25. See Brecht, *Short Organon*, sec. 3, in *Brecht on Theatre*.

26. Christian Metz, in *The Imaginary Signifier* (9), expounds on the viewers' reactions to "good" and "bad" object relations (along the lines of psychologist Melanie Klein) with films; he cites as an example the denunciation of the "French quality film": "This attack was no pretence, it went much further than a mere disagreement at the intellectual level, it conveyed a real and profound antipathy for the films denounced: it constituted them as bad objects, for the denouncers themselves first of all, then for the audience that attached themselves to them and a little later guaranteed the success of their films (thus restoring good cinema)." The same violent reactions and hostility are obvious when confronted with disturbing "bad" plays.

27. For a brilliant discussion on this discourse, see Susan Sontag's "Fascinating fascism" in *Under The Sign of Saturn*.

28. By "tragedy" I mean the object of Aristotle's definition: dramatic texts depicting personages "of defined moral character" (*Poetics* 9.6), nobler than average (*Poetics* 3.2), which show pain in order to give pleasure (*Poetics* 6) and are informed by notions of heroism, inevitability, and transcendence—not the adjective "tragic," which Murray Krieger in *The Tragic Vision* (1) uses to describe the vision that is "the most spectacular and the most expressive of the crisis-mentality of our time." Krieger assertively continues: "Fearful and demoniac in its revelations, this vision needed the ultimate soothing power of the aesthetic form that contained it—of tragedy itself—in order to preserve for the world a sanity which the vision itself denied" (3). My point is that this theatre, though tragic in its vision, refuses to give the soothing reassurance and the sense of sanity inherent in tragedy as a dramatic form. It seems oddly incongruous and anachronistic for Robert Skloot (in *The Theatre of the Holocaust*, but particularly in *The Darkness We Carry*), to analyze the drama of the Holocaust in the traditional dramatic terminology of "tragedy," "tragicomedy," and the like.

29. John Berger, in *Ways of Seeing* (46), argues that "the social presence of a woman is different in kind from that of a man. A man's presence is dependent upon the promise of power he embodies. . . . The promised power may be moral, physical, temperamental, economic, social, sexual—but its object is always exterior to the man. . . . By contrast, a woman's presence expresses her own attitude towards herself, and defines what can or cannot be done to her. . . . To be born a woman has been to be born, within an allotted and confined space, into the keeping of men. The social presence of women has developed as a result of their ingenuity in living under such tutelage within such a limited space. But this has been at the cost of a woman being split in two. A woman must continually watch herself. She is almost always accompanied by her own image of herself. . . . She has to survey everything she is and everything she does because how she appears to others, and ultimately how she appears to men, is of crucial importance for what is normally thought of as the success of her life.

30. "Perverse" is defined by Robert J. Stoller (*Sexual Excitement*, xii) as having "the urge to harm one's sexual object."

31. Jean Franco in "Self-Destructing Heroines" curiously, also uses the word "lure" to describe Emma's role in this scene. However, I disagree with her reading insofar as she perceives Emma as an almost willing accomplice in her annihilation: "She aspires to the kind of power known as art. She does not aspire to create in the true sense but rather to perform on a public stage" (110). Franco sees the concert scene not as an act of torture, as I do, but as "the State's gift to Emma for seducing Martin" (110). The public humiliation of a woman is, however, a form of torture in keeping with the one described by Ximena Bunster-Burotto (309): "[The woman] becomes the pathetic jester who amuses the torturers by her aimless movements directed to make her fall, roll on the floor, crawl on all fours, and jump over obstacles that are non-existent. Fun is made of the shape of the woman's breasts, her birthmarks, or the scars left on her abdomen after a cesarean birth. This stage of torture is marked by the captors' sadistic objectification of the women at their mercy."

32. Again, as in *The Siamese Twins*, the face is the target of annihilation. Levinas (198) explains violence directed at the face: "The alterity that is expressed in the face provides the unique 'matter' possible for total negation. I can wish to kill only an existent absolutely independent, which exceeds my powers infinitely, and therefore does not oppose them but paralyzes the very power of power. The Other is the sole being I can wish to kill." Stoller (*Sexual Excitement*, 8) also observes a different kind of violence directed at the face than at other parts of the body. In fetishizing others, he notes, one dehumanizes them, but "this is easier to do with breasts, buttocks, legs, and penises than with faces. We reside in our faces; it takes more to annihilate a person in the face."

33. Cited by Vivian Patraka in "Fascist Ideology and Theatricalization."

34. Marguerite Feitlowitz's 1987 translation of *Information for Foreigners* is unpublished and reached me after I had completed this study; hence, the translations used in this text are my own.

35. Rock (355) explains the intensification of violence in the early 1970s, the kidnappings, abductions, and disappearances carried out by extreme right-wing groups called *Mano* (Hand): "Most of these victims simply vanished without a trace, and the few to reappear spoke of torture. By the early months of 1971 one such 'disappearance' occurred on average each eighteen days." He adds that "these incidents are detailed in press reports from April to December 1970; see *La Prensa*, *La Nación* and *Clarín*, for example" (441 n.56).

36. Bunster-Burotto also emphasizes the prevalence of attacks on the woman's sexual organs.

37. Franco, in "Self-Destructing Heroines" (105), indicates that the "division of the traditional city into public (male) spaces and private space where women's power derives from motherhood or virginity has deeply affected both political life in Latin America and the imaginary repertoire on which literature draws. . . . women characters [are allegorized] in their virtually invariant positions of mother, prostitute or love object." See also Bunster-Burotto.

38. Stanley Milgram, in "The Perils of Obedience," describes his experiment: two subjects, one assigned the role of "teacher" and the other of "learner," are asked by the experimenter to participate in a test of "the effects of punishment on learning." The learner is strapped to a miniature electric chair in one room, and the teacher, in the adjoining room, is given a sample electric shock of 45 volts to establish the authenticity of the punishment. The teacher then recites a list of

associations which the learner must subsequently repeat. When the learner makes a mistake, the teacher inflicts ever intensifying electric shocks, reaching the potentially lethal dose of 450 volts. The teacher is told that the learner suffers from a heart condition and, as the shocks become stronger hears screams and pleas for help from the next room. The experimenter instructs the teacher to carry on with the experiment. The teacher's willingness to comply with these commands are of course the real focus of the test.

39. Levin, 606. General Jacques Massu was a general in the Algerian war who strongly supported the legitimacy of torture (see Peters, 176-79): hence *massuisme* in French, "massuism" in English.

40. Joan Dassin, in *Torture in Brazil* (xii), notes that the victims and their families were accused of seeking "revenge, not justice" by calling for official investigations into the atrocities carried out by the Brazilian military dictatorship between 1964 and 1985.

41. See Chomsky and Herman, *The Washington Connection and Third World Fascism*, 266-70.

## 4. Emilio Carballido

1. Emilio Carballido was born in Córdoba, Veracruz, in 1925; the family moved to Mexico City in 1926. He began writing plays in 1946, and premiered his first major play, *Rosalba y los Llaveros* (Rosalba and the Llaveros) in 1950. Since then he has written more than a hundred plays; his major ones include *La hebra de oro* (1957, trans. by M.S. Peden, *The Golden Thread and Other Plays*, 1971), *El día que se soltaron los leones* (1957; Oliver's translatation of *The Day They Let the Lions Loose* appeared in his 1971 *Voices of Change*), *El relojero de Córdoba* (1960, trans. by M.S. Peden as *The Clockmaker from Cordoba* in *The Golden Thread*), *Un pequeño día de ira* (1961, trans. by M.S. Peden as *Short Day's Anger*, 1975), *Medusa* (1960), *Te juro Juana* (1965), *Yo también hablo de la rosa* (1965, trans. by Oliver in Woodyard's 1971 *The Modern State in Latin America*), *Orinoco* (1979), *Ceremonia en el templo del tigre* (1983), and *La rosa de dos aromas* (1986). Carballido won the Casa de las Americas award in 1962 for *Un pequeño día de ira*, as well as numerous other awards. His plays have been translated into English, French, Italian, Russian, Czech, Norwegian, and other languages. Carballido currently lives in Mexico City.

2. Arif Dirlik, in "Culturalism as Hegemonic Ideology and Liberating Practice" (13), verbalizes a position similar to Carballido's when he insists on the importance of studying culture as a "liberating" practice and "argues the radicalism of cultural activity against efforts to subsume the question of culture within other, seemingly more radical activities upon which individuals attempting to change the world have increasingly focused their attention. In a world where economic necessity and political crisis confront us daily, this argument may seem superfluous or even self-indulgent. This is especially the case where the question of culture relates to the non-Western world where millions of lives await the urgent resolution of practical problems for their survival. Yet I will argue in the face of necessity that the realm of culture, as the realm of activity that

is bound up with the most fundamental epistemological questions, demands priority of attention."

3. Dirlik (14), who, in turn, is paraphrasing E.P. Thompson.

4. Translations from *The Day They Let the Lions Loose* (in Oliver's *Voices of Change*) and *I Too Speak of the Rose* (in Woodyard's *The Modern Stage in Latin America*) are by William I. Oliver except as otherwise noted; page numbers cite these editions.

5. This is my translation. Oliver's "I don't think people are the way they say" misses the sexual innuendos of Carballido's original: "Yo no creo que las gentes hagan esas cosas que dicen" (233; page numbers of the Spanish correspond to *Teatro*, the Fondo de Cultural Económica edition of three Carballido plays).

6. In 1880, Cunninghame Graham observed a phenomenon foreshadowing Carballido's play: "The giant cypresses, tall even in the time of Moctezuma, the castle of Chapultepec upon its rock . . . did not interest me so much as a small courtyard, in which, ironed and guarded, a band of Indians . . . were kept confined . . . their demeanour less reassuring than that of the tigers in the cage hard by" (116).

7. My translation of Carballido's "huele a orilla de lago, a tierra levemente podrida" (263); Oliver has "it smells of rotting leaves" (37).

8. See Davis, *Latin American Thought*, chap. 5, for a study of positivism in Latin America.

9. My translation of Carballido's "Entre más sabe la gente, más difícil resulta disciplinarla" (241), erroneously translated by Oliver as "The more people you know, the more difficult it is to keep order" (15). Carballido is referring here to an uneasy contradiction in Mexico's educational system. On one hand, the government is obliged and theoretically "committed" to provide an education for its population. Schools and universities are free in Mexico, and the large national universities are "autonomous," meaning that the government cannot send in police or directly influence their functioning. But like the Teacher, the government finds itself in the situation of having to educate people who are potentially threatening to its continued existence. Its way of solving this contradiction without directly meddling with university education has been to unionize the university workers—janitors, watchmen, and the like. When the political situation becomes heated, this union goes on strike, and the universities must be shut down for lack of personnel.

10. "Musica de la persecución" (246), not "percussive music" as Oliver has it (20).

11. My translation. I approve of Oliver's substitution of "we" in Carballido's original "they are surgeons, butchers" (39) insofar as the scene emphasizes that we (as victims and outcasts) are responsible for our leaders; however, the original distinction between "we" and "they" is an important one in that we are responsible for our roles as *victims* but not as butchers—we are not the oppressors.

12. Oliver's translation (331) except that he has "what Toña's wedding looked like."

13. I am indebted to my colleague Raul Bueno for the observation of the double dynamic of the oral/literate paradigm. Though the vertical class tensions are evident throughout the chapter, I concentrate on the horizontal aspect be-

cause *Rose* provides an example of the passage of cultural material from one society to another, which is at issue throughout this work.

14. Ong defines primary orality as "the orality of cultures untouched by literacy" (6) and says of its coexistence with literacy: "Today primary oral culture in the strict sense hardly exists, since every culture knows of writing and has some experience of its effects. Still, to varying degrees many cultures and sub-cultures, even in a high-technology ambiance, preserve much of the mind-set of primary orality" (11).

15. My translation. In the original, the mother implies that Toña is not about to go around derailing trains for the rest of her life, whereas Oliver's translation, "Oh, well, if she's going to go on derailing trains . . . " (54) seems to leave that possibility open.

16. I disagree with Kerr's reading (52) of these lines as Jungian, a product of the "collective unconscious" manifesting itself through the dreams and visions of the individual psyche. Rather, I think Carballido is referring here to a much more concrete social process, the transmission of knowledge and cultural traditions from one generation to another through speech.

17. I hasten to add, with Susan Sontag: "Of course, I don't mean interpretation in the broadest sense in which Nietzsche (rightly) says, 'There are no facts, only interpretations.' By interpretation, I mean here a conscious act of the mind which illustrates a certain code, certain 'rules' of interpretation" (*Interpretation*, 15).

18. See M.M. Bober, *Karl Marx's Interpretation of History*, 5.

19. My translation of "man is Economy." Oliver's "Man is economy" misses some of Carballido's humor.

20. For an interesting essay on "common sense," see Geertz, "Common Sense as a Cultural System," in *Local Knowledge*.

21. My translation.

22. Alice Lakwena's "Holy Spirit Movement" in Uganda in 1987 graphically illustrates the devastating consequences of relying on ritual to solve violent social crisis. Her warriors, armed only with stones, felt that the ritual preparation for combat made them impervious to attack from the heavily armed enemy. An interview with one of her followers describes their beliefs: "If you throw a 'stone' grenade it will explode. I threw them in battle but it was difficult to tell if they worked because other people were throwing real grenades. . . . This woman [Lakwena] can reach Kampala because when they are moving the NRA do not see the Holy Spirit soldiers. That happens. . . . People in ambush will sleep as you pass." This, the soldier explains, is because the soldiers rub over themselves a powder made of burned squirrel bones, which makes them invisible. An eyewitness report of a battle, however, saw things differently: "They [the Holy Spirit Movement] came in three groups totalling around 500 men and women singing religious hymns. . . . they were received by a shower of bullets from the NRA soldiers who had taken cover," and nearly half the group were killed or captured (qtd. in Uganda's *New Vision* 26 (Oct. 1987): 1-11.

23. Transculturation is also discussed by Carl Weber in a 1989 article, "AC/TC: Currents of Theatrical Exchange." Weber seems unaware of the earlier uses of the term as I outline them here, stating that the word "is as new as the phenomenon" of international arts festivals dating from the 1950s onward (11). He

notes that "the trend labeled 'transculturation' has, indeed, pervaded [the media] on a global scale. . . . 'Western,' which in this context means European or North American ideology, its values, structure, and contents are inscribed in the predominant models of performance accepted by most contemporary societies, models that partly ingest, partly destroy indigenous cultural values and forms" (12). However, Weber does accept that the process is not merely one-directional and that original, culturally specific art forms can develop from it: "Even when early efforts still bordered on copies, soon the models became infused and mediated with native literary and/or performance tradition" (18).

24. Kerr (53) associates the Medium with Brecht's narrators and asserts that, like them, she functions to distance the audience from the action: "The fact that she evokes the other scenes avoids any semblance of reality in her representation. She transforms the spectator into an observer, rather than participant, of the action. These elements, and the effects of distancing that they produce, represent the theatrical norms that we associate with Brecht's epic theatre."

25. See Artaud's *México y Viaje al país de los Tarahumaras* (Fondo Cultura Económica) or the extract "Concerning a Journey to the Land of the Tarahumaras" in the *Artaud Anthology.*

26. The fluidity I have associated with orality is also, according to Josette Féral (550), a characteristic of feminine discourse, which is "closer to the liquid (and therefore intangible) state of fluids rather than contained in the rigid system of solids."

27. Dirlik (26) makes a similar observation in discussing E.P. Thompson's *Making of the Working Class:* "The centering of the working class must necessarily be accompanied by the 'decentering' of the ruling, hegemonic class, since the two groups by definition make contradictory claims upon history."

## 5. Enrique Buenaventura

1. Enrique Buenaventura was born in Calí, Colombia, in 1925. He began writing plays in 1960, and has worked with the Teatro Escuela de Calí, which later became the Teatro Experimental de Calí (TEC), since the early 1960s. He wrote *A la diestra de Dios Padre* in 1960 (*On the Right Hand of God the Father,* translated by William I. Oliver and included in his anthology, *Voices of Change*). This was followed by *La tragedia del Rey Christophe (The Tragedy of King Christophe)* in 1962 which won the Instituto Internacional de Teatro award. *Un requiem por el Padre Las Casas (Requiem for Father Las Casas)* appeared in 1963. In 1966 his *La trampa (The Trap)* resulted in the loss of governmental funding and support for the TEC. In 1968 he wrote *Papeles del infierno (Documents from Hell)* and has thenceforth worked mainly on collaborative pieces such as *Los soldados* and *La denuncia. Historia de una bala de plata (Story of a Silver Bullet),* a collective creation of Buenaventura and the TEC, won the Casa de las Américas award in 1980. He has also written numerous theoretical pieces, the most notable being "Teatro y cultura" ("Theatre and culture") in 1968 and "Teatro y política" ("Theatre and politics") in 1974. Buenaventura continues to work with the TEC in Calí.

2. William Oliver, Beatriz Risk, and Luys A. Díez all call Buenaventura a *magister ludi*, 49; Fernando de Toro, Beatriz Risk, and Carl Weber discuss him in relation to Brechtian theatre.

3. Buenaventura himself says, "I have proposed that the history of Colombia and of Latin America be widely discussed and known. . . . A country cannot think of a future if it does not know or discuss its past" (qtd. in Espener, 45).

4. Luzuriaga (42-46) describes Buenaventura's popular methodology; Risk uses Buenaventura as her model for "new theatre."

5. Quoted in Penny A. Wallace, "Enrique Buenaventura's *Los papeles del infierno*," 37 (the prologue does not appear in the 1977 edition of the play).

6. "We artists are not going to decolonize culture by ourselves. We alone are not going to achieve a fusion of the European and North American elements which—although the folklorists and indigenists protest—are embedded in us. We are not able to join those elements with the timid—because colonized—culture of the majority. The abyss between the two, like the abyss between productivity and misery, can begin to be closed only by revolutionary violence, and only new forms of society born out of revolution can heal the split permanently" ("Theater and Culture," 152-53).

7. For descriptions of the collaborative project, see Collazos, "Buenaventura"; and Buenaventura's own "Esquema general."

8. These questions, requiring prolonged workshop experimentation and rigorous examination, will be investigated by a research group in residence at the University of California's Humanities Research Institute at Irvine. Enrique Buenaventura and Augusto Boal plan to join theatre practitioners Jorge Huerta (author of *Chicano Theatre*, founder and director of Teatro de la esperanza), Sue-Ellen Case (author of *Feminism and Theatre*, drama director at the University of Washington), Diana Taylor (director of Primer Acto), and Juan Villegas (author of *Ideología*) to rehearse Buenaventura's *La maestra*, approaching it from different ideological and critical perspectives. At this writing, the results are scheduled for presentation at a conference on Representations of Otherness in October 1990.

9. Foucault, in *The Archaeology of Knowledge* (24), describes the problem of *oeuvre*: "At first sight, what could be more simple? A collection of texts that can be designated by a proper name. But this designation (even leaving to one side the problems of attribution) is not a homogeneous function: does the name of an author designate in the same way a text that he has published under his name, a text that he has presented under a pseudonym, another found after his death in the form of an unfinished draft, and another that is merely a collection of jottings, a notebook? The establishment of a complete *oeuvre* presupposes a number of choices that are difficult to justify or even to formulate."

10. My translation, from the 1977 edition of Buenaventura's work published as *Teatro*. William Oliver's translation of this play appears in his anthology, *Voices of Change*.

11. Quoted in Espener, who says she is citing Buenaventura's "Theatre and Culture"; however, this particular statement does not appear in either the Spanish or the English version of the essay. There, Buenaventura states something similar, though more militant: "What we need for the revolution is to be able to

use freely the colonizers' conquests in science and art in developing our peoples' buried traditions" (155; Pottlitzer's translation).

12. Ngugi Wa Thiong'o, the Kenyan dramatist-novelist, told me that his (and others') search for a decolonizing theatre took him through Brecht to other "Brechtians" (such as Augusto Boal) from countries that shared a similar history of colonization.

13. Huerta, in *Chicano Theatre* (3), uses the term "people's theatre" to denote theatre in which "the message is more important than the medium" and plays that "place politics above aesthetics."

14. See Susanne Zantop's "Re-presenting the Present" for a discussion of other views on the fictionalization of history.

15. De Toro (59) speaks of *"La tortura, La orgía, La maestra,* and *La auto-pista";* the last I assume to be an intended reference to *La autopsia (The Autopsy),* since *autopista* means "highway."

16. Wallace (37-46) states that *The Menu* was added to the cycle in 1970 and that the date of *The Dream* is unknown.

17. All references to Buenaventura's plays are from *Teatro* (1977). The translations are my own unless otherwise noted.

18. Donald M. Lowe, in *History of Bourgeois Perception* (176), states that "the changes within a period are always alluvial, and do not fundamentally transform its structure; changes between periods are seismic, involving transformations from one structure to another."

19. See Ximena Bunster-Burotto's "Surviving beyond Fear." Because I deal with torture and gender-related violence specifically in the chapters on Gambaro and Wolff, I focus on other issues in this one.

20. See Jan Vansina's *Oral Tradition as History,* 4-5. Vansina acknowledges, however, that because witnesses are only partially reliable, "the hypercritical analyst can . . . deny validity to an eye-witness account" (5).

21. White does admit that there are limits to the kinds of emplotment the audience will accept: "I do not suppose that anyone would accept the emplotment of the life of President Kennedy as comedy, but whether it ought to be emplotted romantically, tragically, or satirically is an open question" (84). White also makes it clear, however, that although emplotment is basically a literary "fiction-making operation," this "in no way detracts from the status of historical narratives as providing a kind of knowledge" (85). Furthermore, he stresses that we would be mistaken "if we were to believe that literature did not teach us anything about reality" (99).

22. While this may sound disrespectful of tragedy, traditionally regarded as the epitome of the dramatic form, I hasten to assure the reader that what I attack here is the manipulation of the aristocratic genre rather than the genre itself. The Greek theatres and tragedies, considered strictly from the point of view of *theatre,* belie notions of progress (as does Buenaventura's *spirale du pire).* My distinction between "tragedy" and "the tragic" is the standard one, as defined in chapter 4, n. 28, above.

23. "It's Hideously True" is the title of an article by cartoonist Al Capp, in which he describes his farcical characters, Li'l Abner and Daisy Mae (in Corrigan, *Comedy: Meaning and Form*).

24. Sander Gilman's *Jewish Self-Hatred,* as I noted in chapter 1, analyzes the

mechanism of self-hatred by means of which the rejected self identifies with the defining group and distances him- or herself from the characteristics associated with rejection.

25. For a study of the struggle for the historical record in resistance movements, see Barbara Harlow's *Resistance Literature*, chap. 1.

## 6. Egon Wolff

1. Egon Wolff was born in Chile in 1926 of German parents. Although he is a chemical engineer by training, he started writing plays in 1957 with *Discípulos del miedo (Disciples of Fear)*. He won the Premio Nacional de Literatura for this play in 1959 and continued writing; his other plays: *Mansión de lechuzas (The Mansion of Owls)* in 1957, *Parejas de trapo (Rag couples)* in 1960, *Niñamadre (Girl Mother)* and *Los invasores (The Intruders)* in 1963, *El signo de Caín (The Sign of Cain)* in 1967, and *Flores de papel (Paper Flowers)* in 1968 or 1970. *Paper Flowers* received an award from Casa de las Américas and the Laurel de oro in 1970. The play was performed in Argentina, Mexico, United States, Belgium, France, England, Germany, Greece, Sweden, Denmark, Norway and Finland among other countries. This play was followed by *Kindergarten* (1977) and *Espejismos* (1977 or 1978). Wolff continues to live in Chile.

2. The date of *Paper Flowers* is given as 1970 in Leon Lyday's introduction in *9 dramaturgos*, but Teodosio Fernández (146) puts it at 1968 and says that it was first performed in November 1970. Juan Villegas says the play premiered in 1971. Orlando Rodríguez-Sardiñas and Carlos Miguel Suárez-Radillo (113) also date it from 1968.

3. All page numbers refer to Egon Wolff, *Flores de papel*, in *9 dramaturgos hispanoamericanos*. *Paper Flowers* was translated by Margaret S. Peden and published in 1970 by the University of Missouri Press; however, all the translations from the play in this chapter are my own.

4. See Jean Franco's "Beyond Ethnocentrism" (505-6) for an analysis of the subordination of gender by Third World intelligentsia, "the last category to be desconstructed." Franco shows (following Nancy Hartsock's argument in *Money, Sex and Power: Towards a Feminist Historical Materialism*) "how the sexual division of labor that subordinated reproduction to the lowest level of human creativity has led to the valorization of intellectual creations 'born to the minds of those not contaminated by the concerns or necessities of the body.'"

5. Leon Lyday, "Whence Wolff's Canary?"; Margaret S. Peden, "The Theater of Egon Wolff," 190-201; Daniel López, "Ambiguity in *Flores de papel*"; and Myra S. Gann, "Meaning and Metaphor in *Flores de papel*," all illustrate this approach.

6. Other interpretations along political lines include the one by Orlando Rodríguez-Sardiñas and Carlos Miguel Suárez-Radillo (113), which has more than a touch of mythification: "In this play [*Paper Flowers*] the author confronts two antagonistic worlds through his two characters, the same worlds he confronted in *Los invasores* [*The Intruders*]. The establishment—represented by a middle-aged woman, with all the prejudices, atavism, repression, and false

values typical of the bourgeoisie—and the 'intruders,' embodied by a man who represents the marginals, with all the powerful, spontaneous joy, the uninhibited instincts, and the force (which, though apparently brute force, is actually intelligent) which characterizes them."

7. Aside from the contribution of 50 percent of Frei's election campaign fund in 1964 and support for the right-wing candidate, Jorge Alessandri, in 1970, there was an assassination attempt on Allende's life shortly after he won the election, even before his presidency was ratified by the Chilean congress. After he was officially recognized, sabotage continued, mainly through the CIA. However, there was also Nixon's "invisible blockade," the freeze on accounts and loans, the black-market undermining of the Chilean economy, and the subsidy of strikes designed to harm the Allende administration. Skidmore and Smith (142) conclude that whether the U.S. government's "'destabilizing' (that is overthrowing) the Allende regime . . . caused the government's downfall remains unclear, since the Allende administration had a mountain of troubles of its own. Nonetheless, the U.S. once again placed itself squarely on the side of the counterrevolutionaries" (see their *Modern Latin America*, 124-42, for an overview of this period).

8. Teodosio Fernández (145) quotes Wolff as saying that "two-thirds of the men nowadays live suppressed, and those two-thirds cannot wait any longer. It's not just a question of condemning the problem as one of ignorance, and wrapping it in a flag of one color or another. That is a comfortable strategy to postpone the hour in which the violence from one side of the river responds to the violence from the other side if we do not act intelligently and make a better world for all of us, a human world . . . one made up of spirit, reason, and tenderness." Fernández adds that "people have interpreted these words as an attempt to convert [Wolff's] allegory into a warning for the privileged minorities that their egoism is undermining the foundation of the established order."

9. Saul Friedländer (25) discusses kitsch as "a faithful expression of a common sensibility, of harmony dear to the petit bourgeois."

10. Wolff is quoted by Gann (32), who does not seem to disagree with his evaluation.

11. Jean Franco illustrates "the meaning borne by the feminine" in Latin America, from colonial times to the present, with the following diagram:

| mother | | virgin |
|--------|---------|--------|
| | phallus | |
| not virgin | | mother |
| not mother | | virgin |
| (whore) | | (Mary) |

Franco explains that "the central term of the quadrangle is the phallus, which is the bearer of meaning and the active element that determines social reproduction. One term of the semiotic quadrangle is occupied by the mother, who is not a virgin but the bearer of children and whose space is the home. . . . The opposite term to the mother is the virgin—that is, the nun who is pure and uncontaminated and whose space is the convent. The negation of the mother and the virgin is the whore, whose body is open to all men" ("Beyond Ethnocentrism," 507).

12. "The woman is the condition for recollection, the interiority of the Home, and inhabitation" (Levinas, 155).

13. Shoshana Felman (*Writing*, 82-84) describes a similar ironic inversion of reason and madness: "Beneath the mask of accusation, the accused becomes the accuser, pointing his finger at the exposed faces of the 'fools': madness designates as its opposite not sanity but stupidity. It is as though reason did not exist at all, or existed only as a term of negative comparison. What enters into *opposition* are two ways of *being opposed* to reason: either through pettiness, which characterizes the 'category of fools' (what is commonly called reason—bourgeois good sense, the logic of self-interest); or through greatness, in the case of the 'category of madmen.' There is obviously in 'madness' more than a touch of complacency and pride. . . . the term 'madness' demonstrates not only that the *outside* is, in reality, *inside*—that what society rejects under the name of 'madness' as its *exterior*, in fact constitutes the very *interior* of subjectivity—but also that the non-mad are fools, that those who believe themselves to be *inside*, inside society and inside reason, are actually 'out of it,' in the realm of stupidity."

# BIBLIOGRAPHY

## WORKS BY THE PLAYWRIGHTS

### Enrique Buenaventura

*Selected Plays*

*A la diestra de Dios Padre. Teatro: Enrique Buenaventura*. Bogota: Ediciones Tercer Mundo, 1963.

_____.*Enrique Buenaventura: Teatro*. Bogota: Instituto Colombiano de Cultura, 1977.

_____.*In the Right Hand of God the Father*. Trans. William I. Oliver. *Voices of Change in the Spanish American Theatre*. Austin: Univ. of Texas Press, 1971.

*La audiencia. Enrique Buenaventura: Teatro*.

*La autopsia. Enrique Buenaventura: Teatro*.

*La denuncia*. In collaboration with Teatro Experimental de Calí. *Conjunto* 19 (Jan.-Mar. 1974): 40-80.

"The Dream." Typescript. Trans. José Barba-Martín and Robert E. Louis as "Leave from Hell" from an unspecified original.

*The Funeral*. Trans. Anthony Sampson from an unspecified original. Errol Hill, ed., *A Time and a Season: 8 Caribbean Plays*. Jamaica: Carifesta, 1976.

*Historia de una bala de plata*. In collaboration with Teatro Experimental de Calí. Havana: Casa de las Américas, 1980.

*La maestra. Enrique Buenaventura: Teatro*.

_____.Frank Dauster and Leon Lyday, eds. *En un acto: Diez piezas hispanoamericana*. Boston: Heinle and Heinle, 1990.

_____.*The Schoolteacher*. Trans. Gerardo Luzuriaga and Robert S. Rudder. *The Orgy: Modern One-Act Plays from Latin America*. Los Angeles: Univ. of California Press, 1974.

*El menú. Enrique Buenaventura: Teatro*.

_____.Carlos Solórzano, ed. *El teatro actual latinoamericano*. Mexico City: Ediciones de Andrea, 1972.

_____."The Menu." Trans. Diana Taylor, 1990. Unpublished.

*La orgía. Enrique Buenaventura: Teatro*.

_____.Bogota: Editorial Oveja Negra, 1985.

_____.*The Orgy*. Trans. Bogota: Editorial Oveja Negra, 1985.

———.*The Orgy.* Trans. Gerardo Luzuriaga and Robert S. Rudder. *The Orgy: Modern One-Act Plays from Latin America.*

———.*The Orgy.* Trans. Anthony Sampson. Errol Hill, ed., *A Time and a Season: 8 Caribbean Plays.*

*Un requiem por el Padre Las Casas. Teatro: Enrique Buenaventura.* Bogota: Ediciones Tercer Mundo, 1963.

*La requisa. Enrique Buenaventura: Teatro.*

*Los Soldados.* In combination with Carlos José Reyes, Jaqueline Vidal, Jorge Herrera, Sergio Gómez, Gilberto Ramírez, Guillermo Piedrahita. *Enrique Buenaventura: Teatro.*

*La tortura. Enrique Buenaventura: Teatro.*

———.Trans. José Barba-Martin and Louis E. Roberts as *The Twisted State. Drama Review* 14, no. 2 (Winter 1970): 157-59.

*La tragedia del Rey Christophe. Teatro: Enrique Buenaventura.*

## Critical Writings

"El arte no es lujo." *Teatros y política.* Buenos Aires: Edición de la Flor, 1969.

"El arte nuevo de hacer comedias y el Nuevo Teatro." Calí, Colombia: Publicaciones del TEC, 1983.

"Bird's Eye View of the Latin American Theatre." *World Theatre* 9, no. 3 (Autumn 1960): 265-71.

"Esquema general del método de trabajo colectivo del Teatro Experimental de Calí." *Popular Theatre for Social Change in Latin America,* ed. Gerardo Luzuriaga, 42-66.

"Teatro y cultura." *Revista de la Escuela de Teatro,* 1970.

———."Theater and Culture." Trans. Joanna Pottlitzer. *Drama Review* 14, no. 2 (Winter 1970): 151-56.

"Teatro y política." *Conjunto,* 22 (Oct.-Dec. 1974): 90-96.

## Interview

Diez, Luys A. "Entrevista con Enrique Buenaventura." *Latin American Theatre Review* 14, no. 2 (1981): 49-55.

# Emilio Carballido

## Selected Plays

*Acapulco los lunes.* Monterrey: Ediciones Sierra Madre, 1969.

*Las cartas de Mozart.* In edition with *Orinoco* and *Felicidad.* Mexico City: Editores mexicanos unidos, 1985.

*Ceremonia en el templo del tigre.* (In edition with *La rosa de dos aromas* and *Un pequeño día de ira*). Mexico City: Editores mexicanos unidos, 1986.

*El censo.* Part of his collection of one-act plays, *D.F.* Mexico City: Colección teatro mexicano, 1957.

———.Wilberto Cantón, ed. *12 obras en un acto.* Mexico City: Ecuador O O'O, 1967.

_____.Frank Dauster and Leon Lyday, eds., *En un acto: Diez piezas hispanoamericanos.* Boston: Heinle and Heinle, 1990.

*Conversación entre las ruinas.* Trans. as *Conversation among the Ruins.* Presented at Kalamazoo College, Michigan, 1971, and at Puerto Rican Travelling Company, New York City, 1989.

*D.F.* Mexico City: Colección teatro mexicano, 1957.

_____.*D.F.: 13 obras en un acto.* Editorial Novaro, 1973.

*El día que se soltaron los leones. Emilio Carballido: Teatro.* Mexico City: Fondo de Cultura Económica, 1960, 1976, 1979.

_____.Trans. William I. Oliver as *The Day They Let the Lions Loose, Voices of Change in the Spanish American Theatre.* Austin: Univ. of Texas Press, 1971.

*La hebra de oro. El lugar y la hora.* Mexico City: Universidad Nacional Autónoma de México, 1957.

_____.Trans. Margaret S. Peden as *The Golden Thread. The Golden Thread and Other Plays.* Austin: Univ. of Texas Press, 1971.

*Orinoco.* In edition with *Las cartas de Mozart* and *Felicidad.* Mexico City: Editores mexicanos unidos, 1985.

*Un pequeño día de ira.* Havana: Casa de las Américas, 1962.

_____.*Textos de teatro de la Universidad de México.* Mexico: UNAM, 1972.

_____.Trans. Margaret S. Peden as *A Short Day's Anger. Drama and Theatre,* 1975

_____.In edition with *Ceremonia en el templo del tigre* and *La rosa de dos aromas.* Mexico City: Editores mexicanos unidos, 1986.

*El relojero de Córdoba. Emilio Carballido: Teatro.*

_____.Trans. Margaret S. Peden as *The Clockmaker from Córdoba. The Golden Thread and Other Plays.* Austin: Univ. of Texas Press, 1971.

*La rosa de dos aromas.* In edition with *Ceremonia en el templo del tigre* and *Un pequeño día de ira.* Mexico City: Edtiores mexicanos unidos, 1986.

*¡Silencio, pollos pelones, ya les van a echar su máiz! La Palabra y el Hombre* 31 (July/Sept. 1964): 509-71.

_____.Antonio Magaña Esquivel, ed., *Teatro mexicano 1963.* Mexico City: Aguilar, 1965.

*Te juro, Juana que tengo ganas. La Palabra y el Hombre* 35 (July/Sept. 1965): 487-560.

_____.*Te juro, Juana que tengo ganas* and *Yo también hablo de la rosa.* Mexico: Editorial Novaro, 1970.

*Teatro para obreros.* Anthology ed. by Carballido. Mexico City: Editores mexicanos unidos, 1985.

*Yo también hablo de la rosa. Revista de Bellas Artes* 6 (Nov./Dec. 1965): 5-22.

_____.*I Too Speak of the Rose.* Trans. William I. Oliver. *Drama and Theatre* 8, no. 1 (Fall 1969): 47-60.

_____.Ruth S. Lamb, ed. *Three Contemporary Latin American Plays.* Waltham, Mass: Xerox College Publishing, 1971.

_____.*I Too Speak of the Rose.* Oliver translation. George Woodyard, ed., *The Modern Stage in Latin America: Six Plays.* New York: E.P. Dutton, 1971.

_____.*Yo también hablo de la rosa.* Frank Dauster, Leon Lyday, and George Woodyard, eds., *9 dramaturgos hispanoamericanos.* vol. 3 Ottawa: Girol Books, 1979.

*Interviews*

Taylor, Diana. "Entrevista con Emilio Carballido." Videotape. Hanover, N.H.: Dartmouth College, Spring 1983.

Vargas, Alfredo. "Dos horas perdidas de Emilio Carballido." In *La Capital*. Mexico City, July 26, 1970: 71-80.

Vélez, Joseph F. "Una entrevista con Emilio Carballido." *Latin American Theatre Review* (Fall 1973): 17-24.

## Griselda Gambaro

*Selected Plays*

*Acuerdo para cambiar la casa. Griselda Gambaro Teatro 3*. Buenos Aires: Ediciones de la Flor, 1989.

*Antígona furiosa. Gestos* 5 (April 1988): 177-94.

————.*Griselda Gambaro Teatro 3*. Buenos Aires: Ediciones de la Flor, 1989.

————."Antígona furiosa." Trans. Marguerite Feitlowitz, 1988. Unpublished.

*El campo*. Buenos Aires: Ediciones Insurrexit, 1967.

————.*El teatro argentino*, vol. 15. Buenos Aries: Centro Editor, 1981.

————.*The Camp*. Trans. William I. Oliver. *Voices of Change in the Spanish American Theatre*. Austin: Univ. of Texas Press, 1971.

*Cuatro ejercicios para actrices. Griselda Gambaro Teatro 3.*

*Dar la vuelta. Griselda Gambaro Teatro 2*. Buenos Aires: Ediciones de la Flor, 1987.

*Decir sí. Hispamérica* 21, 1978.

————.*Antología Teatro Abierto*. Buenos Aires: Editorial Teatro Abierto, 1981.

————.*Antología del teatro hispanoamericano del siglo XX*, vol. 5. Ottawa: Girol Books, 1983.

————.*Teatro breve contemporáneo*. Buenos Aires: Ediciones Colihue, 1983.

————.*Griselda Gambaro Teatro 3.*

————.Frank Dauster and Leon Lyday, eds. *En un acto: Diez piezas hispanoamericanas*. Boston: Heinle and Heinle, 1990.

————.*Saying Yes*. Trans. Diana Taylor and Holly Silvestri. Unpublished; produced, Dartmouth College, Oct. 1987

*Del sol naciente. Griselda Gambaro Teatro 1*. Buenos Aires: Ediciones de la Flor, 1984.

*El desatino*. Buenos Aires: Emecé Editores, 1965.

————.Buenos Aires: Editorial del Instituto Di Tella, 1965.

————.*Griselda Gambaro/Teatro*. With *Las paredes* and *Los siameses*. Buenos Aires: Editorial Argonauta, 1979.

*El despojamiento. Tramoya* 21/22, 1981.

————.*Escandalar* 6, no. 1/2, 1983.

————.Buenos Aires: *Tiempo Argentino*, August 1983.

————.*Griselda Gambaro Teatro 3.*

————.Trans. Marguerite Feitlowitz as *Strip*. Forthcoming in *Performing Arts Journal*.

*Dios no nos quiere contentos*. Barcelona: Editorial Lumen, 1979.

*Una felicidad con menos pena*. Buenos Aires: Editorial Sudamericana, 1967.

*Ganarse la muerte*. Buenos Aires: Ediciones de la Flor, 1976.

*La gracia. El Urogallo* (Madrid) 17 (1972).

————.*Griselda Gambaro Teatro 3.*

*Lo impenetrable*. Buenos Aires: Torres Aüero Editor, 1984.

*Información para extranjeros. Griselda Gambaro Teatro 2.*

_____. "Information for Foreigners." Trans. Marguerite Feitlowitz. Unpublished; performed in workshop, River Arts Repertory Theatre, New York, 1987.

*Madrigal en ciudad.* Buenos Aires: Editorial Goyanarte, 1963.

*La malasangre. Griselda Gambaro Teatro 1.*

_____. Trans. Evelyn Picon Garfield as "Bitter Blood." Unpublished.

*El miedo. Griselda Gambaro Teatro 3.*

*Nada que ver.* with *Sucede lo que pasa.* Ottawa: Girol Books, 1983.

*Nosferatu. Griselda Gambaro Teatro 3.*

*El nombre. Hispamérica* 38 (1984).

_____. *El Cronista* (Buenos Aires), Supplement, Sept. 1975.

_____. *Griselda Gambaro Teatro 3.*

*Las paredes. Griselda Gambaro/Teatro.* with *El desatino* and *Los siameses.*

_____. Trans. Marguerite Feitlowitz as "The Walls." Unpublished, staged in workshop at River Arts Repertory, N.Y., 1989.

*Puesto en claro. Griselda Gambaro Teatro 2.*

*Real envido. Griselda Gambaro Teatro 1.*

*Los siameses.* Buenos Aires: Ediciones Insurrexit, 1967.

_____. *Griselda Gambaro/Teatro.* With *El desatino* and *Las paredes.*

_____. Frank Dauster, Leon Lyday, and George Woodyard, eds., *9 dramaturgos hispanoamericanos,* vol 2. Ottawa: Girol Books, 1979.

*Solo un aspecto. Griselda Gambaro Teatro 3.*

*Sucede lo que pasa. Griselda Gambaro Teatro 2.*

_____. With *Nade que ver.* Ottawa: Girol Books, 1983.

*Viaje de invierno. Griselda Gambaro Teatro 3.*

*El viaje a Bahía Blanca. Griselda Gambaro Teatro 3.*

## Selected Critical Writings

"Algunas consideraciones sobre la mujer y la literatura." *Revista Iberoamericana* 51 (1985): 471-73.

"Así de claro, de claro e incómodo (sobre la crítica)." *La Razón/Cultura* (Buenos Aires) 25 Aug. 1985.

"Cambiar el ritual." *Tiempo Argentino* (Buenos Aires), 1 Dec. 1985.

"La castidad del escritor." *Diario Clarín* (Buenos Aires), Cultural Supplement, May 1981.

"Discépolo, nuestro dramaturgo necesario." *Revista del Teatro Municipal General San Martín* (Buenos Aires), 2, no. 3, 1981.

"Disyuntivas de un autor teatral que se convierte en novelista." *La Opinión* (Buenos Aires), March 1977.

"¿Es posible y deseable una dramaturgia especificamente femenina?" *Latin American Theatre Review* 12, no. 2 (Fall 1980): 17-21.

"Algunas consideraciones sobre la crisis de la dramaturgia." *En busca de una imagen: Ensayos críticos sobre Griselda Gambaro y José Triana,* ed. Diana Taylor. Ottawa: Girol Books, 1989.

## Interviews

Betsko, Kathleen, and Rachel Koenig (with Maria Irene Fornes). "Griselda Gambaro." *Interviews with Contemporary Women Playwrights.* New York: Beech Tree Books, 1987.

Garfield, Evelyn Picón. *Women's Voices from Latin America: Interviews with Six Contempo-rary Authors*. Detroit: Wayne State Univ. Press, 1985. 53-71.
Giella, Miguel Angel. "Entrevista con Griselda Gambaro." *Hispamérica* 14 (April 1985): 35-42.
Giella, Miguel Angel, Peter Roster; and Leandro Urbina. "Entrevista. Griselda Gam-baro: La ética de la confrontación." *Griselda Gambaro: Teatro. Nada que ver. Sucede lo que pasa*. Ottawa: Girol Books, 1983.
———."Griselda Gambaro: La difícil perfección." *Griselda Gambaro: Teatro. Nada que ver. Sucede lo que pasa*. Ottawa: Girol Books, 1983.

## José Triana

### Selected Plays

*Ceremonial de guerra*. Honolulu: Editorial Persona, 1990. Prologue by George Wood-yard.
*El Mayor General hablará de teogonía*. With *El parque de la fraternidad* and *Medea en el espejo*. Havana: Unión de Escritores y Artistas de Cuba, 1962.
———.Rine Leal, ed., *Teatro cubano en un acto*. Havana: Ediciones Revolución.
Frank Dauster, ed., *En un acto: nueve piezas hispanoamericanas*. New York: Van Nostrand, 1974.
*Medea en el espejo*. With *El Mayor General* and *El parque de la fraternidad*. Havana: Unión de Escritores y Artistas de Cuba, 1962.
*La muerte del ñeque*. Havana: *Casa de las Americas* 3, no. 20/21 (Sept.-Dec. 1963): 53-63.
———.Havana: Ediciones Revolución, 1964.
*El parque de la fraternidad*. With *El Mayor General hablará de teogonía* and *Medea en el espejo*. Havana: Unión de Escritores y Artistas de Cuba, 1962.
*La noche de los asesinos*. Havana. Casa de las Américas, 1965.
———.Frank Dauster, Leon Lyday, George Woodyard, eds., *9 dramaturgos his-panoamericanos*, vol. 1. Ottawa: Girol Books, 1979.
———.The Criminals. Trans. Pablo Armando Fernández and Michael Kustow. Adap-tation by Adrian Mitchell. George Woodyard, *The Modern Stage in Latin America: Six Plays*. New York: Dutton, 1971.
———.*The Criminals*. Trans. Pablo Armando Fernández and Michael Kustow. Adapta-tion by Adrian Mitchell. *The Drama Review* 14, no. 2 (Winter 1970): 104-29.
"Palabras comunes." Unpublished manuscript in the author's possession.
———.*Worlds Apart*. Trans. Kate Littlewood. Adapted by Peter Whelan for production by Royal Skakespeare Co. Stratford-upon-Avon, England, 1986.
"Revolico en el campo de marte." Unpublished manuscript in the author's possession.

### Selected Critical Writings

"Apuntes sobre un libro de Arrufat." *Gaceta de Cuba* 18 (1963): 12-13.
"La poesía actual." Havana: *Casa de las Américas* 4, no. 22/23 (1964): 34-48.
"Biografía de un cimarrón: ¿un relato etnográfico como confiesa su autor o una novela?" *Gaceta de Cuba* 52 (1966): 12.
"Coloquio de sombras." *Cuadernos Hispanoamericanos* 374 (1981): 317-21.

"Por qué escribo teatro." *Escandalar* 5, no. 1-2 (Jan.-June 1982): 130-36.
"Alusiones al delirio." *En busca de una imagen: Ensayos sobre Griselda Gambaro y José Triana*, ed. Diana Taylor. Ottawa: Girol Books, 1989.

### Interviews

Estorino, Abelardo. "Destruir los fantasmas." Interview with Triana and Vicente Revuelta. *Conjunto* 2 (1967): 6-13.
Fernández-Fernández, Ramiro. "José Triana habla de su teatro." *Románica* 15 (1978-79): 33-45.
Taylor, Diana. "Entrevista con José Triana." *En busca de una imagen*. Ed. Diana Taylor. Ottawa: Girol Books, 1989.

## Egon Wolff

### Selected Plays

*Alamos en la azotea. Teatro chileno contemporáneo.* Santiago: Andres Bello, 1978.
*La balsa de Medusa.* With *Parejas de trapo.* Santiago: Universitaria, 1988.
*Discípulos del miedo.* With *El signo de Caín.* Santiago: Ediciones Valores Literarios, 1971.
*Flores de papel.* Havana: Casa de las Américas, 1970.
————.Orlando Rodríguez-Sardiñas, and Carlos Miguel Suárez Radillo, eds., *Teatro selecto contemporaneo hispanoamericano.* Madrid: Escelicer, 1971.
————.Frank Dauster, Leon Lyday, George Woodyard, eds., *9 dramaturgos hispanoamericanos*, vol. 2. Ottawa: Girol Books, 1979.
————.*Paper Flowers.* Trans. Margaret S. Peden. Columbia: Univ. of Missouri Press, 1971.
————.Juan Andrés Piña, ed. *Niñamadre, Flores de papel, Kindergarten.* Santiago: Editorial Nascimento, 1978.
*Kindergarten.* Juan Andrés Piña, ed. With *Niñamadre* and *Flores de papel.* Santiago: Editorial Nascimento, 1978
*Háblame de Laura. Revista Apuntes* 96 (1988): 125-71.
*Los invasores. Teatro hispanoamericano contemporáneo*, ed. Carlos Solórzano. Mexico City: Fondo de Cultura Económica, 1964.
————.Julio Durán-Cerda, ed. *Teatro chileno contemporáneo.* Mexico City: Aguilar, 1970.
*Mansión de lechuzas. Teatro chileno actual.* Santiago: Empresa Editora Zig-Zag, 1966.
*Niñamadre.* Juan Andrés Piña, ed. With *Flores de papel* and *Kindergarten.* Santiago: Editorial Nascimento, 1978.
————.Santiago: Instituto Chileno-Norteamericano de Cultura, 1966.
*Parejas de trapo.* With *La balsa de Medusa.* Santiago: Universitaria, 1988.
*El signo de Caín.* With *Discípulos del miedo.* Santiago: Ediciones Valores Literarios, 1971.
*El sobre azul.* UTIEH/C, 40 91983: 89-109.

### Selected Critical Writings

"Sobre mi teatro."*Teatro chileno actual.* Santiago: Empresa Editora Zig-Zag, 1966.

*Interviews*

Otano, Rafael. "Egon Wolff: Un dramaturgo entre el nacimiento y el suicidio." *La dramaturgia de Egon Wolff,* ed. Pedro Bravo-Elizondo. Santiago: Editorial Nascimento, 1985.

Bravo-Elizondo, Pedro. "Entrevista." Edmonton, Alberta, April 1980. Referred to in *La dramaturgia de Egon Wolff.*


OTHER WORKS CITED


Adorno, Theodor, Walter Benjamin, Ernst Bloch, Bertolt Brecht, and Georg Lukács. *Aesthetics and Politics.* London: Verso, 1986.

Alegría, Fernando. *Literatura y revolución.* Mexico City: Fondo de Cultura Económica, 1976.

Anderson, Martin Edwin. "Dirty Secrets of the 'Dirty War.'" *Nation,* Mar. 13, 1989, 339-41.

Arendt, Hannah. *On Revolution.* Harmondsworth: Penguin Books, 1963.

———.*On Violence.* San Diego: Harcourt Brace Jovanovich, 1970.

Arriví, Francisco. *El autor dramático.* San Juan, P.R.: Instituto de Cultura Puertorriqueña, 1963.

Arrom, José Juan. *Historia del teatro hispanoamericano: Epoca colonial.* Mexico City: Ediciones de Andrea, 1967.

Arrufat, Antón. *Los siete contra Tebas.* Havana: UNEAC, 1968.

Artaud, Antonin. *Artaud Anthology,* ed. Jack Hirschman. San Francisco: City Lights Books, 1965.

———.*México y Viaje al país de los Tarahumaras,* prologue by Luis Mario Schneider (Mexico City: Fondo de Cultura Económica, 1984).

———.*The Theater and Its Double.* Trans. Mary Caroline Richards. New York: Grove Press, 1958.

Artiles, Freddy. "Teatro popular: Nuevo heroe, nuevo conflicto." In Gutiérrez, *Teatro popular y cambio social en América Latina.*

Barber, Karin. "Popular Reactions to the Petro-Naira." *Journal of African Studies.* 20, no. 3 (1982): 431-50.

Barthes, Roland. *Camera Lucida.* Trans. Richard Howard. New York: Hill & Wang, 1985.

Baudrillard, Jean. *Simulations.* Trans. Paul Foss, Paul Patton, and Philip Beitchman. New York: Semiotexte, 1983.

Beckett, Samuel. *Waiting for Godot.* Trans. by the author. New York: Grove Press, 1954.

Benvenuto, Bice, and Roger Kennedy, eds. *The Works of Jacques Lacan.* New York: St. Martin's Press, 1986.

Berger, John. *Ways of Seeing.* Harmondsworth: Penguin Books, 1972.

Blanchot, Maurice. *The Writing of the Disaster.* Trans. Ann Smock. Lincoln: Univ. of Nebraska Press, 1986.

Blau, Herbert. *Take Up the Bodies: Theater at the Vanishing Point.* Urbana: Univ. of Illinois Press, 1982.

Boal, Augusto. "A Note on Brazilian Agitprop." *Drama Review,* 14/2 (Winter 1970): 96-97.

_____. "Sobre teatro popular y antipopular." In Luzuriaga, *Popular Theater for Social Change in Latin America*.

_____. *Teatro del oprimido*. Vol. 1. Mexico City: Editorial Nueva Imagen, 1980. Trans. Charles McBride and Maria-Odilia Leal McBride as *Theatre of the Oppressed*. New York: Theatre Communications Group, 1985.

Bober, M.M. *Karl Marx's Interpretation of History*. New York: Norton, 1965.

Boudet, Rosa Ileana. *Teatro nuevo: Una respuesta*. Havana: Editorial Letras Cubanas, 1983.

Bourdieu, Pierre. *Distinction: A Social Critique of the Judgement of Taste*. Trans. Richard Nice. Cambridge, Mass.: Harvard University Press, 1984.

Bravo Eliondo, Pedro. *La dramaturgia de Egon Wolff*. Santiago: Editorial Nascimento, 1985.

Brecht, Bertolt. *Brecht on Theatre: The Development of an Aesthetic*. Trans. John Willett. New York: Hill & Wang, 1957; 1964.

Brown, Norman O. *Love's Body*. New York: Vintage Books, 1966.

Bruckner, Pascal. *The Tears of the White Man: Compassion as Contempt*. Trans. William R. Beer. New York: Free Press, 1986.

Bunster-Burotto, Ximena. "Surviving beyond Fear: Women and Torture in Latin America." In Nash and Safa, *Women and Change in Latin America*.

Burns, Elizabeth. *Theatricality*, New York: Harper & Row, 1972.

Burns, Elizabeth, and Tom Burns, eds. *Sociology of Literature and Drama*. Harmondsworth: Penguin Books, 1973.

Calderwood, James L., et al., eds. *Perspectives on Drama*. New York: Oxford Univ. Press, 1968.

Callois, Roger. *Man, Play, and Games*. Trans. Meyer Barash. New York: Schocken Books, 1979.

Carlson, Marvin. *Theories of the Theatre*. Ithaca: Cornell Univ. Press, 1984.

Carpentier, Alejo. *The Kingdom of This World*. Trans. Harriet de Onís. Harmondsworth: Penguin, 1975.

Carrasco, Pedro. "La sociedad mexicana antes de la conquista." In Cosío Villegas, *Historia general de México*, vol. 1.

Chaudhuri, Una. "The Spectator in Drama/Drama in the Spectator." *Modern Drama* 27, no. 3 (1984): 281-92.

Chomsky, Noam, and Edward S. Herman. *The Washington Connection and Third World Fascism: The Political Economy of Human Rights*. Vol. 1. Montreal: Black Rose Books, 1979.

Christian, Barbara. "The Race for Theory." *Cultural Critique* 6 (1987): 51-63.

Cirlot, J.E. *A Dictionary of Symbols*. Trans. Jack Sage. New York: Philosophical Library, 1962.

Cixous, Hélène. "Aller à la mer." Trans. Barbara Kerslake. *Modern Drama* 27, no. 4 (1984): 546-48.

Clark, Barrett H. *European Theories of the Drama*. New York: Crown, 1965.

Cleaver, Eldridge. *Soul on Ice*. New York: Dell, 1968.

Collazos, Oscar. "Buenaventura: Quince años de trabajo creador." *Conjunto* 10 (1971): 6-11.

Concha, Jaime. "Juan Ruíz de Alarcón." In Iñigo Madrigal, *Historia de la literatura hispanoamericana*.

Cooper, J.C. *An Illustrated Encyclopedia of Traditional Symbols*. London: Thames & Hudson, 1984.

Corrigan, Robert W. *Comedy: Meaning and Form*. Scranton: Chandler, 1965.

———. *Tragedy: Vision and Form*. San Francisco: Chandler, 1965.

Cosío Villegas, Daniel, ed. *Historia general de México*. 2 vols. Mexico City: El Colegio de México, 1981.

Cypess, Sandra Messinger. "I, Too, Speak: 'Female' Discourse in Carballido's Plays." *Latin American Theatre Review*, 18, no. 1 (Fall 1984): 45-52.

———. "Physical Imagery in the Works of Griselda Gambaro." *Modern Drama* 18 (1975): 357-64.

Dassin, Joan, ed. *Torture in Brazil:* Prepared by the Archdiocese of São Paulo. Trans. Jaime Wright. New York: Vintage Books, 1986.

Dauster, Frank. *Ensayos sobre teatro hispanoamericano*. Mexico City: Setentas, 1975.

———. "The Game of Chance: The Theatre of José Triana." In Lyday and Woodyard, eds., *Dramatists in Revolt*.

———. *Historia del teatro hispanoamericano*. Mexico City: Ediciones de Andrea, 1966.

———. *Teatro hispanoamericano: Tres piezas*. New York: Harcourt, Brace & World. 1965.

Dauster, Frank; Leon Lyday; and George Woodyard, eds. *9 dramaturgos hispanoamericanos* vols. 1-3. Ottawa: Girol Books, 1979.

Davis, Harold Eugene. *Latin American Thought: A Historical Introduction*. Baton Rouge: Louisiana State Univ. Press, 1972.

Debord, Guy. *Society of the Spectacle*. Detroit: Black & Red, 1983.

Debray, Régis. *Revolution in the Revolution?* New York: Grove Press, 1967.

De la Campa, Román V. *José Triana: Ritualización de la sociedad cubana*. Madrid: Cátedra, 1979.

Deleuze, Gilles, and Félix Guattari. *Anti-Oedipus*. Trans. Robert Hurley, Mark Seem, and Helen R. Lane. Minneapolis: Univ. of Minnesota Press, 1983.

———. *Kafka: Toward a Minor Literature*. Trans. Dana Polan. Minneapolis: Univ. of Minnesota Press, 1986.

Del Saz, Agustín. *Teatro hispanoamericano*. Barcelona: Editorial Vergara, 1963.

Derrida, Jacques. *Writing and Difference*. Trans. Alan Bass. Chicago: Univ. of Chicago Press, 1978.

De Toro, Fernando. *Brecht en el teatro hispanoamericano contemporáneo*. Ottawa: Girol Books, 1984.

Dirlik, Arif. "Culturism as Hegemonic Ideology and Liberating Practice." *Cultural Critique*, 6 (Spring 1987): 13-50.

Dragún, Osvaldo. "El teatro argentino en 1985." In Pianca, *Diógenes*, 1985.

Dumouchel, Paul, ed. *Violence and Truth*. Stanford, Calif.: Stanford Univ. Press, 1988.

Duvignaud, Jean. *Les ombres collectives sociologie du théâtre*. Paris: Presses Universitaires de France, 1973.

———. *El Sacrificio Inútil*. Mexico City: Fondo de Cultura Económica, 1979.

———. *Sociologie du théâtre*. In Burns and Burns, *Sociology of Literature and Drama*.

———. *Spectacle et Societé*. Paris: Denoël/Gonthier, 1970.

Ehrenreich, Barbara. Foreword. In Theweleit, *Male Fantasies*, vol. 1.

Eidelberg, Nora. *Teatro experimental hispanoamericano, 1960–1980: La realidad social como manipulación*. Minneapolis, Minn.: Institute for the Study of Ideologies and Literature, 1985.

Eliade, Mircea. *The Myth of the Eternal Return*. Princeton, N.J.: Princeton Univ. Press, 1974.

———. *Myths, Dreams and Mysteries*. Trans. Philip Mairet. New York: Harper Torchbooks, 1957.

_____.*The Sacred and the Profane.* Trans. William R. Trask. New York: Harcourt Brace Jovanovich, 1959.

Else, Gerald F. *Aristotle's Poetics: The Argument.* Cambridge, Mass.: Harvard Univ. Press, 1957.

_____.*The Origin and Early Form of Greek Tragedy.* Martin Classical Lectures 20. Cambridge, Mass.: Harvard Univ. Press, 1965.

Esslin, Martin. *The Theatre of the Absurd.* Harmondsworth: Penguin Books, 1968.

Etherton, Michael. *The Development of African Drama.* New York: Africana, 1982.

Euripides. *The Bacchae and Other Plays.* Trans. Philip Vellacott. Harmondsworth: Penguin Books, 1967.

Fanon, Frantz. *The Wretched of the Earth.* Trans. Constance Farrington. New York: Grove Press, 1968.

Feder, Lillian. *Madness in Literature.* Princeton, N.J.: Princeton Univ. Press, 1980.

Felman, Shoshana. *The Literary Speech Act.* Trans. Catherine Porter. Ithaca, N.Y.: Cornell Univ. Press, 1983.

_____.*Writing and Madness.* Trans. Martha Noel Evans and Shoshana Felman with Brian Massumi. Ithaca, N.Y.: Cornell Univ. Press, 1985.

Féral, Josette. "Writing and Displacement: Women in Theatre." Trans. Barbara Kerslake. *Modern Drama* 27, no. 4 (1984): 549-63.

Fernández, Teodosio. *El teatro chileno contemporaneo (1941-1973).* Madrid: Editorial Playor, 1982.

Foucault, Michel. *The Archaeology of Knowledge* and *The Discourse of Language.* Trans. A.M. Sheridan Smith. New York: Panther, 1972.

_____.*Discipline and Punish.* Trans. Alan Sheridan. New York: Vintage Books, 1979.

_____.*Madness and Civilization: A History of Insanity in the Age of Reason.* Trans. Richard Howard. New York: Vintage Books. 1973.

_____.*Power/Knowledge.* Trans. Colin Gordon, Leo Marshall, John Mepham, and Kate Soper. New York: Panther, 1980.

Franco, Jean. "Beyond Ethnocentrism: Gender, Power, and the Third-World Intelligentsia." In Nelson and Grossberg, *Marxism and the Interpretation of Culture.*

_____."The Crisis of the Liberal Imagination and the Utopia of Writing." *Ideologies and Literature* 1 (1976-77): 5-24.

_____."Dependency Theory and Literary History: The Case of Latin America." *Minnesota Review* 5 (1975): 65-80.

_____."Self-Destructing Heroines." *Minnesota Review* 22 (1984): 105-15.

Freire, Paulo. *Pedagogy of the Oppressed.* Trans. Myra Bergman Ramos. New York: Continuum, 1988.

Freud, Sigmund. *A General Selection from the Works of Sigmund Freud.* Ed. John Rickman. Garden City, N.Y.: Doubleday/Anchor, 1957.

Friedländer, Saul. *Reflections of Nazism: An Essay on Kitsch and Death.* Trans. Thomas Weyr. New York: Harper & Row, 1984.

Fuchs, Elinor, ed. *Plays of the Holocaust: An International Anthology.* New York: Theatre Communications Group, 1987.

Galbraith, W.O. *Colombia: A General Survey.* London: Oxford Univ. Press, 1966.

Gálvez Acero, Marina. *El teatro hispanoamericano.* Madrid: Taurus, 1988.

Gann, Myra S. "Meaning and Metaphor in *Flores de papel.*" *Latin American Theatre Review* 22, no. 2 (1989): 31-36.

Garibay K., Angel Maria. *Historia de la literatura Náhuatl.* Vols. 1-5. Mexico City: Editorial Porrua, 1987.

_____.*Panorama literario de los pueblos Nahuas.* Mexico City: Editorial Porrua, 1987.

Geertz, Clifford. "Anti-Anti-Relativism." *American Anthropologist* 86, no. 2 (1984): 263-348.

_____.*Negara: The Theatre State in Nineteenth Century Bali.* Princeton, N.J.: Princeton Univ. Press, 1980.

_____.*Local Knowledge.* New York: Basic Books. 1983.

Genet, Jean. *The Balcony.* Revised version. Trans. Bernard Frechtman. New York: Grove Press, 1966.

Gilligan, Carol. *In a Different Voice.* Cambridge, Mass.: Harvard Univ. Press, 1982.

Gilman, Sander L. *Disease and Representation: Images of Illness from Madness to AIDS.* Ithaca, N.Y.: Cornell Univ. Press, 1988.

_____.*Jewish Self-Hatred.* Baltimore, Md.: Johns Hopkins Univ. Press, 1986.

Giordano, Enrique. *La teatralización de la obra dramática: De Florencio Sanchez a Roberto Arlt.* Mexico City: Premia Editora, 1982.

Girard, René. *Deceit, Desire, and the Novel.* Trans. Yvonne Freccero. Baltimore, Md.: Johns Hopkins Univ. Press, 1980.

_____.*The Scapegoat.* Trans. Yvonne Frecerro. Baltimore, Md.: John Hopkins Univ. Press, 1986.

_____.*Violence and the Sacred.* Trans. Patrick Gregory. Baltimore, Md.: Johns Hopkins Univ. Press, 1981.

González Torres, Yolotl. *El sacrificio humano entre los mexicas.* Mexico City: Fondo de Cultura Económica, 1985.

Gorostiza, Celestino. *El color de nuestra piel.* In Gerardo Luzuriaga and Richard Reeve, eds., *Los clásicos del teatro Hispano Americano.* Mexico City: Fondo de Cultura Económica, 1975.

Graham, R.B. Cunninghame. *Selected Writings of Cunninghame Graham.* Cedric Watts, ed. East Brunswick, N.J.: Associated Univ. Presses, 1981.

Grotowski, Jerzy. *Towards a Poor Theatre.* New York: Simon & Schuster, 1968.

Guevara, Ernesto Ché. *El diario de Che en Bolivia.* Prologue by Fidel Castro. Mexico City: Siglo Veintiuno Editores. 1968.

Gutiérrez, Sonia, ed. *Teatro popular y cambio social en América Latina.* Ciudad Universitaria "Rodrigo Facio," Costa Rica: EDUCA, 1979.

Habermas, Jürgen, *Legitimation Crisis.* Trans. Thomas McCarthy. Boston: Beacon Press, 1973.

Hallie, Philip P. *Cruelty.* Middletown, Conn.: Wesleyan Univ. Press, 1983.

Hampden-Turner, Charles. *Maps of the Mind.* New York: Collier Books, 1981.

Harlow, Barbara. *Resistance Literature.* New York: Methuen, 1987.

Hegel, Georg W.F. *The Phenomenology of Mind.* Trans. J.B. Baillie. New York: Harper & Row, 1967.

Heilbroner, Robert. *Behind the Veil of Economics: Essays in Worldly Philosophy.* New York: Norton, 1988.

_____."The Triumph of Capitalism," *New Yorker,* Jan 23. 1989, pp. 98-109.

Henriquez Ureña, P. *Historia de la cultura en América Hispánica.* Mexico City: Fondo de Cultura Económica, 1986.

Hill, Errol. *A Time and a Season: 8 Caribbean Plays.* Jamaica: Carifesta, 1976.

Hitler, Adolf. *Mein Kampf.* Trans. Ralph Manheim. Boston: Houghton Mifflin, 1943.

Holzapfel, Tamara. "Griselda Gambaro's Theatre of the Absurd." *Latin American Theatre Review* 4 (Fall 1970): 5-11.

Huerta, Jorge A. *Chicano Theatre: Theme and Forms*. Ypsilanti: Bilingual Press, 1982.

Huizinga, Johan. *Homo Ludens*. Boston: Beacon Press, 1955.

Iñigo Madrigal, Luis, ed. *Historia de la literatura hispanoamericana*, vol. 1, *Epoca colonial*, Madrid: Ediciones Catedra, 1982.

Ionesco, Eugene. "Remarks on My Theatre and on the Remarks of Others." In Daniel Seltzer, *The Modern Theatre: Readings and Documents*. Boston: Little, Brown, 1967.

———. "Still about Avant-Garde Theatre." In Daniel Seltzer, *The Modern Theatre: Readings and Documents*.

Irigaray, Luce. *Speculum of the Other Woman*. Trans. Gillian C. Gill. Ithaca, N.Y.: Cornell Univ. Press, 1986.

———. *This Sex Which Is Not One*. Trans. Catherine Porter. Ithaca, N.Y.: Cornell Univ. Press, 1985.

Jacobi, Jolande. *The Psychology of C.G. Jung*. Trans. Ralph Manheim. London: Routledge and Kegan Paul, 1968.

Jameson, Fredric. Afterword. In Adorno et al., *Aesthetics and Politics*.

JanMohamed, Abdul R., and David Lloyd. "Introduction: Minority Discourse—What Is to Be Done?" *Cultural Critique* 7 (Fall 1987): 10.

Joes, Anthony James. *Fascism in the Contemporary World: Ideology, Evolution, Resurgence*. Boulder, Colo.: Westview Press, 1978.

Johnson, Barbara. *A World of Difference*. Baltimore, Md.: John Hopkins Univ. Press, 1987.

Jung, Carl G. *The Undiscovered Self*. Trans. R.F.C. Hull. Boston: Little, Brown, 1958.

Kaplan, Alice Yaeger. *Reproductions of Banality: Fascism, Literature, and French Intellectual Life*. Minneapolis: Univ. of Minnesota Press, 1986.

Kaplan, Caren. "Deterritorializations: The Rewriting of Home and Exile in Western Feminist Discourse." *Cultural Critique* 6 (1987): 187-98.

Katz, Steven T. "Central and South American Indians." In *The Holocaust in the Context of History*. In progress.

Kavanagh, Robert. *Theatre and Cultural Struggle in South Africa*. London: Zed Books, 1985.

Kayser, Wolfgang. *The Grotesque in Art and Literature*. Trans. Ulrich Weisstein. 1957; New York: Columbia Univ. Press, 1981.

Kerr, R.A. "La función de la Intermediaria en *Yo también hablo de la rosa*." *Latin American Theatre Review* 12, no. 2 (1978): 51-60.

Kirby, E.T., ed. *Total Theatre*. New York: Dutton, 1969.

Kline, Harvey F. *Colombia: Portrait of Unity and Diversity*. Boulder, Colo.: Westview Press, 1983.

Kobralka, Michal. "Let the Artists Die? An Interview with Tadeusz Kantor." *Drama Review*, Fall 1986, 177-83.

Kojève, Alexandre. *Introduction to the Reading of Hegel*. Trans. James H. Nichols, Jr. Ed. Allan Bloom. New York: Basic Books, 1969.

Krieger, Murray. *The Tragic Vision*. New York: Holt, Rinehart & Winston, 1960.

Kristeva, Julia. *Desire in Language*. Trans. Thomas Gora, Alice Gora, and Leon S. Roudiez. New York: Columbia Univ. Press, 1980.

———. *Powers of Horror*. Trans. Leon S. Roudiez. New York: Columbia Univ. Press, 1982.

Kubayanda, Josaphat B. "Minority Discourse and the African Collective: Some Examples from Latin American and Caribbean Literature." *Cultural Critique* 6 (1987): 113-30.

Kubiak, Anthony. "Disappearance as History: The Stages of Terror." *Theatre Journal* 84 (March 1987): 78-88.

Lacan, Jacques. *Écrits: A Selection.* Trans. Alan Sheridan. New York: Norton, 1977.

Laing, R.D. *The Divided Self.* Harmondsworth: Penguin Books, 1960.

―――.*The Politics of Experience and the Bird of Paradise.* Harmondsworth: Penguin Books, 1967.

Landes, Joan B. *Women and the Public Sphere in the Age of the French Revolution.* Ithaca, N.Y.: Cornell Univ. Press, 1988.

Langer, Lawrence L. *The Holocaust and the Literary Imagination.* New Haven, Conn.: Yale Univ. Press, 1975.

Leach, Edmund, ed. *The Stuctural Study of Myth and Totemism.* A.S.A. Monographs 5. London: Tavistock, 1976.

Leal, Riné. *Breve historia del teatro cubano.* Havana: Editorial Letras Cubanas, 1980.

―――, ed. *Teatro bufo, siglo XIX.* Vol. 1. Havana: Editorial Arte y Literatura, 1975.

León-Portilla, Miguel. *Los antiguos mexicanos.* Mexico City: Fondo de Cultura Económica, 1988.

―――.*Pre-Columbian Literatures of Mexico.* Trans. Grace Lobanov and Miguel León-Portilla. Norman: Univ. of Oklahoma Press, 1986.

Lernoux, Penny. "A Society Torn Apart by Violence." *Nation,* Nov. 7, 1987, pp. 512-16.

Levin, Michael. "The Case for Torture." In *The Norton Reader: An Anthology of Expository Prose,* ed. Caeser R. Blake et al. New York: Norton, 1988.

Levinas, Emmanuel. *Totality and Infinity.* Trans. Alphonso Lingis. Pittsburgh, Pa.: Duquesne Univ. Press, 1979.

Ley-Piscator, Maria. *The Piscator Experiment.* New York: Heineman, 1967.

Lifton, Robert Jay. *Boundaries: Psychological Man in Revolution.* New York: Touchstone, 1976.

―――.*The Nazi Doctors: Medical Killing and the Psychology of Genocide.* New York: Basic Books, 1986.

Liss, Sheldon B. *Marxist Thought in Latin America.* Berkeley: Univ. of California Press, 1984.

López, Daniel. "Ambiguity in *Flores de papel.*" *Latin American Theatre Review* 12, no. 2 (1978): 43-49.

Lowe, Donald M. *History of Bourgeois Perception.* Chicago: Univ. of Chicago Press, 1982.

Luzuriaga, Gerardo, ed. *Popular Theater for Social Change in Latin America.* Los Angeles: UCLA Latin American Center Publications, 1978.

Luzuriaga, Gerardo, and Richard Reeve, eds. *Los clásicos del teatro hispanoamericano.* Mexico City: Fondo de Cultura Económica, 1975.

Lyday, Leon. "Whence Wolff's Canary? A Conjecture on Commonality." *Latin American Theatre Review* 17, no. 1 (1983): 23-29.

Lyday, Leon, and George Woodyard. *Dramatists in Revolt: The New Latin American Theatre.* Austin: Univ. of Texas Press, 1976.

Lyotard, Jean-Francois. *Driftworks.* New York: Semiotexte, 1984.

―――."On the Strength of the Weak." *Semiotexte* 3, no. 2 (1978): 206-14.

Macdonell, Diane. *Theories of Discourse.* Oxford: Basil Blackwell, 1986.

Malloy, James M., and Mitchell A. Seligson, eds. *Authoritarians and Democrats: Regime Transition in Latin America.* Pittsburgh, Pa.: Univ. of Pittsburgh Press, 1987.

Mannoni, O. *Prospero and Caliban: The Psychology of Colonization.* Trans. Pamela Porvesland. New York: Praeger, 1968.

Marcuse, Herbert. *Reason and Revolution: Hegel and the Rise of Social Theory.* Boston: Beacon Press, 1968.

Mariátegui, José Carlos. *7 ensayos de interpretación de la realidad peruana.* Lima: Amauta, 1975.

Marrus, Michael, R. *The Holocaust in History.* New York: New American Library, 1987.

Memmi, Albert. *The Colonizer and the Colonized.* Boston: Beacon Press, 1965.

Méndez-Faith, Teresa. "Sobre el uso y abuso de poder en la producción dramática de Griselda Gambaro." *Revista Iberoamericana* 51 (1985): 831-41.

Merleau-Ponty, Maurice. *Humanism and Terror.* Trans. John O'Neill. Boston: Beacon Press, 1969.

Metz, Christian. *The Imaginary Signifier.* Trans. Celia Britton, Annwyl Williams, Ben Brewster, and Alfred Guzzetti. Bloomington: Indiana Univ. Press, 1982.

Milgram, Stanley. "The Perils of Obedience." In Caesar R. Blake et al., *The Norton Reader: An Anthology of Expository Prose.* New York: Norton, 1988.

Miller, Alice. *For Your Own Good: Hidden Cruelty in Child-Rearing and the Roots of Violence.* Trans. Hildegarde Hannum and Hunter Hannum. New York: Farrar, Straus & Giroux, 1988.

Miranda, Julio. "José Triana o el conflicto." *Cuadernos Hispanoamericanos* 230 (Feb. 1969): 439-44.

Mitchell, W.J.T. *Iconology: Image, Text, Ideology.* Chicago: Univ. of Chicago Press, 1986.

Moi, Toril. Study of Simone de Beauvoir. In progress.

————. "Politics and the Intellectual Woman: The Reception of Simone de Beauvoir." Lecture at School of Criticism and Theory, Dartmouth College, 1989.

Monsiváis, Carlos. "La naturaleza de la onda." In Skirius, *El ensayo hispanoamericano del siglo XX.*

Monterde, Francisco, ed. *Teatro indígena prehispánico: Rabinal Achí.* Mexico City: Universidad Nacional Autónoma de México, 1979.

Moore, R.I. Preface. In Peters, *Torture.*

Moreno, Jacob L. *Psychodrama.* Vol. 1. 3d ed. New York: Beacon Press, 1964.

————. *Theatre of Spontaneity.* 2d ed. New York: Beacon Press, 1973.

Munk, Erika. "TDR comment: A Repressive Theatre." *Drama Review* 14, no. 2 (1970): 33-34.

Murch, Anne C. "Genet-Triana-Kopit: Ritual as 'Danse Macabre.'" *Modern Drama* 15 (March 1973): 369-81.

Murena, H.A. "El estridor del conformismo." In Stabb, *In Quest of Identity.*

Murray, Timothy. "Comment." *Theatre Journal* 37, no. 3 (1985): 272.

Nash, June, and Helen Safa, eds. *Sex and Class in Latin America.* New York: Praeger, 1976.

————, eds. *Women and Change in Latin America.* Massachusetts: Bergin & Garvey, 1986.

Ndlovu, Duma, ed. *Woza Afrika! An Anthology of South African Plays.* New York: Braziller, 1986.

Neglia, Erminio G. "El hecho teatral contempráneo en Hispanoamerica." *Texto Crítico.* 10 (1978): 110-19.

————. *El hecho teatral en Hispanoamerica.* Rome: Bulzoni, 1985.

Nelson, Cary, and Lawrence Grossberg, ed. *Marxism and the Interpretation of Culture.* Urbana: Univ. of Illinois Press, 1988.

Ngugi wa Thiong'o. *Decolonising the Mind: The Politics of Language in African Literature.* Portsmouth: Heinemann, 1986.

Nigro, Kirsten. "Discurso femenino y el teatro de Grisleda Gambaro." In Taylor, *En busca de una imagen.*

_____."*La noche de los asesinos*: Playscript and Stage Enactment." *Latin American Theatre Review,* Fall 1977, pp. 45-47.

*Nunca más: The Report of the Argentine National Commission on the Disappeared.* New York: Farrar, Straus & Giroux, 1986.

O'Connor, James. *The Meaning of Crisis.* Oxford: Basil Blackwell, 1987.

Olaniyan, Richard, ed. *African History and Culture.* Lagos: Longman Nigeria, 1982.

Oliver, William, ed. *Voices of Change in Spanish American Theatre.* Austin: Univ. of Texas Press, 1971.

Ong, Walter J. *Orality and Literacy: The Technologizing of the Word.* London: Methuen, 1984.

Oquist, Paul. *Violence, Conflict, and Politics in Colombia.* New York: Academic Press, 1980.

Ortega, Julio. "*La noche de los asesinos.*" *Cuadernos Americanos* 164, no. 3 (1969): 262-67.

Ortiz, Fernando. *Contra punteo cubano del tabaco y el azircar.* Caracas: Biblioteca Ayacucho, 1978.

Otano, Rafael. "Egon Wolff: Un dramaturgo entre el nacimiento y el suicidio." In Bravo Elizondo, *La dramaturgia de Egon Wolff.*

Palls, Terry L. "The Theatre in Revolutionary Cuba." Thesis, Univ. of Kansas. Brief summary in "The Theater of the Absurd in Cuba after 1959." *Latin American Theatre Review* 4, no. 7 (1975): 67-72.

Patraka, Vivian M. "Contemporary Drama, Fascism, and the Holocaust." *Theatre Journal* 39, no. 1 (1987): 65-77.

_____."Fascist Ideology and Theatricalization." Paper presented at New Languages for the Stage Conference, University of Kansas, 1988.

Paz, Octavio. "Invencion, subdesarrollo, modernidad." In Skirius, *El ensayo Hispanoamericano del siglo XX.*

_____.*The Labyrinth of Solitude: Life and Thought in Mexico.* Trans. Lysander Kemp. New York: Grove Press, 1961.

_____.*Sor Juana; or The Traps of Faith.* Trans. Margaret S. Peden. Cambridge, Mass.: Harvard Univ. Press, 1988.

Peden, Margaret S. *Emilio Carballido.* Boston: Twayne, 1980.

_____."Emilio Carballido, Curriculum operum." In Carballido, *Orinoco, Las cartas de Mozart, Felicidad.* Mex. City: Editores Mexicanos unidos, 1985.

_____."Three Plays by Egon Wolff." *Latin American Theatre Review* 3, no. 1 (1969): 29-35.

_____, ed. and trans. *The Golden Thread and Other Plays.* Austin: Univ. of Texas Press, 1971.

Peters, Edward. *Torture.* New York: Blackwell, 1985.

Pianca, Marina, ed. *Diógenes: Anuario crítico del teatro latinoamericano* 1 (1985) and 2 (1986). Ottawa: Girol Books, 1987.

Plato. *The Republic.* trans. H.D.P. Lee. Baltimore, Md.: Penguin Books, 1967.

Quackenbush, L. Howard, ed. *Teatro del absurdo hispanoamericano.* Mexico City: Editorial Patria, 1987.

Quigley, Austin E. *The Modern Stage and Other Worlds.* London: Methuen, 1985.

Rama, Angel. *La ciudad letrada*. Hanover, N.H.: Ediciones del Norte, 1984.

_____. *Transculturación narrativa en América Latina*. Mexico City: Siglo XXI, 1982.

Rank, Otto. *Art and Artist*. Trans. Charles Frances Atkinson, New York: Agathon, 1968.

Retamar, Roberto Fernández. *Calibán*. Mexico City: Editorial Diógenes, 1972.

_____. *Para una teoria de la literatura hispanoamericana*. Mexico City: Editorial Nuestro Tiempo, 1981.

Reyes, Carlos José. "Introducción: El teatro de Enrique Buenaventura." In Buenaventura, *Teatro*.

Ricoeur, Paul. *History and Truth*. Trans. Charles A. Kelbley. Evanston, Ill.: Northwestern Univ. Press, 1965.

Risk, Beatriz. *El nuevo teatro latinoamericano: Una lectura histórica*. Minneapolis, Minn.: Prisma Institute, 1987.

Roach, Joseph R. "Theatre History and the Ideology of the Aesthetic." *Theatre Journal* 41, no. 2 (1989): 155-68.

Rock, David. *Argentina: 1516-1987*. Berkeley: Univ. of California Press, 1987.

Rodríguez Monegal, Emir, ed., with Thomas Colchie. *The Borzoi Anthology of Latin American Literature*. Vol. 1. New York: Knopf, 1984.

Rodríguez-Sardiñas, Orlando, and Carlos Miguel Súarez-Radillo, eds. *Teatro selecto contemporaneo hispanoamericano*. Vol. 1. Madrid: Editorial Escelicer, 1971.

Rose, Jacqueline. *Sexuality in the Field of Vision*. London: Verso, 1986.

Rouquié, Alain. *The Military and the State in Latin America*. Trans. Paul E. Sigmund. Berkeley: Univ. of California Press, 1987.

Said, Edward W. *The World, the Text, and the Critic*. Cambridge, Mass.: Harvard Univ. Press, 1983.

Sangari, Kumkum. "The Politics of the Possible." *Cultural Critique* 7 (Fall 1987): 157-86.

Sartre, Jean-Paul. *Being and Nothingness*. Trans. Hazel E. Barnes. New York: Washington Square Press, 1969.

_____. Introduction. In Fanon, *The Wretched of the Earth*.

_____. *No Exit and Three Other Plays*. Trans. Stuart Gilbert and Lionel Abel. New York: Vintage, 1955.

Scarry, Elaine. *The Body in Pain*. New York: Oxford Univ. Press, 1985.

Schechner, Richard. *Between Theater and Anthropology*. Philadelphia: Univ. of Pennsylvania Press, 1985.

_____. "Conformists in the Heart: An Interview with Richard Schechner," by Joanne Pottlitzer. *Drama Review* 14, no. 2 (1970): 39-42.

Scheler, M.F. *Ressentiment*. Trans. William W. Holdheim. New York: Schocken Books, 1972.

Seltzer, Daniel, ed. *The Modern Theatre: Readings and Documents*. Boston: Little, Brown, 1967.

Shelley, Kathleen, and Grínor Rojo. "El teatro hispanoamericano colonial." In Iñigo Madrigal, *Historia de la literatura hispanoamericana*.

Simon, Jean-Marie. *Guatemala: Eternal Spring, Eternal Tyranny*. New York: Norton, 1987.

Simpson, John, and Jana Bennett. *The Disappeared and the Mothers of the Plaza*. New York: St. Martin's Press, 1985.

Skidmore, Thomas E. and Peter H. Smith. *Modern Latin America*. New York: Oxford Univ. Press, 1984.

Skirius, John, ed. *El ensayo hispanoamericano del siglo XX.* Mexico City: Fondo de Cultura Económica, 1981.

Skloot, Robert. *The Darkness We Carry: The Drama of the Holocaust.* Madison: Univ. of Wisconsin Press, 1988.

————,ed. *The Theatre of the Holocaust: Four Plays.* Madison: Univ. of Wisconsin Press, 1982.

Skura, Meredith Anne. *The Literary Use of the Psychoanalytic Process.* New Haven, Conn.: Yale Univ. Press, 1981.

Solórzano, Carlos. *El teatro latinoamericano en el siglo XX.* Mexico City: Editorial Pormaca, 1964.

Sontag, Susan. *Against Interpretation.* New York: Dell, 1966.

————.*Illness as Metaphor.* New York: Vintage Books, 1979.

————.*A Susan Sontag Reader.* New York: Vintage Books, 1983.

————.*Under the Sign of Saturn.* New York: Noonday Press, 1989.

Sorel, Georger. *Reflections on Violence.* Trans. T.E. Hulme. London: Collier, 1969.

Soyinka, Wole. Foreword. In Ndlovu, *Woza Afrika!*

————."Theatre in African Traditional Culture." In Olaniyan, *African History and Culture.*

Stabb, Martin S. *In Quest of Identity: Patterns in the Spanish American Essay of Ideas, 1890-1960.* Chapel Hill: Univ. of North Carolina Press, 1967.

Stallybrass, Peter, and Allon White. *The Politics and Poetics of Transgression.* Ithaca, N.Y.: Cornell Univ. Press, 1986.

Sten, María. *Vida y muerte del teatro Náhuatl.* Xalapa: Editorial Universidad Veracruzana, 1982.

Stoller, Robert J. *Perversion: The Erotic Form of Hatred.* New York: Pantheon Books, 1975.

————.*Sexual Excitement: Dynamics of Erotic Life.* New York: Pantheon Books, 1979.

Súarez, Pablo. Letter. *Drama Review* 14, no. 2 (1970): 103.

Szanto, George H. *Theater and Propaganda.* Austin: Univ of Texas Press, 1978.

Taussig, Michael. *Shamanism, Colonialism, and the Wild Man: A Study in Terror and Healing.* Chicago: Chicago Univ. Press, 1987.

Taylor, Diana. "Art and Anti-Art in Egon Wolff's *Flores de papel.*" *Latin American Theatre Review* 18, no. 1 (1984): 65-68.

————,ed. *En busca de una imagen: Ensayos sobre el teatro de Griselda Gambaro y José Triana.* Ottawa: Girol Books, 1989.

————."Framing the Revolution." *Latin American Theatre Review,* forthcoming.

————."Mad World, Mad Hope: Carballido's *El día que se soltaron los leones.*" *Latin American Theatre Review* 20, no. 2 (1987): 67-76.

Theweleit, Klaus. *Male Fantasies.* Vol. 1, trans. Stephen Conway with Erica Carter and Chris Turner. Vol. 2, trans. Carter and Turner. Minneapolis: Univ. of Minnesota Press, 1987, 1989.

Timerman, Jacobo. *Chile: Death in the South.* Trans. Robert Cox. New York: Vintage Books, 1988.

————.*Prisoner without a Name, Cell without a Number.* Trans. Toby Talbot. New York: Vintage Books, 1982.

Tschudi, Lilian. *Teatro argentino actual (1960-1972).* Buenos Aires: Fernando García Cambeiro, 1974.

Turner, Victor. *From Ritual to Theatre: The Human Seriousness of Play.* New York: Performing Arts Journal Publications, 1982.

Usigli, Rodolfo. *El gesticulador.* In Luzuriaga and Reeve, *Los clásicos del teatro hispanoamericano.*

———.*Mexico in the Theater.* Trans. Wilder P. Scott. University Miss.: Romance Monographs, 1976.

Vacs, Aldo C. "Authoritarian Breakdown and Redemocratization in Argentina." In Malloy and Seligson, *Authoritarians and Democrats.*

Vajda, Mihaly. *Fascism as a Mass Movement.* New York: St. Martin's Press, 1976.

Vansina, Jan. *Oral Tradition as History.* Madison: Univ. of Wisconsin Press, 1985.

Varela, José R. "Origen y función de la amigüedad en *Flores de papel* de Egon Wolff." *Gestos* no. 3 (1987): 87-101.

Vásquez Amaral, Mary. *El teatro de Emilio Carballido (1950-1965).* Mexico City: 1974.

Vega Carpio, Lope de. *Arte nuevo de hacer comedias en este tiempo.* Trans. William T. Brewster. In Clark, *European Theories of the Drama.*

Vélez, Joseph F. "Una entrevista con Emilio Carballido." *Latin American Theatre Review* 7 (Fall 1973): 17-24.

Vidal, Hernán. Prologue. In de Campa, *José Triana.*

Vieta, Ezequiel. "Cuba: Dramaturgia y revolución." *Primer Acto* 108 (1969): 22-30.

Villegas, Juan. *Ideología y discurso crítico sobre el teatro de España y América Latina.* Minneapolis, Minn.: Prisma Institute, 1988.

———.*Interpretación y analisis del texto dramático.* Ottawa: Girol Books, 1982.

———. "Los marginados como personajes: Teatro chileno de la década de los sesenta." *Latin American Theatre Review* 19, no.2 (1986): 85-95.

Wakashe, T. Philemon. "*Pula:* An Example of Black Protest Theatre in South Africa." *Drama Review* 30, no. 4 (1986): 43.

Wallace, Penny. "Enrique Buenaventura's *Los papeles del infierno.*" *Latin American Theatre Review* 9 (Fall 1975): 37-46.

Watson Espener, Maida. "Enrique Buenaventura's Theory of the Committed Theatre." *Latin American Theatre Review* 10, no. 1 (1976): 43-47.

Weber, Carl. "AC/TC: Currents of Theatrical Exchange." *Performing Arts Journal* 33/34 (1989): 11-21.

White, Hayden. *Tropics of Discourse.* Baltimore, Md.: Johns Hopkins Univ. Press, 1986.

Wilden, Anthony. *The Language of the Self: The Function of Language in Psychoanalysis.* Baltimore, Md.: Johns Hopkins Univ. Press, 1968.

Wilson, Edwin. *The Theater Experience.* New York: McGraw-Hill, 1980.

Winnicott, D.W. *Playing and Reality.* London: Tavistock, 1971.

Woodyard, George. *The Modern Stage in Latin America: Six Plays.* New York: Dutton, 1971.

———. "Perspectives on Cuban Theater." *Revista Interamericana* 9 (1979): 42-29.

———. "Threads, Roses and Music: Life Forces in Carballido's Theatre." Paper read at the Conference of Latin American Theatre, Pennsylvania State Univ., Oct. 1976.

Zalacain, Daniel. "El personaje 'fuera del juego' en el teatro de Griselda Gambaro." *Revista de Estudios Hispánicos* 14, no. 2 (1980): 59-72.

Zamyatin, Yevgeny. *A Soviet Heretic.* Ed. and trans. Mirra Ginsburg. Chicago: Univ. of Chicago Press, 1970.

Zantop, Susanne. "Re-presenting the Present: History and Literature in Restoration Germany." *Modern Language Notes,* April 1987, pp. 570-85.

Zatlin, Phyllis. "La presencia argentina en el teatro español contemporaneo." In Taylor, *En busca de una imagen.*

# INDEX